D1432117

SOUL LIBERTY

OTHER BOOKS BY WILLIAM G. McLOUGHLIN

*New England Dissent: The Baptists and the
Separation of Church and State, 1633–1833*

Isaac Backus and the American Pietistic Tradition

The American Evangelicals

Rhode Island: A Bicentennial History

Revivals, Awakenings and Reform

*Modern Revivalism from Charles Grandison Finney
to Billy Graham*

Billy Sunday Was His Real Name

Billy Graham: Revivalist in a Secular Age

The Meaning of Henry Ward Beecher

Cherokees and Missionaries

*The Cherokee Ghost Dance and Other Essays on the
Southeastern Indians*

Evan and John B. Jones: Champions of the Cherokees

Cherokee Renascence

Religion in America (edited with Robert Bellah)

The Diary of Isaac Backus (editor)

William G. McLoughlin

SOUL LIBERTY

The Baptists' Struggle in New England,
1630-1833

Brown University Press
Published by University Press of New England
Hanover and London

The University Press of New England

is a consortium of universities in New England dedicated to publishing scholarly and trade works by authors from member campuses and elsewhere. The New England imprint signifies uniform standards for publication excellence maintained without exception by the consortium members. A joint imprint cf University Press of New England and a sponsoring member acknowledges the publishing mission of that university and its support for the dissemination of scholarship throughout the world. Cited by the American Council of Learned Societies as a model to be followed, University Press of New England publishes books under its own imprint and the imprints of Brandeis University, Brown University, Clark University, University of Connecticut, Dartmouth College, University of New Hampshire, University of Rhode Island, Tufts University, University of Vermont, and Wesleyan University.

Printed in the United States of America

∞

LIBRARY OF CONGRESS CATALOGING-IN-PUBLICATION DATA
McLoughlin, William Gerald.
    Soul liberty : the Baptists' struggle in New England, 1630–1833 / William G. McLoughlin.
        p. cm.
    Includes bibliographical references and index.
    ISBN 0-87451-532-7 (alk. paper)
    1. Baptists—New England—History—17th century. 2. Baptists—New England—History—18th century. 3. Baptists—New England—History—19th century. 4. Church and state—New England—History. 5. Freedom of religion—New England—History. 6. New England—Church history. I. Title.
BX6239.M26 1991
286'.0974—dc20   90-43369
                  CIP

5   4   3   2   1

The book is dedicated to my friends and colleagues in the
History Department at Brown University

Contents

Preface

Congress shall make no law respecting an establishment of
religion, or prohibiting the free exercise thereof. . . .
—First Amendment to the U.S. Constitution, 1791

Most of the essays in this collection were written over a ten-year
period when I was engaged in research for a book about the struggle to disestablish the Puritan churches in New England. That study
helped to clarify for me some basic confusions with regard to the
history of separation of church and state in North America. One
such misunderstanding holds that separation as we know it today
came primarily, if not entirely, from the rationalistic spirit of the
Enlightenment and received its essential expression in the 1780s
when Thomas Jefferson and James Madison overthrew the established Anglican Church in Virginia. The second most common misunderstanding holds that the concept of separation sprang fully
formed from the mind of Roger Williams in the early 1630s. A
third assumption pushed the principle of separation even further
back, to the Anabaptist movement of the Reformation in Germany
in the 1520s, holding that it was brought to America by early English Baptists. But whichever assumption is emphasized, the common view is that its ideology was perfectly clear and that over the
centuries in colonial America numerous dedicated individuals fought
heroically to implement it. A final misunderstanding affirms that
separation and religious freedom for all was finally achieved in
1791 with the adoption of the First Amendment to the Constitution.

In various ways these essays may help to dispel such myths. The
development of the unique American tradition of separation of
church and state was far more ambiguous and pragmatic. It evolved
neither from Jefferson, Williams, nor the Anabaptists, nor did the
First Amendment conclude the struggle. Most historians today believe it can never be concluded. However, the tensions between the
state authority and private religious freedom have been, on the
whole, central to the expansion of liberty in America from its first
settlements, and they remain a vital element in the dynamics of
American culture today. The manner in which the concept of re-

ligious freedom evolved, both in the southern colonies against the Anglican establishment and in the northern colonies against the Puritan establishment, had less to do with ideology than with the very practical exigencies of finding spiritual self-expression within the limited bounds available to dissenters within these establishments.

After the "Dark Ages," Europeans slowly evolved a tradition of unity between church and state, imposed from the top down by the papacy in Rome in harmony with the emperors and kings of what was called the Holy Roman Empire or Christendom. The Reformation caused a sharp break with the definition of what was holy in Christendom, but the mainstream varieties of Protestant Christianity that challenged the old Roman Catholic definition—Lutheranism, Calvinism, and Anglicanism—did not alter the concept of state support for an established church. It merely created smaller establishments of different kinds in different Christian kingdoms. Efforts were made to transplant this ideal of a confessional state, supported by tithes or religious taxes, to most of the English colonies in the New World. In Rhode Island, and to a lesser extent in the Jerseys and Pennsylvania, the concept of religious toleration was experimented with in various forms but was never perfected. Once the concepts of separation and voluntary support for religion became a live option, the sectarian impetus within Christendom took on new power. Individuals who had hitherto kept their dissenting views to themselves and groups that had secretly led a hole-in-the-corner existence sought ways and means to worship more freely. Throughout the colonial era the efforts to suppress dissent were harsh, but the impetus was irresistible.

For a variety of reasons (chief of which were the salutary neglect of English colonialism and the scattered settlements in the howling wilderness) dissent multiplied despite persecution. But whereas a few, like Roger Williams, seemed to have a pretty clear idea of what they wanted, most did not. The history of the struggle for religious freedom became a prudent and pragmatic effort, over many generations, to work out a modus vivendi within the established order. At first little more than a hope for toleration, however grudgingly given, was the goal. In the New World, their closest neighbors became the "authorities" with whom dissenters had to cope. When, after many years, the dissenters achieved toleration, they then began to seek relief from religious taxes. Not until the chaotic years of the Revolutionary era was it possible to hope for full religious liberty and equality for all kinds of Christians.

As this problem has assumed new importance and taken new forms in our own day—and as the two-hundredth anniversary of the First Amendment is upon us—it seems essential to distinguish more clearly than we have done between the diverse origins of the tradition of separation of church and state and to note that neither a rationalist nor a pietistic approach has prevailed. No sooner did Christian dissenters achieve their goal of voluntarism in the early nineteenth century than they formed an alliance against those outside the prevailing Evangelical Protestant consensus. National unity seemed to require some measure of conformity. By the mid-nineteenth century a second establishment had emerged, upheld by the tyranny of the majority; non-Protestants were instructed to be satisfied with toleration and second-class citizenship or to go back where they came from. "This is a Christian republic," said the Presbyterian preacher S. M. Campbell of Rochester, New York, in 1867, "our Christianity being of the Protestant type. People who are not Christians, and people called Christians but who are not Protestants, dwell among us; but they did not build this house. . . . they must take up with such accommodations as we have. . . . If any one, coming among us, finds this arrangement is uncomfortable, perhaps he will do well to try some other country."[1] The Native Americans, having no other country, were placed on reservations to "accommodate" their refusal to become Protestants. Irish Catholics, Mormons, and others outside the norm found that both legal and popular intolerance undermined their right to free exercise of religion. The irony continues today, when a tripartite pluralism includes Protestants, Catholics, and Jews but finds less space for those of various Oriental persuasions, Moslems, Native Americans, or the new wave of sectarian dissent often pilloried as "cults."

This volume, though limited to the story of Baptist dissent in colonial New England (when they were a dangerous sect), examines some of the earlier ironies, inconsistencies, and contradictions within the concepts and practice of toleration and religious liberty. They do not exhaust the varieties within the Baptists' struggle.[2]

Nonetheless, they are illustrative of the complexity of the notion of separation of church and state. Essentially, the individual chapters are vignettes, illustrative by striking detail of the constant struggle of one particular group of dissenters to find some breathing space within the tightly knit church–state system of the Puritans (later called the Standing Order). Among these vignettes are several colorful firsthand accounts in the words of various Baptists describing their personal difficulties. These self-portraits by ordinary people struggling with their neighbors to determine how much freedom there could be in America shed new light on the present as well as the past. We know from the history of the civil rights movement and the feminist movement that deeply held convictions and the willingness to suffer for them are required of many ordinary citizens over long periods of time before legal discrimination and popular prejudice can be overcome. The Baptists here may seem unusual in their courage and conviction, but they were part of a continuing effort of ordinary people everywhere to evolve a broader meaning of liberty and justice for all.

Providence, Rhode Island   W. G. MCL.
February 1990

Acknowledgments

The articles reprinted here owe much to the editors of the various scholarly journals in which they were originally printed and to the referees and copy editors who helped to improve them. I want also to thank in particular Winthrop S. Hudson and Edwin S. Gaustad who made very helpful suggestions in the early stages of putting this anthology together (not to mention their friendship and collegial assistance over the years as we worked together in the field of religious history in America). And, as always, I want to thank my wife, Virginia, for her continued help and unfailing common sense whenever I need it.

I am grateful to the following for permission to reprint these articles that have appeared previously in different publications: "The Rise of the Antipedobaptists in New England, 1630–1655," from *New England Dissent,* Harvard University Press, 1971; "The Baptist Debates of April 14–15, 1968" (edited with Martha Whiting Davidson), *Proceedings* of the Massachusetts Historical Society, 1964; "Barrington Congregationalists vs. Swansea Baptists, 1711," *Rhode Island History,* 1973; "Free Love, Immortalism, and Perfectionism in Cumberland, Rhode Island, 1748–1768," *Rhode Island History,* 1974; "The First Calvinistic Baptist Association in New England, 1754?–1767," *Church History,* 1967; "Ebenezer Smith's Ballad of the Ashfield Baptists, 1772," *The New England Quarterly,* 1974; "The First Anti-slavery Church in New England," *Foundations,* 1972; "Massive Civil Disobedience as a Baptist Tactic in 1773," *The American Quarterly,* 1969; "Patriotism and Pietism. The Dissenting Dilemma: Massachusetts Rural Baptists and the American Revolution," *Foundations,* 1976; "Mob Violence Against Dissent in Revolutionary Massachusetts," *Foundations,* 1971; "The Balkcom Case (1782) and the Pietistic Theory of Separation of Church and State," *William and Mary Quarterly,* 1967; "Isaac Backus and the Separation of Church and State in America," *American Historical Review,* 1968; "A Brief Account of the Life of James Manning, D.D., President of Rhode Island College, by Isaac Backus," *Books at Brown,* 1968; "The Life of Elder Jabez Cottle (1747–1820): A Spiritual Autobiography in Verse," *New England Quarterly,* 1965. *Note:* I have changed some of the titles of these articles in order to provide more coherence to this volume, but except for some omissions of repetitive material, these articles remain as originally published.

SOUL LIBERTY

Introduction: An Overview

The Baptists of New England played an important role in American religious history from their first emergence as a group of dissenters in Massachusetts Bay in the early 1630s. Only grudgingly were they granted limited toleration in 1691. The Massachusetts authorities continued to tax them, distrain their property, and jail them throughout the eighteenth century. Finding little help at first from their Puritan neighbors or their legislators, the Baptists occasionally turned to the king and his counselors for assistance. But although the kings provided some help against the Congregationalists, they were hardly advocates of separation of church and state. Essentially, the Baptists had to rely on themselves.

Baptist grievances and complaints became louder in the 1760s, when new ideas about "the rights of Englishmen" and "inalienable natural rights" became popular. However, their fellow colonists did not like or trust them. On the eve of the colonial rebellion against the king and Parliament, many American patriots in New England doubted whether the Baptists would be on their side. The leading Congregational minister in Rhode Island (later the president of Yale), the Reverend Ezra Stiles of Newport, said of one of the foremost New England Baptists on July 16, 1776:

Mr. Manning, President of the Baptist College [in Rhode Island] is a Tory affecting Neutrality. He never prayed for the Congress or [for] Success to our Army till Gen. Washington, returning from Boston last Spring, being at Providence on Lordsday, he went to Mr. Manning's meeting [at the First Baptist Church]—then, for the first time, he prayed for the Congress and Army. But he and most of the Heads of the Baptists, especially Ministers, thro' the Continent are cool in this Cause, if not rather wishing the King's side Victory. . . . [Mr. Manning lately made] some sneering reflexions on the public affairs—he suggested that this was a Presbyterian [Congregational] War—the Congregationalists to the Northward had prevailed upon the [Anglican] Churchmen to the Southward [in Virginia] to join them—and that it was worth considering [whether] the Baptists would be crushed between them both if they overcome [the king]. This is the heart of the bigotted Baptist Politicians.[1]

Most of the doubts about Baptist patriotism grew out of the fact that the Congregationalists and Anglicans had been anything but fair toward the Baptists. Nevertheless, when the Revolution got underway, the Baptists enlisted overwhelmingly on the side of the patriot cause.

But something happened to the Baptist movement in America after the Revolution. The Baptists became the victims of their own success. With the victory of Thomas Jefferson (for whom most Baptists voted) in the election campaign of 1800, the Baptists entered the mainstream of American life. Though they did not succeed in overthrowing the remnants of the Congregational establishment in New England until 1833, they grew so numerous and popular that they were one of the two major denominations in the United States. They were no longer a small sect of outcast and downtrodden martyrs. It is not too much to say that the Baptists (especially in the south and west) embodied the basic outlook of the American people for most of the nineteenth century.

By entering the mainstream the Baptists ceased to be critics of American society; their piety relaxed, and they became the captives of the culture against which they had fought for so long. As the embodiment of American values, they were guilty of what Reinhold Niebuhr called "absolutizing the relative." That is, they came to believe that because the American social order had accepted their evangelical views, then America must be the equivalent of a Christian society. They concluded that the United States was, in fact, the most Christian society the world had ever known and that the Baptist cause must sink or swim with America. To be a good Baptist one should be a good American, and to be a good American one should be a good Baptist. Which meant, in effect, that the Baptists began to act as though they were the establishment. In short, between 1630 and 1833 the Baptists went through the classical evolution from a dissenting sect to an established church. In a way, the history of the Baptists is a paradigm of the American success myth: from rags to riches, from outcast to respectability, from pariah to pillar, from heresy to orthodoxy, from criminal deviant to authoritarian standard-bearer.

Although the first Baptist church in America still exists in Providence, the history of Rhode Island does not hold the key to either the history of the Baptists or the history of "soul liberty" in America. Rhode Island's "lively experiment" in freedom suffered from being at least 150 years ahead of its time. Rhode Island was called "rogue's island"—a scandal to decent order and propriety. It was not a model the other colonies wanted to imitate. The key to the history of religious liberty in New England lies in the story of the Baptists who did not run away to rogue's island but who stuck it out in Massachusetts, Connecticut, and Plymouth colonies. In some of those early battles for soul liberty the Baptists had to join forces with the Quakers (a sect that Roger Williams considered the worst form of heresy) because the Quakers in the early eighteenth century had powerful allies in England who had the ear of the king, which the Baptists did not. In the seventeenth century the Quakers suffered far crueler persecution in Puritan New England than did the Baptists. No Baptist was ever hung on Boston Common.

The Baptists were saved from the cruelties meted out to Quakers because they were not so different from their neighbors and did not invade the colony suddenly from outside. Most Baptists started as good Calvinistic members of the Puritan congregations. Some of them were deacons in the Puritan churches. Because the Puritans were themselves very uncertain about the question of infant baptism, the Baptists were able to argue with them pretty much on their own terms. In fact, it was the view of the earliest Baptists in Massachusetts, like Thomas Goold, that the mode and subject of baptism was a minor and "non-essential" matter about which good Puritans might differ without splitting the churches. We know that John Cotton and Charles Chauncy, two outstanding Congregational ministers, both agreed that baptism by immersion was as proper a mode as baptism by sprinkling. We know that the Puritans believed in gathered churches of baptized believers and in a congregational autonomy. We know that at first the Puritans favored voluntary support of the ministers and churches, not compulsory taxation.

Hence, the early Baptists had much common ground on which to stand with their neighbors.

But if the Baptists had the advantage of arguing from within the Puritan system as respectable, hardworking, pious farmers and churchgoers, they also had several disadvantages. There was no college-educated Baptist who could stand up and speak for them (Henry Dunster, the president of Harvard, tried to do so briefly in 1654, but he was immediately silenced and left for Plymouth Colony). Second, their opponents were quick to associate their views with the wild and revolutionary Anabaptists of 1535, who took over the city of Munster, Germany, and practiced polygamy and rebellion against their rulers. Third, some of these early Baptists were not the most tactful and reasonable of men, and when the Puritans tried to tell them to shut up, some of them got very angry and raised a great fuss. One early Baptist in Charlestown was sentenced to pay a fine of ten pounds or be openly whipped ten stripes because he stomped to the front of the meetinghouse one Sunday morning when an infant was being baptized and threw the baptismal basin on the floor. A Rhode Island Baptist who had the temerity to enter Massachusetts to baptize a believer by immersion in 1651 was given thirty-nine lashes with a three-corded whip.

Despite these and other early examples of contumely and persecution, the Baptist faith persisted. In 1665 a small group of Baptists in the town of Charlestown, just across the river from Boston, formed a little church in the home of Thomas Goold. Goold and his friends were threatened with banishment and fled to Noddles Island in Boston harbor until things cooled down a bit. Then, in 1679, these Baptists secretly built a meetinghouse in the very center of Boston, telling those who asked what they were building so close to the millpond that it was to be a brewery. When it was completed and they tried to worship in it, the authorities boarded up the doors. But by that time Massachusetts was under considerable pressure from Puritans in old England to go easy on the Baptists. English Puritans were themselves being persecuted under the Restoration government of Charles II. Fearing that the king might revoke their charter, in 1682 the Puritans of Massachusetts finally relented to the point of allowing the Baptists to worship freely in their Boston meetinghouse.

So the first stage of Baptist martyrdom ended, and toleration was obtained. It is worth noting that in none of the early debates with the Puritan authorities did the Baptists argue against the system of compulsory religious taxes to support the Congregational churches (a system Massachusetts adopted in 1646). Under this practice every town in the colony (and in those of Plymouth, Connecticut, New Hampshire, and Vermont) was required to levy taxes on all inhabitants to pay the salary of the Congregational minister in that town and also to build and maintain the Congregational meetinghouse (where town meetings were also held). There were no exemptions from this tax. But not until they first obtained sufficient toleration to worship as they pleased did the Baptists try to take the next step toward soul liberty by demanding that they be excused from paying these ecclesiastical taxes.

The main scene for this stage of their development was in southeastern Massachusetts in the area of the old Plymouth Colony. Plymouth had been somewhat more tolerant toward dissenters than had Massachusetts, and many Baptists and Quakers had settled in towns like Rehoboth, Swansea, Dartmouth, and Tiverton as well as on Cape Cod. In some of these towns the Baptists and Quakers constituted a majority of the residents, and they refused to pass laws levying taxes to support Congregational ministers. When, after 1691, Plymouth Colony was merged into Massachusetts Bay Colony, the legislature in Boston tried to force the Baptist and Quaker towns to hire Congregational ministers and to lay taxes for their support. At the instigation of the Quakers in Dartmouth and Tiverton an appeal was carried to the king in 1723, claiming that this was contrary to the Toleration Act that had been passed by Parliament in 1689. The king agreed and demanded that the Congregationalists stop taxing other dissenters for the support of their churches. Although the king had no objection to Anglican churches taxing dissenters, he saw no grounds for Congregationalists to assume this right.

In 1728 Massachusetts began passing a series of laws that eventually granted the right of Anglicans, Baptists, and Quakers to tax exemption for the support of Congregationalism. Strangely enough, this seemed to satisfy the Baptists. They quietly agreed to the idea of an established church as long as they did not have to support it.

During the 1730s the Baptists in Massachusetts did everything they could to gain the respect of their Congregational neighbors. As early as 1708 they had begun to send some of their young men to Harvard to be educated. Moreover, they agreed not to spread the Baptist cause by evangelizing among the Congregationalists. And some of the Baptists around Boston began to lose interest in Calvinistic theology; they adopted the Arminian doctrines that were popular among Rhode Island Baptists and becoming popular at Harvard. As a result, the Baptist movement ceased to grow after 1710.

It might well have died out entirely had it not been for the Great Awakening, which occurred in the 1740s. For obvious reasons the Arminian Baptists were not interested in that revival. In the first place most of the revivalists were, like Jonathan Edwards and George Whitefield, strict Calvinists in their theology. Second, the Awakening was seen in New England as essentially a Congregational movement. George Whitefield, for example, never preached in a Baptist meetinghouse when he toured New England, and Jonathan Edwards, Gilbert Tennent, and other revival preachers had nothing but scorn for Baptists.

Ultimately, however, the Awakening did revive the Baptist movement. Many of the Congregationalists who were converted during the revival of the 1740s became dissatisfied with their ministers either because they were not sufficiently ardent in their preaching or because they admitted unconverted persons into the churches or because they allowed ecclesiastical councils to interfere with the congregational autonomy of the churches. These newly converted or reawakened Congregationalists were called New Lights. They were ardent believers in voluntarily gathered churches of converted believers. Thwarted in their efforts to reform the Old Light conservatives, they separated from the established churches and began what historians now called the Separate movement. Scores of new Separate churches were formed throughout New England, creating, in effect, a new denomination (sometimes called Strict Congregationalists or Separates). By the middle of the 1750s there were more than 125 Separate churches in New England. The town and colony magistrates refused to recognize them as a new denomination and continued to lay taxes on their members to support the "old light" churches from which they had separated.

These devout and earnestly pious New Light Calvinists began to study their Bibles more carefully, and they tried to make their churches as free of corruption as possible. Many of them came to the conclusion that the source of corruption within the Puritan churches was the unscriptural practice of infant baptism. Within a few years, more than half of the Separate churches had adopted the principle of believers baptism by immersion. The churches that did so were then called Separate-Baptist churches. Their growth provided a new impetus to the Baptist movement and a return to Calvinist theology for the denomination. By 1760 the Baptists and their principles were spreading far and wide across the Puritan colonies; Baptist principles found new popularity, and because the Separates and Separate Baptists opposed being taxed to support corrupt Old Light churches, they began to agitate for tax exemption. New leaders, such as Isaac Backus, Ebenezer Smith, and Thomas Green, arose out of the Separate-Baptist movement. They wrote petitions and memorials for religious freedom and lobbied against the "certificate system" through which the old Baptists had obtained tax exemption.

The rise of a large Baptist movement in New England attracted the attention of Baptists in the middle colonies. Men from Pennsylvania and New Jersey, who were themselves learned ministers— Hezekiah Smith, Samuel Stillman, David Howell, John Davis, and James Manning—came to New England to urge the founding of a Baptist college in Rhode Island, where Baptists could train pastors for their growing churches. They also urged the Baptist churches to unite in an association or confederation to provide stability, unity, and order to the denomination in New England. From this point on, the Baptists of New England combined their efforts for soul liberty with their efforts at institution building.

The founding of the Baptist College in Warren, Rhode Island, in 1764 was one of the first major achievements of the reinvigorated Baptist movement. It would never have been founded without the Great Awakening, the Separate movement, and the influx of leadership from the Baptists to the south. It had to be founded in Rhode

Island because none of the Puritan colonies would grant a charter
to a Baptist institution. James Manning became its first president.
In 1767 Manning also drafted a constitution for the first permanent
Baptist association in New England, the Warren Association. Many
Baptists were at first suspicious that such associations would assume
power over the individual churches, and Elder Peter Werden (the
Baptists preferred the term "Elder" to "Minister") of the Baptist
church in Coventry, Rhode Island, explained that his church would
not join such an association because it could not find anything in
the Bible that "supports a classical government over the churches
of Christ." Werden's church members also said that an association
would "overthrow the independence of the churches of Christ."[2]
Elder Isaac Backus of the First Baptist Church in Middleborough,
Massachusetts, a trustee of the new college, wrote to Manning saying that he and his church did not believe "that the rights and
liberties of particular churches are sufficiently secured by what is
said in your plan."[3]

There is little doubt that Manning did want the association to
exercise some measure of order and regulation over the constituent
churches. Some of them were tending toward heterodoxy and perfectionism. He also wanted to assure that all Baptist churches were
Calvinist in theology and to give the association the power to adjudicate disputes between or within churches. But he had to make
some concessions before the majority of Baptist churches agreed to
join the association. Over the next twenty years some forty-five
churches, most of them in Massachusetts, joined, but many others
did not. Eventually, new associations were formed: the Stonington,
Connecticut, Association in 1772; the New Hampshire Association
in 1776; and the Shaftesbury, Vermont, Association in 1781.

Despite the strength that this new unity gave the Baptist cause,
the established (or Standing) order continued to lay taxes on Separate Baptists, who, they said, were wholly different from the Baptists exempted from taxation in the law of 1729. Isaac Backus wrote
a history of the Baptists in 1776 in which he gave dozens of examples in which Separate Baptists were sent to jail or had their
property distrained and sold at auction for refusing to pay ecclesiastical taxes. He told the story of an elderly widow, Esther White,
in his own church who spent thirteen months in jail because she

would not pay the eight-penny tax levied on her. In the face of this continued persecution, the members of the Warren Association agreed in 1769 to create a Grievance Committee, which would assist any Baptist unfairly taxed, distrained, or jailed. Elder John Davis was its first chairman; in 1773 Isaac Backus succeeded him. The members of the Grievance Committee collected affidavits from the persecuted and their friends, wrote petitions to the courts and legislature, appeared before the legislative committees to lobby for revision of the exemption laws, and in some cases carried appeals to the king of England. In 1773 this committee organized a campaign of massive civil disobedience in an effort to fill the jails with Baptists who would refuse to cooperate in any way with the tax laws. This effort failed, but it indicated a new turning point in the evolution of the New England Baptists' position on separation of church and state. Hitherto, they had worked only to make tax exemption through certificates of Baptist membership more workable; now they concluded that ecclesiastical taxes in any form were contrary to the higher principle of separation of church and state. It is significant that until this date no Baptist had ever cited Roger Williams as an authority on this point.

The Revolution brought a temporary lull in Baptist agitation as they joined in the fight for political liberty. They assumed that one of the principles of the revolutionary cause was freedom of religion. To their astonishment, when Massachusetts adopted its first constitution as a state, in 1780, it included the right and duty of every town to lay taxes for the support of religion. Although the majority in almost every town was Congregational, the constitution of Massachusetts stated that "every denomination of Christians . . . shall be equally under the protection of the law and no subordination of any one sect or denomination to another shall ever be established by law." What Massachusetts intended by this apparent contradiction was that the churches of every denomination in every township should also have the right to support from ecclesiastical taxes. The taxes for religious support in each town were to be divided up among the denominations in proportion to the number of members in each. The writers of the constitution, assuming that most citizens were too stingy to provide adequate support for religion, wished to use the power of the state for that purpose. This same procedure was advocated in Virginia by Patrick Henry and others in the 1780s and was called "a general assessment for the support of religion." In Virginia the people rejected the general assessment bill and adopted instead the bill for religious freedom drafted by Thomas Jefferson and sponsored by James Madison. In 1785 Virginia abolished the tax-supported system for religion, but in New England the general assessment compromise was tried with disastrous results for over half a century.

The difficulty arose from the fact that few towns could devise or sustain a fair and nondiscriminatory means of dividing up the ecclesiastical tax. Some towns tried to reinstate the old certificate system (though it was no longer on the law books). Some were dominated by stubborn Congregationalists who required dissenters to sue the town before they would return their taxes. The courts inclined toward the view that dissenting congregations could not legally obtain a share of the ecclesiastical taxes in their township until they had applied to the state legislature for incorporation: only corporate bodies were "public" and thus entitled to a share of ecclesiastical taxes under the constitution. On this point, however, juries often disagreed with the judges. Dissenters who tried to give in certificates found that, as before, they were not always honored. Those who refused to pay such taxes continued to be distrained and jailed. As for seeking incorporation, many dissenters (like Isaac Backus among the Baptists) fiercely opposed any such obeisance to "Caesar" in order to worship according to conscience; they continued to struggle for total disestablishment and voluntary support for religion.

The final phase in the history of disestablishment (discussed more fully in chapter 15) involved the complex efforts by various court decisions, legislative acts, and dissenting protests to discover whether a general assessment system could be made fair and workable. Some Baptists were willing to accept the system, but only a minority. Those who did so sought incorporation and made the most of the taxes raised for them by the state. But this was not the only inconsistency in the Baptist struggle for religious freedom in these years. In 1781, at the very time when Backus and the Grievance Committee were making their most eloquent pleas for religious equality, a prominent Baptist minister in the town of Pittsfield, Elder Valentine Rathbun, helped to write (and then signed) a statement urging the selectmen to arrest, imprison, or drive out of the town all of those irregular and disorderly persons called Shakers.[4] In Massachusetts, Vermont, and New Hampshire there were instances in which the Baptists, finding themselves to be a majority in a town, laid taxes for the support of their Elder and then forced Congregationalists and others to give in certificates or sue for their share. Although Isaac Backus wrote some of the most stirring tracts on religious liberty of the eighteenth century, nonetheless he supported the test oath in the Massachusetts Constitution, which discriminated against Roman Catholics.[5] He also proclaimed fast days and thanksgiving days from his pulpit at the request of the governors, knowing full well that failure of any citizen to attend church on such days was punishable by law. In fact, he never thought it necessary to oppose the existing New England laws that required church attendance on the Sabbath, nor did he oppose inculcating the Westminster catechism in the public schools. The Baptists never opposed state-supported legislative chaplains, and several Baptist elders served in that capacity. The Baptists in Rhode Island ardently sought license from the state to issue lottery tickets to raise money for their college in 1795. And in 1792 Backus joined with the Congregationalists of New England in petitioning Congress to establish a committee to license the publication of Bibles (though the right to license would seem to include the right to censor). All of which indicates that it was as difficult then as now to draw a precise line between church and state, especially when the Baptists, like most Christians in the early nineteenth century, considered that the United States was, and of right ought to be, a Christian nation.

When Isaac Backus died in 1806, the fight for separation of church and state was still far from over in New England. Vermont did not disestablish its Congregational churches until 1707; Connecticut followed in 1818, New Hampshire in 1819, and Massachusetts in 1833.[6] But the political power of dissenters grew steadily after 1776, making disestablishment ultimately necessary. The institutional growth of the Baptist denomination hardly needs documenting. In the year 1740 there were only twelve Baptist churches in New England (outside the colony of Rhode Island). Between

1740 and 1800 these had grown to one hundred. By 1830 there were more than 250. In addition to Rhode Island College (after 1805 called Brown University), the Baptists founded Colby College in 1820, Hamilton College in 1821, and Newton Theological Seminary in 1825. In 1802 the Baptists founded their first home missionary society and in 1814 their first foreign missionary society. They began their first monthly magazine in 1802 and their first weekly newspaper in 1819. In the 1820s they organized state conventions to unite the various associations, and with the formation of the Triennial Baptist Convention in 1814 they tied the New England movement into the even larger Baptist movements in the middle, southern, and western states. By 1830 they were engaged in all kinds of voluntary reform societies and had eminent national leaders like Francis Wayland and Thomas Baldwin in New England.

As they became one of the most prominent denominations in the nation, the Baptists assumed the right to speak for the nation and even for the city of Boston. In an editorial in their Boston newspaper in 1828, they deplored the fact that the radical British lecturer Frances Wright "has been permitted to come into the heart of our city with the avowed object of contesting the dearest principles of our social state."[7] Three hundred years after the law banishing them from Massachusetts, the Baptists were claiming that the city upon a hill was "our city" in "our state." Victory seemed to have gone to their heads.

On the long route to this victory, the Baptists presented a colorful and valiant panoply of defiance and protest in the name of disestablishment and the free exercise of religion, one that needs to be better known. The mighty and respectable should not forget their own humble origins.

[1]

The Rise of the Antipedobaptists in New England, 1630-1655

It is no more possible to speak of "the Baptists" than it is to speak of "the Indians" in seventeenth-century America because there were too many different kinds of them. Lumping varieties of peoples together is usually a way of stereotyping them under certain pejorative characteristics. Just as all Indians were considered pagan, savage, cruel, and untrustworthy, so early New Englanders tended to lump all Baptists (or in their term, "Anabaptists"—meaning "rebaptizers") under the heading of heretics, schismatics, troublemakers, and fanatics. Once such a stereotype takes hold, it is easy to rouse the populace against such "enemies" of good order and Christian truth and then to pass discriminatory laws or to tolerate popular harassment of these deviants from decency. Persecution then becomes respectable.

The wide variety of Baptists in the early nineteenth century indicates something else equally important here. They were a comparatively new group, still seeking self-definition, coherence, and uniformity even among themselves. The Puritans of New England suffered from the same incoherence as part of a general dissatisfaction among Englishmen with the beliefs and practices of the Church of England. Pilgrims in Plymouth Bay thought a good Puritan should separate himself from that polluted sepulcher. Puritans in Massachusetts Bay thought they ought not to separate but to reform the Anglican church from within. The whole of England became a seething mass of new sects and schismatics in the mid-seventeenth century. It is well to start any discussion of religious liberty by understanding the variety of Baptists who claimed that title. This will help us to remember that the Baptists were themselves part of the Puritan movement against the Anglican establishment.

When they first arose in the early part of the seventeenth century, those who eventually were to be known as Baptists did not know whether to advocate complete or partial separation from the churches they left, whether they wanted open or closed communion with other Reformed Protestants or among themselves, whether they believed in baptism by sprinkling or immersion, whether they should worship on the seventh or the first day of the week, whether there were five or six principles fundamental to their faith, whether they should stand for pacifism, communism, faith healing, anti-magistracy, the priesthood of all believers, or, after all, for only a slightly modified form of Puritanism. In England and in Rhode Island they did not even know whether they stood for Calvinism or Arminianism. Ultimately, it proved to be the most conservative wing of the movement, that closest in principle and practice to the Puritans from whom they separated, who dominated the denomination and carried the day.

Because the Baptists did not know at first who they were or what they stood for, it is not surprising that the Puritans also misunderstood them. At first the Puritans looked upon them as eccentric fanatics—a dangerous resurgence of sixteenth-century Munsterite Anabaptism. At other times they equated them with Brownists, Antinomians, Levellers, Familists, Quakers, and even "Papists." In the battle of words and whips that the Puritans of Massachusetts waged to extirpate these dissenters between 1635 and 1682 the basis of the differences between them was slowly hammered out. The truth was that both the Puritans and the Baptists changed gradually with the times and with experience. Yet each group was convinced that it, and it alone, constituted the vanguard of the "new Reformation" that was to carry forward in the realm of Britain the work begun a century earlier by Luther and Calvin on the continent. They argued not in terms of denominationalism but in terms of which of them had the clearer insight into the revealed will of God and which of them, therefore, knew best how to establish and maintain the true church and the true faith. As there was only one true church and one true faith, those who were not with God were against him.

In addition to religious principles there were certain pragmatic problems raised by the claim of the minority to be tolerated. Regardless of the theological merits of the Baptists' claim, the Puritans were convinced that Massachusetts Bay was not big enough for two rival groups of true believers. Those who did not agree with the principles of the founders and leaders of the colony had "free liberty," as Nathaniel Ward put it in *The Simple Cobbler of Agawam* (1647), "to keep away from us." After all, the plantation was a private company. It had the right by royal charter to establish its own rules of church and state as long as they did not contradict those of England; and until Oliver Cromwell came to power, no Baptist could claim he was tolerated in England. Throughout Christendom the policy of *cuius regio, eius religio* prevailed. The Puritans were convinced that if the Baptists ever became a majority they would not tolerate deviants from *their* way. Even when, under Cromwell's regime, England did tolerate Baptists, the New England Puritans pointed out that what might be allowed in an ancient, large, and well-established country like England would be a grave danger to a small, unstable young frontier plantation like Massachusetts Bay or Connecticut. The Baptists, adding their own pragmatic arguments, replied that nothing was less conducive to peace and order than persecution of respectable persons for conscience. Abstract and absolute principles of religious faith and order thus mingled indiscriminately with questions of expediency, law, custom, and majority rule.

Because religion was so deeply imbedded in the social and political principles of the era, the quarrel involved more than toleration or the separation of church and state. It displayed all of the fundamental antinomies of human social behavior and private belief. It could be roughly subsumed under such headings as church versus sect, conservatism versus radicalism, corporate welfare versus individual freedom, aristocracy versus democracy, in-group versus out-group. The solutions that were worked out in colonial New England to settle this struggle (insofar as it can ever be settled) were those that, for better or worse, shaped the history of liberty in modern America.

Although evolution of the Baptist persuasion was simultaneous in old England and New England, direct connection between the two groups was relatively slight. The first so-called Baptist church was founded in England in 1611 or 1612, when Thomas Helwys and John Murton returned to London from Holland (where they had gone in 1608 as Separatists). In Holland, Helwys and Murton had been influenced by the Mennonites to the extent of giving up infant baptism, but they did not agree with the Mennonites in rejecting oaths, war, and civil magistracy. Nor did they believe that baptism should be by immersion. But they did follow the Mennonites in adopting an Arminian revision of Calvinism, notably in believing that Christ died to save *all* men who would accept him on faith, not just the predestined or particular elect. Hence, the Baptist church of Helwys and Murton began the wing of the Baptist movement known as the General Baptists, as differentiated from the Calvinistic or Particular Baptists. During most of the seventeenth century there were more General Baptists than Particular Baptists, though their relationship with the New England Baptists was even more tenuous, except among those in Providence Plantations.

The founding of the first Particular Baptist church in England is usually dated from 1638, though its members did not practice baptism by immersion until 1641—two years after the Baptists in Providence, Rhode Island, appear to have adopted it. Significantly, the Particular Baptists in London, led by John Spilsbury, derived from the Non-Separatist Congregational church founded by Henry Jacob in Southwark in 1616.

Jacob was an Oxford graduate and a Puritan minister within the Anglican church. He is credited with being among the founders of that branch of Congregationalism that contributed most to the settlement of Massachusetts. He also persuaded John Robinson, whose followers settled the Plymouth Colony, to modify his early Separatism after 1612 to the extent of sanctioning open communion with the Church of England, at least in preaching and prayer.

The fact that John Spilsbury and his antipedobaptist congregations derived directly from Jacob's Non-Separatist Congregational principles is characteristic of the whole Calvinistic Baptist movement in England and New England. Yet the Anglo-American relationships even with this Calvinistic wing of the movement were minimal. Several individuals baptized in Spilsbury's church and in other Baptist offshoots from Jacob's church found their way into New England Baptist churches. One of these was Hanserd Knollys, who had a stormy career as a minister in New England from 1638 to 1641, returned to London, and became a Particular Baptist in 1644. That same year Spilsbury, William Kiffin, and several other Calvinistic Baptist ministers drew up the first confession of faith for the Particularists and thus gave the beginning of unity to the movement. The adherence of several college-educated former Puritans to the Baptists in the 1640s (men like Knollys, Henry Jessey, and John Tombes) gave the denomination some able scholarly apol-

ogists whose books were quoted in New England. In 1645 Tombes
sent one of his books to the magistrates of Massachusetts in the
hope of persuading them to reconsider their recent law banishing
Anabaptists from the colony. Knollys and Jessey (though not Kiffin)
adopted a policy of open or mixed communion with the Independents and Presbyterians who would accept it, and over the years
(especially after 1660) the open-communion Congregationalists in
England urged toleration for Baptists in New England. But except
for this kind of general encouragement and example, the English
Baptists provided little help or stimulus to their New England
brethren. Knowledge of intolerance in Massachusetts prevented any
mass exodus of Baptists to the Puritan colonies even after the Clarendon Code led to their persecution in England. Only one leading
Baptist minister, John Myles of Wales, ever came to New England
to provide the leadership sorely needed for the movement there,
and he settled in the Plymouth Colony in 1663.

In short, the Baptist movement in New England was essentially
an indigenous, parallel movement to that in England and not an
offshoot or extension of it. It stemmed from a common source in
the theological and ecclesiological principles of the general Puritan
movement and needed no other source or stimulus than the ideas
the Non-Separatist Congregationalists brought to New England.

The spectrum of the seventeenth-century pietistic movement,
which Increase Mather called "the new Reformation," went from
Presbyterianism on the right to Quakerism and Seekerism on the
left. Roger Williams ran the spectrum from right to left, as did
many other Englishmen. To the Anglicans and Presbyterians the
settlers of the Massachusetts Bay Colony "were separatists and
would be Anabaptists." For the New England Puritans, however,
the difference between their own views and those of all varieties of
the antipedobaptists was the difference between the civilized frontier of the true Reformation and the wilderness of anarchy and
chaos: "the briars of Anabaptisme," Cotton Mather called it. He
added, "Most of the Quakers that I have had occasion to converse
with were first Anabaptists." Once a man began to have scruples
about infant baptism, he had started down the slippery road to
Antinomianism, Familism, Ranterism, Quakerism, and all of the
other heresies to which Satan lured the ignorant, the arrogant, and

the self-righteous. The Reverend William Hubbard of Ipswich, writing his history of New England in 1680, concluded, "It is too often seen that these new sectaries that go about to unchurch all other christian societies do at last unchurch themselves and from anabaptists become sebaptists then seekers and at last ranters"—all "out of a giddy unstable mind."

In one sense the fight for toleration that the Baptists waged in New England in the seventeenth century was an attempt to prove that they were not ignorant, irresponsible enthusiasts like the Munsterites or the Quakers, that they were in fact just as respectable and law-abiding and correct in their interpretation of Scripture as were the Puritans. Because they were former members or adherents of the Puritan churches and generally respectable inhabitants of the commonwealth—not wild invaders like the Antinomians and Quakers—they had one advantage that these immigrant sects lacked. As offshoots from the Puritan churches they had the additional advantage of being orthodox Calvinists who argued within the accepted philosophical and social framework of the community. And finally, because the New England Puritans themselves could not make up their minds precisely what the correct practice of baptism involved, the Baptists had a third advantage: they waged their fight for reform on the most controversial and unsettled ground in the whole Puritan system. Increase Mather went so far as to say that "the right to baptism" was to "the new Reformation" of the seventeenth century what the argument over transubstantiation was to the Reformation of the sixteenth century. The question of baptism reached not only to the heart of the complex problem of the true form of church policy but also to the church's relationship to the state. It challenged the very structure and purpose of the Puritan social and political order. Was the Massachusetts Bay Colony a corporate, collectivist, Christian order in which, as John Winthrop said, "the care of the publique must oversway all private respects"? If so, were the magistrates, as nursing fathers to the church, obligated primarily to follow the will of God rather than the will of those who elected them? Or was it essential for the purity of the churches, and ultimately for the prevalence of Truth, that the magistrate keep scrupulously out of religious affairs and confine himself basically to the role of an umpire in public affairs? Was every man to be free, not only in his conscience but also in his actions (insofar as he caused no direct harm to the body or property of others), to follow his own judgment in all of the affairs of this world because ultimately he alone must answer to God in the next?

The questions were not phrased precisely in these terms in the seventeenth century, and the Baptists often denied that they were trying to raise them. Yet they lay at the heart of the controversy, and Americans were a long time finding answers to them.

Roger Williams began the struggle for separation of church and state in 1635 with a magnificent failure. His inability to define his own beliefs or to remain for long in any church or denomination is symbolic of the amorphous quality of religious dissent in old and New England during his lifetime. Williams, like the Baptists, whose claims he accepted for only a few months in 1639, knew better what he was against than what he was for. Soul liberty, as he explained it, was a negative, not a positive ideal. It asked the state to stop interfering in religious affairs because interference had, as experience demonstrated, led to the oppression of true saints and the persecution of true churches. But precisely what true saints and true churches, Williams spent the whole of his life seeking unsuccessfully. Some of those who came to share the freedom of his "lively experiment" in Rhode Island and Providence Plantations found the answer in mysticism, others in Socinianism, some in Quakerism, and still others in the several varieties of the Baptist persuasion.

Roger Williams's experiment was a failure because of the inability of Rhode Islanders to shape, by example or evangelism, the destiny of either New England or any of the other colonies. Despite the valiant efforts of Williams, almost no one in colonial New England ever praised his experiment, sought his advice, quoted his books, or tried to imitate his practices. Even in Rhode Island he was often assailed as unsound—and to the other New England colonies, Rhode Island was always the prime example not of the virtues but of the horrors of religious liberty. Those who fought hardest for religious freedom in Massachusetts, Connecticut, Vermont, and New Hampshire considered Rhode Island an embarrassment rather than an asset to their cause. During and after the colonial period, Rhode Island, "the licentious Republic" and "sinke hole of New England," was an example to be shunned.

Hence, Rhode Islanders were always on the periphery of the battle for religious liberty. What happened in their precariously held corner of New England counted for little unless the citadel of Puritanism was taken. The Rhode Islanders rightly saw themselves not as the center of an expanding crusade but as a wilderness shelter for outcasts, a precarious experiment in nonconformity, a furtive supplier of succor for those who waged the real fight within the gates of the enemy. Because they had separated themselves from the corruptions of the Puritan system (or had been banished for their separatism), they went their way alone. The lump of compulsory conformity from which they separated had to be leavened from within by the saving remnant who stayed behind—the non-separating dissenters.

In the fight for separation of church and state in New England, the Baptists were only one of several battalions of dissenters. Ultimately, however, they proved to be the most consistent, the most numerous, and the most effective. During the seventeenth and early eighteenth centuries they often received valuable assistance from the parallel (but seldom cooperative) efforts of Presbyterians, Anglicans, and Quakers. In the middle and latter parts of the eighteenth century and the early nineteenth century they received similar assistance from the Separates during the Great Awakening and from the Methodists and Universalists afterward. Without this help they could not have won the fight for religious liberty. Generally, however, the Baptists bore the brunt of the fighting from 1635, when Roger Williams was banished, to 1833, when compulsory religious taxation was abolished.

Because the term Anabaptist was so loosely applied to a wide range of dissenters from Puritan orthodoxy, it is impossible to assess with any accuracy the generation and growth of the Baptist movement in the seventeenth century. Almost any person to the left of the Puritan position was termed an Anabaptist or said to be "tinged with Anabaptistry."[1] Contemporary private and public records mention some forty to fifty incidents in New England between 1635 and 1680 involving "Anabaptists" or persons "with anabaptistical tendencies"; but since these terms were used to describe Antinomians like Anne Hutchinson, as well as Separatists, these incidents tell us more about Puritan fears than about Baptist growth. Baptism was a controversial issue, but it was difficult at the outset to distinguish Baptists as a sect. Charles Chauncy was called a Baptist by some simply because he advocated the baptism of infants (and adults) by immersion, though he differed from his colleagues in the Massachusetts ministry on nothing else. Henry Dunster was called a Baptist though he was never excommunicated from the Puritan church in Cambridge and never was more explicit in his dissent than to oppose infant baptism.

There is no record of many forerunners of the Baptist movement because they feared to reveal themselves. The promptness with which ecclesiastical and civil authorities pounced on suspected Anabaptists gave pause to any who leaned in that direction. However, the fact that the First Baptist Church of Boston grew from its nine original founders in 1665 to more than eighty members by 1680 indicates that an inert potential existed for the movement.

The authorities usually discovered an incipient Anabaptist by his own action—his refusal to have a child baptized or his unwillingness to participate in the baptismal services for the infants of others. The certainty of punishment for such overt acts of nonconformity undoubtedly led many to prefer emigration from the colony. No doubt some who were punished for failing to attend church regularly were covert Baptists who chose that alternative to the more severe penalties they could have received had they attended a baptism and felt obligated in conscience to turn their backs on it or to walk out of the church rather than participate. Once a Baptist church was formed, many admitted that they had long held antipedobaptist views but had not dared express them.[2]

By the end of the seventeenth century there were six Baptist churches in Rhode Island, three in the old Plymouth Colony area, one in Boston, and none in Connecticut.[3] Rhode Island and the towns on its indeterminate boundaries (Seekonk, Dartmouth, Tiverton, and Little Compton on the east and New London and Westerly on the west) acted as safety valves for the dissenters from the Puritan colonies. Even after 1682, when Baptists and other dissenters in Massachusetts ceased to be subject to civil punishments, social discrimination continued to drive them off to unsettled areas between villages, to the frontier, or to other colonies. Toleration, as it turned out, did not lead to any rapid increase in dissent. Intolerance after 1682 merely became secularized. Not until the Great Awakening did the Baptist movement in New England really attain sizable proportions. According to the best estimate that can be made, not more than one in one hundred persons in New England (including Rhode Island) was an acknowledged Baptist in the year 1700. Not more than two in one hundred belonged to any other dissenting denomination—Quakers, Anglicans, Presbyterians. Most of the ten thousand people living in Rhode Island at that time, however, may be considered as opponents of the Puritan system, and many silent dissenters still existed within the Puritan colonies.

The first group openly advocating antipedobaptism in New England, and the first to adopt baptism (for them, rebaptism) of adult believers by immersion as the only proper basis for church membership, was the small band of exiles from Salem who formed the First Baptist Church in Providence in 1639. Roger Williams and Ezekiel Holliman baptized each other and then ten more persons, most of them former members of the Salem church. According to John Winthrop, Williams was led to adopt "anabaptism" by the wife of Richard Scott, a sister of Mrs. Hutchinson, who had come to Providence with her husband that year.[4] But it is just as likely that Williams's own incessant search for the true form of the true church led him to adopt Baptist views at this time. Four months after his baptism Williams left the Baptist church because he doubted the validity of adult immersion, and in subsequent trips to England he found the friendship of Congregationalists like Harry Vane and John Milton more congenial than that of Baptists.[5] In 1652 the Baptist Church in Providence split over two questions: the "laying on of hands" upon all believers ("the sixth principle") and Arminianism. The Six Principle and Arminianism both prevailed, and the Five Principle Calvinists in Providence soon died out. The lack of strong leadership among the Providence Baptists and their break with Calvinism prevented their playing a significant role in the spread of Baptist views among the Puritan colonies thereafter, for the Baptist movement outside the Rhode Island area, especially around Boston, was Calvinistic.

Thus, it was the First Baptist Church in Newport, which had good leadership and remained Calvinistic, that had the closer relationship with the Baptists of Massachusetts Bay. Founded by John Clarke in or about 1644, it lost some members in a schism over the laying on of hands in 1656, and others became Seventh Day Baptists in 1671. But these schisms failed to stem its growth. Clarke, born in Suffolk, England, in 1609 and educated as a physician (possibly at the University of Leyden), arrived in Boston in the fall of 1637.[6] He appears to have sympathized with the Antinomians and was among those disarmed by the Puritan leaders out of fear of insurrection. He left Boston after a few weeks, spent the winter with a group of Antinomian emigrants in New Hampshire, and moved to Portsmouth, Rhode Island, the next spring. Why Clarke assumed religious leadership over the church founded in Portsmouth is not known. It does not appear that he was a Baptist at this time, and the church that he led in Portsmouth (and after 1639 in Newport) probably was a Separatist Congregational church until 1644. That some of the Antinomians became Baptists and others became Quakers after 1641 can be explained only in terms of their own intense pietistic striving (through the help of the Holy Spirit) to discover or to recover the basic doctrines of divine revelation and the basic policy of the primitive church. It may be that the immigration of some Baptists from London, like Henry Lukar, influenced Clarke's decision to found a Baptist church, but there is no record of this.[7]

While the Baptist (and later the Quaker) movement flourished in the tolerant antinomian atmospheres of Providence, Portsmouth, Newport, and other Narragansett Bay settlements, the dissenters in Massachusetts Bay found life very difficult in the seventeenth century. One of the proudest claims of the New England Puritans was that their system retained its uniformity and its stability, simultaneously maintaining a strict division between the things that are God's and those that are Caesar's. Not only did they have no bishops or ecclesiastical courts but no creeds, no rituals, no liturgies, no disciplines, no book of common prayer imposed on their autonomous churches by the state. One of their claims to being a more purified Christian commonwealth lay in their careful attempt to maintain a rigid line between the rights of the churches and the duties of the magistrates. Though they were accused of establishing a theocracy, they called their establishment a coordinate system, and they laid down careful regulations to keep the ministers and the magistrates within their respective spheres. These two spheres, said John Cotton, were not to be confused "either by giving the Spiritual Power which is proper to the Church into the hands of the Civil Magistrate . . . or by giving Civil Power to church officers, who are called to attend to Spiritual Matters and the things of God."[8] When a Baptist published a list of what he called the "Ecclesiastical laws" of the Bay Colony in 1652, he was firmly corrected by the Reverend Thomas Cobbett, who said, "We profess against any such title or thing . . . for Civil Power to make laws properly ecclesiastical, were an usurped power."[9] What seemed like ecclesiastical laws to dissenters were simply laws for keeping Christian peace and order. The Puritans had had sufficient experience with ecclesiastical interference in religious affairs in England to make every effort to avoid this in New England. "It is not so long since our own Necks bled under an intolerable yoke of Imposition on conscience as that we should forget what it is to be so dealt with," said Increase Mather.[10] "God's institutions (such as government of church and commonwealth be)," John Cotton concluded, "may be close and compact, and coordinate to one another and yet not be confounded."[11]

But if Puritans have received too little credit for the step they took toward separating church and state in their opposition to Erastianism, prelacy, and sacerdotalism, they have nevertheless been rightly charged with failing to maintain in practice the sharp division that they advanced in theory. Many times the Puritans quarreled among themselves over whether the clergy and the magistrates were not still too closely intertwined in New England, a problem that grew out of the firm belief of the leaders of Massachusetts Bay that the principal duty of the magistrates was to act as "nursing fathers to the churches," preserving the churches from disorder and the commonwealth from offending God. But did this mean that the magistrates could decide when a church had chosen an improperly qualified minister? Could they prohibit any new church from being formed without their permission? Could they lay taxes on all inhabitants for the support of the churches? Could they command the ministers to hold a synod? There was less quarrel, however, over the assumption, universal then in Christendom, that the magistrates were duty bound, as the Cambridge Platform put it in 1648, to suppress all "Idolatry, Blasphemy, Heresy, venting corrupt & pernicious opinions, that destroy the foundation, open contempt of the word preached, prophanation of the Lord's day, disturbing the peacable administration & exercise of the worship & holy things of God."[12] As for those who would separate from the existing churches and seek to lead souls into error by challenging the uniformity and conformity to truth that God required of his people in "the new Jerusalem," "the modern Canaan," the "new Israel" of New England, the Cambridge Platform, sustaining a law of 1631, declared: "If any church one or more shall grow schismaticall, rending it self from the communion of other churches, or shall walke incorrigibly or obstinately in any corrupt way of their own, contrary to the rule of the word; in such case the Magistrate is to put forth his coercive power as the matter shall require."[13]

Fighting a desperate battle to prove to Episcopalians and Presbyterians in England that the congregational polity could be sustained in good order and orthodoxy, the Puritans' coordinate system necessitated a delicate balance that they could not always maintain. But the effort had to be made, for life itself was a delicate balance between good and evil, and it required that every man be made to abide by Truth and be subject to lawful authority, that he know his place and mind his duties lest Satan make use of him to cause evil to church and state and arouse the wrath of God against those who tolerated such delinquents. In an era of pietistic ferment the Puritans took a practical view: "While the liquor is boiling it must needs have a scumming." The banishments of Roger Williams, Anne Hutchinson, Robert Childe, and the Quakers are simply the best-known incidents of scumming—the Puritans' attempt to maintain at least outward conformity and uniformity in faith and worship. Their effort was praised by most contemporaries but condemned by their descendants.

What differentiated the Baptists from the other dissenters in Massachusetts was their disorganized and sporadic evolution. Until the First Baptist Church was organized in Charlestown in 1665, they had no leader or spokesman, no coherence or unity of purpose. The history of the movement, if it can be called that, during the first thirty-five years of the colony is a history of scattered individuals maintaining a furtive hole-in-the-corner existence, occasionally bursting out in mild or vigorous dissent only to be summarily dealt with and then lapsing back into obscurity. Those who might have provided leadership (Williams, Clarke, Obadiah Holmes, Henry Dunster) were bludgeoned into silence or exile. Nor did the Baptist movement in England, which had many leaders, send any significant disturbers of the peace to Massachusetts or Connecticut. What force the Baptist persuasion developed in New England in the early years derived largely from internal disagreements among the Puritans themselves.

Although the dynamic personality of Roger Williams seems to have left a decided mark on the inhabitants of Salem and Lynn, which had more than their share of dissenters from 1630 to 1655, antipedobaptist views were not limited to any area. Cases of prosecution that reached the courts occurred in almost a score of towns at one time or another in the seventeenth century, though there appear to have been a few that occurred prior to 1639. William Wickenden and William Wolcott of Salem were accused of antipedobaptist views in 1639; they left that same year for Providence.[14] During the next five years, as the revolution in England loosed a flood of dissent, declared Baptists increased rapidly, first in one place and then another in Massachusetts. But wherever the Baptist movement raised its head, the authorities proceeded vigorously to lop it off.

First the delinquent was presented to the county court by the grand jury for failing to present his child for baptism or for turning his back on God's ordinance; then he was warned or fined by the court (or whipped if he was too truculent in defending his views or too poor to pay his fine). If he persisted, he was again presented, warned, fined, or whipped. Refusal to pay the fine meant imprisonment for an indeterminate period. Meanwhile, if he was a church member, as many of them were, he was warned, censured, and ultimately excommunicated by his church. The prosecution was unrelenting unless the Baptist either left the colony or publicly repented, confessing his sinfulness and humbly asking forgiveness, promising to sin no more. There are records of some individuals in the Middlesex County Court who were brought to trial at least twenty times in as many years for persisting in their Anabaptist views. But the majority of these early Baptists either left the colony very quickly once the authorities hailed them in or else they recanted—at least to the point of conforming and keeping their views to themselves.

There is no doubt that the social persecution by their neighbors and fellow church members was at least as potent a force in their suppression as the punishments meted out by the courts. Throughout the colonial period Baptists were the pariahs of New England society. Known Baptists could not attain the rights of freemen in the seventeenth century; thus, they could not vote or hold office. Their children were the butts of childish malevolence, their sons and daughters were considered unfit for marriage to the orthodox (after a time the Baptists defensively refused to have *their* children "unequally yoked with unbelievers," thereby making a virtue of necessity). Adults were shut out from the closed circle of social, political, and economic control. Even after 1682, when they dared to build a few meetinghouses, they did so in an outlying corner of their township, far from the Puritan meetinghouse on the village green. Baptists were to the respectable churchgoers of the colonial period what the Mormons and Adventists were to respectable Baptists and Methodists in the nineteenth century and what the Holiness and Pentecostal sects are to respectable Presbyterians and Episcopalians in the twentieth century: eccentric, fanatical, ignorant enthusiasts. Prior to 1682 they were deemed even worse—they were subversives, dangers to civil and political safety, threats to the peace and order of the commonwealth, men whose presence was apt to bring down the vengeance of God upon the community. Denouncing the Baptists as *un-American* subversives, a convention of Massachusetts ministers told the legislators in 1668, "if once that party becomes numerous and prevailing, this country is undone, the work of reformation ended."[15] As a result, the Baptists pursued such a *sub rosa* existence that it is still difficult to discern their activities. To the descendants of the Puritans who wrote the history books, they were little more than a distasteful footnote.

Among the more notable cases of Anabaptism in the 1640s was that of Lady Deborah Moody, one of the few persons of education and wealth in the colony to take up the persuasion. In 1649 she settled in Salem and was admitted to the church. But in 1642 she came to the conclusion that infant baptism was not justified by Scripture and began to persuade other women in the church not to have their children baptized. After the minister and elder were unable to dissuade her from this error, the church censured her and two of her friends, and she was brought before the quarterly court of sessions in Salem and admonished publicly. She would not give up her views, but not seeing any way to make them prevail, she left for Long Island in 1643, where her wealth and intelligence brought her considerable influence among the more tolerant Dutch. But as the Puritans would have predicted, her Anabaptism eventually carried her into Quakerism.[16]

More typical of the early advocates of antipedobaptism in Massachusetts was Thomas Painter, a poor, stubborn laborer in Hingham. Painter, said John Winthrop, "on the sudden turned anabaptist" in 1644: "having a child born, he would not suffer his wife to bring it to the ordinance of baptism, for she was a member of the church, though he himself was not."[17] Painter was taken to court, where he told the judges he thought infant baptism was "antichristian." The judges, with "much patience," tried to dissuade him from this view, but he persisted. Whereupon "because he was very poor, so as no other but corporal punishment could be fastened upon him—he was ordered to be whipped, but not for his opinion, but for his reproaching the Lord's ordinance, and for his bold and evil behavior both at home and in the Court." Painter soon left the colony for Newport, where he joined John Clarke's church.

Whipping, as Winthrop said, was a last resort with the more obstinate and stubborn fanatics and with those who were so poor that it was impossible to fine or distrain them. The court record for the case of Christopher Goodwine of Charlestown reveals more clearly the type of behavior that warranted whipping. Goodwine,

being convicted of contempt & violence to ye publ: dispensac[io]n of ye ordinance of Baptisme at Charlestowne, throwing done [down] the Basin of Water in the meeting house & strikeing the constable in ye meeting House & kicking him on ye Lords day & expressing himselfe in Court with High contempt of ye Holy ordinance, justifying himselfe in his former acc[i]ons & highly contemning the Court, is sentenced to pay ten pounds or to be openly whipt 10 stripes.[18]

It is doubtful whether Goodwine had ten pounds in cash or property to pay the fine.

More than once, whole families were brought into court for Anabaptism. Benanual Bowers, his wife, and his son George of Charlestown and Cambridge were among those who refused to be suppressed and yet who would not leave the colony. Between 1655 and 1682 the Bowerses were brought into court at least a dozen times on various charges, including absence from worship, "abetting vagabond quakers," and turning their backs on infant baptism at worship. The Bowerses were poor, vociferous, and irascible. Bowers himself went insane in his old age, but his various petitions to the courts indicate that he was neither ignorant nor stupid. When they were first whipped for their actions is not known, but in 1683 Bowers complained that he and his wife had been whipped several times for their religious views.[19] Bowers's petition to the Court of Assistants in 1673 reveals the extent to which the Massachusetts authorities were prepared to go when faced with a particularly stubborn and outspoken opponent of the system:

I have been formerly sentenced at Cambridge & Charlestowne Court much after this manner of proceeding five or six times, fined imprisoned and three times whipt privately at the house of correction at Cambr. My hands being put in the irons of the whipping post for the execution, which hard usidge did cause my neighbours hearing it to be so much [disturbed that they] did desire me to let them see the signs of the stripes which I did, at which they were much troubled and grieved for my sore sufferings, and my imprisonment was in ye dead & cold time of the winter and in seed time, and they kept me in prison two weeks, and after that whipt me and sent me [away?] . . . and my maid servant which was hired for one year was forced away from my wife when she had five small children, one of them sucking, and against the maids own will and threatened by Capt. Gookin if she would not go away he would send her to the house of correction and also my wife have suffered much when I was in prison by coming to me in the extremity of winter having noe maid, being destitute of any assistance or other help, and also my wife have bine forced to come to Court when she had lain in bed but three weakes and condemned for contempt of authority in not coming to Court when she had laine in but three daies and my wife have bine likewise whipt upon the same account or pretense as I have bine and all this hath not satisfied the will and desires of some of my judges but do still continue their cruel proceedings against me mostly every Court still; & magistrate Danforth expressing his fury yet further in open Court against me saying unto me, if I be not hanged he would be hanged for me.[20]

This was probably the most extreme case of Baptist persecution. The extant records indicate that only a few of those prosecuted for Anabaptist views were whipped.[21] Nor were the whippings as vicious as those given to the Quakers in this same period.

The case of William Witter is more typical than those of Painter, Goodwine, or Bowers, though he appears to have been just as contemptuous of authority. Witter, born in 1584, was a farmer who lived in Swampscott and was a member of the Salem church until he was excommunicated for being rebaptized in 1651. He was presented to the county court in Salem in February, 1643/4 "for entertaining that baptism of infants was sinful" and for calling the ordinance "a badge of the whore." The court sentenced him to confess his fault before the church and to apologize to Thomas Cobbett, the minister in Lynn, whose services he had interrupted to make these blasphemous statements. But Witter neither changed his opinion nor confessed his fault. Two years later he was again presented to the court, this time for saying "that they who stayed while a childe was baptised doe worshipp the dyvill." He was again sentenced to make a public confession of his error, and again he refused. In May 1646 he was ordered to appear before the General Court, but he did not. Probably old age and increasing blindness, plus greater reticence, saved him from continuing harassment, for there is no further record of his being prosecuted, though he was censured by the Salem church for his views. At some time between 1646 and 1651 he apparently was immersed and joined the Newport Baptist church. He continued to live in Lynn, however, and evidently the Salem church was not aware of his rebaptism until after he became involved in one of the most celebrated cases of American Baptist martyrology. This occurred in the summer of 1651, when Witter requested the church in Newport to send some brethren to visit him in Lynn, presumably because he had some friends who wished to be immersed.[22]

John Clarke knew that he was courting trouble when he acted on Witter's request, but he and his church believed that God had called them to make this trip into the Puritan citadel and to bear witness for the Baptist persuasion. Perhaps he was deliberately testing the authorities. On Saturday, July 19, 1651, Clarke and two leading members of his church, Obadiah Holmes and John Crandall, arrived at Witter's home late at night. The next morning they held a private religious service there that was attended by several of Witter's friends. Apparently, the Rhode Islanders had planned to attend the services at Thomas Cobbett's church in Lynn and there make a more public witness against infant baptism, but, said Clarke, we did not have "freedom in our Spirits for want of a clear Call from God to goe into the Publike Assemblie to declare there what was the mind and counsell of God concerning them."[23]

Almost at once, knowledge of the invasion from Rhode Island reached the local magistrate, Robert Bridges, and during the service in Witter's home two constables arrived to arrest the three visitors. That afternoon the constables compelled the visitors to attend the service at the church in Lynn. When they walked in, Clarke and Holmes refused to remove their hats, which were "plucked off " by the constable. After the sermon Clarke stood up to rebuke the Puritan churches publicly, saying that they were not instituted "according to the visible order of our Lord" because they were based on infant baptism. The next day, having somehow escaped the surveillance of the constables, the three men conducted another service at Witter's home at which Holmes administered the Lord's Supper and baptized two or three persons, including Mrs. William Bowditch (Bowdish), a member of the Salem church.[24]

On Tuesday, July 22, the three Rhode Islanders were taken to Boston and imprisoned. A week later they were tried by Governor John Endecott and the Council with several ministers in attendance (one of whom, John Wilson, angrily struck Holmes). They were found guilty of holding a private meeting on the Lord's Day, showing disrespect to God's ordinance by keeping their hats on in church, disturbing the congregation during worship, denouncing the basis of church organization, administering the Lord's Supper to persons not entitled to it, rebaptizing persons, and denying in court the lawfulness of baptizing infants. "All of this," said the court, "tends to the dishonour of God, the despising of the ordinances of God among us, the peace of the Churches, and seducing the subjects of this Commonwealth from the truth of the Gospel of Jesus Christ, and perverting the strait waies of the Lord."[25]

Holmes was sentenced to pay a fine of thirty pounds; Clarke, twenty; and Crandall, five, "or else to be well whipt." They were to remain in prison until the fines were paid or the whipping executed. The three men refused to pay their fines, but some friends paid Clarke's, and Crandall was released after he paid bail. Holmes persuaded his friend that he would be offended if they paid so unjust a fine for him.[26] Clarke and Crandall returned to Rhode Island. Holmes remained in prison until September, when the court decided that he should receive thirty lashes with a three-corded whip. The sentence was executed, the executioner "spitting on his hand three times" to get a good grip on the whip.[27] Holmes said that God sustained him through the ordeal: "You have struck me as with roses." The bloody public spectacle aroused the sympathy of several bystanders who offered afterward to assist Holmes. Two, known to be Baptists, shook his hand saying, "Blessed be the Lord"; they were fined and imprisoned for implicit contempt of the justice of the sentence.[28]

This incident received wide notoriety when John Clarke published a detailed account of it in London a year later under the title *Ill-Newes from New England* in which he tried, unsuccessfully, to persuade Parliament to force a policy of toleration on New England. It was the last time Baptists from Rhode Island invaded Massachusetts to immerse converts; the movement continued to lack organization and leaders for another fifteen years.

Still the incidence of Baptist tendencies increased. The most significant involved Henry Dunster in 1654. Dunster's case had far more serious implications for the Massachusetts ministers and magistrates than the invasion from Rhode Island. When the president of Harvard College, a graduate of Cambridge University, refused to have his child baptized and publicly stated his disbelief in the ordinance, it was no longer possible for the Puritans to argue that antipedobaptism was simply a fanatical delusion held only by ignorant enthusiasts. Nor was it possible to treat Dunster with the same summary justice given to less important men. The shock to the community called for more extraordinary action.

Jonathan Mitchell, the pastor of the Cambridge church, first tried to persuade President Dunster of his error. But the learned Dunster almost succeeded in shaking his young pastor's faith. The General Court then instructed nine ministers and two ruling elders to meet with Dunster in Boston to try by private conference and debate to correct him. Dunster wrote an account of this futile two-day discussion in which he defended himself by insisting that "all instituted Gospel Worship hath some express word of Scripture. But pedobaptism hath none."[29] Nor did Dunster find any precedent for it in the practice of the primitive church: "John the Baptist, Christ himself, & [the] Apostles did none of them baptize children." The crux of the matter to Dunster was the "*Soli visibiliter fideles sunt baptizandi,*" and since infants were not, in his view, "visible believers," they should not be baptized.

Since the conference proved fruitless, the General Court in May 1654, passed a law requiring that all teachers at Harvard or in the public schools who were "unsound in the faith" should be relieved of their offices. Dunster compounded his crime by openly stating his views during a baptismal service at the Cambridge church on July 30, 1654. For this he was sentenced to receive a public admonition by one of the magistrates on a lecture day in the Cambridge church, to which he submitted. Not only was he also required to give bond for his future good behavior, but his resignation from Harvard was demanded; it took effect in October of the same year.

Dunster evidently recognized the consequences it would have for the colony if he were to assume leadership of the Baptist movement; he chose instead to view the dispute as a private matter of conscience. Unlike Roger Williams and Anne Hutchinson, he saw no need to conduct an ecclesiastical revolt. Consequently, he held his peace, and in March 1655 he left Massachusetts Bay for the more tolerant atmosphere of Plymouth Colony, where he spent the remaining four years of his life. He seems to have preached occasionally to some members of the Standing church in Scituate, though he was never ordained over them. His preaching evidently did not touch on the controversial aspects of the Baptist persuasion, which even the Plymouth authorities would not have permitted. Nor did he leave any known Baptist followers behind in Scituate at his death. But he did express his distaste for the persecution of the Quakers.[30]

Dunster's significance for the Baptist movement was considerably diminished by his failure to seek rebaptism for himself. He neither advocated his antipedobaptist views in print nor attacked the intolerance of the Massachusetts system. He was not excommunicated from the Cambridge church, and he continued to own property in Cambridge. His desire to be buried in the Cambridge burial ground was granted. Like many Congregationalists in England at this time, he may have approved open or mixed communion between pedo- and antipedobaptists, but he never said so. By holding his peace he probably proved an embarrassment rather than a help to the Baptists, for he gave truth to the Puritan claim that uniformity and conformity were not insisted upon by them so long as dissenting opinions were "not vented." According to Cotton Mather, Dunster "died in harmony of affection with the good men who had been the authors of his removal from Cambridge."

The failure of Dunster, Holmes, Clarke, Williams, Witter, Painter, Bowers, Lady Deborah, and many others to advance either the organization of Baptist churches or the toleration of Baptist views within Massachusetts Bay indicated the coherent strength of the Puritan community and its conviction that "he that corrupteth a soule with a corrupt religion, layeth a spreading leaven which corrupteth the state."[31] Nothing reveals more clearly the radical danger that the Puritans sensed in these sporadic Baptist outbursts than the laws they wrote to eradicate them. When the first Baptists appeared in the colony in the 1630s and early 1640s, they were tried under the existing general laws requiring civil order, subjection to authority, and preservation of the churches. Under these laws many Puritan deviants or malcontents were also tried for one reason or another: failure to attend church, contempt of religious authority, reading heretical books. But when, as Winthrop noted in 1644, "Anabaptistry increased and spread in the country" and when Baptist tracts and sermons began to arrive in large numbers from England, the Puritans recognized the beginnings of a distinct new movement in their midst. And so, in November 1644, the General Court passed the following act to name, define, and stamp out this heresy:

Forasmuch as experience hath plentifully and often proved that since the first arising of the Anabaptists about a hundred years since they have been the incendiaries of the commonwealths and the infectors of persons in main matters of religion and the troublers of churches in all places where they have been, and that they who have held the baptizing of infants unlawful have usually held other errors or heresies together therewith though they have (as hereticks use to do) concealed the same till they spied out a fit advantage and opportunity to vent them, by way of question or scruple; and whereas divers of this kind have since our coming into New England appeared amongst ourselves, some whereof (as others before them) denied the ordinance of magistracy, and the lawfulness of making warr, and others the lawfulness of magistrates, and their inspection into any breach of the first tables; which opinions, if they should be connived at by us, are like to be increased among us, and so must necessarily bring guilt upon us, infection and trouble to the churches, and hazard to the whole commonwealth; it is ordered and agreed that if any person or persons within this jurisdiction shall either openly condemne or oppose the baptizing of infants or go about secretly to seduce others from the approbation or use thereof, or shall purposely depart the congregation at the ministration of the ordinance or shall deny the ordinance of magistracy or their lawful right and authority to make warr or to punish the outward breaches of the first table, and shall appear to the Court willfully and obstinately to continue therein after due time and means of conviction, every such person or persons shall be sentenced to banishment.[32]

There is no record that any of the early Baptists in Massachusetts opposed the lawfulness of making war or the lawfulness of magistrates or even the enforcement of the first table by the civil authorities, but there were some in old England and a few in Rhode Island who did so. The concept of toleration, however, was implicit in the Baptists' requests to be indulged or connived at.

In addition to this law to protect the civil peace by banishing antipedobaptists, another law was passed in 1646 to maintain the dignity of the ministers and the good order of the churches by punishing those who turned their backs on infant baptism or who walked out of the churches or stood up to speak against the ordinance when it was performed. Though it did not specifically mention Anabaptists, it had them clearly in mind. By this law, anyone who

shall contemptuously behave himself toward ye word preached or ye messengers thereof . . . either by interrupting him in his preaching or by charging him falsely with error . . . or like a sonn of Corah, cast upon his true doctrine or himselfe any reproach . . . and making God's wayes contemptible and ridiculous . . . shall for the first scandall be convented and reproved openly by ye megistrates at some lecture and be bound to their good behavior [and for the second offense pay a fine of five pounds] stand two howres openly upon a block for foote high on a lecture day with a paper fixed on his breast with this: A WANTON GOSPELLER, written in capitall latters.[33]

Thus, social opprobrium and humiliation were added to the more drastic law of banishment.

The existence of open dissent constituted an affront to the uniformity and conformity of the Standing Order even though it was not until 1648 that the doctrines and practices of that order were codified in the Cambridge Platform. The need to codify their own position, like the need to define the position of the dissenters, is indicative of an increasing formalism in Puritan New England. A consensus could no longer be taken for granted. Yet the mere act of defining the Baptists as a distinct group (however unfairly or inaccurately) undoubtedly served to give coherence to a formless malaise among certain pietistic colonists who had previously considered themselves part of the community. Even to deny that to be an antipedobaptist was also to be a pacifist or an opponent of magistracy helped to give these nonconformists a new coherence. As the frontier community codified its own beliefs and structure, so it simultaneously formalized dissent. Massachusetts was forced to profess and develop a homogeneity it had assumed but had not possessed. The spontaneity of the new reformation was slowly congealing in New England, and it continued to do so through the ensuing century.

[2]

The Baptist-Puritan Debate of
April 14-15, 1668

The Puritans of New England believed in trying to reason with dissenters who seemed to have strayed from the path of Truth. Consequently, when civil punishments (whipping, jailing, banishment) failed to stamp out the movement called Anabaptism in the years 1630–1668, the authorities in Massachusetts decided to hold a public debate in the meetinghouse in Boston. The learned ministers and civil magistrates would allow the Baptists to make their arguments for antipedobaptism, and then they would so thoroughly refute them that their movement would collapse.

The debate took place over two days in April 1668. Baptists traveled from Rhode Island to speak on behalf of their cause, and local Baptists in the Bay Colony brought forth their best speakers. A large crowd filled the meetinghouse. A court stenographer took down the debate word for word. When it was over, no one had changed his mind. The Baptist movement continued to grow. The authorities continued to persecute it.

The court record of this debate was never transcribed. It lay in its original shorthand in the archives of the Massachusetts Historical Society for three centuries. Some historians tried to transcribe it but failed to find the key to the shorthand. Finally, in 1964 Martha Whiting Davidson (a descendant of one of the Puritan magistrates who took part in the debate) succeeded in breaking the code, and I have tried to put the debate in its historical context. It was the first significant statement of the major issues underlying the Baptist movement. It indicates also that the Baptists were still far from advocating what we now consider disestablishment and equal religious liberty.

INTRODUCTION

Although the Baptist Debate, or disputation, that took place in the meetinghouse of the First Church of Boston on April 14 and 15, 1668, was unique and significant in the annals of the Massachusetts Bay Colony, it has received little attention by historians. Perhaps this was because the Debate itself, though taken down in shorthand by Thomas Danforth, was never transcribed or pub-

lished.[1] Historians have assumed that the basic issues debated on
that occasion were merely recapitulations of the published polemics
between the Puritans and Baptists (or Anabaptists, as they were
then called) that filled hundreds of pages in scores of tracts and
sermons in the preceding thirty years since the founding of the first
Calvinistic Baptist church in London in 1638. Contemporary Puritans considered the debate an open-and-shut case of willful sin-
ning against conscience by the Baptists and made little note of the
affair; later Puritans were too embarrassed by the intolerance of
their ancestors to discuss it. Baptist historians, unaware of the shorthand account, have been misled by a contemporary statement of
Mary Goold, the wife of the principal Baptist participant, who
claimed that the Baptists, "desiring liberty to speak" at the outset
of the Debate, found that the Puritans "would not suffer them, but
told them they stood there as delinquents and ought not to have
liberty to speak." Thus, as she put it, the "two days were spent to
little purpose."[2] However, the Debate, as transcribed below, indicates clearly that Baptists not only had liberty to speak but that they
did so often and to considerable purpose.

Unfortunately, we do not have the whole of the debate. Danforth
evidently tired of transcribing it toward the end of the morning of
the second day, so we may be missing as much as a quarter of it.
Nevertheless, even in this truncated form the Debate reveals more
clearly and vividly the long and bitter fight of the Baptists for toleration in the seventeenth century than does any other document.
This is not only because it speaks in the accents of the contemporary
speech nor because of the dramatic tension produced by the direct
confrontation of the two groups; it is because in the give-and-take
of spontaneous debate both sides reveal more starkly than in their
written arguments what was really gnawing at them and not merely
what they could say in cold print.[3] Moreover, and perhaps more
significant, this is the only document we have in which the founders
of the first Baptist church in the Bay Colony defended their actions
and principles at length.

It adds considerably to the value of the document that the Debate
occurred when the Baptist movement was still in its formative state.
It therefore reveals a great deal more disparity among the Baptists
than historians have recognized, particularly in regard to their rea-

sons for separation from the Puritan churches and their attitudes toward separation of church and state. As the Debate indicates, the Baptist position was so ambiguous and so poorly defined that its defenders frequently argued at cross purposes.

The background of the Debate is generally well known: how Thomas Goold, a respectable member of the Puritan church in Charlestown, first began to have scruples about infant baptism in the years 1652–1655;[4] how he refused in the year 1655 to have a newborn daughter baptized; how first the church and then the magistrates took steps to persuade him of his error; how he was censured by the church, forbidden to take communion with his former brethren, and admonished and fined by the courts for turning his back when the children of other members were baptized and for absenting himself from public worship; how, finally, in 1663, as Goold put it, "God sent out of Old England some who were Baptists," who came to Charlestown, where they joined Goold, Edward Drinker, John George, John Farnum, Sr., and others in holding private meetings in their homes; how the authorities tried in vain to prohibit this; how on May 28, 1665, nine of these Baptists (seven men and two women) decided to form a church, rebaptized each other by immersion,[5] and signed articles of faith and order drawn up by Goold; how the Charlestown church proceeded to excommunicate those of its members who had joined this "schismatical" and "pretended" church; how it nevertheless grew in size though the authorities relentlessly took them to court to warn them, fine them, disfranchise them, and finally imprison three of them (Goold, Farnum, and George) in April 1666 when they refused to pay the fines levied against them; and how these three were released in October 1666, although Goold and Farnum, with William Turner, were imprisoned again on March 3, 1668, after a jury trial that precipitated the decision to hold a public debate.

The question obviously arises: why, when a law had been passed in 1644 authorizing the banishment of Anabaptists, and why, in the face of the fierce persecution of the Quakers in these same years, the Puritans acted so slowly and comparatively mildly in their treatment of Goold and his brethren? So far as is known, none of the members of his church was ever whipped, and not until after the Debate was a sentence of banishment finally passed against the three leaders. In part the reasons for this delay grew out of the comparative peaceableness with which Goold and his friends had conducted themselves and out of their own inherent respectability as church members, freemen, and hardworking, God-fearing, honest yeomen and artisans.[6] In such cases the Puritans habitually moved slowly, hoping to persuade their erring brothers by patience and firmness to return to the fold. But there were two other important factors in the reluctance of the Puritans to proceed to the ultimate lengths of the law in this case. One of these was the state of religious unrest and dissension within the colony preceding and following the adoption of the Halfway Covenant by the Synod of 1662; the other was the increasing political pressure being brought on the colony by the authorities in England to make it conform more closely to English law and practice.

It probably would not be too great an exaggeration to say that over the years the Baptists gained as many converts to their views out of the negative resentment against the Halfway Covenant (and its logical extension into "Stoddardeanism") as they did out of their own positive proselyting. For the Halfway Covenant revealed the most serious flaw in the whole "New England way," a flaw that stemmed directly from the confusion over infant baptism. To the Puritans, of course, the question of whether to extend baptism not only to the children of visible saints but also their grandchildren was in no way a justification of the antipedobaptist position (i.e., the refusal to allow children to be baptized under any circumstances). Yet the very fact that this was a quarrel over baptism and over the subjects of baptism, not the mode, helped to reinforce the position of the Baptists and their sympathizers. It enabled them to argue that infant baptism was a matter of such complexity and so much disagreement even among the learned and "godly-wise" that differences over it ought to be tolerated. This point is clearly made in the Debate. But equally important, some of the Puritan ministers who opposed the Halfway Covenant, men as influential as Increase Mather, Charles Chauncy, and John Davenport, became so vehement in attacking it that they were charged by the defenders of the synod with having adopted as rigid a position as that of the antipedobaptists. "This arguing" against the synod, said Richard Mather in 1664 in condemnation of the position of his own son,

Increase, "is but too like that of the Antipaedobaptists"; in fact, he went on, the proposals of the synod "cannot be denied but by joining with the Antipaedobaptists."[7] And within a year after the Baptist Debate had ended the people of Massachusetts were treated to the horrifying spectacle of a schism occasioned by the Halfway Covenant among the members of the First Church of Boston (in whose meetinghouse the Baptist Debate had taken place)—a schism, moreover, that was condoned by the governor, the Assistants, and the majority of the clergy, to the outrage of the House of Deputies. Such indications of the breakdown of authority and harmony in both church and state indicated only too clearly that the golden era of the Bible Commonwealth was passing.

As for the political pressure from England, this was manifest in countless ways, the most obvious of which in the religious sphere were the efforts of the king to enforce toleration in Massachusetts, at least for members of the Church of England (though he also prohibited hangings of his loyal Quaker subjects), and the presence of royal commissioners in 1664–1665 who forced a modification of the law limiting freemanship (and hence the franchise) to full members of the Puritan churches in the colony. It may well have been that Goold was relying on the protection of these commissioners when he formally organized his church in May 1665. During the Debate one of the Baptists, stretching a point, tried to claim that the Massachusetts Charter guaranteed liberty of conscience to the Baptists presumably because King Charles II in his letter to the General Court of Massachusetts confirming the charter in 1662 stated that "the principle and foundation of that charter was and is the freedom of liberty of conscience."[8]

The fact that public confidence in the magistrates and clergy was shaken, and that perhaps the fear of England had increased by 1666, may well explain why the House of Deputies struck from the resolution passed by the Assistants in September of that year, a paragraph that threatened Goold and Thomas Osborne with banishment if they persisted in disobeying the court's previous injunction against holding any further meetings of their church.[9] In addition, when Goold was given a jury trial on March 3, 1668, in connection with his refusal to pay a fine for failure to attend the parish church, the jury first brought in a verdict acquitting him and had to be sent out again by the court to hew more closely to the line of justice. It was only five days after this that the governor and Assistants decided to hold the Debate, a time-honored device in the "coordinate system" of Massachusetts for using the spiritual resources of the clergy to persuade a reluctant populace to live up to the commandments of Scripture and the laws of the magistrates. As John Allin, the Puritan moderator of the Debate, put it, this was a case of Moses and Aaron, the civil and spiritual "shepherds of the flock," meeting together "to reduce those that have gone out of God's way."

That the clergy succeeded, as they had done before in the cases of Roger Williams, Anne Hutchinson, and Robert Childe, was evidenced by the vote of the General Court on May 27, 1668: "Whereas Thomas Gold, William Turner, and John Farnum, Senr, obstinate & turbulent Annabaptists, have some time since combined themselves with others in a pretended church estate, without the knowledge or approbation of the authority here established . . . to the great greife & offense of the godly orthodox . . . this Court doe judge it necessary that they be remooved to some other part of this country or elsewhere . . . before the twentieth of July next."[10] The three men were released from prison to make ready for their departure, but when July 20 came and they had still not left the colony, they were arrested again and returned to prison. In October 1668 the General Court made public its order of banishment, hoping no doubt to get support for the forcible ejection of the Baptists. But to its astonishment it received instead a petition signed by sixty-six inhabitants, some of them very prominent citizens, asking that Goold and his colleagues be pardoned and freed.[11] Shocked by this affront to its justice, the court forced the more prominent signers to retract their names and fined two of the main instigators of the petition. Shortly afterward, John Farnum, Sr., won release by promising to return to regular attendance at the Second Church of Boston, from which he had been excommunicated. Goold and Turner stayed in prison through the winter and were granted a three-day release in March 1668/69 to attend to some private business. They took the opportunity to go into semibanishment on Noddles Island in Boston Harbor.

The court evidently considered this a fair compromise, and the

Baptist leaders remained unmolested for the next five years, conducting services regularly for those of the faithful who cared to row over to Noddles Island and back. Those who did not care to row out attended services in Woburn conducted by John Russell, Sr., a former deacon of the Woburn church, who in 1669 joined Goold's church and was made a ruling elder. The authorities continued to prosecute the increasing number of Baptists in Charlestown, Woburn, Billerica, and a dozen other towns, warning, fining, and imprisoning them. But the movement would not die down, and the Puritans could not muster the will nor the public support to crush it. After Governor Bellingham died, the more lenient John Leverett declined to take any action when Goold moved his church to Boston in the summer of 1674. The Baptists held their meetings there in a private home until 1679, when they built a meetinghouse. For two years the authorities harassed them, nailing the door shut and calling their leaders into court. But after May 1681 the authorities decided to tolerate even this direct affront to uniformity and conformity. The Baptists were in Massachusetts to stay, and Thomas Goold (who had died quietly in his bed on October 27, 1675) had succeeded where Roger Williams, John Clarke, and Henry Dunster—all more learned and talented men—had failed.

To say that the Debate marked a crucial turning point in the Puritan attitude toward the Baptists in particular or toward toleration in general is perhaps to put too much stress on one incident out of many that took place in the 1660s. The fact that the clergy succeeded in bolstering the Court in a final effort to banish Goold and his two friends might be the basis for claiming the Debate as a Puritan success. But if so, it was a minor success and the last of its kind. The banishment could not be made to stick, and the petition of the sixty-six proponents of toleration in October 1668 indicates that the clergy had not really been very convincing in their arguments. Apart from the continued pressure from England and the growth of the so-called moderate faction that sought to concede certain charter privileges to the king for the sake of peace, the failure of the Puritans to stamp out the Baptist movement was part of a much larger trend toward toleration.

Massachusetts had been behind the rest of Britain on this issue since the late 1640s, and perhaps the surprising thing is that the

Puritans maintained their policy of intolerance as long as they did. The pressure that was hardest of all to resist was that from their Congregational brethren in England, whom they admired and respected not only for their faith and learning but also because they had lived through the experience of the Revolution and were now called on to suffer for its failure. On March 25, 1669, thirteen of the leading Independent ministers in England sent a letter concerning Goold and his friends to the governor of Massachusetts, urging that he "put an end unto the sufferings and confinements of the persons censured and return them to their former liberty."[12] They urged this, they said, in part because such persecution "put an advantage into the hands of some who feel pretences and occasions against our liberty" and in part because "assuredly you need not be disquieted, though some few persons (through their own infirmity and weakness, or through their ignorance, darkness and prejudices) should to their disadvantage turn out of the way, in some lesser matters, into by-paths of their own." If such men as Thomas Goodwin, John Owen, and Philip Nye, who in the 1640s had been as anti-Baptist as anyone in Massachusetts, now felt that the Baptists differed from the Puritans only "in some lesser matters," it was difficult to maintain the pitch of zeal needed to suppress such stubborn men as Thomas Goold and his church. The clergy tried to do it, and as late as 1681 they published bitter attacks on these "scandalous," "dangerous," "prophane," and "arrogant" men. But it was shouting into the wind. Massachusetts had passed into a new era. As for the Baptists, having won toleration, they still faced a century and a half of continued fighting to establish religious equality.

Although the issues raised in the Debate are not easy to follow for anyone unfamiliar with the details of the numerous polemics and apologetics published by both sides over the years, the Debate is by no means a mere recapitulation of these controversies.[13] Since only two tracts were published by New England Baptists in the seventeenth century (both of them narrow in scope),[14] the Puritans carried on the publication warfare primarily with the more learned Baptists of England. It is not surprising, therefore, that in this debate a somewhat different emphasis emerges. The emphasis is that of a group of Puritan lay Baptists, many of them former members or adherents of the Massachusetts churches, arguing within the context of the "New England way" and trying desperately to prove not how much they differ from their brethren but how much they have in common with them. Or to put it another way, the Debate represents a quarrel between two groups of left-wing pietistic Calvinists, each of which claims to know better what the gospel ordains as the proper basis of church order and polity; one says the Reformation must go one step further (and abolish infant baptism), and the other says it has gone far enough. In this respect the Debate substantiates Increase Mather's statement that "the question of baptism" was to "the New Reformation" of the seventeenth century what the question of transubstantiation was to the Reformation of the sixteenth century.

The central issue of the Debate is clearly defined in the order that instituted it:

The Governor and Council, accounting themselves bound by the law of God and of this Commonwealth to protect the churches of Christ here planted from the intrusion thereby made upon their peace in the ways of godliness, yet being willing by all Christian candor to endeavor the reducing of the said persons from the error of their way, and their return to the Lord and the communion of his people from whence they are fallen, do judge meet to grant unto Thomas Gould, John Farnum, Thomas Osburne, and company, yet further an opportunity of a full and free debate of their grounds for their practice: and for that end this court doth nominate and request the Rev. Mr. John Allen, Mr. Thomas Cobbett, Mr. John Higginson, Mr. Samuel Danforth, Mr. Jonathan Mitchel, and Mr. Thomas Shepard, to assemble with the Governor and magistrates, upon the 14th day of the next month, in the meeting-house at Boston, at nine in the morning; before whom, or so many of them, with any other of the Reverend elders or ministers, as shall then assemble, the above-said persons and their company shall have liberty, freely and fully, in open assembly, to present their grounds as above said, in an orderly debate of this following question: Whether it be justifiable by the word of God for these persons and their company to depart from the communion of these churches, and to set up an assembly here in the way of Anabaptism, and whether such a practice is to be allowed by the government of this jurisdiction.[15]

Or as John Allin put it to the Baptists at the opening of the Debate, "Your work is to give the reason of your separation from the people of God and setting up a meeting in the way of Anabaptism and whether this commonwealth be to allow it." The issue then was not primarily the scriptural proofs for or against infant baptism, and there is no debate concerning the practice of immersion.[16] Nor was there any quarrel concerning the doctrinal matters of Calvinist theology. The issue was purely and simply the justification for separation, or "schism," a crime that in the Bible Commonwealth was tantamount to civil as well as religious revolution. For how could anyone leave the true church of Christ without automatically condemning himself as one who preferred to follow Satan?[17]

It is not strange, therefore, that the major part of the Debate centered on the extent to which the members of Goold's church differed from the Puritan churches and whether or not this difference constituted "separation" (or "schismatical rending"). As the Debate reveals, the Baptists were not themselves agreed on this point, and a careful reading will disclose that there were three different answers offered at various times to this question. First, there were those like Thomas Goold, Edward Drinker, and John Thrumble, who seemed to argue that despite the fact that they had formed another church, they could not fairly be called Separatists. "I own no separation," Goold said. "We hold communion with you in preaching and praying and in the sacraments"; they held the parish churches to be "true churches of Christ." According to this argument, the difference between the Baptists and the Puritans in Massachusetts Bay was simply over the ordinance of baptism, and this point not being so plain and explicit in Scripture, they ought to "bear with one another," as Thrumble said, until all have further light on the matter from God. In the minds of these Non-separating, open-communion Baptists, their position in regard to the established church in Massachusetts was precisely parallel to that of the Non-Separating Puritans who left the established Church of England in 1629. The argument of this group of Baptists might be stated in a paraphrase of Francis Higginson's famous farewell sermon in 1629: "We will not say, as the Antinomians were wont to say at their leaving Massachusetts, 'Farewell, Babylon!' . . . but 'Reform thou Church of God in Massachusetts! . . . We do not set up new churches as separatists from the Church of New England, though we cannot but separate from the corruptions in it.'"

Needless to say, the Puritan ministers found this line of reasoning infuriating and insulting; nevertheless, there was a decided parallel. In this respect the position taken by this group of Baptists differed markedly from that of the early Separatist Baptists who left Massachusetts (or were driven out) between 1638 and 1660 to form the Baptist churches of Rhode Island. That Goold, Drinker, and Thrumble were not alone in taking this approach and that in fact it was probably the prevailing attitude among the Baptists of Massachusetts at this time is testified to by the efforts of many antipedobaptists to remain within their parish churches as communicants despite the opposition of their ministers and most of their former brethren. Cases of this kind occurred in Charlestown, Woburn, and Billerica, and there is even evidence that some of the Puritan ministers in New England, influenced by the growing policy of open communion between Baptists and Independents in England, were willing to toy with this idea for a time.[18] Had this line of development succeeded, the history of the New England Baptists, and perhaps the development of separation of church and state, might have taken a very different line. But it failed, and were it not for this debate, we would have much less convincing evidence that it had been seriously raised as a solution by responsible leaders of the movement.

A second point of view on the question of separation was put forward by William Turner and John Johnson. These Baptists seemed to be arguing not for open communion or nonseparation but for the right of a different form of Puritanism to exist as a parallel denomination with its own churches but nevertheless within the existing framework of the Puritan system. That is to say, they recognized that there was too important a difference between the two groups to make open communion possible or to permit churches to leave the question of infant baptism optional with individual members, and they were willing to acknowledge that a separation (as opposed to a mere "withdrawal" or "secession") was necessary. But they still did not think the matter so important as to justify their banishment; they still considered the Puritan churches to be true churches though somewhat corrupt on this particular point. They offered no revolutionary alterations in the Bible Commonwealth such as a policy of complete religious liberty would entail. In short, they were fighting for the right of their own form of Puritanism to exist but not for the right of any or all kinds of religious views.[19]

And finally, there were some Baptists in the debate who seemed flatly to assert that they had not only separated from the Puritan churches but that the corruption of those churches was so great that they were, in fact, not Christian churches at all but "nullities" or even "anti-christian." These views were not expressed fully because they might have subjected their advocates to punishment on the spot, but there is little doubt that such were the views held by men like John Crandall (called "Grendall of Narragansett" by Thomas Danforth) and by Benanuel Bowers. Crandall, who had come up from Westerly (where he was the elder of a branch of John Clarke's church), had been arrested and fined in Massachusetts in 1651 because he joined with Clarke in making a public protest, in the Puritan church in Lynn during a Sunday afternoon service, that the churches of Massachusetts were not instituted "according to the visible order of our Lord" because they practiced infant baptism. Benanuel Bowers had not only been fined and imprisoned but had been whipped for his denunciation of the Puritan churches.[20] From the viewpoint of these radicals there was no solution, no compromise, but the overthrow of the Puritan system and the establishment of complete religious liberty. In the free marketplace of ideas, they believed, the Baptist views would soon prevail and the Puritan corruptions wither away.

Because the Baptists were still unclear as to how far they wanted to separate from the established churches, the issue of toleration played a secondary role in the Debate. Presumably, if the Puritans had accepted the policy of open communion with antipedobaptists, there would have been no need of toleration, no need even to rescind the law against Anabaptists since the disputants all denied that they were Anabaptists (how could they be rebaptized when they did not consider their infant baptism valid in the first place?). In answer to the question posed at the outset of the Debate, whether the commonwealth should allow such separation, the Baptists simply said, in effect, "Yes, it should allow it because it is within the bounds of Scripture to deny infant baptism." But as to the broad implications of toleration in general, that was not something they wished to go into. It was the Puritans who forced this issue into the Debate because in their view the allowance of antipedobaptism was the first step down the slippery road to Quakerism, Seekerism,

Ranterism, and the chaos that overtook Rhode Island after 1639 and England once Cromwell had foolishly adopted a policy of toleration in 1647. The very presence of a Baptist church in Massachusetts, as the General Court said, would be "opening the door for all sorts of abominations to come among us, to the disturbance not only of our ecclesiastical enjoyments but also contempt of our civil order and the authority here established."[21] One or two of the Baptists ventured the view that the magistrate was not entitled to use the civil sword in spiritual affairs, but they did not push the argument. And when John Thrumble raised the example of Holland as a place where "the magistrates maintain peace among the Baptists and presbyterians, and all the rest, Lutherans, Anabaptists, Presbyterians," he was nonplussed by Thomas Shepard's rejoinder that Holland also tolerated "Papists." No Baptist was ready to take up the gauntlet and argue for Roger Williams's policy of soul liberty for Jews, Turks, and papists.[22]

Looked at from this point of view the Debate makes the Puritans seem terribly intolerant and even hysterical in their fear of the horrors opened up by the separation of a few conservative, non-separatist, open-communion Baptists in the town of Charlestown. But there is another dimension of the Debate, which the Puritans grasped more clearly than the Baptists and which the modern reader, living in the world the Baptists helped to create, may forget. It is true that England in the 1650s and Rhode Island throughout most of that century were brought close to chaos by their policies of toleration; a conservative historian might well agree with the Puritans that in an age of illiteracy and fierce religious fanaticism no sensible man advocated complete religious freedom. But the issue went beyond that. What the Puritans foresaw, even if dimly, in the thrust of the principles advocated by the Baptists was the overthrow of the medieval ideal of the corporate Christian state and the substitution for it of a voluntaristic, pluralistic, individualistic, or atomistic social order. This, in their eyes, was tantamount to anarchy. For no matter how conservative the Baptists claimed to be in pushing the New Reformation just one step further toward absolute purity, their method of justifying this step had more far-reaching consequences.

For example, the doctrine of "further light," put forward in the

Debate by some of the Baptists to explain their abandonment of infant baptism, if adopted as a regular policy for action could be used to justify the wildest kind of perfectionist delusions. And the doctrine of individual judgment, as stated by Turner ("Is it not a reasonable thing that every man have his particular judgment in matters of faith seeing we must all appear before the judgment seat of Christ"), also enabled every man to make himself the judge of all institutions and to rebel against them, using the name of God as justification when it might be only his own confusion, ambition, presumption, or pride. Or the claim of the Baptists that unlearned laymen had the right to ordination by their brethren in the church and their complaint that a salaried (hireling) ministry was contrary to Scripture—what endless grounds these views provided for disorder! As Calvinists, the Baptists claimed to believe in the depravity of man, but they had so exalted a view of the wisdom of visible saints that they seemed utterly to lose sight of the fact that no man attained perfection on earth, nor any church. Or conversely, the Baptists so disliked the restraints that the institutions of church and state placed on the visible saints that they failed to see how essential such restraints were on the unregenerate populace.

Of course, the Puritans themselves held all of these doctrines ("further light," "individual judgment," and "lay ordination") and had in the past used them to justify their own secession from the Church of England and the tyranny of the king. But they held them in moderation. They were suspicious of their tendencies. They applied them in caution. And they set up every possible restraint to guard against their misapplication—which is precisely what the Bible Commonwealth was, a pietistic utopia that utilized all possible restraints of tradition, law, Scripture, and social custom to prevent its adherents from rushing headlong into individualism and perfectionism. The tradition of a learned ministry with a veto power over the congregation, of the magistrates as "nursing fathers of the church," of the coordinate rule of spiritual and civil shepherds, of a set of laws based in part on the Mosaic code and in part on the medieval conception of the just price and the just wage, of a social order where lower and upper orders were forever fixed in their respective spheres ("All men being thus [by divine providence] rancked into two sorts, riche and poore," as John Winthrop said)—

in short, the whole conception of a Christian corporate collectivist state was created and sustained as a purposeful counterweight to the tendencies within Puritan pietism that the Baptists were seeking to unleash.[23] Thomas Shepard struck this corporate note in the Debate when he denied Goold's argument that individual members may depart at will from sinful churches: "A particular person may not judge the whole: but is to be subject to the whole." And when Goold, seeking Scriptural support, insisted that "a private member may cast off " when he sees his brethren committing any sins "for which God may cast them off," Cobbett snapped: "A dangerous inference: Because the all-seeing God may do it, therefore Goodman Goold, a fallible judge and running to many errors, may."

But the heart of this crucial distinction between the corporate views of the Puritans and the individualistic views of the Baptists did not lie really in the question of which of the two pietistic groups was pushing the doctrine of the priesthood of all believers too slowly or too fast. It lay rather in their conceptions of the true basis of a church. Both groups claimed, of course, to believe that a church must be made up of visible saints gathered out of the world and united in autonomous congregations from which the unregenerate and visible sinners were excluded. But according to the covenant theology of the Puritans, the infants of visible saints were themselves assumed to be visible (at least until adulthood) and were thus entitled to the seal of baptism under the right of "federal holiness" in the external covenant (as opposed to the right to communion and full church membership, which was granted only to those who had received internal grace or "real holiness" through a conversion experience). The Puritans justified infant baptism by the terms of God's covenant with Abraham and "his seed," and they considered the sprinkling or immersion of infants (the mode was immaterial) the gospel form of circumcision. And just as the continuity, stability, and preservation of the Jewish church was maintained by the circumcision of the children of those in the covenant, so the continuity, stability, and preservation of the Christian church was to be maintained by the baptism of the children of the visible saints in the Puritan or Reformed churches. Circumcision united those who had faith in the Messiah yet to come; infant baptism united those who had faith in the Christ who came. And of course, the stability and order of society depended on the stability and order of the individual churches within it, Roger Williams to the contrary notwithstanding.

For the Baptists to challenge infant baptism was to challenge the covenant theology. And the Baptists made no bones about the fact that they saw no justification for infant baptism as the gospel form of circumcision because, at the coming of Christ, a new covenant was established, replacing the old one. To prove baptism by circumcision, as John Thrumble said in the Debate, was "to mix law and gospel" or the doctrine of works and the doctrine of faith. Under the terms of "the new covenant" only those who were converted through grace by faith and could give an account of the workings of the Holy Spirit in their souls and a profession of their faith with their mouths were entitled to be members of the churches of Christ. Infants could not give such an account (though they might perhaps be predestined saints) and therefore were not entitled to baptism. And certainly the grandchildren of visible saints, as under the Half-way Covenant, could not be baptized. And insofar as the Puritan churches insisted, as they did, that sainthood flowed through the loins of the saints, thus creating a kind of hereditary sainthood as well as aristocracy, the Baptists believed that they were following in the path of "the Whore of Babylon," the Church of Rome.[24] For infant baptism was not the seal of federal holiness but "the badge of the whore." From the practice of this false rite the creation of a national church was inevitable (as Stoddardeanism and the Saybrook Platform were to prove in New England). And a National Church (which the Puritans vehemently denied they had in Massachusetts) inevitably led to the persecution of the true saints as, said the Baptists, our fathers who settled this wilderness well knew.

Thomas Cobbett summed up the social consequences of anti-pedobaptism some years after the Debate in a letter to Increase Mather. In doing so he revealed clearly why the seemingly mild request of Thomas Goold and his brethren for open communion or toleration in this Debate aroused such heated opposition:

theyr very principle of makeing infant Baptisme a nullity, it doth make at once, all our churches, & our religious, Civill state & polity, & all the officers & members thereof to be unbaptised, & to bee no Christians, & so, our churches to bee no churches; & so we have no regular freemen, which by our laws, are to bee members of churches; & so we have no regular power to choose Deputies for any Generall Courts, nor to chuse any Magistrates; but all beeing, according to that pernicious doctrine, non members of any true church, and all our holsom laws & orders made a nullity; & that hedge is pulled downe, & all left open to state destroyers . . . so that our very fundaments of civil & sacred order, here in New England, are at once thereby . . . overturned.[25]

No matter how orthodox the Baptists were in their adherence to the theological doctrines of Calvinism, they were heretical in the fundamentals concerning church order and hence could not be tolerated even though they might plead for it with tears in their eyes. What was ultimately at stake in this debate, as in the whole movement of the Baptists and other sects for toleration and religious liberty in the seventeenth century, was the breakdown of the corporate Christian state and the substitution for it of a state of free individuals relying on their own judgment to create the city of God upon the American hill. The two groups recognized in each other the essence of a struggle not just for the souls of men in the next world but for the truth of God in the social order of this world. And it was this direct confrontation between the medieval and modern worlds that gave the heightened tension and wider drama to that debate in the old wooden meetinghouse on the outskirts of Western civilization.

TRANSCRIBER'S NOTE
by Martha Whiting Davidson

The shorthand text of the Baptist Debate of April 14–15, 1668, is in the Massachusetts Historical Society, in a small volume of manuscripts labeled on its spine "MASS./PAPERS/1662–6/DANFORTH." It covers thirty-four unnumbered leaves and is accompanied by copies of other papers of the 1660s made by Thomas Danforth (1622–1699). "Communicated" to the Society by James Savage on August 25, 1818,[26] the longhand portions of the papers were printed in the 1819 volume of the Society's *Collections*[27] under the running head "DANFORTH PAPERS." But the Debate, which was not printed there, was suspected of being unedifying because it contained so many brief speeches. A note by "C.H.S." (probably Caleb H. Snow, the historian of Boston), bound into the manuscript volume at the start of the Debate, records his failure in 1829 to decipher its shorthand.[28]

The transcript seems clearly to be Danforth's, for there are fragments of the same shorthand scattered throughout other parts of the same manuscript volume as well as through the contemporary court records of Middlesex County, where Danforth was recorder. There is some question, however, whether this is the document Danforth meant to preserve, for the introduction to this part of the manuscript volume concludes: "Whereupon at a Counsell held at Boston in march 1667–8 an act was passed for their [the Anabaptists'] orderly conviction, by the labours of some of the Reverend Elders a coppie whereof here followeth."

The shorthand is based on the alphabet of Edmond Willis,[29] the second really effective shorthand system in English. There is a symbol for every letter, but internal vowels, which are omitted, are shown by the position of the following consonant, above or below the waist of the one preceding. Silent letters, as in doubled consonants, are not set down, and repeated syllables are suppressed, but there are relatively few abbreviations or arbitrary symbols.

I have in all cases attempted to supply a meaning for doubtful words, indicating my hesitation by brackets and question marks. The shorthand symbols for "*be*" and "*is*" are the same, the straight line meaning "*b*," and I may have erred in the direction of modern usage in choosing between them, as also in the case of verbs ending in "*th*." The diagonal line for "*t*" and "*th*" is very similar to the shorter stroke used for a final "*s*." I have supplied "'*s*," which the shorthand omits.

Because of the phonetic aspects of the shorthand, modern spelling has been used throughout, except in transcribing the few longhand words, which are indicated by *italic* type. The speakers' names (here given in SMALL CAPITALS) are also in longhand, except where shown, and the spelling and abbreviation of the original have been followed. In a few cases the insertion of missing words seemed to help the flow of language. These are shown within brackets.

The only mark of punctuation in the original is the colon, which I have retained, feeling that this unusual pointing does something to preserve the stenographic character of the documents. I have, however, closed abbreviations and sentences, so far as sentence endings could be determined, with periods. In several places the recorder drew a line halfway across the page, indicating perhaps omission or merely the conclusion of a subject. These lines are rendered typographically by centered horizontal rules.

CAST OF CHARACTERS

Participants on the Baptist side:[30]

BENANUAL BOWERS, a resident of Charlestown, Cambridge, Woburn, in the years 1650–1693, was first arrested, fined, and whipped as a Quaker in the 1650s and later regularly attended Thomas Goold's Baptist church in Charlestown and Boston, for which he suffered many arrests and fines. He never joined the Baptist church. In 1693 his wife reported that he had gone insane.

JOHN CRANDALL (Grendall of Narragansett) was born in Providence and married a daughter of Samuel Gorton; he moved to Newport and joined John Clarke's Baptist church. In 1651 he was arrested and fined in Boston with Clarke and Obadiah Holmes for proselyting in Lynn and for denouncing the Puritan churches. In 1660 he moved to Westerly, where he became pastor of a branch of the Newport church, which in 1671 adopted Seventh Day worship. Savage says he was born in 1637, and John Callender says he died in 1737.

EDWARD DRINKER (d. 1700), born in England, became a potter in Charlestown, where he was elected constable in 1652; he moved to Boston in 1668. A constituent member of Goold's church in 1665, he was arrested and disfranchised with him in 1666. He fought in King Philip's War as a lieutenant. He became a deacon and teaching elder in the Baptist church in Boston but was excommunicated in 1695, apparently because he joined another Baptist group in Newbury without proper dismissal from the Boston church.

JOHN FARNUM, SR., was a founder and deacon of the Second Congregational Church in Boston in 1650. He became a member of Goold's Baptist church in 1666 and was arrested and banished with him in 1668. He then recanted and in 1683 was readmitted to membership in the Second Church of Boston. In 1695 he returned to the Baptist Church, and in 1709 he said he had become a Quaker.

THOMAS GOOLD (d. 1675), wagon-maker and tenant-farmer of John Winthrop's Tenhills farm in Charlestown, adopted Baptist views in 1655 and founded the First Baptist Church of Boston (originally at Charlestown) in 1665, serving as its pastor from 1665 to 1675. Imprisoned and disfranchised in 1666, he was imprisoned again and banished in 1668, but the authorities failed to enforce the sentence.

ISAAC HULL (d. 1699) joined Goold's church in 1666 and became a leading figure in it. He was made a teaching elder in 1679 and served as pastor from 1682 to 1689 and co-pastor from 1694 to 1699.

JOHN JOHNSON, a resident of Woburn, joined Goold's church in 1666 but was excommunicated in 1671 when he recanted.

THOMAS OSBORNE left the Charlestown Congregational Church to become a constituent member of Goold's Baptist church in 1665; later he moved to Woburn. He was imprisoned and disfranchised with Goold but remained a leader in the Baptist church until at least 1676.

JOHN THRUMBLE (1607–1687), born in Newcastle-on-Tyne, arrived in Charlestown in 1642. He was captain of a trading vessel and, after 1673, a shopkeeper. He does not appear to have joined the Baptist church but regularly attended its services and was arrested and fined for that.

WILLIAM TURNER (d. 1676) had been a member of a Baptist church in Dartmouth, England, before emigrating to Boston, where he became a constituent member of Goold's church. He was arrested with Goold in 1666 and banished with him in 1668. In 1675 the General Court refused to let him raise a company to fight in King Philip's War because of his Baptist views, but in the spring of 1676 he was commissioned as a captain. He won a notable battle in May 1676 at what is now Turner's Falls but was killed by the Indians the next day at Green River.

Participants on the Congregational side:[31]

JOHN ALLIN (Allen) (1597–1671) was minister at Dedham. He was an experienced moderator and the author of an official defense of the Halfway Covenant. (There is no evidence that James Allen [1632–1710], soon to become minister of the First Church, took part in the Debate).

RICHARD BELLINGHAM (1592?–1672) was governor of the Massachusetts Bay Colony in 1641, 1654, and 1665–1672.

THOMAS COBBETT (1608–1685) was minister at Ipswich.

SAMUEL DANFORTH (1626–1674), Thomas's brother, was minister at Roxbury.

DANIEL GOOKIN (Gowkin) (1612–1687) was a trader, colonist, and soldier who served frequently as deputy or assistant.

JOHN HIGGINSON (1616–1708) was a minister at Salem and notably hard on Quakers.

JONATHAN MITCHELL (1624–1668) was minister at Cambridge and a leading advocate of the Halfway Covenant. Fifteen years earlier he had attempted to dissuade President Dunster of Harvard from his antipedobaptist views and had suffered scruples about whether infant baptism was not, after all, an invention of man.[32]

RICHARD RUSSELL (1611–1676) was a selectman in Charlestown. For twenty years he was treasurer of the Massachusetts Bay Colony, and he was an assistant from 1659 until his death.

THOMAS SHEPARD, JR. (1635–1677) was Symmes's colleague at Charlestown and thus involved in the case of Thomas Goold from the beginning.

ZECHARIAH SYMMES (Simes), SR. (1599–1672?) was minister at Charlestown.

THOMAS THACHER (d. 1678) was minister at Weymouth and later at the Old South Church in Boston.

SAMUEL WHITING (Whiteing) (1597–1679) was minister at Lynn.

THE DEBATE

[*In the margin:*] *Boston*: 14:2: 1668.

Mr. John Allin and Mr. Whiteing Senr, were chosen for moderators and Mr. John Allin made this following speech.

The scope of this meeting is to reduce those that have gone out of God's way to Anabaptism a noble and high end it is. So the apostle saith: he that saveth a brother from the error of his way:[33] where we may take notice it is possible to save a brother from the error of his way though hard: sinners whose souls are in danger of death if not converted; sinners that have a multitude of sins. Error leadeth a soul into many corrupt ways. This is the end that the honored *magistrates* have propounded to themselves and us: who are shepherds of the flock in a civil way. They have endeavored to stop men from running out by wholesome laws: spiritual shepherds by instruction and censure have endeavored to reduce also: but now it pleaseth God to give this opportunity wherein spiritual and civil shepherds doth both join together: if it may please God to give us a blessing. It is hard to turn men from their opinion: but yet such a sinner may be converted: and may it please God to save one soul from death by this day's work it will be an attendant recompence. It is true evil men and seditious will wax worse and worse: and who can help that? That this assembly may be more equally minded: in the work before us: I shall be bold to propound 3: or 4: considerations.

1: Consider who were the 1: promoters of this opinion against infant baptism. [Creditable histories?] do declare strange things of it. Such as came in sheeps' clothing they appeared to be devouring wolves: allowing [polygamy?][34] and running out into many false prophecies which never came to pass. Let not these be thought lies and slanders. They were [acted?] in the open sight of the sun: and their error confuted. Now I would appeal to the consciences of this assembly whether ever they heard or read that God made use of such instruments as these to make known his truth to [the] world: especially such as do oppose all the instruments of reformation Luther Calvin etc.

2: Let all consider whether this be a thing creditable to [be] believed that that God which hath in all ages extended his covenant to the seed of the church: that now the Lord should cast off the seed of his faithful people. Is not God the God of the gentiles as of the Jews? Can we think that the love of God to the children of believing parents is now dried up: and are his bowels restrained? Had the Lord Jesus said so when children were brought to him then a man might have believed this: but when the Lord Jesus pronounced of them that such was the kingdom of God: I know not how to believe that the Lord should now restrain his love to children and love them no better than pagans as some have affirmed.

3: Consider the sad consequences of this opinion: 1: how it renders godly parents mourn with hope for their children that die in infancy: if they be not the subjects of election that die in their infancy. What a sad state are those parents in for their children that die in infancy. 2: Consider how this opinion undermines all the protestant churches and ordinances of God for if infant baptism is *nulled*: where shall we find visible churches? Though some are more modest than to own them: yet some are bold to profess: these churches wherein God hath so wonderfully appeared. Shall we think that a truth which undermineth man?

4: Consider with what spirit this opinion have been acted: in all this much profession of near acquaintance with God. But saith the apostle try the spirits whether of God or not.[35] Two things are evident in the spirit of Anabaptism which show it not to be the spirit of God: 1: The spirit of God is uniting but this is a spirit of division. 2: Observe the character that John giveth of the spirit of truth: he that is of us heareth us. If we look into all books: false teachers have been the great [opposers?] of the truth of God. Jeremiah was a mad man: and made himself a prophet:[36] and false apostles how did they also turn the spirit of the people from Paul. These sort of people they disgrace the faithful ministers of Christ. Now to cast off them: and as Christ saith John 13:20: whoever receiveth him that cometh in my name receiveth me: it can't be denied but that the Lord hath raised up many eminent faithful ones in his church: but what is the reproach and despite that is cast on the ministers by this sort: it is too evidently known to all. Can you beloved brethren that look that way approve your hearts to God that you highly esteem those that [are] over you in the Lord? Do you hear this with due respect to the truth of God? By this you may know the spirit of truth and error.

A word or 2: let me speak to these persons that are [charged?] in the work of this place. You see the [fairness?] of our Christian magistrates. Abuse it not by running into thy matters. Your work is to give the reason of your separation from the people of God: and setting up a meeting in the way of Anabaptism: and whether this commonwealth is to allow it. Keep to the business you are to attend I do beseech ye: and I hope we shall with all love and faithfulness endeavor to manage matters as need shall require: the Lord assisting us therein. If it please the honored magistrates to direct.

GOVR. I know nothing to be said. Whether they will give account of the matters propounded?

GOOLD: I should desire to propound 2: or 3: questions. I should desire to speak a word or 2: to what hath been delivered concerning our separation: but I think that will come in with your things: and therefore we shall forbear at present. One or 2: things I shall propound to the honored Governor.

We are here in his *magistrate's* name [by?] warrant to appear here this day. I should desire to know whether we as appear are before a court or no.

GOVR. Ye are to appear here to answer for setting up another way than we are in: and we desire them to speak without any such question.

[GOOLD.] We are free to do it: but we would know whether we speak before a court or no.

Another thing I would speak. It is in the writing a free debate. Then we should desire and I hope it will be so: that what passeth from us we may not lie under the penalty of any law.

GOVR. You may speak so offensively against God and man that you can't be suffered therein.

ALLEN. So far as you speak to the cause in hand.

GOOLD. We are but man: and we would not be made offenders for a word.

COBBITT. Keep to the question. If you go besides it you may thank yourselves.

MITCHELL. It is a mixt meeting: and it is no wry thing for Moses and Aaron to meet together. The paper brings you no time and place: that is a civil act. You may choose whether you will say anything or no.

GOWKIN. The paper [rather?] declareth the mind of the church: and at no meeting we may take liberty to sin: to reproach persons or blaspheme God so you may speak what you will according to reason. We come not to ensnare you: but to inform you.

GOOLD. Have not we liberty to choose moderators?

COBBITT. You come not on equal terms: but as a delinquent: to answer for what you have done. You come not here to choose moderators.

RUSSELL. You have this liberty: come to what you are called.

GOOLD. We would make known the truth of our hearts and would not give offence to one and another.

HIG. Propound some of your grounds for the affirmative of your question.

GOOLD. We have the grounds in the writing.

COBBITT. That is the matter: but it is the grounds [*thus in MS*].

GOOLD. We have given our grounds to the General Court.[37]

ALLEN. If those be all the grounds let us know them.

GOOLD. We are not called to give them free.

MITCHELL. You are left to your own way to give them as you please.

GOOLD. We shall begin when you please.

GOOLD. May any other speak?

ALLEN. You or any of your company.

TURNER. I hope it will not be offensive if any of the company take liberty to speak in this assembly. I own myself to be of this way and order. I hope I shall not be ashamed of it in the day of the Lord. Then friends: the question we are appointed to answer is as followeth. And so he recited the question.[38] Now in answer to it. If you please to hear: we think it necessary 1: to clear how far any of these have departed from the communion of these churches.

MITCHELL. I suppose it is not the best way to teach: to make intermitted speeches.

TURNER. Let one speak at a time that we may keep due order.

COBBITT. The council declares you have done thus and thus: you must not put us to prove it.

TURNER. We account ourselves guilty of such a charge [is?] to depart from the churches of Christ.[39]

WHITING. What mean you the churches of Christ?

TURNER. All that follow the Lord Jesus Christ. The Lord knows who is his: every man must judge for himself.

MITCHELL. He declines the owning of these churches of Christ.

TURNER. We own all that are followers of Christ.

GOVR. This man declares himself to be a Baptist and confesseth that his father was so before him.

TURNER. There hath been a precious scripture mentioned: he that converteth a brother. We desire to have it cleared up what be the mind of God. I hope it is the desire of our souls to lie under the truth of God. You are to prove yourselves to be churches by the last will and testament of Christ before we own you so. Whatever is not of faith is sin: and if we have not faith it will be sin for us to act in it. You all own the Lord Jesus Christ to be the [head corner-stone?]: and he giveth power to his servants to go unto all nations and baptize them and teach them what he command them. We conceive the souls ought to be taught in the doctrine of Christ before they be baptized.

MITCHELL. It is a piece of confusion to wind to and again into interrogatory.

GOOLD. Lay down then the things we are to hold to.

MITCHELL. Let us have an argument.

TURNER. God is a spirit: and they that worship him be to worship him in spirit and truth. Show us where any mortal man is able to constrain him to worship him in spirit and truth. Therefore I judge that the assemblies of God's people may wait on him when he appoints.

You would persuade us to sin against God and the light of our own souls.

If a soul be not first born of God: how can he worship God in spirit and truth? And if you judge God otherwise: I wonder you should enjoin us to worship with you.

GOOLD. I shall desire to come to the particular thing. 1: We are charged with separation. For my own particular I have as much to say as another. Only let me ask 1: question first.

COBBITT. We are come to hear your grounds.

GOOLD. Whether may not a member depart from a church for the same sin that a church may separate a member?

MITCHELL. No. They ought to have put away that wicked person: but while he was among them it was not lawful for any particular to depart.

SHEPARD. A particular person may not judge the whole: but is to be subject to the whole.

GOOLD. By the rule of Christ he may: too. [*Three or four words undeciphered*] is not my people. I do not say excommunicate but withdraw.

Many answers are given but no scripture given. If convincing arguments be laid it is that which answers. I gave convincing arguments to the church why I did separate from them.

Holding up the Bible in his hand he said: We have nothing to judge but this.

COBBITT. The church and not the brother is to be [true witness?] before the judge.

[*In shorthand:*] SHEPHARD. I will give you 2: scriptures to show that a private brother is to submit to the judgment of the church. Matt. 18:12: if he shall neglect to hear the church. I Cor. 5:12: Do not yet judge them that are within. If a private brother will separate from the church for an evil therein; upon his peril it lieth.

GOOLD. The church is to be the judge: but the church is to judge according to the rule of Christ. When my spirit is with you: the spirit of Christ is with them.

SHEPD. Must the offender judge or the church that they have the spirit of Christ?

GOOLD. The church may pass sentence and yet not according to the rule of Christ.

SHEPD. Churches may sin as well as private persons.

GOOLD. If those sins may be committed in a church for which God may cast them off: then a private member may cast them off.

COBBITT. A dangerous inference. Because the all-seeing God may do it: therefore Goodman Goold a fallible judge and running to many errors may.

GOOLD. Let me give you 2: or 3: scriptures to show you wherein a member may separate from a church.

ALLEN. Consider this whether on your principles you will have any communion with any church in the world. You own yourselves a church. Will there not be differences among you and will you own that particular member may cast you off?

GOOLD. If they go out from us: it is a sign they were not of us.

MITCHELL. Goodman Goold's notion is this: that a particular person may put away a church where a church may a particular person. It is plain [*one or two words undeciphered*] of God towards churches: where he doth not allow particular persons nor are churches to allow them. Show but a shadow of a scripture for what you say.

GOOLD. Anything that is unclean I am to withdraw from. II Cor. 6: Wherefore come out from among them and touch no unclean thing and I will be your God.

MITCHELL. That is not from the church but from infidels: and you put it upon the church.

GOOLD. Would he bid them come out from pagans?

MITCHELL. The scope is to dissuade them from partaking with idolaters: and you apply it to separation from the church of Corinth.

GOOLD. Was the discourse about the [fasts?]:[40] confined to pagans?

MITCHELL. We speak not of the [wise?]: but of the [*one or two words undeciphered*].

SHEPARD. II Cor. 6:16.[41]

Wherefore come out from among them and be yet separate with the Lord. God requires them not to separate themselves from those among whom they did dwell: and from his temple.

GOOLD. Be not ye unequally yoked to unbelievers. They were saints by calling: but had gross corruptions among them. Christ dwelleth in no temple but in the heart of a believer: whose house ye are.

MITCHELL. Is not the church God's habitation?

GOOLD. They are lodging sins that be this house that Christ dwelleth in.

[*In shorthand:*] SHEPARD. I will dwell in them: and therefore it is not true that he dwelleth only in a particular person.

The Lord dwelleth in the holy and upright believer. The church of Christ is but one take it in substance.

MITCHELL. In Salem is his tabernacle and his dwelling place is in Sion.

TURNER. A church that receiveth unbelievers: it dwelleth not in the unbeliever: though he dwelleth in that church.

COBBITT. Doth he dwell in every believer and not in them together: as made up in a house?

GOOLD. From such we would not separate: and it is impossible that a true believer should separate from a church of Christ.

COBBITT. Any sin but blasphemy may be committed by a believer: but this is a sin and not blasphemy and therefore a believer may fall into this.

GOOLD. A believer may separate from a society of believers: and yet notwithstanding his separating from them doth not separate from Christ.

COBBITT. If the church of Corinth were to separate from the church: then they were to separate from themselves.

GOOLD. Come out from among them saith the Lord. The believer is to come then from the unbeliever: although of the same church.

GOOK. According to this notion every man must separate from himself: for who is free from sin?

ALLEN. I will gather up the scope of your argument. You justify your separation.

GOOLD. I own no separation.

ALLEN. You own it in your judgment. Your arguments run upon this: that a believer must withdraw from an unbeliever: and upon invisible grace: how can you judge this unbeliever? The scripture is very plain that all that are in the church are to be judged believers.

MITCHELL. I hope yourself will own the strange absurdity of this reasoning.

BOWER. It is said that John wrote to the 7: churches of Asia: and in all *minor* part was only the true church: and from such as have only a form of godliness we are to turn away: for alas the true church consisteth of the fewest members.

MITCHELL. When Christ saith they are golden candlesticks: and yet you say they are in form.

GOOLD. One of them was such a golden candlestick that the Lord threatens to spew them out of his mouth.[42]

[*In shorthand:*] SHEPARD. Christ called on them to repent: and therefore he owns them.

BOWERS. The spirit of God in every Christian tells them whether the other be right or in form only.

[*Another speaker:*] The question is whether those that have the form and the power are the true church.

BOWER. Christ hath but one church.

COBBITT. Those worthy names were in this and not separate from them.

[*In shorthand:*] A MAN: MODERATOR.—If you charges them with separation from the church then it is necessary to make the charge appear.

———————

COBBITT. Their meeting was for the worse and not the better: in that place you mentioned in Corinthians. Why because they did meet with a schismatical spirit.

GOOLD. The apostle speaks not there of schism: but of excess in eating and drinking: and dividing one from another. I shall give you but one scripture more. Acts. 19:9: And when divers were hardened and believed not: he departed from them and separated the disciples.

MITCHELL. Because he withdrew from the blasphemous *Jews*: therefore we may withdraw from these churches?

COBBITT. He preached in a synagogue of the Jews: who seemed to hear him gladly: but when the *Jews* did contradict: then saith he Lo we turn from you. When the churches turn from Christ here: then this place will help [*word undeciphered*].

GOOLD. The *Jews* spoke evil of the way of life: and on this he turns away and separates the disciples.

MITCHELL. From obstinate blasphemous Jews such as rejected the fundamentals of salvation Christ separates. Will you compare the churches here to it? You mean because we speak evil of your way of Anabaptism and that it is your ground to turn away from us.

[*In shorthand:*] THRUMBLE. You speak well.

[*In shorthand:*] GOOLD. You have put words into our *mouth*.

SHEP. Doth the apostle require the disciples to separate: or did he separate the disciples from the disciples?

GOOLD. He separated the disciples from those who spake evil of the way.

MITCHELL. When we speak against Anabaptism we speak against an error: and if it were all evil is this parallel to the fundamentals of religion?

GOOLD. If they speak of the way: they are to be separated from.

ALLEN. It is the wise providence of God to leave these people to propound such places of scripture as are most clear against them.

GOOLD. We find there is scripture for which persons may withdraw from societies: and such as be called the churches of Christ.

ALLEN. Prove these things against these churches for which a man may separate.

MITCHELL. We [abhor?] separation from the churches of *England*.

GOOLD. So do we.

WHITING. You seem to *renounce* them by your *renouncing of* your baptism.

MITCHELL. There is difference between separation and secession. They came 3000: miles from them rather than oppose them.

GOOLD. You did withdraw from the corruption there: and so we witness against your corruption.

We will hold communion with you so far forth as you keep to the rule of Christ.

Do not we hold communion with you in preaching and praying: and in the sacraments?[43]

Though every one hear not in every assembly: yet they may hold communion.

We only withdraw from you in some things: and set up those things that are according to the mind of Christ.

I have set up another way which I believe to be the mind of God. I judge there are such corruptions in your way that I can't approve of.

ALLEN. What not *Arminians* and others do the same?

GOOLD. You did the same when you came from *Eng.* and many go when dissatisfied.

THRUMBLE. Master Mitchell hath been pleased to say that this company do so separate as that they will not join in word and prayer: and I know none of the company but that do join in word and prayer: and I do not believe he can prove what he saith.

MITCH. Do not we know many of us: that some here refuse to join with the church in Charlestown?

THRUMBL. It is grievous to hear such [aggravations?] and [offences] as are laid upon these brethren here. I suppose the whole country can't make it appear that they do schismatically rend.

And is this to clear the truth of God: for 6: or more persons to speak to one poor man: before he hath done: not permitting him to speak. And every man must have his saying before he can give a right answer.

———

A stranger [*in the margin:*] *Hull of Bass River* now recited the question and read his answer to the civil parts thereof. We desire no further toleration than Deacon [Owen?][44] pleads for.

GOOLD. Those be the main things we are to answer: [brethren?]. As for the confession of our faith we gave it to the court: and you may hear it again if you please.

[*In shorthand:*] THRUMBLE. Here you hear the desire of these friends. It is to walk according to truth. If they walk uncivilly: they are willing to suffer by the authority: if irregularly: they are willing to hear it from the counsel of God.

We desire nothing more to plead for us than the grounds of your withdrawing from *Engl.* But it may be you will say you did not set up Anabaptism. We understand not what the word means: unless it render a man to deny all baptism.

ALLEN. *Ans.* it is rebaptizing.

THR. John baptized none but those that confessed their sins. John told them they must not plead Abraham's right: think it not enough to say we have Abraham to our father. And why should the gentiles have more privilege than the *Jewes*? I have stood to maintain what now I oppose: but when God clears up his mind I can't shut my [eyes?] against it.

You bring baptism only to believers' children: and now we fall to enlargement: some to the 2: sort: some to all.[45] Now if you can confine and enlarge and none [*word undeciphered*] you: [are?] the subjects of [*one or two words undeciphered*] authority and look at one another as godly men: we desire that we may have no more privilege. If we go about to take away government: or desire any office deny it to us. If we walk not according to the rules of Christ then deny it to us: but as our conversation speaks for us that we desire to walk with God: to pay every one his own. If not then turn us aside for such as do deny the rules of Christ.

Did every church well with you for your differing one with another: or excommunicate you?

GOOLD. We will now read the confession of our faith.

ALLEN. We desire not that it be the grounds of your practice.

TURNR. We believe we own communion with all believers in the world.

HIG. These grounds for the practice will be every one of them answered. I shall only propound one argument for the *neg.*: *i.e.*: to prove that your way is not justifiable by the word of God.

1: argument. It is not justifiable by the word of God for Thomas Goold and company to depart from the communion of these churches: and set up a meeting in way of Anabaptism. They are 3: of them excommunicate persons: and others do join with excommunicate persons in this their meeting: who are according to their order wicked persons. Put away from you this wicked person delivered over to Satan: and being justly cast out of one church: they are [verily?] cast out of all the churches of Christ on earth: and therefore uncapable of such communion in any place while they continue in that state: and meeting together in that way they are a synagogue of Satan: [Greeks?] who say they are *Jewes* and are not: they are so called. This is the cause of those and of those that join with them: as a synagogue of Satan. They may say they are a church of Christ but are not but do lie.

GOOLD. We desire you now that we may come to our particular answer.

In the after noone

TURNER. We desire that the grounds of our faith and practice may be read.

ALLEN. An account of your faith is not now called for in the *question*.

THR. It is said they have set up a place of their own. They are willing to own.

DRINKER. We present these to be our grounds: these testimonies of scripture which we are ready to present to you: so that the grounds of our thus acting are from these professions of [*word undeciphered*].

TUNR. [I serve?] the people of God as a holy [presider?]. *Hee* now read the confession of their faith.[46]

MITCHELL. So far as we agree what need of reading this: but what argument is there here for our separation?

TURNER. Our baptizing of believers the scripture warrants.

MITCHELL. We baptize believers as well as you.

TURNER. 3: things I separate from you for. 1: Baptizing infants. 2: Denying prophecy to the brethren. 3: A spirit of persecution of those that differ from you. These are the reason why I differ from you.

DRINKER. I can't see how we can be said to be separated from the churches here: and that for these reasons. 1: Because many of us were never joined to the churches here. For my own part I have lived many years: but in the conclusion I did not see the way and order of these churches to be so according to rule of the gospel as the pattern laid down by Christ Jesus: and therefore how am I chargeable with schismatical rending from you? It is the liberty of every believer before his joining to weigh what particular society he can best close with: and the confession read as the grounds of our acting in this way: for several others of your brethren who were with you: I [*word undeciphered*] declare the imminence of their coming from you: whether they separated from you: or you from them.

MITCHELL. He that professeth himself to be a Christian he separates by refusing to join as well as by breaking away after he hath joined. 2: You make yourself a separatist by joining with those that are so.

THR. You did say if we would withdraw from you as you from old *Engld.*: then you could allow of us: although I suppose yourself *Mr. mitchell* and some others that set by you did not come over upon that *account*. We would not go from under the [benefit?] of your government.

ALLEN. Will you submit to the government?

THRUMB. To any rule of Christ we are willing to submit [*word undeciphered*].

HIG. How can your profession of submission to the government here be believed: whenas in this way of yours you have transgressed many of the laws of this commonwealth: with [*one or two words un-deciphered*] being presumptuous and self-willed: despising govern-ment: no new thing for such as you to quarrel with *magistrates* [nor?] government in matters of religion.

TRUMBL. Let us have the same liberty you desire and give as your reasons to the ministers at Westminster[47] and they shall serve our turn.

HIG. The people of this place came hither in an orderly way that they might enjoy their liberty in a peaceable way.

THR. Was your patent to settle just a form of church government and no other?

HIG. The generality of the people of God that came to this coun-try: they did not separate from the churches of *Engl* but came from the disordered there: with full desire of reformation without dis-turbance to any.

THR. We came for liberty of conscience as well as yourselves. You had not a patent for such a form: and you are not perfect. We are daily exhorted to be growing [in] grace and knowledge: and if you be not perfect: we are to look for light as well as you. If you [coun-sel?] one thing and we another: bear one with another. If we un-dermine church or commonwealth burn us hang us we beg no farther. It is the Lord and not you that must reduce us.

HIG. You are in a degree an apostate from that which you pro-fessed to come over for.

THR. I did as you say walk 20: years with the churches: and was as clear in my fancy for infant baptism as any other: but I told some of you that you were about at the synod to make [an] Anabaptist.

Because we would not grieve people in going out from the sprin-kling of children: therefore we did withdraw to meet by ourselves. If we any way interrupt you or exclaim against you: then spare us not.[48]

MITCH. You speak to so many things the once: as now the cause of the nonconformist and of the patent: etc.

You say the patent give us liberty of conscience. Lo there is no such word as liberty of conscience. This people had made a sad bargain for themselves and their posterity if they had come hither for [an infirmity and?] liberty.

2: To whom gave it liberty? Surely to no company and citizen:

who have fixed on the present government: in church and commonwealth. The liberty was not to every single person: and it us against the fundamental liberties of the patent for people to act here contrary to the patent and the laws here made. And I suppose there was not an Anabaptist of all the patentees: and is any bound to let another have a room in his house whether he will or not?

THR. The patentees did not obtain it for themselves but for others. I have been at charges as well as others.

COBBITT. We came over hither for liberty of conscience: and so did Master Thrumble: and we keep to him. He chose the lawmakers: and it may be Goodman Goold did the like: and chose these men that have made these laws. They engage to submit to all the laws that are made and established by this government: and they have sworn to it. Now if you go from your own oaths and acts: who is to *blame*?[49] We keep to the patent and you go from it.

THRUMBL. I was an unworthy member of a church: and I was then engaged to walk up to all the rules of Christ that ever I knew or should know. If that form of church order had still been continued in: I had remained where I was for aught I know.

WHITING. Take heed Master Thrumble of the flying roll.[50] A swift curse will come upon them that break their oath.

DRINKER. I suppose the expectation of the company may be to hear something to Master Higginson's speech just before we break up.

Turnr. was now desired to read what he read in the morning.

TURNER. Where is the rule of Christ that we must follow the churches here farther than they follow Christ?

MITCHELL. The sum of what you say is a mere cloud of words: and to deny your [free?] separation of the churches here.

Yet you and Goodman Gould have declined to own us to be churches: and this is the height of separation.

2: It was said here that you did not join with us in word and prayer. Upon this ground he that separates from one church in communion with the rest: separates from all. You refuse to join with them in word and prayer upon considerations that are common to all the churches in the country.

3: It is so to answer we do and will hold communion with you.

SHEPD. A Papist will say as much: that we will hold communion with these churches so far as the word of God do direct. Your word is general.

TURNR. Is it not a reasonable thing that every man have his particular judgment in matters of faith seeing we must all appear before the judgment seat of Christ?

THR. You say a Papist may say as much as this friend saith. I know not but that 20: Papists may say as much as you say in point of holding communion.

The Synod book saith for 3: causes a man may separate from a church in being.[51] 1: For avoiding pollution. 2: For his further edification. 3: For peace of his conscience.

MITCH. The Synod book is mistaken by therein they speak of withdrawing unto another place: and not separating.

THR. Abraham and others lived in the sin of *Apurgama*[52] and yet that is not a warrant for others to do the like.

DRINKER. We plead not for separatism. There may be a separation partly and not fully.

MITCH. Total separation and [*thus in MS*].

GRENDALL OF NARRAGANSETT. One thing I take notice of. I think that Master Allen did declare that this Anabaptism did declare in the beginning: the meaning of the word Anabaptism: and forestalled the minds of the people. It is not for [person's?] sake that make things true or false. I did believe when I was in *Engl.* that the church there was a true church: and after I came hither: and [lodged?] at *Dorchester.*

HIG. I look upon it a wrong to the company called that others should take up the time.

[CRANDALL] I do not look at myself as having separated from you all: and I am willing to give you my reasons.

GOOLD. We were promised that we should return to the thing we were to come [word undeciphered]: which was some scripture alleged about separation. I did then believe it was not separation: but withdrawing from some things that we could not close with all in the churches. To say you are not a church of Christ I dare not: but wherein I do not walk with you in some things I do declare freely. But I am also to give you an account that I did not go away from you until I was put away from you: and the church would not let me communicate with them.[53]

SHEP. Explain that particular that you did not withdraw until the church did put you away.

GOOLD. I shall speak fully and freely to that *matter.*

COBBITT. We are bound to believe the church and not a delinquent.

GOOLD. Then do with us what you will. I am ready before all this congregation: that I was put away from the church before I did withdraw.

Let it be reckoned up what the church did with [*word undeciphered*] from *mee.* When I can see that I have broke a rule I am ready for to give answer: and to make satisfaction according to any rule of Christ.

MITCH. Putting away by the Church is no warrant for separation.

THR. If a child be corrected he must not run away: but if a member of a body be so tied up as that he can't receive nourishment: is not the way to starve the body?

Mr. Shepd. gave an account of the casting out of Goold out of Charlestown Church: in writing.[54]

1655. The 1: occasion was the not bringing of his child to baptism: to which he answered he saw no warrant for it from the word of God.

He was thought fit by many brethren for the highest censure not for casting off the ordinance of infant baptism: but for reproaching and casting dirt upon it. Upon motion of an admonition to be given to him: it was propounded that he should withdraw from the sacrament of the Lord's supper until satisfaction which he yielded [*word undeciphered*]. The grounds of his admonition was his open renouncing of children's baptism: with many reproachful speeches.

6:4:58: He was called forth for withdrawing from the ordinances on the Lord's day. He answered he had not turned from any ordinance of God: but attended the word in other places.

He was admonished for his breaking from the church in the way of schism: occasioned by his denying his child infant baptism: and bearing witness against it: and reproaching it saying it was as bad as the cross and since that he hath appeared obstinate in his own and till now hath spoke to the endangering of his soul and the souls of others.

*Novemr.*9:63: *Osburn* was examined by the eldership for withdrawing from the public worship of God on the Lord's day: confessed he was at Thomas Goold's and discovered himself to be an Anabaptist, Having had often discourse with Goold: he objected that we gave not leave to prophesy. He laid much on the freeness of his spirit to as being the rule of duty.

*Novemr.*15:63: The church was informed of *Osburne* when he still justified himself in his sinful way: because he did not see it to be the mind of God to continue some churches by way of natural generation.

Novem. 18:63. *Osburn* being called forth: would not confess his sin: though very unsteady in his expression: but *Goold* denied himself to stand related to the church: when he was called to give an account for his withdrawing from public ordinances. When a copy of the 2: admonition to Goold was read: he stiffly denied that he had been twice admonished.

He replied to some brethren that would have him cast out that he did not care how soon they did it.

Reasons why he lay so long unexcommunicated.

Some that were against his opinion and practice moved that the utmost censure might be forborne: hoping that he would not press to the sacrament of the supper until that he had given satisfaction. To this day he never sought to be reconciled to the church in any meet way.

The issue of the meeting was *Osburn's* admonition: and *Goold* declared to be under the great offence of the church and rebuked for this great sin of his.

Janr. 63/4: *Osburne* is again sent for.

*Febr.*7:63/4: *Osburn & Goold sent for. Osburne* saith that he sees no sin what he was charged with and this he declares himself to be firm in.

He had with the consent of the breathren a 2: admonition.

Feb. 28: *Goold* again admonished.

June 9:65: Information being given that Goold *Osburne* and others had embodied themselves in a church way: were again sent for by the deacon: a negative answer returned to the church: and denied himself to be a member of our church. At refusing to appear: according to that of *Corah* Numbers 16: 12: who said we will not come up. At another time he giveth the like answer: and saith plainly that he will not come: and *Osburne* to the like purpose.

And they proceeding thus incorrigibly: it did further increase the offence of the church against them. Not one brother objected against his excommunication. With the consent of the brethren in the name of the Lord Jesus they are delivered up to Satan for their schismatical withdrawing themselves from the churches of Christ.

GOOLD. I desire liberty to clear my innocence in this cause. There be some [*word undeciphered*] of things: but in regard to the *matter* of time they are not so as they are now read.

HIG. This is a church *record* attested by a public officer: and signed by the church.

All this time you never sought for reconciliation with the church: nor yet for a hearing by others in an orderly way.

GOOLD. I apprehend I was wronged: in the 1: admonition. One time I was called a liar and another time a blasphemer: which things were cleared up. I yielded my child to be baptized if they would do it as their act. I said not that word if they would come by way of authority to take my child out as they may take goods out of my home. Let the transcript speak.

MR. RUSSELL. I do verily believe by way of authority was used: and something in that way of your goods fetching out of your house was spoken: and for the sum of this *narrative* I can attest to it if I was going out of the world. You forget yourself when you say you did not argue as you might fetch your goods. Deacon Lynde attests to the same.[55]

[GOOLD.] I was charged with schism for withdrawing from the church.

GOOLD. I thank God I have that which upholds me.

MITCHELL. You pleaded that the church put you away whereas it is apparent by the *narrative* that the church dealt with you for putting away yourself from the communion of the church.

GOOLD. I desired a clear rule for their baptizing infants: but they could not give it me.

SIMES SENR. If this was the least that I should speak: I do declare against your way of being very sinful.

MITCH. He that is ecclesiastically unclean ought not to eat of the holy things.

COB. Nothing cuts off a man from the church but excommunication.

GOOLD. I have but 2: things to say.

While I lay under admonition and could not partake of the ordinance of Christ as I ought to have: that of breaking bread: the Lord did convince me and let in such a gracious light unto my soul whereby I saw that I was an unbaptized person: and therefore if the church should have released me and let me enjoy the same liberty I could not close with them therein because I was an unbaptised person. And the church they baptized infants: which I could not close with: and also the means as well as the subject I could not close with: it not being the sprinkling of a little water but dipping of a professed believer. Now God did give me an opportunity to gather into society with those that were of the [like] apprehension and judgment. The Lord had brought some out of *Engl.* of that judgment: and others here that were of the same mind: and we have held out our grounds: and this we apprehend to be according to God's mind in his gospel. If any of you can show us our error we desire to see it.

ALLEN. That will be the work of tomorrow. I could desire to hear from the church of Boston something of that grounds of the excommunication of the other from their church.

GOOLD. I sent them word by 3: brethren that I would come the next Lord's day. You have done as far as ye can go I have no more to say [*word undeciphered*] it.

The *narrative of the ch. of Boston* proceeding with John *Farns-worth*:[56] sometime member of the new church: by *Mr. Mayo*: (and] *Mr. Mather* charged with breaking the rule of truth: [saying?] that Thomas Goold was cast out of the church of Charlestown by Master Symmes and Master Shepard without the consent of the church and that it was a wicked act.

2: Rash and sinful judging of the whole church of Charlestown: for rash and wicked proceeding.

3: Your breaking covenant with the church and becoming guilty of schism.

4: By holding communion with excommunicated persons: thereby approving their way.

5: Adding thereto contumacy and hardness of heart: saying he cared not though elders were offended at it: and that there was never an elder in [the] country that would have read the scriptures besides themselves.

The narrative being fully read: *Farnam* said many things were left out: and not true: *and* that it was the best day that ever dawned upon him: or words to that effect.

The meeting was adjourned until the morrow morn 8:a clock.

15:day: the assembly met again

Mr. Allen began with prayer.

GOOLD. What we have confessed before the court is in writing. It was spoken yesterday: that he that converteth a sinner from the error of his way shall save a soul: and clear a load of sins. I hope that is your end. Now then show us where the error of our way appear.

2: What means Christ hath appointed for the reducing of such persons. We conceive the spiritual weapons of Christ as to be used. Christ never appointed carnal means to draw off any soul from the error of his way: and as Cornelius said to Peter we are all here before God to hear what God hath commanded you to speak: to show us from the error of our way: and the means for to reduce us therefrom.

Allen now readeth their confessions before the court: of their being rebaptized by some of their own company.[57]

DRINKER. We deny not what is read in the least: for it may be many things are eloped out of our memories.

This public Anabaptism: baptizing those that have been baptized already.

TURNER. We are attending the practice of the Lord Jesus Christ. I hope you are not able to contradict it.

GOOLD. Let it be done by a rule of Christ. Carnal weapons will not do it.

DANF. S. The question is whether it is justifiable by the word of God if persons in question do withdraw from the churches here: etc. In answer here [*word undecipherable*] let me propound 2: or 3: scriptures.

Chro. 12: When David called on the priests and Levites to sanctify themselves: the action they did in carrying home the ark was good for the substance: but they failed in the means of it. I *Chr.* 15:12: at the 1: they carried the ark of God on a new cart: whereas the command of God was that the Levites the sons of *Koath*: should bear the ark on their shoulders. Herein they transgressed the order of God's house. Therefore the Lord made a breach in *Uzza*.

There was no wagons given to the sons of *Koath* because the ark of God was to be carried on their shoulders: and now King David he commands that they observe the due order that God had commanded. Therefore: I observe that the open violation of the order of God's house it is not justifiable by the word of God nor ought it to be allowed by the government of this jurisdiction but so is the practice of these persons.

Such order it is of God instituted by him. God is the God of order. He is not the author of confusion but of order. He is not the author of confusion but of peace: which is the tranquility of order. The civil magistrates may not allow the transgression of that order which God himself hath appointed. It was commanded: Ezra 7:26: Whosoever will not do that law of thy God and of this king let judgment be executed speedily on him. This was the decree you will say of a pagan prince: but holy Ezra thanketh God for it: that had put such a thing into the king's heart to beautify the house of the Lord which is Jerusalem.

Now the practice of the persons in question is an open violation of the order of God's house. The order of gospel requireth that all church members walk in holy fellowship with the churches of Christ: frequent their public meetings. Heb. 10: 25: Not forsaking saith the apostle the assembling of yourselves together as the manner of some is. This he taxeth as a great error: and the way of apostacy.

I John 2:19: The apostle declares it to be the spirit of the truly faithful: that they continue in communion with the churches: and all that do otherwise he thinks them hypocrites and strangers: and had they been of us they would have continued with us.

Cor: The apostle reproved them for their inferior division and bids him mark those that cause divisions and avoid them. Romans 16:17.

But the persons in question have withdrawn from the communion of the churches of Christ; and attend not the public meetings and assemblies.

2: The order of the gospel requires that delinquents: and such as fall under church censure should reform themselves: and confess their sin and manifest their repentance: yea even in the cause of private offence their gift must be left at the altar and reconciliation made with a brother: but the persons in question are delinquents: that is the chief of them: and the rest of them do partake with them in their evil way. They do not hold themselves before God and his people and seek reconciliation with the church of God.

3: The order of the gospel that none be admitted to administer the holy things but such as are qualified according to the rule. No stranger shall draw near to give instance that he is not as *Korah* and his company. By a stranger is meant he that is not of the family of *Aron*.

Now the persons in question they are not qualified according to the rule of God's word: for this service: for they are not [cleansed?] as the rule requireth.

2: scripture I would propound is in *Hag.* 2: 12: 13; 14: If one bear holy things in the skirt of his garment: and touch a dead body shall he be clean: *etc.* So are this people and this nation before me saith the Lord. External performances render no man holy: but his personal uncleanness do render his work vile and abominable. The pollution of holy things is not justifiable before God nor to be allowed by the government here.

That they pollute holy things I thus prove. If any man that is morally and ecclesiastically unclean do intermeddle with holy things he doth pollute and defile the same: but the persons in question are morally unclean and ecclesiastically unclean. According to church reputation they are as heathen: and according to scripture reputation: they are to be looked at as heathen and publicans. The chief are so and the rest partake with them in their wicked words and therefore may be looked at [as] such. They do not hear the church which have been abundantly proved.

3: scripture: Ezekiel 43: 7: 8: Son of man the place of my throne where I will dwell: shall the house of Israel no more defile: in setting their threshold by my threshold. Whatever is of man's devising in the worship of God: it defileth the name of God his throne and sanctuary. It is a reproach to God his worship and sanctuary that the devices of man should stand cheek by jowl with God's holy worship. Therefore: I thus argue that the profanation of God's holy name: is not warrantable by God's word nor to be allowed by the authority of this jurisdiction.

By setting up their posts by God's posts they profane the holy name of God.

That I thus prove. They set up a church and a ministry of their own devising: by the churches and ministry of Christ which is according to divine institution: and therefore they set up their posts by God's posts. The churches of Christ according to divine institution consist of visible saints: but this pretended church consists at least some of them and the chief of them: and the rest approve their way: they consist of such as are visibly unclean: unholy: such as are to be looked at as heathen men and publicans. Again: the ministry of Christ are to be meet qualified persons: furnished with ministerial abilities: and orderly called to this holy function. They are not cleansed: they hold not fast the covenant I will be a God to thee and to thy children: and therefore this pretended church and ministry is not of God. It never came into God's heart to appoint such a way but they are mere human inventions to the dishonor of Christ who is the lord of his house and king of his body.

And let me speak a word to the person in question. Consider that in the 16: of Numbers: to mention the names of those great men I know is odious: *Korah* and his company pretended to as much holiness as you can do and as much set apart to the priesthood as Aaron: and they pretend to God's gracious presence with them and among them. And is not the Lord among us? And they had their new and gracious light as well as any of you: and were bold to appeal and stand to the judgment of God: and were ready with their censers in their hands: but remember on the morrow that God made these men a sign and he manifested to all who was holy: and who he would have to draw near to him. *Korah* indeed was holy: but not set apart to the office of the priesthood. We expect not now that God should make men signs as he did then: but let me tell you this: the spiritual judgments that the Lord doth inflict on such persons they are far more dreadful and tremendous than those judgments that the Lord did inflict on *Korah* and company: signal and fearful [*word undeciphered*]: hardened: and confident of their evil work.

THRUMB. I do not own myself to be any of these persons spoken [*word undeciphered*].

It was propounded to be a free debate and dispute: but if ever there was such a dispute as this: I leave it to all the company to judge. That one man shall stand and judge and pass sentence: I leave it to the assembly and I hope that they will vindicate. 1: and foremost: you instanced in King David. Whether will you parallel New Testament government with Old? I suppose there is no king in the world that will assume that which David did. He was a type of Christ: who was dead and is ascended: and I hope he is here this day to behold these actions: now for you to bring in David as though we were under legal ceremonies. You say the gospel requires this and that: and instance the 10: of the Hebrews:25.[58]

That these people here spoken [*word undeciphered*] had any public assembly I bid defiance to all that can oppose. The Hebrews were a people persecuted and opposed.

MITCH. They had a church assembly: and therefore a public assembly. A church is a public society.

GOOLD. So is ours.

THRUMB. Had they any public assembly allowed by civil power?

THR. If wheresoever a persecuted people did meet together to edify one another: and to provide one another to love and good works. I will forfeit all the estate I have that Master Danforth have abused the scripture that he hath mentioned as to this.

[*In shorthand:*] DANFORTH. The word in the original: Heb. 10: doth signify a public assembly.

Not forsaking the assembling of yourselves together as the manner of some is.

[*In shorthand:*] THRUMBLE. The scripture saith they lived in caves and holes of the earth.

HIG. The apostle writed to the Hebrews: that were Christian *Jews*: of the churches of Jerusalem and Judea. 2: 3: 4: 5: 6: of Acts: we read of the churches of God in Judea: now the apostle he rebukes them for forsaking these assemblies.

THRUMB. The apostle writed to the people of God [*word undeciphered*].

SHEPD. An organical church assembly is a church assembly. A people orderly seated under public officers: are a public assembly. *Heb.* 13: Obey them that have the rule over you.

THR. When they had them they were to do so: but they had not any then.

MICHELL. Salute them that have the rule over you. He speaks of them that they had.

THR. All this makes it not that they were an assembly that were maintained by public authority.

SHEP. Notwithstanding their persecution: they did so continue together as that the elders did watch over the church. They watch for your souls.

GOOLD. When the apostle giveth this exhortation to provoke one another to love and good works: he telleth them in the same chapter that they suffered the spoiling of their goods with joy.[59]

THR. Yourselves do own that an assembly of a people of God though persecuted are a church of Christ and ought to meet together.

MITCH. An orderly assembly ought so to do.

DANF. You owned in the confession of your faith: that the Old Testament as well as the New was the rule and canon of faith and order: and do I do amiss to prove it from that which you own to be the rule?

MITCH. In the 10: of the Hebrews: the Old Testament?

GOOLD. We desire to speak of the particulars as they be laid down: and let us see whether we be the sons of *Korah*: as hath been said.

THR. The Old Testament rules are not parallel to the rules of the gospel: nor are no way binding to us: and to mix law and gospel together: the apostle saith is to bring a new gospel.

COBBITT. If Christians that have their elders among them and do meet together in covenant: their assemblies are not to be forsaken: much more they who may come to assemblies that are Christian assemblies: and encouraged by the authority of the place.

THR. If they would have attended their meetings to their synagogues as formerly they had not then [been] persecuted: but they could not do it because they saw other light: and according to your own Synod book they might allow this.[60]

[*In shorthand:*] DANFORTH. That which is the rule of faith and order is binding to us.

THR. We are on another account. If you will own yourselves to be priests and Levites: then we must look for a new Christ.

For my part I do thank God I desire not to be [favored?] in any thing: but that Christ should be advanced.

ALLEN. You are as unwilling to see the truth as ever I saw any.

THRUMBL. You say you convince these men: whom you never showed them a rule of Christ wherein they were found breaking any rule of Christ.

THR. Let me speak one word more and I shall [strive?] to speak no more. We desire to keep to God's word. If besides it I desire you would show it to us. We are commanded if ye love me to keep my commands. Gospel commands we are to observe. By the gospel we shall be all judged: John 14. It hath been delivered in that [*word undeciphered*] that whoever take up anything that Christ hath not commanded he is a rejecter of Christ.

DANF. 1: argument the open violation of the order of God's house is not justifiable by the word of God: nor to be allowed by the government of this jurisdiction. But the practice of the persons in question is an open violation of the order of God's house: *etc.*: and that was proved by these scriptures: Heb. 10: 25: Romans 16: 7: I

Cor. 2: 8: John 1. The order of the gospel requires the frequenting of Christian assemblies.

TURNER. We do not well understand this proposition. It will be good 1: to consider what the order of the gospel is. Moses is said to be faithful in all things as a servant: Christ as a son. Matt. 17: 5. While he yet spake a bright cloud overshadowed him: and said this is my beloved son hear him. We must take the institutions of the gospel from Christ Jesus. We must consider what it is to assemble: for that Heb. 10: they must be 1: gathered together according to the gospel of Christ. All the work is not to lie on one person or teacher as you do: but you are to build up one another.[61]

MITCH. Your meaning is that our churches here are not according to the constitution of the gospel: and therefore that of the 10: of Hebrews: do not forbid to forsake us.

GOOLD. We are a church of Christ and ought not though persecuted to forsake our assembling together.

TURNER. What is not of faith is sin.

MITCH. You did forsake the orderly church assemblies for to set up your own.

GOOLD. If you had not put us from you: we could not have joined with you in your practices.

ALLEN. Observe this whether this tends not to undermine all our churches.

COBBITT. There is the pinch. They think you speak not to them because they forsake not their own assemblies.

GOOLD. All the churches of Asia kept to their assemblies.

COB. They that keep to their own so as to reject others they break that rule.

You deny communion with ours.

THR. Whether did the magistrate bring in those that do forsake the assembly by the civil authority?

ALLEN. If this be cleared sufficiently that these do not observe the order of the gospel: and setting up sufficient men to administer the ordinances: then we will go to another cause.

GOOLD. We desire to see where our error lies that we are not fit matter for a church.

MITCH. They that be as heathen and publicans are not fit matter for a church.

GOOLD. Divers that were the founders of churches here: were excommunicated in *Engld.*

MITCH. You have often had this over. Not the punishment but the cause makes the matter: and so in this. The cause of their excommunication: hath been cleared and suffered for by the body of all reformers from Calvin to this day: and you parallel this by an opinion that hath been condemned by all reformers from Calvin to this day. You know by what power that was done. You are here excommunicated by an orderly walking church: every brother having his liberty. Was any person so excommunicated by a church so constituted and walking? Do you say if you can that the power that excommunicated you had no power from Christ. Was the excommunication of the church of Corinth nothing: because the blind man was excommunicated and Christ received him?[62]

GOOLD. THRUMBL. You say we will authorize excommunication. The Lord keep us from that spirit: and we do own that excommunication may be administered on [false?] grounds. If excommunication is truly administered let all [free men?] tremble under that excommunication: but if it be [misapplied] and not any rule made known: let those that do thus do take heed what they do. Is. 55: 5.[63] Your brethren that hated you shall put you away and say let the Lord be glorified. *Diotrephes*[64] that desires the pre-eminence he casts off the saints and is this [truth?]? Now our friends desire that you will make their excommunication to be according to the rule of God: and they will fall under the rule of God.

MITCH. It is your work for to prove that the power which excommunicated those which you spake of in *Engl.* and their cause was as bad as yours when you will parallel the cause.

THR. These friends say the grounds for which we were excommunicated was not for breaking any rule of Christ: Although you apprehend a rule broken: yet we find it not clear from the word of God.

MITCH. If there shall be no regular excommunication before the party will own it done shall it be right? But those that you instanced in *Engl.* their cause is cleared by all reformed churches.

THR. The prophet saith the brethren saith that your brethren that hated you shall cast you out: and Diotrephes be in place: and he passeth a sentence on a wrong person.

MITCH. Here be the elders with the consent of the brethren.

GOOLD. No church of Christ ought to cast out a member: but it ought to be so plain that all the world may read it. You speak of those that were cast out in *Engl.* Say we the same is here with us: because we could not conform to all those things you would have us conform [*word undeciphered*].

MITCH. Prove your nonconformity to be as good as theirs.

GOOLD. You would compel us to bring our children to baptism. We will tell you we could not see a rule of Christ for it.

MICH. It is all wrong that you say. You were desired to carry yourselves orderly. If you had any scripture: could you not desire light?

[GOOLD.] Let me say this word and I will set down and say no more. There is no sentence of excommunication but it ought to be as clear as the sun in the firmanent.

ALLEN. So it is.

GOOLD. You say so. Let them believe it that can.

ALLEN. It was not for your opinion but for your disorders.[65]

DANF. If a particular administration ought to be so clear: how much more the setting up of a new church in a new way: How much more ought their way to be as clear as the sun in the firmanent.

GOOLD. We shall clear it from the rules of Christ that our grounds for gathering our church are right.

SHEPD. I shall propose an argument to prove the negative to the question.

That practice which is setting up another gospel: is not allowable by the word of God: nor to be allowed by the government of this jurisdiction. That it is the setting up another gospel: I shall thus prove. Your way is to answer by negation or denial. If the practice of these persons is such as is the gospel of non-communion with these churches: then it is another gospel: but yours is such.

GOOLD. We told you our desire is to hold communion with all the churches of Christ.

THR. The gospel that Christ and his disciples: was not communicable with John and his disciples.

Apollos convinced the *Jews* by scripture.

You once told me in private that Christ had his consequence from the scripture.

SHEP. The gospel of Christ is not a gospel of non-communion with itself. If the gospel professed by these churches is the gospel of Christ: and you will not hold communion with them: then your gospel is another gospel.

THR. May we speak without offence.

Prove that infant baptism is any part of the gospel. To indent so much a year before ye preach:[66] prove this to be part of the gospel.

———————

SHEPD. That gospel which is for non-communion with them: is another.

THR. Make you a confession of your faith: and we will of ours and then see where the difference lies.

JOHNSON. I am not excommunicate but one of these. I would only give you my grounds why I separate. If those things that I apprehend to be practiced in your churches be contrary to the order of the gospel: if you will make them appear to be according to the gospel I will join with you.

1: That you are according to an institution of Christ baptized persons. Acts 2: Before they were joined to the church they were baptized.

2: That you give liberty for prophesying and for edifying of one another: which you deny.

3: That whereas such as be added to the church: should be those as be profitable to the body: you add such as be not capable for they can't speak.

Therefore I would entreat you before the assembly now to clear up the right baptism which our savior laid down.

MITCH. I would give a general answer. If we were all unbaptized persons: it were to [unbirth?] us all. Your principles are destructive. If not baptized no sacraments nor no ordinance this 130: years[67] it hath been proved over and over.

JOHNSON. I can't remember what was done 130: years ago.

MITCH. Suppose these were all corruptions. Yet are these so great as was in the church of the *Jews*: with whom Christ maintain communion? We know what we worship. He stands the man to the priests: and forbids separation: and Paul's charge to the *Corinths* forbids separation: where was great separations. And suppose baptizing of children were irregular: at the worst it is but an infirmity.

The argument is this that which is ordinarily [*word undeciphered*] to the best of men on earth is but an infirmity. Now I appeal to all this assembly: whether the generality of faithful and godly men in all ages have not practiced infant baptism. They that will separate for infirmity they will separate from all the men on earth.

JOHNSON. You say you are not so bad as the church in *Corinth*: but I judge not you: still are matter fit for a church: but there may be gross sins in a church: which a man is not to separate from. But if the cart [ark?] is carried on a new cart: the order of the gospel not observed: this I [pause] at.

MITCH. To separate from the churches on infirmity only it is a horrible evil.

JOHNSON. We separate from you because you come not up to the order of the gospel.

MITCH. The positive part the practicing of it is but an infirmity if amiss: but the taking of it away: is a destructive thing. It is an ordinance of God and if we extend it over far: and to take it away it overthrows all.

And there is a [just?] difference between a mere suspicion of the irregularity of infant baptism: and to make it a frailty: for that is the overthrow of religion and the inlet of apostacy.

JOHNSON. I judge it a frailty not only as to the subject: but as to the manner of the administration. John baptized at *Enon*. because there was much water: which he need not to have done if basin water would have done.

The cutting of the [ear?] would never have been accounted for circumcision.[68]

SHEP. I shall propose another argument. I Tim. 2: 1: 1: I exhort therefore that 1: of all supplications be made: for kings and all in authority that under them we may lead a quiet and peaceable life in all godliness and honesty but this principle and practice in the question is destructive to the peace of the churches.

GOOLD. It is not destructive because it is a rule of God.

THRUMBL. For ye were sometimes darkness but now are light in the Lord. Walk as the children of the light: for the fruit of the spirit is in all goods repose and truth.[69] God hath given you his [gospel?] proving what is acceptable to the Lord.

SHEP. I shall prove it both these ways: 1: Because these practices do overthrow communion of churches. Such practice as overthrow communion of churches is destructive to the peace of the churches.

THR. We can't be saved by answering your arguments. We must be saved by the scripture.

GOOLD. If your churches be built on the rock Christ: it is impossible for us to destroy you.

THR. In Christ's time: they had 3: forms: and yet they were all allowed.

ALLEN. It is a popish opinion to say that John's form and Christ's were different.

TURNR. Show me any warrant for the magistrates in the gospel to protect the churches of Christ. Christ saith Matt. 10: Whoever shall deny me before men him will I deny also before my father in Heaven. Think not that I am come to send peace on earth: but to send where the power of God converts a soul from the error of his way. The world is at such enmity with God that God can't endure them in their way. So far as you oppose us in following Christ it is worldly.

THRUMBL. You say that we may lead a peaceable life. Whether is conformity peace: to hold whatever the churches do hold: or the peace that you plead in your Synod book inward peace?[70] Whether that is not better than the *magistrates'* peace? *In Holld. the magistrates* maintain peace among Baptists and presbyterians: and all the rest: Lutherans: Anabaptists: Presbyterians.

SHEPD. And *Papists* also are allowed in *Holld.*

SHEP. I will propound another argument. This practice it tends to nullify the ordinance of excommunication.

THR. I did hear a saying by a *student* that if the elders in a [scholastical?] way might propound things they would drown us.

SHEP. I suppose the women present do understand. I will prove the excommunication of these persons to be according to the rule of Christ. These persons are according to Christ's order excommunicated. Matt. 18: If they neglect to hear the church let them be a heathen man and publican.

GOOLD. Doth he appoint their not hearing church a day? You

never dealt with me according to the rule of Christ for not hearing the church: for that which themselves say they cast me out for: which was for not hearing the church: it was for not coming that day they sent for me.

SHEPD. That is not true. That was an aggravation. The church had had so much experience of your obstinacy in not [*thus in MS*] refusing to submit to the ordinance of Christ that they had no hope of your repentance.

THR. We know God hath his time to convert: some about 9: and 12: wherefore: had they waited that time: how do they know but that Christ might convert him? You did not well with him as a heathen man: but you gave him up to the devil.

MITCH. The heathens are in the kingdom of Satan. To make a man a heathen is to deliver him to Satan.

THR. Were Cornelius and his company heathen?

MITCH. They were religious devout persons.

THATCHER. I plainly perceive here is [*word undeciphered*] to deceive the whole congregation of their expectation: in the way of argumentation. The rule have been delivered and the appellation: and both orderly published. Why this honored and great assembly should be [wearied?] with words I [truly?] desire it may be considered: and the matter close kept [*word undeciphered*].

ALLEN. We have patience with many extravagant discourses: because we would avoid reproach which these persons are [*one or two words undeciphered*].

SHEP. That practice which opens the door to let in upon us the worst of false worship: and the greatest abomination in any Christians is not to be allowed by the government here and such is the practice of these persons.

I will prove that it doth so: because that way is contrary to the wholesome laws of this commonwealth. It opens the door to let in the worst sort of false worships at the same door they may come in at: for the laws and government here is their only wall. Break down that what abomination may not come in.

You have broken down this hedge I shall thus prove. In the Platform of discipline: when a company of believers intend to gather into such fellowship: they are to signify the same to their neighbor churches: G L: 2: I: 2: 9.[71]

And then he read the law of the country about churches gathering: to [*word undeciphered*] error. This disorder of yours is such as the vilest of heretics may come in at the same door.

TH. If they have transgressed in not asking leave of the *magistrates* I hope there may be a remedy. I hope it is not the unpardonable sin. If they be [*word undeciphered*] for it.

GOOLD. In the General Court we desired our freedom: but they did not [*word undeciphered*] us to our freedoms.

GOOLD. By your own judgment worse than we can't come in.

MITCH. Any 10: or 12: persons may set up a church according to practice.

GOOLD. Suppose those be put out that are under excommunication will you allow the rest?

MITCH. An assembly in the way of Anabaptism is apart of the question and may not be granted here.

[*In shorthand:*] SHEPARD. They that hold communion with those that are delivered up to Satan they are bad themselves.

GOOLD. If they put us away: then they may walk together without that blame.

MITCH. For you to set up a church in the midst of us in opposition to us: this is schism although you had never been among us.

SHEP. I might parallel your causes with divers causes in scripture that are not justifiable.

TURNER. I pray repeat the former argument. I have forgot it.

[*Answer:*] At the same principle you go upon any man may come in among us.

TURNER. Acts 17: God that made the world and all things therein: dwelleth not in temples made with hands. Now from hence I challenge there is a liberty given to every man to seek after the Lord: and that some may find him and others may not and must they be cast out of the world because they can't find God? [*Here the account abruptly ends.*].

[3]
Baptists Tax Congregationalists in Swansea, 1711

Although it is well known that the Puritans taxed Baptists and other dissenters for the support of their established Puritan churches in each town, it is less well known that the Baptists occasionally reversed the procedure. By law in the Puritan colonies of New England all towns were required to lay taxes for the maintenance of religion (i.e., paying a ministerial salary, building and maintaining a meetinghouse). When a town had more Baptists than Puritans among its voters, the majority could in theory lay taxes of this kind, which the minority was required to pay. This situation arose in the town of Swansea, Massachusetts, when that town was incorporated as part of the colony of Plymouth in 1667. The Pilgrims, being more tolerant than the Puritans of Massachusetts Bay, had allowed a group of Baptists to settle on their western frontier and to lay taxes for their support. The Baptists prospered and grew numerous. In 1691 the king decided to merge the Plymouth Colony into the Massachusetts Bay Colony. When the Swansea Baptists refused to discontinue the practice of laying religious taxes to support their minister and church, the Massachusetts authorities decided to stop them; in the Bay Colony only orthodoxy (defined as Calvinist pedobaptism) could be supported by taxes. To tax the orthodox Congregationalists for the support of the unorthodox Baptists was a gross perversion of order.

This affair is not exactly an example of the soul liberty that later became the hallmark of the Baptist persuasion. The Baptists had a long way to go before they fully understood the meaning of religious liberty.

A petition purchased by the Rhode Island Historical Society at auction in Providence in 1969 is of important historical interest to Rhode Island. It offers unique insight into one of the most curious episodes in the religious history of New England. For in this document Congregationalists in the western part of Swansea, Massachusetts (an area that in 1717 became the town of Barrington), complain that they are being persecuted by Baptists, who constituted the majority of inhabitants in Swansea at that time.

Almost any history of New England will inform readers that from the earliest days of its settlement the colony of Massachusetts dealt harshly with Baptists—sending them to jail, fining, whipping, and banishing them—during the first half century after the founding of the colony. Yet here is an instance in which the tables appear to be turned and Baptists were persecuting Puritans. How did it happen, and what does this episode have to tell us about the founding of Barrington, Rhode Island?

The story is long and complicated. Readers are urged to see the detailed account in Thomas W. Bicknell's *History of Barrington Rhode Island* (Providence, 1898); a variant form of the petition appears on pages 187–189 in Bicknell. The story in brief concerns the founding of a Baptist church in New England in 1663 by Rev. John Myles. Myles was a Baptist who, during the Cromwellian interregnum, had founded a Baptist church in Swansea, Wales, and played a significant role in the ecclesiastical system established by Cromwell and the Long Parliament. After the return of the king, Myles was forced to flee from Wales in 1662, and along with several of his parishioners he settled in the town of Rehoboth in old Plymouth Colony. There he began to hold Baptist services in 1663, which brought protests not only from Congregational ministers in the colony but also from authorities in Massachusetts. In 1667 he was ordered to leave Rehoboth, but the tolerant legislators of Plymouth agreed to allow him and Baptists who worshipped with him to settle in the new town of Swansea. Except for a brief sojourn in Boston during King Philip's War, Myles preached in Swansea until his death in 1683. After his death the Baptists chose Samuel Luther to be their pastor.

According to regulations adopted when Swansea was founded, John Myles agreed to practice open or mixed communion in the only church in town. That is, he agreed to allow both Baptists (who opposed infant baptism) and Congregationalists (who believed in the necessity of infant baptism) to be members of the church. (Fortunately, Congregationalists and Baptists agreed on the doctrines of Calvinism.) Samuel Luther continued mixed communion until about 1705, when he decided that it was unscriptural to allow persons who believed in baptizing infants to join the church. This greatly offended many people, and they began to petition the legislature of Massachusetts (which gained control over the old Plymouth Colony under the charter of 1691) to have Samuel Luther expelled from his position.

According to ecclesiastical laws passed by the Massachusetts legislature in 1691–1692, every parish in the province was required to support by taxes a "learned, pious and orthodox minister." Samuel Luther was not "learned" by the legal definition of that time because he did not know Greek and Latin (he had never attended college), nor had he studied theology. He was not considered "orthodox" by Massachusetts standards because he opposed infant baptism (an offense for which Henry Dunster had been removed from the presidency of Harvard College in 1654). But the legislature of Massachusetts was reluctant to expel him from his pulpit because the majority in Swansea were Baptists and because of the special agreement that the legislature of Plymouth had made with John Myles when it established Swansea for him and his followers in 1667. Baptists of Swansea claimed that under the new charter of 1691 they were granted not only "liberty of conscience" by the king but also the same rights and privileges they had held under the Plymouth charter.

The Massachusetts legislature tried to persuade the Congregationalists of Swansea to hire their own minister and establish their own church, where they could have their children baptized. In 1708 the Congregationalists did persuade a Harvard graduate named John Fiske (class of 1702) to help them form a church. But the selectmen of the town—Baptists all—ordered the town constable to eject Fiske as a vagabond who lacked visible means of support. Fiske left town in a huff.

In addition to complaining that there was no learned and orthodox minister to preach to them as the law required, Congregationalists—most of whom lived in the western part of town, which then bordered on Narragansett Bay—complained that they were being taxed to help repair and maintain the meetinghouse of Samuel Luther, where they could not in conscience worship. Although there is no evidence that the Baptists laid religious taxes for the salary of Luther, they did lay taxes for the maintenance of their meetinghouse. But they felt justified in this because, as in every other New England town, the parish meetinghouse also served as the town hall. In towns in which all inhabitants were of the same denomination the fact that parish church and town hall were the same building posed no difficulty. But as dissident sects arose in the eighteenth century, taxes for the meetinghouse raised perplexing questions about the separation of church and state.

As the petition (see below) indicates, the Congregational minority in Swansea concluded in 1711 that the only way they could resolve their dilemma was to ask the legislature to divide Swansea into two parts. The western part of town—where Congregationalists were most numerous—should, they argued, be separated from the eastern part and incorporated as a new and distinct township. Swansea, like most New England towns, was already divided into militia districts for the purpose of raising and training troops to fight Indians. It so happened that the western militia district was roughly the area in which most Congregationalists resided. Hence, petitioners suggested that the legislature make the boundary of the new town the same as that of Captain Samuel Low's military district.

Unfortunately for Congregationalists in Captain Low's district, the legislature did not think that they were sufficiently numerous or sufficiently well off to be constituted as a township in 1711. Their petition was turned down. The Congregationalists then made a second attempt to hire a minister, and in 1712 they persuaded John Wilson (Harvard, 1705) to preach to them. He was just about to form a church when he died untimely in 1713. Four years later the Congregationalists again petitioned to be set off as a separate town, and this time the legislature granted their petition. Thus, in November 1717 Barrington was incorporated as a haven for Congregationalists from what they considered Baptist persecution.

From 1717 until 1746 Barrington was part of the province of Massachusetts Bay. But in 1746 the king settled the long-standing boundary dispute between Massachusetts and Rhode Island. As a result, Barrington (along with Little Compton, Tiverton, Bristol, and Warren) became part of Rhode Island. Hence, in a unique way, the petition of 1711 marks the beginning of Barrington, which in 1970 celebrated its two-hundredth anniversary. The reason 1970 rather than 1917 is the two-hundredth anniversary is that from 1746—when the town came under the jurisdiction of Rhode Island—until 1770 Barrington was part of the township of Warren. It therefore had two birth dates—or perhaps three: its first birth was November 18, 1717, when it became a separate town in Massachusetts; its second was in 1746, when it became part of Rhode Island (but was immediately made part of Warren); and its third birthday was in 1770, when it was separated from Warren. But whatever its birth date, its date of conception was May 30, 1711, when the people in "the Westward End of Swanzey" first petitioned the Massachusetts legislature to become a town.

Two small footnotes are needed here. If, as is true, Baptists of Swansea did to a certain extent persecute the Congregational minority from 1705 to 1717 by making them pay taxes to support the Baptist meetinghouse, the Congregational majority in Barrington returned the persecution from 1717 to 1735, when it taxed not only the Baptist minority within its own limits but also the Anglican minority to support the Congregational church and its minister. Not until 1735 did the laws of Massachusetts give sufficient protection to dissenting minorities to save them from paying taxes to support the religion of the majority in any town.

Second, it should also be noted that Thomas Bicknell's otherwise excellent town history contains one important error. Bicknell states that the first minister of the Congregational church (now the White Church) in Barrington was the Reverend Samuel Torrey. But a closer look at the original records shows that the first pastor, ordained in 1720, was Samuel Terry (Harvard, 1710).

THE PETITION

To his Excellency Joseph Dudley Esqr
Captain General and Governor in Chief in and Over her Majesty's Province of the Massachusetts Bay in New England. The Honobl Council and Representatives in General Court Assembled At Boston this Thirtieth Day of May
The Petition of us the subscribers Inhabitants in the westward End of Swanzey Most Humbly Sheweth,

That among all the outward & External blessings with which the god of all Mercy blesseth any people with all in this world That of the house of God Among them. The Gospell purely preached, and the Ordinances of Christs kingdom duly Administered, and Fathers and Children settled under Pastorall Watch, Care and Governmt under Pious, Learned Orthodox

Ministers being in our esteem the Greatest. And We your Petitioners being under the Deplorable Privation thereof Do most Humbly and Earnestly petition This Honoured General Court That Some Methods may be taken (as in wisdome may be thought best) for Our Releife. And we being well perswaded and Assured of this Honourd Generall Courts power and Good will to help in Such Cases from their Repeated Acts of the Like Nature, Do the more Freely Open our Mallady which bespeaks Pitty and Cure. Not to Mention the Ill Circumstances (which Our different Opinion in Matters of Religion from our Neighbours) brings our Estates under in whose power they are in all taxes (Though bad enough in it self) is Yet Little and Light compared with the bitterness we Feal at present and fear for the Future for the very mention of no Settled Minister, Learned and Orthodox, No Church of Christ Settled in Gospel Order, No Pastour to feed Christs Lambs among us; this as We believe is an uncomfortable thought unto all the Holy and Reverend Ministers of Christ that know our State. So is it a heart breaking Thought to us to think that when We are Called out of this World to Consider into what State we Leave Our posterity Exposed to a Ruinating inticement from pure Gospell and Gospell Ordnances. All which Sorrow and Misery either felt or feared if this Honoured General Court do in Mercy & Pitty prevent by Granting us a Township According to the Limits of Captain Samuel Lows Military Company in Swanzey Thereby enabling us to Settle and Maintaine A Pious Learned, Orthodox Minister for the Good of us & our posterity, God will be Glorified, Christs Kingdom Inlarged

And shall Oblige yor Most Humble Petitioners Ever to pray

Samuel Low	*Joseph Chaffe*
Daniel Allen	*Daniel Allen Junr.*
Benjn. Viall	*Obadiah Bettis*
Israel Peck	*Elisha May*
Samuel Humphrey	*William Corbet*
Zecha Bicknell	*John Toogood*
Nathanl. Peck	*Samuel Guy*
Josiah Turner	*John Rogers*
James Smith	*Joshua Finney*
Benjamin Cary	*William Salisbury*
Ebenezer Allin	*William Salisbury Junr.*
John Chaffe	*Jonathan Phiney*
Simon Davis	*Ebenezer Tiffany*

Thomas Turner   *Thomas Tiffany*
Jonathan Viall
    June 7: 1711   *In Council*
    Read and Ordered
        That the Selectmen of Swanzey Be served with a Copy of this Petition And that they be heard thereto upon the Second Wednesday in the Next Session of this Court if any thing they have to say against Granting the Prayer thereof.

    Sent down for Concurrence   *Isa. Addington, Secty.*

[4]

Separate Baptists and the "Free Love" Problem, 1748-1749

Many religious movements have produced some pious believers who assumed that their piety was so pure as to raise them above ordinary human sin and to make them perfect even as their Father in Heaven is perfect. Frequently this perfectionism takes the form of a conviction that true believers need not obey the laws of man because they are obedient to a higher law. Sometimes this leads to what opponents of such movements call free love and the true believers call soul marriage.

Such a movement took place in Cumberland, Rhode Island, shortly after the start of the Great Awakening, just about the time Jonathan Edwards was preaching about sinners in the hands of an angry God. The incident described here concerned chiefly Separates, a group of pious Congregationalists who separated from what they considered the corruptions of the established churches of New England and formed their own churches. Scores of these Separate churches were formed throughout New England as a result of the great New Light revival movement.

Because many Separates later became Separate Baptists, the problem of perfectionism and free love caused the Baptists considerable concern. Orthodox ("Old Light") Congregationalists used the perfectionist heresy to taunt the Baptists, asserting that all of those who broke from orthodoxy would end in this kind of fanaticism. Separate-Baptists, like Elder Isaac Backus, had to work hard to keep the good name of their denomination from being tarred with the brush of Cumberland perfectionism.

As Ebenezer Ward of Cumberland lay in prison in Providence in the early summer of 1749, he must have been puzzled by the mysterious ways of God. He was not only a wealthy man but a pious man, well respected until then in his community. He had been leading a number of his neighbors in weekly prayers and exhortations in his home for more than a year. They were about to form a church and call a pastor who would preach a purer form of the gospel than prevailed in the existing churches. Now his religious friends were in total confusion and disorder, and he was being sued by his son-in-law for alienating the affections of his daughter Molly. He had allowed his daughter to live with another man while her husband, Joseph Bennet, was at sea—though, as he told a friend, he believed this man "and his daughter meant no harm lodging together for they lay with the Bible between them."

What was more, Ward thought he had not only a good spiritual case to make for permitting his daughter to live with a man more in harmony with her, he could also cite extenuating circumstances. For one thing, his daughter, a very pious girl, was "subject to fits." For another, it was her husband who first suggested that their marriage was improper. Ward had witnesses who could testify that Bennet had surprised a group of neighbors one night more than a year before by telling them that "Ward's daughter was not his wife and that he had no more right to lie with her than any other woman." Ward had protested against this and urged Bennet to reconsider. He had perhaps been wrong to insist, after their marriage in 1745—when Molly was only sixteen—that the couple should live with him, and if that was the cause of Bennet's discontent, Ward said they might move into a home of their own. In fact, if Bennet "would provide a place suitable anywhere within ten miles, he [Ward] was willing his daughter should go with him and that he would furnish her with things suitable to keep house and if he [Bennet] would get a good maid or nurse to be constantly with her . . . he would pay her [the nurse] yearly himself." What was more, he would give his daughter one thousand pounds for her comfort (though this may have been a figure of speech to express his extreme concern for her welfare).[1]

But Joseph Bennet (or Bennett) had not taken this offer. Instead he had squandered what funds he did have and had then taken ship and gone to sea. Hearing nothing from him for many months, Ward and his neighbors assumed that the ship had been lost. Only then had Ward allowed his daughter to move into Solomon Finney's home, and even then he had extracted a promise from the two that they would sleep with a Bible between them to prevent any carnal relations. The arrangement was to be a purely spiritual one. Molly and Solomon had convinced Ebenezer Ward, and themselves, that they were spiritual soulmates.

Bennet returned and, finding his wife with another man (by her

father's permission), demanded an explanation. Ward tried to mol-
lify him, saying that he was glad to find Bennet alive and that he
would make his daughter return to him; he renewed his offer to
support Molly and Bennet (and provide a nurse for her) if Bennet
would promise to live within ten miles of her father's home. But
Bennet would not be mollified. He threatened to go to law. Ward
was convinced that Bennet was a scamp who wanted to bring suit
simply to obtain more money from him, which he would promptly
spend. So when Bennet swore out charges against Ward early in
1749 for alienation of affections and had him imprisoned, Ward
obtained legal counsel and prepared to defend himself. But just as
the case was about to come to trial, Ward's daughter confessed that
she was pregnant. The father of her child could be no one but
Solomon Finney (or Phinney), her spiritual soulmate. This "took
all the heart" from old Ebenezer Ward. And it convinced Bennet
that he should sue for divorce, an action which at that time could
be granted only by an act of the Rhode Island General Assembly.

Such were the facts as Ward and his friends saw them. A pious,
if overprotective, father, he had let himself to be too easily misled
by his daughter and her soulmate (or they had trusted too much
in their own self-restraint). Bennet's story, of course, was rather
different. As he told the General Assembly in his petition for divorce in August 1749, it was Ebenezer Ward who had first "imbibed
and cherished certain wicked and strange tenets and principles"
regarding spiritual marriage. And it was Ward who "did then Suggest unto the said Molly, his Daughter, your Petitioner's Wife, that
your petitioner was in an unconverted State and Condition and that
it was Sinful for her to Cohabit with your petitioner as her Husband." Molly had heeded her father. Ward then compelled Bennet
to leave his house, and no sooner was he gone than "he, the said
Ebenezer, together with one Solomon Finney, a person of like Pernicious and Evil Principles, did Conspire to Seduce the said Molly."[2]

The General Assembly believed Bennet's side of the story, no
doubt because of the clear evidence of adulterous carnal relations.
Ward and Finney were fined, and Bennet got his divorce in October
1749. Despite all of the evidence we have about this incident, it is
still impossible to tell what role Molly Ward Bennet played. We have
no statement, direct or indirect, from her. Was she the innocent

tool of her father? Was she the injured and mistreated wife of Bennet? Was she a giddy religious zealot? Or was she perhaps a rather self-willed hypochondriac who wanted to find a way to live with her lover and who used the religious ferment of the times to deceive the others—and perhaps herself?

It was fortunate for Ward (and the spiritual soulmates) that he was sued when he was, for had the case taken place a month later, he would have been subject to far more than a fine. In October 1749 the same legislative session that granted Bennet his divorce also passed a new law "Against Adultery, Polygamy, and Unlawfully Marrying Persons; and for the Relief of Such Persons as Are Injured by the Breach of Marriage Covenants." According to this law (which seems like a throwback to the days of Hester Prynne and Puritan Massachusetts), any person convicted of breach of marriage contract "shall be punished by being set publickly on the Gallows in the Day Time with a Rope about their Neck for the space of One hour and in their return from the Gallows to the Gaol shall be puplickly whipped on their Naked Body not exceeding Thirty Stripes."

The Ward–Bennet affair might have remained simply a matter of local scandal of no particular interest to historians, but as it turned out, the incident had far wider ramifications. It disrupted not only Ward's incipient church in Cumberland but churches for miles around. Many other couples followed the example of Molly and Solomon. For twenty years the issue reverberated in ecclesiastical disputes in northeastern Rhode Island and southeastern Massachusetts. It affected churches in Cumberland, Attleborough, Norton, Easton, Middleborough, and Taunton. Dozens of families and several ministers were caught up in scandals over the next twenty years. It is more than likely that the Rhode Island law against breaches of marriage covenants was a direct response to the rapid spread of spiritual wifery in this period.

What is more, the Ward–Bennet incident became a subject for discussion in a half dozen tracts and books in the eighteenth century; Joseph Fish of Norwich, Connecticut, and Isaac Backus in Middleborough, Massachusetts, engaged in acrimonious debate over it; Ebenezer Frothingham in Middletown, Connecticut, made a cause célèbre out of it in one of his tracts; subsequent local historians, such as William L. Chaffin, John Daggett, and George F. Clark, also felt obliged to rehash the matter late in the nineteenth century in their town histories.

But psychohistorians and anthropologists of the past ten years have thrown the most light on such incidents. Ronald Knox, Norman Cohn, Geoffrey Nuttall, Kai T. Erikson, Weston LaBarre, and E. J. Hobsbawm have found many periods in history in which members of Christian churches have rebelled against marriage laws and other well-established patterns of social and moral behavior. It is a recurrent phenomenon in Western religious history. The incident in Cumberland can be adequately explained only in terms of these broader patterns of religious behavior. Any study of the documents in this case reveals at once that it was directly related to that astounding outburst of religious excitement in the years 1734–1755 known as the first Great Awakening, and any student of this awakening can cite a dozen or more similar incidents of sexually aberrant behavior in other parts of New England.[3] What is more, these free love movements, generally described as perfectionism, have cropped up in later awakenings in American history, particularly after the Second Great Awakening, which produced the Mormon movement, the Brimfield "bundling," and the Oneida Community.

Nor is sexual experimentation the only eccentric aspect of such episodes. Many perfectionist groups—including the one to which Ward, Bennet, Finney, and their friends in southeastern New England belonged—also considered themselves free from all mortal illness and hence immortal. Some immortalists in the Ward–Finney circle declared that as a result of their religious conversion they were so perfect that they were no longer capable of sin. This is too far-ranging a subject to be summarized in a short chapter, but a brief look at some other aspects of the Cumberland perfectionist, or immortalist, movement in the 1740s and 1750s will help place it in perspective. For despite frequent mention of this group in contemporary and later literature, no one has ever looked closely at all of the documents and tried to make sense of them—at least perfectionist sense.

The Cumberland perfectionists—I shall so call them though they included many people who lived in Easton, Norton, Attleborough, and Taunton—were part of what historians call the "New Light" movement of the Great Awakening. That is, they felt that as a result of the work of God and the Holy Spirit in their hearts they had undergone religious experiences that gave them "new light" into the truth of the Gospel and the mysterious will of God concerning them, their souls, the world in which they lived, and the spiritual world. This is, of course, characteristic of all new religious movements; it justifies pious leaders of such movements in their efforts to reform or rebel against the restrictions, formality, and spiritual deadness of the existing religion—which is simply a way of saying that most religions tend to become lifeless from time to time and fail to meet the emotional needs of their members. The New Lights in America in 1730–1760 were not unlike Wesleyan Methodists in England, in the same years, who disliked the corruption, formality, and spiritual torpor of the established Church of England and who sought through prayer, fasting, revival meetings, hymn singing, and other means to bring new spiritual life into their churches.

In New England established churches were Congregational—remnants of the old Puritan theocracy. Inhabitants of Rhode Island did not have an established church, but until 1748 the eastern side of Narragansett Bay was in dispute between Massachusetts and Rhode Island, and most inhabitants there were considered to be inhabitants of Massachusetts and subject to its laws. So people in Cumberland shared with New Lights to the east of them that spiritual rebellion against established churches that became known as the New Light movement. Most of the New Lights did not want to destroy old churches or the established system; they simply wanted to put new fervor into them. (Similarly, John Wesley had no intention of splitting from the Anglican church and founding the Methodist Episcopal church when he started his spiritual movement in the 1730s.) But ministers of established churches, as well as secular authorities, frowned on many of the views and much of the behavior of the New Lights; for New lights were highly critical of their ministers, and in many places they tried to remove them from office and install more zealous preachers. Religious zeal spilled over into very bitter quarrels about doctrine, church government, and ritual. By the end of the 1740s many fervent New Lights were ready to conclude that it was impossible for them to reform established churches from within, so they would have to leave and start new

churches. The favorite text of these radical New Lights was 2 Corinthians 6:17—"Come out from among them, and be ye separate"—from which they were called "come-outers" or "separates."
In Cumberland, Attleboro, Easton, Norton, and Middleborough
there were come-outers who left their old Congregational churches
and formed separate churches, where they could have preachers
more in harmony with the new spiritual fervor of the times.

The separates in Norton—to which many of the Ward–Finney
group later belonged—started a new church in February 1747, stating the following reasons for leaving their old church:

> 1. *Because that they did not particularly examine those admitted to their com-
> munion as they ought to do.*
> 2. *Because they did not hold a gospel discipline.*
> 3. *They deny the fellowship of the saints.*
> 4. *Their settling ministers by way of salary.*
> 5. *By their allowing of half-way members.*
>
> *All of which particulars we look upon to be contrary to the rules that Christ and
> his apostles practised. . . . Then the Lord put it into our hearts to [look to] him for
> direction, and we set ourselves to seek the Lord by prayers.*[4]

And after "a day of solemn fasting and prayer for the occasion
of his Holy Spirit to direct us in the way he would have us to walk
in," they concluded that they must come out from the old church
and form a new one.

The next step was to set forth the principles on which they would
join together; and here we must pay particular close attention to
the words they used, for these people were Calvinists and they chose
their words carefully to prove that they were acting in strict accord
with the Bible, literally interpreted. Yet their friends and the minister in the church they were leaving insisted that their actions and
beliefs were not strictly orthodox or according to the Bible. We need
not quote all seventeen of their articles of faith nor all of the nine
articles defining their views about church organization. But we do
need to select for consideration those that Old Lights, or conservatives, found most objectionable (I have indicated the important
phrases in roman type):

> 1. We believe that there is one only living and true God who is a spirit; of himself
> from all eternity to all eternity unchangeably the same; infinitely holy, wise, omnip-
> otent, just, merciful and gracious, omniscient, true, and faithful God; filling all

places and not included in any place; *essentially happy in the possession of his own glorious* perfections.

3. *That the Scriptures of the Old and New Testament are the word of God, wherein he hath given us* a perfect rule of faith and practice.

4. *That God hath, for the manifestation of his glorious* perfections *ordained whatsoever comes to pass.*

5. *That* we are of the number that was chosen from eternity in Christ; *and that he hath come and obeyed and suffered, arose and ascended, and doth ever plead before God the Father* for us; *which he hath given us to believe by* sending the holy spirit to convince us . . .

13. *That the life of religion consist [in] the knowledge of God and a conformity to him in the* inner man; which necessarily produced an external conformity to his laws.

14. *That* all doubting in a believer is sinful, *being contrary to the commands of God, hurtful to the soul, and a hindrance to the performance of duty.*

The words in roman type indicate the stress these pietists placed on perfectionism, reliance on the Holy Spirit for inner direction, belief in a literal Bible to which the Christian must conform, absolute faith, and the necessity for external conformity to internal convictions of divine duty. Of course, it takes strong faith to stand up against the established order and declare one's independence from it. Such absolute conviction is necessary if one is to bear sacrifices, scorn, even civil punishment for one's deeply held beliefs. But by the same token this reliance on an inward spiritual power that comes directly from God can lead to extremely radical behavior when it is divorced from any other means of authority or control. In most of the Separate churches control over inner spiritual prompting was asserted by three means: first, by testing all inward feelings against the written word of God; second, by requiring that individuals submit their own inner prompting to the regulation and common wisdom of all of the brethren (or "saints"); and third, in the case of conflict or disharmony, by relying for help and guidance from brethren and ministers of other nearby churches, who might be called on to give counsel and advice.

Nevertheless, even these checks might not suffice. In the case of most of the perfectionist or immortalist groups the individuals concerned have such strong convictions of the necessity of following the divine promptings they feel in their hearts that they refuse to heed any of these restrictions. They ignore the advice and counsel of spiritual brethren and leaders. Such people are termed Antinomians; *nomos* being the Greek word for law, an Antinomian is someone who acts against all law, though the individual insists that he or she is acting according to God's law within his or her heart. The most common means of self-justification used by an Antinomian is to find a literal text or phrase in the Bible that seems to justify the action, thereby conceding at least the validity of the first rule of control.

Unfortunately, "the Devil can quote Scripture to his purpose," and one of the most obvious bits of Scripture to which an Antinomian can turn is the command of Christ to his apostles in Matthew 5:48, "Be ye therefore perfect, even as your Father which is in heaven is perfect." The text most popular among those who would leave their earthly spouses for spiritual soulmates is 2 Corinthians 6:14, "Be ye not unequally yoked together with unbelievers." Clearly, it was this text that Bennet claimed Ebenezer Ward had used to persuade Molly to leave him because Bennet had not been converted to radical New Light views.

There are two other aspects of radical New Light or perfectionist religious thought that we need to consider before we turn to the documents. First is the concept of "the new covenant," and second is "the improvement of gifts." By the new covenant a New Light meant that God's covenant with Abraham and the Jews in the Old Testament had been superseded by his covenant with Christ and the Christians in the New Testament. This was especially important in regard to the ordinance of baptism: whereas baptism by water is a New Testament practice, the Puritans had justified baptism of infants (who cannot profess to a belief in Christ) on the basis of the Old Testament ritual of circumcision. Many radical New Lights, or Separates—intent on living up to the literal word of God—were surprised that they could find no instance in the New Testament where Jesus commanded baptism of infants or where the Apostles practiced it. As one might expect, many of these Separates consequently concluded that their infant baptism in their old churches was not valid and that they should not baptize infants in their new churches. The New Testament covenant seemed to be much clearer in commanding that only persons who publicly profess their belief in Christ were fit subjects of baptism.

As for improvement of gifts, this related to biblical texts that spoke of various gifts or privileges or talents given to certain men and women by the Holy Ghost. The twelfth chapter of 1 Corinthians is a favorite source: "Now there are diversities of gifts, but the same Spirit. . . . For to one is given by the Spirit the word of wisdom, to another the word of knowledge by the same Spirit; . . . And God hath set some in the church, first apostles, secondarily prophets, thirdly teachers, after that miracles, then gifts of healings, helps, governments, diversities of tongues. . . . But covet earnestly the best gifts." In throwing off the yoke of old churches and ministers, radical come-outers had to rely on the Holy Spirit to provide them with new preachers and apostles. Not surprisingly, the Separate church in Norton mentioned this aspect in its articles of faith and practice: "That all gifts and graces that are bestowed upon any of the members [of the church] are to be improved by them for the good of the whole."

Usually, anyone who thought he had a gift of prophesying or preaching was allowed to exercise (i.e., improve) it. It was up to the church members to select the one who had the best gifts to be their preacher. But even after a preacher or minister was chosen, other members of the church were still permitted to exercise their individual gifts, for New Lights believed in the priesthood of all believers. Here again was a broad area in which perfectionism could cause considerable disturbance to good gospel order in a community. Ebenezer Ward had for some years exercised his gift of preaching and prayer in his home and might well have been chosen minister of a New Light church in Cumberland had he not got into trouble over his daughter. Even so, he did frequently exercise the right to baptize, as did others in his group, including John Finney, Jr., brother of Solomon. It became a question of considerable importance whether men who had such perfectionist views as these were proper persons to perform the sacred ordinance of baptism and whether their baptisms were in fact valid. Many of the less radical New Light churches not only refused to accept as members persons baptized by Ward and Finney but even refused to have Christian fellowship with more radical New Light churches that did accept them as members.

Many of the documents related to the Cumberland perfectionists are located among the papers and writings of Rev. Isaac Backus, who, though born in Norwich, Connecticut, became a New Light (Separate) minister in Middleborough, Massachusetts, in 1748. Three years later he gave up the practice of infant baptism, though for five years more he admitted to his church both those who continued to believe in infant baptism and those who were opposed to it (this was known as the policy of "open communion" and was necessary in order to accommodate the diversity of opinion on this subject among the Separates). After 1756 Backus joined a growing number of Separates who turned to "closed communion" principles, refusing to allow "infant baptizers" in his church or have fellowship with any church that followed the practice of infant baptism. In his famous history of the Separate-Baptist movement, written at the end of the eighteenth century, Backus wrote as follows:

The Baptist church in Taunton was first gathered in Norton. Mr. William Carpenter was ordained the pastor of a Separate Church there, September 7, 1748. . . . Some of the members of that church, especially they who lived in Easton, had run into the most delusive notions that could be conceived of; even so as to forsake their lawful wives and husbands and to take others, and they go so far as to declare themselves to be perfect and immortal, or that the resurrection was past already, as some did in the Apostolic Age, II Tim. ii, 18.[5]

This text refers to an early church that contained some erroneous members who said that Christ had already returned to earth, in the Spirit, and had designated those who would never die from those who were doomed to hell. Many perfectionists took the view that they were among those who would never die, utilizing another text (which most learned theologians said applied only to the *souls* of the elect and not to their earthly bodies), John 11:25–26—"Jesus said unto her, I am the resurrection and the life; he that believeth in me, though he were dead, yet shall he live: And whosoever liveth and believeth in me shall never die." Ergo, immortalists!

Let us turn now to some of the documents that deal with the Cumberland perfectionist movement of the 1740s and 1750s to see how its members—friends of Ebenezer Ward and John and Solomon Finney—described and justified the behavior that their neighbors (and the courts) found so "pernicious." One of the first of these is a reference in the diary of Isaac Backus under January 16,

1748/49: "I went to Cumberland where the false spirit has ben working very Powerfully and Some have ben led into awfull Erours. And glory to god he gave me Clearness in laying open the Difference between the true and false Spirit and it was blest to Several of the hearers." To Backus it was a "false Spirit," but obviously to Ward and his friends it was the true Spirit of God. Sometime later Backus went to Attleboro and talked to his friend Elihu Daggett. "He told me how he see[s] this error trying to creap into the Church to make the Spirit the rule instead of the word." To Backus and Daggett the perfectionists were clearly antinomians who made their inward belief rather than the revealed word of God (rightly interpreted) their rule for action.

Samuel Bartlet of Cumberland stated that he had heard Molly Bennet say, on July 11, 1749, "that Solomon Finney and she was man and wife Enternally [internally] but not Externally." That is, they were spiritual soulmates but (she implied) had no carnal knowledge of each other: "She said that they was man and wife in the sight of the Lord and it was made known to them that it was so."[6] The only way this kind of internal marriage, made in heaven, could be "made known to them," of course, was through the Holy Spirit. Referring to rules 12 and 13 of the Separate church in Norton, we can imagine that Molly Bennet did not need to be persuaded by her earthly father to leave the unconverted Bennet and live with Solomon Finney, for God "hath given us to believe by sending the holy spirit to convince us" and "the life of religion consists [in] the knowledge of God and a conformity to him in the inner man; which necessarily produces an external conformity to his laws." Conservative New Lights, like Isaac Backus, might and did argue that this simply meant that men should conform to God's explicit laws, such as the Ten Commandments, in their external lives if they were really inwardly Christians in their faith. But who was to tell which other spiritual laws required conformity? If Backus accepted conformity to "be ye separate," why did he not accept "be ye not unequally yoked"? Should the saints, those who never doubted that they were of the number chosen from eternity to live with Christ in heaven, be obliged to obey the statute laws passed by unconverted (perhaps wicked) men (such as marriage laws or laws to pay taxes to corrupt established churches)? Must not true believers obey a higher law? "Be ye not unequally yoked with un-believers."

American history has had little respect for this kind of Bible exegesis when applied to marriage, immortalism, perfectionism, and faith healing, but it has sometimes had great respect for the higher-law doctrine when it has been applied to social reform—notably, activities of our Revolutionary leaders, abolitionists, opponents of segregation, and conscientious objectors to war. Apart from these exceptions, however, the general view of Christianity holds that only extreme radical fringe groups indulge in such bizarre behavior as to put a higher law above the law of the land.

But it is worth noting that some Old Lights among the established churches also got caught up in perfectionism during the Great Awakening, most notably the wife of Rev. Solomon Prentice of Grafton. Prentice was a minister of the established (Congregational) church, but in 1752 his wife fell under the spell of an immortalist in that town named Shadrach Ireland, and according to Ezra Stiles, "She used to lie with Ireland as her spiritual Husband."[7] Unlike Joseph Bennet, however, Solomon Prentice stuck with his wife. The townspeople could not tolerate this and forced him to leave town. He and his wife went to Easton, where Sarah Prentice continued her eccentric behavior, even inviting some perfectionists and Baptists to meet in her husband's home. Isaac Backus met her one day in June 1752 when she was visiting in Attleboro, and "she declar'd that this night 2 months ago, she passed thro' a change in her Body Equivalent to Death; so that she had been intirely free from any disorder in her Body or Corruption in her Soul ever Since; and expected she ever sho'd be so; and that her body wo'd never see Corruption but wo'd live here 'till Christs personal coming."[8]

Four years later Backus wrote to his brother Elijah, in Norwich, "Mr. Eaton, minister [of the established Congregational church] at Braintree is Put down [dismissed] for having to do with his neighbour's wife." Backus claimed there were similar cases of adultery among other respectable ministers: "I think this is Plainly one of the Signes of Christs Coming when iniquity abounds and ye love of many waxes cold."

Let us turn now to the second aspect of the perfectionist problem, the right to improve one's gifts. Ebenezer Ward and John Finney, Jr., assumed the right to baptize and to conduct communion services, though neither was ever ordained either by a group of their own followers or by any ministerial authority. A number of members of the Separate churches in Easton and Norton preferred to attend the preaching of these men rather than that of their own ministers, and a council was held on March 5 and 6, 1753 by the ministers to decide what should be done about these wayward church members. As Backus tells it,

John Finney junr. had then got the chief lead of the church and the design of this council (at which I was present) was to examine him and others about their principles which the agrieved were disatesfied with and they had much labour upon what he had held and acted about marriage and he [Finney] confessed that he was wrong in openly approving of his brother Solomon's having Ward's daughter as he did, and in other things of that nature.

But he was not ready to confess any error in his (or Ward's) assuming the right to baptize and administer communion.

Finney held forth that when a man is called to preach the gospel by the Spirit of God, he has a right to administer baptism and the [Lord's] supper before he is ordained by the church; and on the day he was baptized, he was at a loss for any administrator, for he feared, he said, that Ebenezer Ward was corrupt in principles and knew he was in practice, but those words came into his mind with power, "Go with him nothing doubting for I have sent him" which removeth all his scruples and he went directly into the water with him and was baptized [by Ward] and then he [Finney] immediately baptised his father [John Finney, Sr.].

There are three distinct issues at stake here: First, was Ward a proper person to baptize Finney? Second, was Finney truly hearing the voice of God when he sought guidance? And third, was he right to baptize his father (and later others) after his baptism by Ward?

These were not easy questions to answer. Many learned theologians and orthodox Christians before and since have contended that in certain circumstances even a layman may perform baptism. It has been even more widely held that if a person is once given the right to perform religious rites, the fact that that person becomes personally corrupt in no way invalidates any rites he may have performed while still in office. There were many New Lights who believed that even a baptism performed by an unorthodox man, like Ward or Finney, if it was performed "in the name of the Father and of the Son and of the Holy Ghost," was of such sanctity that it could not be revoked and that it would be an insult to the Trinity to seek a second baptism. Even many who had been baptized as infants in the spiritually corrupt and dead Congregational churches were fearful of being rebaptized as adults when they came under "the new covenant" of Separate-Baptist preaching.

It is not surprising then that radical New Light churches had a great deal of difficulty dealing with such pietistic believers. Take the case of Daniel Niles, who moved from Easton to Middleborough in 1757 and sought admission to Isaac Backus's Separate-Baptist church.

July 8, 1757, the Church took into consideration the case of Mr. Daniel Niles of Easton who wants to join with us, which is as follows, viz. He was baptized by Ebenezer Ward (a man of very bad principles and practices in many respects) who professed that he was called to God as John the Baptist was, to Baptize, tho' he had not been neither baptized nor ordained himself. He [Ward] coming to Easton and Mr. Niles being convinced before [that time] of his duty of being baptized and not knowing but said Ward had good right to baptize—submitted to ye ordinance by his administration and now, because he acted honestly in himself in ye affair, therefore he holds his baptism to be valid, notwithstanding what he since learns of the character of the administrator. But it appeared to the Church [members] that inasmuch as there was no evidence that said Ward was either internally or externally authorized to baptize and had himself been a great scandal to religion, the integrity of the other's [Niles] heart was not sufficient to make the baptism good, and also for us to allow it to be so tended to open a door to disorder and confusion in the church, therefore they could not admit him.

Some years later, in 1764, the baptism of John Finney, Sr., by his son was challenged by the Separate church in Norton.

Mr. Finney [Sr.] declared that he believed that his son John was called of God to teach and baptize, and that he went into the water with him in obedience to God's command; tho' at the same time he [Finney Jr.] was not ordained, and many knew that he held then several gross errors. And Mr. Finney [Sr.]'s wife now in her relation said that she had no view as to the administrator [of baptism] 'till she went into the water and was being questioned upon it, she said that if persons did but obey the command of God in baptism, their baptism was good if the devil had been the administrator.

The insistence of John Finney's parents that even baptism by the devil was valid in certain circumstances may have been prompted by another aspect of their case. For according to Backus,

In June, 1753, John Woodward was put into Newport jail for counterfeiting dollars and he turned King's evidence and accused John Finney (Jr.) and others to having a hand therein, and Finney was afraid and kept out of the way till September after, when he was taken and was imprisoned and punished at Taunton, from whence after some time he broke jail and run off into New York government and having been sometime in the army [in the French and Indian War] we heard that he came and died at Grafton in March, 1759.

It was hard on those of great and undoubting faith when their leaders proved false. But even this shock seldom shakes all believers in a movement. Having made the serious commitments that perfectionist faith requires, the true believer usually burns too many bridges (personal, social, and psychological) to enable him or her to retreat again. So they "tough it out."

John Finney, Jr., had been unsound on more than baptism and communion. Prior to his counterfeiting he had also imbibed the new covenant view of marriage from the Cumberland perfectionists. Backus recalled a meeting on June 24, 1751,

at elder Carpenter's [church in Norton] when John Finney [Jr.] made a public declaration wherein it was then observed to them that he plainly represented the union betwixt man and wife to be in the new covenant or a spiritual union and also that Christians ought to marry in the church without any regard to Babylon, as he called rulers in the State, and that what was not so acted was to be done away [with]; soon after which he led off a great part of the [Norton] church from elder Carpenter [into perfectionism]. . . . And it is well known that the affair of Solomon Finney's taking Bennets wife and having of it countenanced by a pretence of new covenant marriage and that of John Finney and others taking their wives before religious meetings without the cognizance of civil authority and living with them, as such, was all before any of these baptisms by Ward, Finney, and their associates.

Now here we must look back more closely at another aspect of this rebellion against established civil authority. The Puritans, in reaction against corruptions in the Church of England, decreed when they came to New England that no one could be married in a church by a minister. Perhaps they also feared that their ministers might not be legally accepted as officials of the Church of England (though they claimed not to have separated from that church, merely to be purifying it). Hence, all marriages in New England were for many years legal only if performed by a justice of the peace or some other secular authority. Later the Puritans, being better established and believing that under the Toleration Act of 1689 they were legally entitled to perform marriages, permitted anyone to be married either by secular authority or by a "duly ordained minister."

This meant that dissenters from Congregational churches—Baptists, Separates, or Separate-Baptists—were discriminated against. Their ministers were not "duly ordained" according to Massachusetts law. Perfectionists were perhaps extreme in their reliance on the inward, or internal, call to preach; their emphasis on inner guidance by the Holy Spirit; and their belief in their immortality. But they had a real grievance in regard to marriage. And although it is no defense of those who left duly married spouses for spiritual soulmates, there is some reason to sympathize with the attempt of others "to take their wives before religious meetings." They were in fact simply saying that they thought a marriage performed before a dissenting church was as legal as any performed before a justice of the peace or an established minister. Quakers had won this right long before. Later, all dissenting ministers were given this right. But in 1748 to 1768 perfectionists may have had some grounds for their reliance on a higher law than that of Babylon. At least it is an understandable protest in this respect.

It is not clear when perfectionism died out in southeastern New England, but there were still instances of it as late as 1768—not to mention Jemima Wilkinson and later the adherents to Shakerism. Backus's old friend, Elihu Daggett of Attleboro, became pastor of a Baptist church there in 1765. Three years later Backus noted in his diary, "Several of his church have been ensnared this year with antinomian notions so as not to be content with their own wives. In particular Jedidiah Freeman (whose wife had played the harlot) has laid some claim to elder Daggett's daughter and she to him, and Wm. Atwell (who was not of the church) has left his wife and gone after Patience Freeman, a young woman of the church."

One other point may be made about these perfectionists. This has to do with the first of their articles of faith, in which they refer to God as "filling all places and not included in any place." An anthropologist at Brown University who has been studying recent utopian experiments, notably the communes of the 1960s, has argued that any great awakening or important revival of religion in American history seems to include or contain attempts to redefine the nature of God or reinterpret the meaning of the word *God*.[9]

Professor David Buchdahl describes the counterculture of the 1960s and its communes this way:

> We can now understand that the death of God does not mean the disappearance of the sacred, the "wholly other," but the transformation of the form in which the sacred is found and worshipped. The counter-culture, and especially the rural communes, are a theater of this transformation, and different substitutions compete for men's faith. The demonic and the occult reappear with all their ancient threats and attractions, along with more hopeful designs. God's death was a destruction of a religious idol, and while other idols have come to replace Him, they have transformed the location of the sacred and revived its power. God the father, creator of the universe, has become transformed into Creation, the Mother earth—Spirit has taken the place of Deity as the religious object.

Different manifestations of "the Spirit" in contemporary culture—the new attraction of charismatic cults, of pentecostal and holiness movements, and of Zen Buddhism and transcendental meditation—clearly indicate that we are today in the grip of a new "great awakening." Buchdahl argues that in this religious awakening we are changing our conception of God in America, and "a change in the conception of God is a cultural event of some magnitude." In many respects the Great Awakening of 1735–1760 also concerned a changing conception of God. From the old Puritan Jehovah and the theocratic priesthood who upheld his iron laws of predestination, original sin, total depravity, and hellfire, the American people in the 1640s began a redefinition that put man's direct personal relationship to God as the central and only meaningful relationship.

Buchdahl states that "American culture bears the imprint of a particular conception of God, the God of Abraham, Isaac, and Jacob, mediated through Protestants like Calvin, Cotton Mather and Billy Graham. The counter-culture represents an elaboration of reality independent from that notion." If the old Puritan conception of the power of God was represented in elaborate legal codes enforced by civil authority, there has also been "in the West another and quite different conception of God, one in which God is understood as a substance that permeated the entire Creation, including man and the natural world—a sacred spirit perhaps, of the stuff of the universe, or even the universe itself." Buchdahl finds this view expressed in the natural theology of eighteenth-century deism, as a reaction against Calvinism, and in the panthe-

ism of Wordsworth and the Romantic transcendentalists, as a reaction against the moralistic evangelicalism of a Victorian era. But,
he cautions, this conception of God is not simply pantheism.

It is not exactly Nature itself, but a more diffuse idea of Spirit which exists
as a vital force within it and unites all of nature's manifestations. From this
perspective, it can be seen that the counter-culture is only a specific manifestation of a recurring theme in Western history, a theme which is sustained by the potential diversity of interpretations which a cultural system
will always yield. It is the most recent attempt to find a meaning in an
immanent God and to worship this Being in all its varied forms. . . . In
such a view, God as a transcendent creator has no special place. Divinity
is everywhere.

Buchdahl would not, of course, find the Cumberland perfectionists and the Separates of Attleboro, Norton, Easton, and Taunton
to be similar in precise particulars to the counterculture of today—
though spiritual marriage is common again. He would undoubtedly
find their God more transcendent than immanent. Yet he would
agree, I think, that they were antinomians, not Puritans, and that
they found God in the Spirit rather than in any particular civil or
ecclesiastical code; most of all, he would find them part of the
counterculture of their day. For these perfectionists the spirit of
God was everywhere and available to all men; what's more it was
radically at odds with the prevailing laws and institutions that
claimed to speak so authoritatively about right and wrong. It
opened the way for new interpretations of life and eternity.

In 1774 Isaac Backus went to Philadelphia to attend the First
Continental Congress. While there he pleaded with the incipient
Revolutionary leaders to heed the voice of radical New Lights like
himself and to free them from paying religious taxes to support
the established Congregational churches of New England—where
the Separates and Separate-Baptists could not in conscience worship. On his way home from Philadelphia on October 27 he stopped
off in Greenwich, Connecticut. To his surprise he met there the
aged leader of the Cumberland perfectionists: "Mr. Ebenezer Ward
met me here, who formerly lived in Attleborough and in Cumberland whose daughter parted from her husband. He now appears
to be a steady, solid man." Ward had become a respected Baptist
preacher, his past eccentricities forgotten. He preached regularly

in various churches in New York and New Jersey, and although the date of his death is unknown, he was last seen in Columbia, Ohio, in 1795, where Rev. David Barrows said he was eighty-seven years old, in ill health, and preparing for death: "I was called upon to write Elder Ward's last will and testament. I felt happy to oblige the old saint. . . . After it was done, he seemed composed and observed that nothing remained but to wait his Lord's call."[10] There is no reason to believe he did not die in good spirits.

About the last days of Molly Bennet, Joseph Bennet, and Solomon Finney we know little, except that Molly and Solomon were married in Norton in 1750. She died in 1760. Her son, Ebenezer Ward Finney, born in 1755, lived with his grandfather in Greenwich, served in the Revolutionary army, went to Rensselaer, New York, and from there founded Finneytown, Ohio, in 1798. His descendants are now honorable members of the Sons of the American Revolution and Daughters of the American Revolution—a revolution that in many respects had its beginnings in the New Light movement of the 1740s.

APPENDIX 1

Ebenezer Ward's Story

These are to certifie [to] all christian people to whom it may concern: That we, the subscribers, having heard from Mr. Gano's copy [of Isaac Backus's A Fish Caught in His Own Net] that Mr. Backus has inserted in his piece to the public that Ebenezer Ward took his daughter away from her husband, Bennet and in the event was forced to leave his countery: the which is so false we think it our duty to declare something of what we know concerning that matter.

That in the year 1748 we were near neighbours to the said Ward and that Josiah Streeter and his wife (that some years ago wrote a few lines on that account) lived in the house with us; the said Bennet lived in the house with his father in law. And as he sat discoursing one evening, to our great surprize he told us said Ward's daughter was not his wife and that he had no more right to lie with her than any other woman. Whereupon we discourst with him a great deal, told him he was deluded, which was the first time we ever heard of such discourse from any mortal. And not long after, he made his uneasiness known to some other[s]. And when said Ward came to know about the matter he was very uneasy.

And inasmuch as he then preacht constantly to a great number of people at his own house, he thought proper to call a number of the brethren and neighbours to come to his house to discourse with his son Bennet in order to know what the matter was. And we were both there and a considerable number of people and we discoursed a great deal with said Bennet in order to know what the matter was.

He did not care to say much but discovered a good deal of uneasiness and seemed to incline to go away. But we discoursed so much with him to the contrary that he said at last if he could have his wife and live some where else, he thought he would; whereupon said Ward told him that if he would provide a place sutable any where within ten miles, he was willing his daughter should go with him and that he would furnish her with things sutable to keep house, and if he would get a good maid or nurse to be constantly with her, as she was a person subject to fits, he would pay her yearly himself, and that we would give her £1000 for her comfort.

But, however, he [Bennet] did not provide any place, and after some time he would go away and disposed of what he had. And as near as we can remember, toward the latter part of winter he went off. We heard he went to sea and was lost.

And about this time there was a considerable discourse about marrying in the new covenant, and this Bennet's wife was of the opinion she had not got the right husband and that one [Solomon] Finney was made for her. The first time this was made know was at a conference meeting which was very surprizing. But said Ward gave his duaghter no felloship in any such thing.

After that it was noised about that she was a going to have said Finney. And about that time said Bennet came home from sea and heard the news and came to Attleboro, as it was in his way to where his wife lived, and brought a number of the brethren with him. And a great number of people met together and among the rest I myself was there and not my wife. And among their discourse I heard said Ward declare his willingness that his daughter should live with said Bennet and that he would do for her as he had offered before he [Bennet] went away.

Much more might be said that is true, but we hope this may suffice to satesfie all christians whom it may concern, and that said Ward lived there about seven years afterwards.

Joseph Fisher &

Witness our hands

Rebeckah Fisher

The above I copied from the original in said Ward's hands on October 28, 1774, at James Philips's in Greenwich, Connecticut, and Ward informed me that, as above, he opposed Bennet's motion and his daughter's also for some time till, as he exprest it, their church seemed to be stoped in their travel. And fearing he should stand in their way, he one Lordsday came out publickly and declared his willingness that that Finney should have his daughter and that Bennet should have another woman. Upon which Bennet went the next week to Providence and entered a complaint against him and had him imprisoned and afterward petitioned the Rhode Island General Assembly for a divorce. And as they [Ward and his daughter] were about to make defense against it, his daughter was found to be with child by Finney, which took all heart from them to make any defense, and he obtained his end.

Deacon Joshue Everett of Attleborough has since assured me that when he and other brethren went and laboured with Ward, he said he believed Phinney and his daughter meant no harm lodging together for they lay with the Bible between them.

Witness.   Isaac Backus

APPENDIX 2

Joseph Bennet's Story

Colony of Rhode Island:

To the Honorable the great Assembly of the Colony of Rhode Island to be held at Newport in and for said Colony on the third Monday of August, A.D. 1749
The Petition of Joseph Bennett of Cumberland in the Colony of Providence, Labourer, Humbly Sheweth

That your Petitioner was married unto Molly Ward, the daughter of Ebenezer Ward of Said Cumberland, and did Cohabit with her at the House of said Ebenezer Ward until some time in the month of February, A.D. 1747 when the said Ebenezer Ward, having Imbibed and Cherished Certain Wicked and Strange Tenets and Principles Destructive to Government and against the Matrimonial laws and rights of the English Nation, did then Suggest unto the said Molly, his Daughter, being your Petitioner's Wife, that your Petitioners was in an unconverted State and Condition and that it was Sinful for her to Cohabit with your petitioners as her Husband, and your petitioner's wife, attending unto the Wicked and evil Counsel and advice of the said Ebenezer Ward, he the said Ebenezer, together with one Solomon Finney, a person of like Pernicious and Evil Principles, did Conspire to Seduce the said Molly, the wife of your Petitioner, to leave him, and to that end the said Ebenezer did first compel your Petitioners to leave his House and did keep your petitioner's wife still there, and as soon as your Petitioners was gone, the said Ebenezer did procure the said Molly, his Daughter, to Deliver herself to the said Solomon Finney to be his wife in a most profane and Impious manner and afterward, viz. in June last past, the said Molly, your Petitioner's wife, did receive the said Solomon to her bed and Company and hath ever since cohabited with him in an Adulterous manner, of all which Evil acts the said Solomon and Ebenezer hath in a fair Tryal been lawfully Convicted and fined for the same.

And now your petitioners Humbly prays that your Honors in Justice to him would divorce him from the said Molly by Declaring the Marriage Between your petitioners and the said Molly to be Utterly Dissolved and Void and that the said Molly be served with a Copy of the Petition and Cited to appear before your Honours at your next Sitting to Shew Cause, if any she hath, why this petition should not be Granted, and your petitioners, as in Duty bound, shall ever pray,

Joseph Bennett

Providence, September 4 A.D. 1749

I serv'd the within Named Molly Bennet, the Wife of Joseph Bennet, with a copy of the within Petition and cited her to be and appear at the time and place above mentioned.

Jonathan Ormesby
Deputy Sherif

Octobr. 27, 1749

Resolved that this Petition be granted & that an Act be drawn up

Accordingly—

Voted and past
per Order J. Lyndon, Clerk

APPENDIX 3

Testimony of Samuel Bartlet of Cumberland

Samuel Bartlet of Cumberland, being of lawfull age and Engaged according to Law, testifieth and saith

that on the Eleventh Day of July, A.D. 1749, being at the House of Mr. Daniel Peck in Cumberland and Molley Bennet, wife of Joseph Bennet was there and sundry other persons, and I hear Molley say that Solomon Finney and she was man and wife Enternally but not Externally and further this Deponent Saith that a few days after, Moley was at my House and I asked Her what she meant by telling Squier Lapom that finney and she was man and wife, and she said that they was man and wife in the sight of the Lord and it was made known to them that it was so, and further saith not.

Samuel Bartlet

Cumberland, October the twentyeth A.D. 1749

Israel Whipple, Just. Peace

APPENDIX 4

Rought draft of the Act of divorce

S.[outh] K.[Kingston] October, 1749
At the General Assembly, etc.

Whereas Joseph Bennett of Cumberland in the County of Providence, Laborer, represented unto the Assembly that he married Molly Ward, daughter of Ebenezer Ward of said Cumberland, and did cohabit with her at the House of her said Father till some time in the month of February A.D. 1747 when the said Ebenezer Ward, having imbibed and cherished certain wicked and strange tenets and principles destructive to government and against the matrimonial laws and rights of the English Nation, did then suggest unto the said Molly, his daughter, being then the said Joseph's wife, that he, the said Joseph, was in an unconverted State and Condition, and that it was sinful for her to cohabit with him as her lawful husband, and the said Molly, attending to the wicked and evil council and advice of the said Ebenezer, he the said Ebenezer, together with one Solomon Finney, a person of like pernicious and evil principles, did conspire to seduce the said Molly, the said Joseph's wife, to leave him and to that end the said Ebenezer did first compel the said Joseph to leave his house and did keep his wife still there, and as soon as the said Joseph was gone the said Ebenezer did procure to said Molly to deliver herself up to the said Solomon Finney to be his wife in a most profane and impious manner and afterwards, to wit in June last, the said Molly did receive the said Solomon to Bed and Company and hath ever since cohabited with him in an adulterous manner, of all which Evil acts the said Solomon and Ebenezer have, on a fair trial, been lawfully convicted and fined for the same, and thereupon the said Joseph Bennet prayed the Assembly to divorce him from the said Molly by declaring the marriage between them to be utterly dissolved and void.

All and every whereof being manifestly made to appear, this Assembly do vote and Enact, and it is hereby voted and enacted, that the said Joseph Bennet be, and he is hereby, divorced from the said Molly, and the Marriage between them is hereby declared and made null and void.

[5]
Arminian and Calvinist Baptists

Jacobus Arminius (1560–1609) gave the name Arminianism to a mod-ification of Calvinism that held that Christ had not died only for the elect few but that he died to make salvation available to all people. In 1608 a synod of Calvinists in Dort, Holland, declared this a heresy, and the Pu-ritans who came to New England agreed. But as time passed, some elements of this heresy seeped into the preaching of some Puritans, and by the 1730s Jonathan Edwards, out on the frontier of Northampton, Massachusetts, feared that Harvard College and the clergy of Boston were more than tainted with it.

It is certain that many Baptists in the area of Rhode Island had become Arminians. They were known as General Baptists (Christ having died for the general salvation of all), whereas the early Baptists in Massachusetts were orthodox, or Particular, Baptists (Christ having died only for the particular few elected by the arbitrary grace of God). The General Baptists in Rhode Island were so numerous that they had organized into an asso-ciation of Baptist churches that held annual meetings to discuss religious issues and strengthen their movement. But when the Great Awakening began in the 1730s, it occurred chiefly among the Particular Baptists and Particular Congregationalists. In the years after the Awakening, the Par-ticular Baptists grew so rapidly that they outnumbered the General Bap-tists. Consequently, they wished to organize their own associations to assist each other.

Historians have been interested in discovering when the first group of Calvinistic Baptists formed an association in New England. This chapter tries to shed some light on this important step in the ecclesiastical history of the denomination. It signaled an important turning point in the move-ment.

Baptist historians have frequently asserted that the first Calvin-istic Baptist Association in New England was the Warren Baptist Association, founded under the aegis of James Manning in 1767. Most historians are aware that an earlier association, founded in the 1690s, existed among the Six Principle General, or Arminian, Baptists in New England, but with the great Calvinistic reorienta-tion in the Baptist movement following the Great Awakening this association ceased to be of any significance outside Rhode Island.[1] Little notice has been taken, however, of the Six Principle Calvinistic Baptist Association that developed on the borders of Connecticut, Massachusetts, and Rhode Island in the 1750s to unite and serve a group of Separate-Baptist churches formed in the aftermath of the Awakening. And yet this association, short-lived though it was, merits attention. It represented the first spontaneous effort of the Separate Baptists to seek unity and order in the confusion following the breakup of the Separate movement after 1754. Although it proved to be a false start, it nevertheless prepared the way for the Warren Association, whose importance is acknowledged by all Baptist historians. And it is particularly interesting that the basis of the organization was agreement on the belief that the ritual of laying on of hands was essential to church membership.

The first historical mention of this association (sometimes referred to as a General Conference or General Convention) appeared in the third volume of Isaac Backus's history of the Baptists, written in 1795. The reference, brief and elliptical, occurs in his discussion of Whitman (Wightman) Jacobs's Separate-Baptist Church in Thompson, Connecticut. It implies that Jacobs was instrumental in the founding of the association:

As the great reformation in our land was opposed by the ruling party in Thompson, then a part of Killingly, a separation took place there, and a Baptist church was formed in 1750, and Mr. Whitman Jacobs was ordained their pastor. They held the laying on of hands upon every member as a term of communion, and an Association was formed upon those principles, which increased to about eight churches in 1763; but in two years after the most of them gave up that bar of communion, of whom Mr. Jacobs was one, and a council was called at Thompson in February 1767, who could not unite the church; and as a number of them removed soon after to Royalston, their minister [Jacobs] removed there also in 1769.[2]

Backus omits to mention the very important part he played in the demise of this association.

Backus's remarks were amplified slightly in the extracts from a historical sermon by the Reverend Charles Train, delivered on December 31, 1826, and printed in the *American Baptist Magazine* for 1827. In the course of this sketch of the history of the Baptist church in Framingham, Train remarked:

In 1763 the Baptist Churches in Stafford, Sturbridge, Thomson, Gloucester, South-Hadley, Spencer, and Cumberland, formed a General Conference, and appointed faithful messengers to visit each church at least once
in each year, to inquire after their prosperity, give them suitable advice,
and report at their annual meeting. In June 1764, this Conference met
with their brethren in Framingham. Such were the pious efforts of our
venerable Fathers to build up the churches in faith and holiness. . . . This
General Convention was probably merged in the Warren Baptist Association which was organized in 1767.[3]

Unfortunately, none of the official records of this association appear to have survived, so it is impossible to tell whether Backus is
right in saying that it was formed in the 1750s; or Train, that it was
formed in 1763. Nor is it possible to tell precisely what function
the "faithful messengers" performed in visiting each church, a procedure that seems to imply closer supervision over the member
churches than was customary in Baptist associations. If the records
of the member churches could be found, they might shed some
light on the problem. Neither the published nor the unpublished
records of the Warren Baptist Association mention this association,
and they certainly do not indicate that any merger took place. Only
two of the elders of the churches listed by Train as belonging to the
Six Principle Association attended the first meeting of the Warren
Association in 1767. Eventually, however, most of the churches in
the earlier association did join the Warren Association, but they did
so seriatim.

The only firsthand accounts of this association that are available
are found in the unpublished diaries, travel journals, and papers
of Isaac Backus at Andover-Newton Theological School. It seems
worthwhile to publish these references for the light they throw on
this forgotten association. The reasons for encouraging further research into the activities of this association become apparent once
Backus's scattered references to it are pieced together. Clearly, this
association represented an important phase in the transition of the
Baptist movement in New England from the older Six Principle
Arminian tradition, which had predominated since the late seventeenth century, to the new Five Principle Calvinistic tradition that
replaced it following the Great Awakening. These excerpts also reveal the important role that Isaac Backus played in effecting the
unity of the Separate Baptists, who, in the 1750s and 1760s, were

almost completely disorganized and in danger of falling apart as a result of their intense internal bickerings over organization and practice. Perhaps historians have overemphasized the role played by the Baptists from the Philadelphia Association—Manning, Morgan Edwards, John Gano, and Hezekiah Smith—in uniting the New England Baptists through the Warren Association. Or perhaps they have not emphasized it enough. In any case, it is evident that the Separate-Baptist movement deserves considerably more study if we are to understand how such a divided, disorganized, and pietistic group of come-outers gradually welded themselves into the most dynamic and aggressive dissenting denomination in New England and the group that did the most to break down the Puritan tradition of a tax-supported church–state establishment.[4]

To put the following excerpts from the Backus Papers in perspective, it is necessary to recall that Backus himself had departed from the Congregational church of his ancestors in Norwich, Connecticut, in 1745. Three years later he had become the pastor of a Separate Church in Titicut parish in Middleborough, Massachusetts. In 1751 he had adopted Baptist principles, and for the next five years he tried to sustain his church on a basis of open communion between pedobaptists and antipedobaptists. This proving impossible, he had dissolved his Separate church and in January 1756 had formed a closed-communion Baptist church on New Light Calvinistic principles; it became the First Baptist Church of Middleborough. At once he began a campaign to unite the various Baptist churches in the vicinity of Middleborough in fellowship.

At first Backus worked principally on the so-called Old Baptists, who were Arminian in outlook and who practiced the sixth principle—the requirement that all persons who sought admission to full church membership not only had to be baptized by immersion upon profession of faith but also had to undergo the rite of laying on of hands as described in Hebrews 6:1–2. His proselyting for the Five Principle Calvinistic cause among this group of churches on the southeastern border of Massachusetts and Rhode Island moved forward slowly but surely. Then in 1763 he discovered the existence of the Six Principle Calvinistic Baptist Association farther to the west, and he began a concerted attempt to persuade them to give up the sixth principle as "a term of communion" and thus to enter fellowship with the Five Principle Separate Baptists. The following entries in his diaries, travel journals, and miscellaneous papers record his highly successful efforts in this direction over the next four years. They provide a graphic account of the way he had at the same time to tear down and build up the new denomination with which he had allied himself and in which he soon assumed a leading role.[5]

Saturday, October 29, 1763: A number of Churches met at the house of mr. Jona. Eddy [in Glouster, Rhode Island] for a general Conference, viz. from Stafford, Noah Alden pastor and mr. Nl. Monger: from Thompson, Whitman Jacobs pastor and decan. Coats and Ebnr. Green: South Hadly James Smith pastor and Noah Clark: Spencer Nathl. Green pastor and Daniel Streeter: Sturbridge David Morse and Benjamin Robbins: Gloucester Joseph Winsor and Jona. Eddy with some others and they chose mr. Saml. Hovey [pastor of the Baptist church in Newton, New Hampshire] moderator and mr. Jonathan Eddy Clerk. These Conference meetings were begun some years ago (after the union of the Separate churches was broken)[6] for to promote union among the saints, and to consider how far they might extend their fellowship &c. This day they admitted elder Daniel Millers Church in Cumberland, and the Church in Newton New-Hampshire into their communion, and after conferring upon some things, they open'd the door for me to propose what was upon my mind which was to enquire whether they would hold communion with our Churches[7] who were agreed in general with 'em in principle and practice except in holding the laying on of hands on all after baptism? And they said that they held that as a standing ordinance in the Church and also a term of communion but were willing to give or receive light in the case; so we discoursed a while upon it 'till time being spent they brake off suddenly; which grieved my mind to think of parting thus but afterward they agreed to appint a Committee to confer upon these things, and Elders Alden and Jacobs was nominated on their side to meet some from our way at Cumberland next April.

April 11, 1764: Came to Cumberland upon appointment and met with elder Alden and Jacobs at elder [Daniel] Miller's meetinghouse. Elder Alden was preaching when I came:—Then after dinner we had a conference concerning laying on of hands with prayer after baptism upon all that are receiv'd into the church:[8] and solemnity and love appear'd thro' the whole conference, and in the conclusion these 2 elders gave in that tho' they tho't that they ought to retain that practice, yet they scrupled whether the rule would warrant their holding of it as a term of communion. So after I had preacht a short Sermon we had a friendly parting.

June 2, 1764: We went over to Framingham to a general meeting or conference. Elder Alden was not there: elder Jacobs was chosen moderator and mr. James Miller Clark; and after some discourse upon other things; the case between our churches and theirs about laying on of hands bro't forward, and much was said upon it: but in conclusion I was disappointed in my hope of that bar between us being remov'd which caused grief to many: however I desire to rest the case in Gods hands.

On October 2, 1764, Backus received a letter, dated September 3, from Benjamin Jacobs of Leicester, asking for assistance in a council called to settle a dispute between him and the Baptist church of Elder Nathaniel Green in the western part of Leicester. But Backus wrote on the back of the letter that he could not participate in such a council, presumably because he was not in fellowship with Green's church. Whether the dispute was over the laying on of hands is not clear from the letter.

On June 1, 1765, Elder Whitman Jacobs of Thompson sent a letter to Backus in which he said, "we have had a deap sarchings of hart about laying on of hands. We think the Scriptur dont make it a Church practis upon privet members. We Conclude not to practis It as we have been. It is a grate labur in the minds of many. . . . Our next general meeting Is at Cumberland friday before the last Sabbath in September."

Friday, September 27, 1765: Went over to Cumberlnd. where was a general meeting of our Bretherin who have held laying on of hands as a term of communion; there I met with elders Alden, Jacobs, Nl. Green, [?] Bennet, [Nathan] Young, [Joseph] Winsor, [Peter] Worden, [Ezekiel] Angel, and [Daniel] Miller, but there were much divided in their Conference, for near half of the meeting and more than half of the elders are bro't to think it won't do to hold that point as a bar of communion as they have done.[9]

Backus makes no mention of attending any meetings of this association in 1766, but in that year Noah Alden's church in Stafford dissolved in controversy, and Alden became pastor of a Five Principle Calvinistic church in Bellingham, Massachusetts. Backus assisted in his ordination and thus acknowledged fellowship between that church and his own.

On January 21, 1767, Elder Whitman Jacobs's church in Thompson wrote Backus a request to aid them in a dispute over the laying on of hands. Jacobs visited Backus in Middleborough on January 25 to deliver this request, and Backus promised to attend the council on February 4.

Wednesday, February 4, 1767: We met there [Thompson] and embodied into a council and eld. Hinds[10] was chosen moderator and they chose me scribe, after which the parties in this church each of them laid open their views of their difficulties and upon the whole, it appear'd to us, that a division arose among them 18 years ago from the same cause that the divisions did at Corinth, viz. Some were for mr. Whitman Jacobs and some for mr. James Glesen; and because Jacobs party prevail'd and got him ordain'd the others drew off, and they have held two meetings [i.e., two congregations for worship] ever since, 'till lately, when upon occasion of eld. Jacobs changing his opinion about laying on of hands the two parties came together as such they soon split again, and got into great confusion: but our labours were so far blest as to bring 'em on both hands to confess their wrong temper and language to each other, tho' their different sentiments concerning leaders and laying on of hands is not removed.

The Backus Papers contain the official "Result" of this council as drawn up by Backus and read to the assembled members of both factions. After describing the division of the Baptists in Thompson into two factions in 1749, the result went on:

When by reason of eld'r Jacobs changing his opinion about laying on of hands upon every chh, member the face of things has been altered; and after other labours they drew up their separation & came all to join together as one church. And in a meeting Nov. 28 last [1766] they voted to practice laying on of hands yet not to hold it as a bar of com'n and eld'r Jacobs was rec'd anew in his office notwithstanding he has dropt holding sd practice as having gospel warrant for it. Upon which a number of the bretherin refused to travel with them, because they rec'd such an eld'r.

Now upon the whole it is evident to us that these dissenting bretherin knew how eld'r Jacobs & his bretherin held about laying on of hands, & also that they were confirm'd in the conterary mind themselves before they essayed thus to join together, therefore we must say that their transactions therein carry in them such a face of unfair dealing as never ought to appear among Chr'st'n people. And we solemnly intreat & exort both parties in a close manner to review & search into your conduct in the fear of God, & confess your faults one to another & pray one for anoth'r that you may be heald.

And as to the point which you have had so much controversy upon, we freely declare that if laying on of hands upon every member is a principle given by the apostles to be practiced by the church of God, then the neglect of it ought not in ordinary cases to be dispensed with: but some of the reasons why we can't look upon it so, is that we can find no instanse in Scrip'r of any one persons laying on hands aft'r bap'm but apostles, & then extraord'y effects follow'd, Acts 8.17 & 19.6. as there did also upon their laying hands upon the sick; neither can we find they ever deliver'd it to the church to practice as they did other gospel ordinances: and as to the sixth of Hebs. it is evident that the run of the epistle is to shew that all Jewish sacrifices & cleansings were fulfilled in Christ so that those shadows of Christ was to be left now the substance is come, and tho the ordinance of water baptism is so often mention'd yet no where does it appear in the plural number, baptisms, as it is here nor is it all mentioned in the commission and we earnestly desire all of you to be as noble as the Bereans and daily search the scriptures to see if these things are so.[11]

On April 23, 1767, Backus received a letter from the Cumberland Baptist Church of Elder Daniel Miller requesting his help in a council to settle a dispute "Concerning terms of Communion." The letter stated that "the Difficulty has ben so greate that the Church has not Communed for a great while. But of Late the grater part of the Church is agreed. But not all." Unfortunately, Backus did not receive this letter until the day after the council was held, so there is no reference to it in his diary or papers. The council resulted, however, in another victory for the Five Principle cause.

On September 8, 1767, Backus went to Warren, Rhode Island, to attend the organization meeting of the Warren Baptist Association. Noah Alden of Bellingham and Daniel Miller of Cumberland were the only two elders of the old Six Principle Calvinistic Association who attended this meeting, but of course, Alden was no longer pastor of the Stafford church. Alden's church in Bellingham joined the Warren Association at this first meeting. Daniel Miller's church joined it in 1771. Backus's church, incidentally, did not join until 1770.

The following chart indicates all that is known at present about the rise and decline of the Six Principle Calvinistic Baptist Association of New England.[12]

After 1767 no more is known of the Six Principle Calvinistic Association except for an interesting historical footnote. In February 1769 Elder Nathaniel Green of Leicester was arrested and jailed for refusing to pay his civil taxes. Green claimed exemption from civil taxes as "a settled minister" and sued the assessor, Seth Washburn, for illegal assessment and arrest. Seth Washburn hired John Adams as his lawyer. Striving to win his case, Adams and his associate, James Putnam, claimed that Green was not entitled to claim exemption as a settled minister because at the time he was taxed, in 1767, he was a member of the Six Principle Baptist Association, which was not in fellowship with the more orthodox Five

TABLE 5.1

The Rise and Decline of the Six Principle Calvinistic
Baptist Association of New England

Church	Pastor	Date joined	Date left	Date joined Warren Association	Remarks
Thompson (Killingly)	W. Jacobs	c. 1754	1768	1771	It was the segment of this church that moved to Royalston, which joined in 1771.
Stafford	Noah Alden	Before 1763	1765	—	This church dissolved in 1765. (Alden's church in Bellingham joined the Warren Association in 1767.)
Sturbridge	None	Before 1763	?	1769	
Gloucester	Jos. Winsor	Before 1763	?	1782	
South Hadley (Granby)	Jas. Smith	Before 1763	?	—	
Spencer (Leicester)	N'l. Green	Before 1766	1766	1768	This church moved from Spencer to Leicester to Charlton.
Cumberland	D'l. Miller	1763	1767	1771	
Newton, N.H.	S'l. Hovey	1763	?	—	Sam'l Hovey attended the second annual meeting of the Warren Association in 1768, but his church dissolved soon after.
Framingham	None	1764	?	1778	
Foster, R.I.	Nath. Young	?			
Coventry, R.I.	Peter Worden	?			
No. Providence	Ez'l. Angell	?			

Principle churches. He was therefore a mere schismatic of no fixed principles and without legal recognition. The jury found for Green both in the inferior court and, on appeal, in the superior court. The case was a landmark for the Baptists' claim to the same tax exemption privilege for its ministers as that given to the members of the established Congregational ministers in the colony.[13]

On the basis of such slender evidence it is difficult to draw any broad conclusions about the first Calvinistic Baptist Association in New England. Obviously, Whitman Jacobs and Noah Alden were its leading figures, but they were uneducated men, and it is not known where they drew their notions from for such an organization. There is evidence that Six Principle Calvinistic Baptist churches continued to exist, scattered around New England, for many years after 1767. Laying on of hands, however, gradually died out among the Baptists, and its assumed importance in 1754–1767 merely indicates the extreme literalism and pietism of the Separate-Baptist movement at this stage. Noah Alden later achieved fame as a member of the Massachusetts Constitutional Convention of 1780 and of the convention that ratified the federal Constitution in Massachusetts in 1788. (Like most Baptist delegates he voted against ratification.) Out of all of this the figure of Isaac Backus assumes new importance as a leader in the movement to unify and organize the renascent Baptists of New England.

[6]

A Poetic Plea for Religious Liberty, 1772

By 1768 the Baptists had become so numerous in many New England towns and so determined not to pay religious taxes to support the Congregational churches, that it was becoming difficult for some towns to raise enough money to support their ministers and repair their meetinghouses. Consequently, the Massachusetts legislature (as well as the legislatures in the other Puritan colonies) began to tighten the regulations under which Baptists and other dissenters from the establishment (the Standing Order) were allowed to be exempted from paying such taxes.

The issue of religious taxation took a particularly bitter turn in the town of Ashfield, Massachusetts. When the town was founded in 1761, the Baptists were the most numerous voters; they refused to vote any religious taxes except for their own pastor. When the legislature passed a special law forcing the Baptists in Ashfield to submit to taxes to support the Congregational minister, they refused. To seek relief from this "persecution," they sent a petition to the king for redress. In 1771 the king revoked the Ashfield law, much to the chagrin of the Massachusetts authorities.

Rejoicing over this victory was short-lived, for the leader of the Ashfield Baptists was accused by the Congregationalists of being a counterfeiter of money. The Baptists denied the charge, considering it a spiteful effort to discredit them. Normally, this would have resulted in a pamphlet war to arouse the public to the injustice of the affair. Instead, two of the Baptists decided to put their case in the form of a narrative poem. For some reason the poem was never published. A few years ago I discovered it among the manuscript papers of Isaac Backus in the possession of one of his direct descendants.

The story of the persecution of the Baptists in Ashfield, Massachusetts, from 1761 to 1771 has often been told both in contemporary pamphlets and in the works of subsequent historians.[1] But until recently no one was aware that it had been set to verse. A few years ago Miss Florence Backus of Riverside, California, a direct descendant of the famous Baptist historian, gave to Brown University her large collection of family papers, many of them collected by Isaac Backus for his polemical and historical tracts in the eighteenth century. Among these papers was a forty-eight-page tract written by Chileab Smith of Ashfield on February 14, 1772.[2] The final ten pages of this tract are devoted to a long narrative poem by Smith's son Ebenezer, Elder of the Baptist Church in Ashfield from 1761 to 1798.[3]

Smith titled his poem "A Brief Hint of the Mischief of Envy," but it is essentially a disquisition in verse on the subject of the separation of church and state and the natural right of freedom of conscience. The poem seems worth publishing for several reasons: first, because there are so few extant poems by eighteenth-century American Baptists; second, because there are so few poems written by any American on the subject of liberty of conscience; and third, because it is an excellent example of primitive protest poetry, which must have been common in its day but which has since disappeared from historical view. An enterprising scholar willing to search through old manuscript collections and diaries probably could unearth a sizable body of such poetry (the precursor of twentieth-century protest songs by men like Joe Hill, Woodie Guthrie, or Bob Dylan and of black poets like Langston Hughes and Gwendolyn Brooks). It is to be hoped that the publication of this poem will encourage further study of protest poems and songs written by members of alienated or outcast groups in the colonial era. Such popular verse constitutes an essential counterpart to the work of the poets and writers of the New England establishment—like the Hartford Wits—whose poetry ignores the natural right of freedom of conscience because they belonged to the Standing Order, which taxed the Baptists and other minority sects for the support of the Congregational churches long after the successful revolutionary fight for the rights of Americans against the standing order of British imperialism.

Although Ebenezer Smith's poem, like his father's pamphlet (to which it was appended), deals with a specific incident, it is written like so much British poetry of the Augustan Age, as an allegory. Inasmuch as Smith had no education beyond the common schools of rural Massachusetts, the poem indicates the extent to which academic standards of literary taste and style penetrated to the most remote areas of the empire, inspiring even the most benighted of the king's loyal subjects. (Ashfield, located one hundred miles west of Boston in the Berkshire Mountains, had a population of 628 in 1776, and the Baptists were among the poorest of these.)

The poem is an odd combination of the religious verse of John Milton and the rationalistic poetry of Alexander Pope—the Age of Cromwell and the Age of Reason in a frontier patty pan. It mingles concern for scriptural truth as defined by John Calvin with a commitment to natural rights politics as defined by John Locke—a further example of the American Revolution as a religious revival.

Starting with the fall of Adam and Eve, the poem concludes with the millennial hope that in America the Edenic garden could be re-created if only men of different denominations would grant religious freedom and equality to God's people. But why has this rural Calvinist poet chosen Envy rather than Satan as the malevolent spirit that stalks the earth, frustrating the Second Coming of Christ? His choice seems to symbolize the optimistic faith of the evangelical Baptists following the Great Awakening. Envy of their rapid growth (statistical evidence of God's favor)—like Cain's envy of Abel's righteousness, the Pharisees' envy of Jesus, and the Romans' envy of the Apostles—had aroused the established Congregational churches of New England to persecute them. The Baptists had indeed grown rapidly in New England after the 1740s, and their presence in many towns posed a threat to the uniformity of faith and practice on which the territorial parish and its tax-supported ministry depended.

The poet's personification of Envy signifies both his own spiritual confidence and the final breakdown of the old Puritan ecclesiastical system on the eve of the Revolution; God was rewarding the faithfulness of the Baptists and, as of old, utilizing the weak and despised of this world to confound the powerful and respectable. But to the secular mind of the twentieth century, pluralism seems a more logical term than envy to explain what was at stake in this confrontation.

The style of the poem has less to commend it than its symbolism or its fervor. The author is more intent on telling his story and getting across his point of view than in pleasing the literati by adhering to fine points of style. As in most protest writing, the poet puts his message before his meter or his rhyme. Concerning the rhyme, the local New England vernacular pronunciations assisted the poet in several cases, such as his rhyming "join" (pronounced "jine") with "combine" and "dead (pronounced "daid") with "laid." Yet he is clearly writing within a tradition; rhymed couplet in iambic quatrameter was a standard form of the day. And at one point he breaks up his singsong couplets with a pair of triplets. How much its style owes to the hymns of Isaac Watts and how much to the English verse printed in contemporary newspapers it is difficult to say. The identification of the poet by the simple acrostic at the conclusion of the poem is, of course, a common device of seventeenth- and eighteenth-century poetry.

About its specific content little need be said beyond the annotation. Anyone interested in the story of the Ashfield Baptists and their long fight for religious liberty against the Congregational establishments can find it amply set forth in the works cited in note 1 and outlined briefly below on pages 146–56. All the reader of the poem needs to know is that the ecclesiastical laws of Massachusetts required all inhabitants of new towns to pay taxes for the building of a meetinghouse and the installation of a Congregational minister whether they were themselves Congregationalists or not. The protest of the Baptists in Ashfield resulted from a special law passed by the General Court in 1768 that required the Baptists to pay religious taxes for the support of Congregationalism in Ashfield even after the town became incorporated (at which time dissenters were traditionally permitted to be exempt from religious taxes to the established church).

In the poem Smith refers to the petitions—"many pleading cries / Sent to the court with weeping eyes"—that the Ashfield Baptists addressed to the legislature for the repeal of "the Ashfield law." He also describes how finally the Baptists appealed to the king in privy council. "Till of the king they it obtain'd" (i.e., repeal or revocation of the Ashfield law in July 1771). It was one of the ironies of the American Revolution (an irony of which the Baptists were well aware) that the Baptists, themselves a protest movement developing out of "the rising expectations" of freedom among the colonists, found the king more willing to listen to their pleas for "the native right of men" and freedom of conscience than were the Sons of Liberty in Boston.[4]

One final word needs to be said about the pamphlet of Chileab Smith that this poem was written to support. It was titled: "The Sword of Oppression in the Land of Freedom: A Breef Naritive of the Sufferings of Chileab Smith, a principle member of the Baptist Church in Ashfield in the county of Hampshire and Province of the Massachusetts Bay in New England, with Some Remarks upon the Same to Which is added a Poem upon Envy by another hand." Chileab Smith's "oppression" was not, in this particular instance, a matter of freedom of conscience, though he was undoubtedly correct in seeing this as an indirect cause. He was writing to defend himself against charges of counterfeiting, which had brought him before the county court (Judge Israel Williams, presiding) in November 1771. Smith, protesting his innocence, spent a cold night on the jail floor and was released under a £200 bond to appear before the superior court in the spring of 1772. In the pamphlet he maintains that he was being persecuted by malicious neighbors for leading the Baptists' appeal to the king in 1771. The charges of counterfeiting were trumped up; he had merely been boiling mercury in his shop in order to make some medicine according to a prescription he had read in "Doctor William Salmon's Book (a Great Doctor in England)."

The tract documents all too vividly how spiteful (not really envious) rural New Englanders could be against nonconformist neighbors who challenged their traditions and who appealed to the legislature or the king over the majority will of the town meeting. The story of the Ashfield Baptists is a classic example of the tyranny of the majority over dissenters. But it is important to add that Chileab Smith and his Baptist brethren are also a classic example of the persistence of dissenters in America in fighting against that tyranny and, given perseverance and dedication, their ability to win out. For Smith was acquitted of the charge of counterfeiting;[5] and the Baptists, having proved themselves as dedicated to the revolutionary cause as their Congregational neighbors after 1775, went on to attain a secure place for themselves in the town, as they did in the new state and nation.

Why Smith's tract and his son's poem were not published in 1772 is not known. Clearly, the manuscript, carefully written and paginated, was intended for the printer. Apparently, Smith sent it to

Isaac Backus and John Davis, then leaders of the Baptist protest movement in the province, and they advised against publication because Smith's case at that time was still under adjudication.[6] However, two years later, the persecution of the Baptists having continued, Chileab Smith wrote a new and larger tract (incorporating much of the earlier one) titled *An Answer to Many Slanderous Reports Cast on the Baptists in Ashield* (Norwich, 1774). Unfortunately, Chileab wrote at such length that the later tract had no room for his son's poem, and it was omitted from the published tract. Its resurrection is long overdue.

A Brief Hint of the Mischief of Envy[7]
[Ebenezer Smith]

When God at first Mankind did make
And in his image did create
Male & female him for to praise
Him to obey in all their ways,
In peace & union they did stand
No Envy seen on either hand
Till they the law of God did break
And the forbidden fruit did take.
Then too accuseing they do go,
And the effect of sin do show.
Man on his wife dos lay the blame;
She on the Serpent does the same.
Near unto Edens ancient ground
Two brothers are to gether found;
The one dos there the other kill
And on the ground his blood doth spill.
This is the reson that we find
(All would do well the same to mind)
The murderers works they evil were
His brothers riteous truth declares

This Spirit walking to & from
Four thousand years the Earth upon
What works it did you may behold
Within the sacred pages told.

Perticulars I shall not tell
Least I on them two long should dwel.
Only in general I may say
It always went in the same way—
Condemning those whose works were good
Because it is a foe of God
And sought his Glory to destroy
And his dear children to anoy.

And when the Son of God came down,
Lost man to raise unto a crown,
How they in spite against him join,
The Jews & Gentiles do combine
Against the Lord[s] annointed son
Whose praise the Angels long had sung.
Him they do charge with Blasphemies
And load his name with hatefull lies.
In him no sin was ever found
While he livd on this earthly ground,
And when before the Judge he stood,
Twas Envy made them seek his Blood,
And tho' the Son of God when left
In sinners hands of life bereft,
And in the silent tomb was laid,
He quickly did rise from the dead.
And now in heaven he's set down
With his own father in his throne.
Envy against His servants dear
It very quickly did appear.
Where'er they went to preach Gods word,
O how their Envy 'gainst them stird,
As if they were the worst of men
Because they spoke against their sin.
And as they past through Asia,
And as they preached in Affrica
Envy against them oft apeard
While they the truth of God declared.
In Europe also we may see

Against those that Gods children be
Envy has them afflicted there;
They often persecuted were.
In Briton too Gods saints have been
Envy'd by people and by Queen,[8]
Who Righteous blood have often shed
And brou't the Guilt on there own head.

At length our fathers to be free,
And to enjoy their Liberty,
Chose for to cross the ocean wide
And in this desert to abide.
To them the king this freedom gave
That in this land they might it have
In worship to the Lord to join
As they thought right from time to time.
How happy had New England been
If Envy here had nare been seen,
But love to God & Love to men
Had always guided us herein.

The Gosple of the Lord was brou't
Into this land and many sought
Hither to come the ocean or'e [o'er]
For to git rid of prelates pow'r.
O might the Gosple here alone
Have past this desert up & down,
And found its way in every heart
And caused all evil to depart.
Then would New England have apeard
Like to a garden well prepard.
Where jesus would his blessings grant
And well supply his peoples want.
But, O!, alas, with greif I tell
Envy, that first was hatcht in hell,
has found its way this land into
Sad work has here been done also.
Witnis the Jail & whiping post,
The Gallos where some lives were lost,

The confi[s]cation of mens goods,
And banishment into the woods.[9]

Some say these men disturbers were,
Therefore such things fell to their share;
So said the Jews & Greeks of old
As in the Scriptures we are told.
When I these thing[s] to some did tell,
That rulers in this land do dwell,
They like the Jews of old do say
Had they been in there fathers day
Surely they would not thus have done,
To whip & kill & banish some.[10]
Yet clear it is they do also
The works there fathers once did do.
'Tis not for want of a good will
They do not now with some thus deal,
As dos appear most plain to me
By what I once & twice did see.
Tho' freedom unto all is given,
Thro' the kind Providence of heavin,
In charter grant our soverign from,
Yet some would trample others on.
And tho' their lives they can't destroy,
Yet their estates they would anoy,
Take the support of life from them,
For to uphold the way there in.[11]

Much of this kind is done of late,
More than I here can well relate.
This I affirm, for I it knew,
I could say more and yet be true.
And when of hardship I complain,
I have been told once & again,
    I worship might as I see fit
    Only let us have your Estate—
    Or word[s] near unto this efect.
    So the pharoah did to Moses say:
    Go, to the Lord your worship pay,

   Only your flocks & herds let stay.
Some times ["] 'tis law["], they to me say,
And therefore they will it obey.[12]
So did the Jews to Pilate cry:
["]'Tis by our law Jesus must die["].
But, O, New England, be thou sure,
There will come on a trying hour
Before the Judge of old and young
Who now regards the oppressing throng,
Who will releve the poor oppressed,
And give his suffering children rest
From all that have oppressed them here,
For they to him are very dear.

Some of these things in Ashfield done,
In ten years past that now are gone,
Till by your gracious king's decree
A stop put to the same we see.[13]
Tho' there was many pleading crys
Sent to the court[14] with weeping eyes
That they these sufferers would a[c]quit,
But yet they never would do it.
They plead the native right of men;
They plead there right the charter in;
But all in vain, no help is gain'd
'Till of the king they it obtain'd.
Encoragement, some times tis true,
They gave as if they would it do,
And yet they never did the thing;
Therefore twas sent unto the king.

Do any ask who suffer'd here?
The Baptist twas, I do declare.
Unto what court was it they cryd
So oft and had their suit denied?
Twas to the court in Boston met,
And when in Cambridge they did set,
These crys were sent, hoping they'd hear;
I know it for my self was there.[15]

But I have some thing more to tell
Which many witnis can ful-well,
The truth of which you may reseive
From the fore-going Naritive:
How one there apprehended was,
And under trial made to pass.
And tho no crime could proved be,
Yet is he keept in bonds we see.[16]
So if we mind the false reports,
Thet up & down are told about,
It may put us in mind what they
Did of the good old prophet say:
Report & then we will it tell,
We like to spread slander so well.
But what saith God in 'is word about
Mens raiseing of a false report?
Now all these things I think must spring
from Envy, that accu[r]sed sin,
Which 'bove five thousand years has done
Much hurt the sons of men among.

And now I would intreat all those
That for to read these lines shall chose,
Of cruel Envy to beware
As of a deadly hurt-full snare.
We'er [we're] told that wrath is cruel too,
And that anger rageth also,
But who can Envy stand before
Because it cruel is yet more.
O, when shall Envy be destroy'd,
And love be by all men enjoyed?
Let every one then love persue,
And Envy by the same subdue.
But you that harbour in your breast
Envy as if a pleaseing guest,
Know that the time will quickly come
When you will find your souls undone.
But happy they who do subdue,

Thro' grace, Envy that cruel foe,
And who the Blessed Jesus serve
And from his precepts never swerve.
Tho' they do suffer here in time,
Yet they in heaven ere long shall join,
To sing the praises of the Lamb
With all his saints for aye, amen.

Now if you ask the writers name
Here on these lines doth stand the same:
   E nvy it is a cruel foe;
   B e care-full then it to subdue.
   E nvy was seen in early days
   N ow may it sink no more to raise.
   E nvy it hates what God has chose;
   Z ealously then the same oppose.
   E nvy on earth much hurt has done;
   R ule may the Lord till tis put down.

   S o that Envy no more may wound
   M ay God the sinners hopes confound
   I n bringing them to die to sin,
   T o trust the Lord Jehovah in.
   H appy then be, eternally.

[7]
Baptist Opposition to
Slavery, 1773

New Englanders in general were slow to show concern over the institution of black chattel slavery even after they began to complain that the tyranny of the king was imposing slavery on them. There were black slaves in all of the New England colonies. Not until 1804 was slavery abolished in the northern states of the new nation.

The Quakers were the first to begin a concerted assault on this cruel institution, but their reasons for it were spiritual rather than an assertion of the inalienable rights of man to life, liberty, and the pursuit of happiness. Not until 1776 did the Quakers report that they had eliminated slaveholding among members of their denomination. (They expelled or "disowned" any member who would not voluntarily give up owning slaves or participating in the slave trade.)

In 1776 a Congregational minister, the Reverend Samuel Hopkins, published an attack on slavery and the slave trade. He lived in Newport, Rhode Island, a city heavily involved in "the triangular trade."

But in 1773 the Baptist Church in Ashfield, Massachusetts, where it was unlikely that there were any slaves, issued an official denunciation of the institution. Like the Quakers, the Baptists based their opposition on spiritual principles, not on natural rights. Perhaps their own suffering from persecution for their religious beliefs led to this unusual statement. The Ashfield church was not supported in its plea by any other Baptist church. Not until after the Revolution did New England Baptists take up this cause. Still, as in all major reforms, it is important to try to pinpoint the origins.

There is no doubt that the efforts of the American colonists to free themselves, as they saw it, from imminent "enslavement" by King George III and Parliament after 1765 provided an indirect but potent impulse to reconsideration of the enslavement of black men in America. Not having succumbed yet to the belief that Africans were subhuman, many Americans concluded that the rights of man applied to blacks as well as whites. And in their search for arguments for liberty, it is not surprising that many Americans found evidence in the Bible to confirm the laws of nature. What is not clear is why the American churches lagged behind the patriot political leaders in condemning slavery. Although there are many public statements in the pre-Revolutionary years demanding an end to slavery, there are few examples of action by Christian churches.

It is probably not very important to identify with absolute certainty (even if that were possible) which church in New England, *as a church,* first condemned the practice of Negro slavery in the American colonies. The title of this chapter is designed rather to direct attention to the general question: When did the Christians in that area, as organized believers, consider that it was an essential part of their spiritual commitment to assert their collective opposition to slavery? That antislavery sentiment among individual Christians was often expressed before 1773 is not debatable, but I have yet to find any such action taken by a church that antedates the action of the First Baptist Church of Ashfield, Massachusetts, and its minister, Rev. Ebenezer Smith, in October 1773. Perhaps publication of their statement will stimulate further inquiry and produce more evidence to challenge the current scholarly estimate that slavery was not an important religious issue in New England at the time of the Revolution.[1]

The first antislavery statement generally cited from the Congregationalists, the dominant religious body in New England, is the publication of the Reverend Samuel Hopkins of Newport, Rhode Island: *A Dialogue concerning the Slavery of Africans* (Norwich, 1776). Among the Baptists, notice has been given to some antislavery statements in the appendix added by John Allen to his address, *An Oration Upon the Beauties of Liberty* . . . (Boston, 1773).[2] But neither tract was an official statement of a church; they were individual statements by ministers. John Allen, who signed his anonymously published tract, "A British Bostonian," had only recently come to America from England; he was preaching on trial in the Second Baptist Church of Boston, and the church did not see fit to give him a call to become its pastor. There is no evidence that Hopkins's church adopted his views.

More impressive is the well-known action of the Quakers. But although the Philadelphia Yearly Meeting had taken an official stand against slavery as early as 1758, the New England Yearly

Meeting did not do so until 1773. And even then it was driven to action by visits from John Woolman of New Jersey rather than by local sentiment.[3] Moses Brown, a Baptist turned Quaker, who spearheaded the abolition movement in New England, did not free his own slaves until 1773.

From what we know of the New England Baptists, they were not particularly interested in this issue during the prerevolutionary era. They were too busy fighting for religious liberty against the New England establishment to think about chattel slavery. Several Baptist leaders in this region, such as Hezekiah Smith and Samuel Stillman, owned slaves at this time, and there is no recorded statement by any leading New England Baptist against slavery in the 1770s. James Manning, president of the Baptist college in Rhode Island, joined the abolition efforts of Moses Brown after 1783. Isaac Backus spoke indirectly against slavery at the Massachusetts convention in 1788. But at the time of the Revolution, there was no voice to join the unknown, backwoods minister in Ashfield, though he tried to arouse his brethren elsewhere in the colony to the cause.[4]

As the Ashfield antislavery statement is apparently exceptional, some explanation is in order. There is no evidence that any of the Baptists (of which there were about one hundred) in the town owned any slaves. In fact, in a tax list of 1766 there is no evidence that any of the six hundred inhabitants of the town owned slaves or were slaves.[5] Located one hundred miles west of Boston in the Berkshire mountains, it was an ordinary New England farming community only recently wrested from the virgin forest. None of the inhabitants was rich. None had any particular acquaintance with slavery.

I can offer only two explanations for the Ashfield statement: the first, for which there is no positive evidence, is that Smith had read the fourth edition of John Allen's *Oration* (if it had been published by that time). Allen's appendix, "The Rights and Liberties of the Africans," is a three-page statement in very general terms. Its only resemblance to Smith's statement is that both condemn "man stealing" and both refer to the same biblical text: "God hath made of one blood all nations." But Allen's tract lacks the pietistic fervor of Smith's plea. The second, based on circumstantial and internal evidence, is that people who have themselves suffered persecution are apt to be sympathetic to the oppression of others. Since Smith neither cites nor refers to Allen's tract, it seems that the second explanation is the more likely.[6] For a dozen years prior to the issuance of their statement, the Baptists of Ashfield had, they believed, been the subject of intense persecution by their fellow townsmen, the Congregationalists of the Standing Order. And when they took their problem to the courts and the legislature, they found that the whole establishment of Massachusetts was against them. That they were not paranoid in their feelings of persecution was proved by the action of King George III, who, upon their appealing to him, disallowed the law of the Massachusetts legislature under which the Baptists had seen their farmlands, pastures, orchards, and hayfields sold at auction to pay taxes levied on them by the town for the support of the Congregational minister. Their story is well known to history and need not be recited here.[7] But a word is in order about the little-known pastor of the Ashfield church, who, in rejoicing at the release of his own people from bondage, took thought for the bondage of others.

EBENEZER SMITH, CHAMPION OF LIBERTY FOR ALL

Ebenezer Smith was born in South Hadley, Massachusetts, October 4, 1734. His father, Chileab Smith, was a deacon in the Congregational church, a successful farmer, and, like many Yankees, a man who dabbled in medicine. Chileab Smith was also a pious and righteous man, who took his Bible and his place in the community seriously. Accused by another member of his church of injuring the man's son by using some homemade tools of dentistry, Chileab first proved his innocence and then sought to have the man censured by the church for slandering him. When the church refused, Chileab Smith began to question the righteousness of the church. Finding that it was founded on principles that he (and Jonathan Edwards, whom he consulted on the matter) considered contrary to true scriptural practice (i.e., they practiced Stoddardeanism, admitting to membership persons who had not experienced a conversion), he separated from the church. Shortly thereafter he left

South Hadley to take up residence in the new plantation of Huntstown (later Ashfield) about twenty-five miles to the northwest.

Thus, in 1751, Ebenezer Smith moved to the frontier town with
his father and several other New Light families. Every Sabbath
these pioneers held religious services in Smith's cabin. Chased from
their homes for a time in 1755–1756 out of fear of Indian raids
during the French and Indian War, they returned in 1757. Ebenezer Smith, like his father, became a lay preacher, having heard
the call to preach in 1753. Early in 1761, nine of those who worshipped together in the Smith homestead became convinced of the
truth of believer's baptism. That is, they could no longer feel justified
in the practice of infant baptism, convinced as they were that Jesus
and his disciples baptized by immersion only those who could give
a convincing account to their brethren of their conversion. In June
of that year these nine Baptists were rebaptized (most of them
having belonged to Congregational churches where they had been
baptized as infants) by Elder Noah Alden of the Stafford, Connecticut, Baptist Church. Alden helped them to form themselves
into the First Baptist Church of Ashfield (they called it the First
Church of Baptized Believers in Ashfield), and on July 2, 1761,
they voted to call Ebenezer Smith as their pastor. He was duly
ordained as minister over the church on August 20, 1761. Among
those assisting in the service were Elder Alden, Elder Whitman
Jacobs of the First Baptist Church of Killingly, Connecticut, and a
deacon from the Sturbridge Baptist Church.

Ebenezer Smith had married Remember Ellis on July 1, 1756,
and together they began to raise a family. Highly respected by his
fellow townsmen, he often was elected to local office. But most of
his energy went into farming. His church members were too poor
to pay him a salary, and like most rural Baptists at that time, they
did not believe that ministers should "preach for hire."

According to the custom in Massachusetts, one section of land in
every new town was reserved for the support of the minister of the
established church. Every new town was required to select a minister, build him a meetinghouse for worship, and pay him a salary
by means of annual taxation on the polls and estates of every inhabitant. In 1761 there were nineteen families living in Huntstown,
fourteen of whom belonged to or attended Smith's Baptist church.

They decided that they would levy a tax to build themselves a meetinghouse, and they also decided that their pastor was to be exempt from all civil taxes (by Massachusetts law the minister of each parish was so exempt). In other words, the Baptists decided that they would become the established church in Huntstown. At least so it appears from the records we now have, though the Baptists later said they intended to tax none but themselves for support of their pastor or for building their meetinghouse.

At the thought of Baptists gaining control of the religious life of a Massachusetts town, the Congregationalists marshaled their forces and fought back. The first thing they did was to challenge in the courts the right of Elder Ebenezer Smith to be exempt from civil taxes. And in 1762 they won their case on the grounds that only a minister educated at college or whose orthodoxy and learning were certified by the majority of the ministers in the county (all Congregationalists, of course) could be considered a duly settled minister according to law.[8]

Next they moved sufficient Congregational families into town so that, together with the votes of nonresident proprietors, they outnumbered the Baptist voters and took control of town affairs. In 1763 the Congregationalists brought their own minister, Jacob Sherwin of Yale, to the town and laid taxes to build him a meetinghouse and pay his salary. This was the beginning of a decade of bitter interdenominational wrangling that finally brought the Province of Massachusetts Bay into conflict with the king in privy council. Smith and his father played a leading role in this controversy, not only writing and presenting many petitions to the Massachusetts legislature but gathering the support of other Baptists throughout New England. Later, in 1774, Chileab Smith traveled to the First Continental Congress to join Isaac Backus and James Manning in trying to persuade the Massachusetts delegates (led by John and Samuel Adams) to grant religious equality to dissenters.

Ebenezer Smith was a good pastor but evidently not such a good farmer. At any rate, with a growing family he found that he needed more than voluntary gifts from his congregation to make ends meet. So in 1786 he requested that his church pay him a regular salary. This provoked a schism in which his father sided with those who opposed Ebenezer's request. A council of ministers upheld

Ebenezer, but his father nevertheless started a second Baptist church over which he became a pastor (though this church was never officially recognized by the Baptist association to which the First Baptist Church of Ashfield belonged). At some time in the 1790s Chileab Smith died at a ripe old age, and the two churches agreed to reunite in 1798. By this time Ebenezer was in ill health and had decided to move west for his declining years. His brother Enos succeeded him as pastor. Ebenezer Smith dropped out of sight after that, except that we know that he itinerated in western New York until 1816, when he settled in Stockton. He preached among the Baptists of that town until his death in 1824.

SMITH AND THE ASHFIELD STATEMENT
AGAINST SLAVERY

Unlike his father, who published a tract in 1774 in defense of the Ashfield Baptists, Ebenezer Smith published nothing. There are, however, among the Backus Papers at Andover Newton Theological School, more than two dozen letters, affidavits, and memoranda in Smith's hand concerning the Ashfield church. Among these is a thirty-seven-page autobiographical letter detailing the sufferings of the Baptists, which he sent to the Reverend Dr. Joseph Stennett in England in 1772. Smith was obviously not a great man, but he was typical of the Baptists who fought so doggedly for the principle of liberty of conscience and separation of church and state in his generation. More than once he risked jail for conscience's sake, and more than once parcels of his land were sold at auction by constables because he engaged in civil disobedience: refusing to pay religious taxes, which he believed the state had no right to levy on him. In the end, like most Baptists of his day, he acquiesced in the policy of turning in a certificate for himself and his church members so that the state might exempt them from such taxes. Not until 1833, ten years after his death, did the system of compulsory taxation for the support of religion end in Massachusetts.

Nevertheless, as the letter below indicates, Ebenezer Smith and his brethren believed in 1773 that God was angry with America. Trouble with the mother country was mounting, and continued oppression of God's chosen people (the Baptists) signified the coming of "a day wherein (I believe) god is a Returning the Captivity of Zion." Because God was showing his displeasure so clearly, it behooved his people "to hold up what we think to be true, that others may Judge, and try it by the standard of Eternal truth." In short, it was up to the Baptists to lead the way, to hold up the Word of God and to show Americans why God was displeased with them. Looking into the Bible to discover the cause of their own perse- cution, the Ashfield Baptists found the cause of "the poor Ne- groes." Perhaps this was the key to their sufferings as well as America's? For "We complain of Bondage and shall we at the same time keep our fellow men in bondage?"

The Ashfield statement seems to speak not only for freedom of the Baptists and the black man; it also speaks to the condition of the American colonies, pointing out why they are being put in bondage to the king and Parliament. Ever since the Stamp Act crisis the people of Massachusetts had been calling for their rights as Englishmen. Baptist pamphleteers, like Isaac Backus and John Al- len, had been quick to denounce the sins of Congregationalism and to apply the arguments of the Sons of Liberty to the Baptists' de- mands for religious liberty at home. Ebenezer Smith and his breth- ren took the matter a step further than most Baptists and two steps further than most New Englanders.

Smith's arguments for abolition anticipate those of William Lloyd Garrison and Theodore Weld. The biblical argument against slav- ery was easy for a frontier Baptist to read: "for god hath made of one Blood all nations"; "all men in the sight of god are brethren"; "woe to him that useth his Neighbours service with out Wages"; and "that men should do to you, do ye even so to them." Like Garrison, Smith believed that "it is High time for the watchmen to sound an alarm against this practice and for Churches to purge themselves from these." Slavery was not just a social problem, a regrettable misfortune, but a spiritual sin for which God would hold all men responsible; no Baptist Church should henceforth have communion with anyone who participated in it.

Having written his thoughts to Isaac Backus, the pastor of the First Baptist Church of Middleborough, Massachusetts, and the leading lobbyist, pamphleteer, and historian of his denomination, Smith decided to bring the matter before his church. He read them his statement, and they concurred with it, thereby transforming his personal views into a spiritual commitment by the church; they called on their brethren to join with them in witnessing against slavery, just as all Baptists had joined to witness against religious persecution through the union of church and state.

But it was not to be. The Baptists did not heed the call to denounce man stealers and to purge their churches as the Quakers were doing. Ironically, many historians believe that it became the honor of the secular state in Massachusetts, in the same courts that continued to tax the Baptists for the support of religion, to put an end to slavery under the constitution of 1780.[9] There is no extant answer to Smith's letter, nor was any action taken by the associations that spoke for the denomination in the Revolutionary era.

STATEMENT OF THE FIRST BAPTIST CHURCH OF ASHFIELD, MASSACHUSETTS, AGAINST SLAVERY

[Ebenr. Smiths letter about Negro's, Oct. 16, 1773. Received Nov. 6. I.B.][10]

Dear Sir,

Wishing Grace mercy and truth to be with you—I take this opportunity to write to you and communicate some of my thoughts to you. It is a day where in (I believe) god is a Returning the Captivity of Zion, and a discovering to his chh [church] the things that are contrary to his mind and will. And I think it agreeable to the gospel to hold up what we think to be true, that others may Judge and try it by the standard of Eternal truth. Therefore I take the Liberty to offer to your consideration one thing that I verily believe ought to be Razed out of the Church of Christ: and that is makeing slaves of the poor Negroes.

We complain of Bondage, and shall we at the same time keep our fellow men in bondage? Tho I know of but few in our Churches that have Negroe slaves, yet the thing is allowed and not Witnessed against as I think it ought to be. For altho under the Law the Jews wer alowed to make slaves of the Gentiles, yet not of thier brethren. And Jesus came to take away the wall of Partition and to set all mankind upon a Level, for god hath made of one Blood all nations

for to dwell on all the Earth. That I think all men in the sight of
god are brethren by Blood and birth as really as the Jews were one
with another, as we all sprang from the first—Adam. Under the
Law he that stole a man was to be put to death. And the apostle
saith, the Law is made for men stealers. And I have been often told
(and I believe truely) that this is the way that they often take to get
slaves from Affrica, even to steal them and bring them here and
sel them. And tho the buyer may try to excuse himself, yet he that
is a Companion of thieves is an abomination in the sight of God.

And there is a woe to him that useth his Neighbours service with
out Wages, and giveath him not for his work. Is not this the very
case with them that keep the Negroes in bondage? They must
spend all thier Life in thier Masters service and thier Children after
them, and Have no wages for it. Is this not keeping back the Hire
of Labourers by fraud, the cry of which will Enter into the Ears of
the Lord of sabaoth? The divine Direction is, all things whatsoever
ye would that men should do to you, Do ye even so to them, for
this is the Law and the Prophets. Which of us would love to be
treated or have our Children treated as we treat them? And thier
Children to be sold as Cattle in a market, and that dureing life. It
is some of the marchandize of Babylon that is to be destroyed.

That it appears to me it is High time for the watchmen to sound
an alarm against this practice, and for Churches to purge themselves from these. I am well senseable it will come across the profits
of them that have slaves and are Enriching themselves with thier
Labour. But they that shall behold the king in His Beuaty, Despiseth
the gain of Oppression. And if we will be Christs Desciples, self
must be Denyed.

These things appear Weighty to me, and I desire you to turn to
the following scriptures and Compare them together (viz): Acts:
17:26, Exodus: 21:16; Deu: 24:7, I Timothy 1:10, Isaiah 1:23, Jeremiah 22:13, James: 5:4, Matt. 7:12, Revel. 18:13, 2 Timothy 2:21,
Isaiah 33:15:17.

I trust that you will not take it amise that I have used this freedom
to write to you, but Hope you will take the matter into serious
consideration before god. And if you can have Opportunity, send
me your thoughts about it. If I have made any mistake, I Desire it

may be Rectifyed, but if the thing be true, as it appears to me at present, then it ought to be Received. I leave it with you to communicate what I have write to as many as you think proper.

And so praying that you may ever be found a burning and shineing Light in the Church of God, beging your pryaers for me, I beg leave to subscribe myself your poor unworthy brother and fellow Labourer in the gospel of Jesus Christ,

Ebenezer Smith

From the House of my pilgrimage in Ashfield in the 16th day of the 10th month

AD 1773

P.S. Give my love to Mr. [Samuel] Stillman and Dea[con Philip] Freeman when you see them and all the brethren that are with you. I read the above Lines to the Church and they Gave thier fellowship to Have them sent to you.

Massive Civil Disobedience as a
Baptist Tactic in 1773

*In 1729 the Baptists in Massachusetts and Connecticut were exempted
from religious taxes to support the established Congregational churches if
they provided a certificate proving that they were bona fide members of a
Baptist church. However, they usually found it very difficult to have such
a certificate validated by the town clerk, tax assessor, or justice of the peace
(always Congregationalists). The authorities charged with carrying out
this law were not only prejudiced against Baptists but realized that the
more certificates they validated, the higher it would be necessary to raise
the taxes on members of the established church. Furthermore, even when
their certificates were validated, Baptists lived under the stigma of being
"certificate men" or "tax dodgers."*

*Chafing under these harassments and roused in 1773 by the mounting
cries of freedom from the tyranny of the king and Parliament by the Sons
of Liberty in New England, the Baptists decided that they should no longer
submit to the restraints on their religious liberty. In 1767 the Baptists had
formed a Grievance Committee (modeled on the earlier Quaker committees
"for sufferings"), and in 1769 Elder Isaac Backus, pastor of the First
Baptist Church of Middleborough, Massachusetts, became its chairman.
As "the Agent for All Baptists in New England," Backus struggled to help
his brethren obtain fair play under the certificate system. In 1773 he concluded that it was unworkable and also contrary to the whole concept of
separation of church and state. He thereupon issued a call to all of his
fellow Baptists in New England to cease turning in certificates and to
refuse to pay religious taxes. He hoped that, by filling the jails of New
England, the Baptists could point out the hypocrisy of the Sons of Liberty.
It was not a tactic likely to win support for the Baptist cause, but like the
Sons of Liberty, they were appealing to a higher law.*

Two years before the Battle of Lexington and three years after
the Boston Massacre, the Baptists of New England launched a remarkable protest for religious liberty that has been all but forgotten
by historians. It was the year 1773, the year of the Boston Tea Party,
one of the most celebrated examples of violent civil disobedience

in our history. But the protest of the Baptists employed a different tactic, a calculated policy of massive, *nonviolent* civil disobedience. And they used it not against the king and Parliament but against the legislature and people of Massachusetts, to fill the Massachusetts jails, disrupt the established system, and focus the attention of the whole world on unjust discriminations against a persecuted religious minority.

Appropriating the slogan of the Sons of Liberty (to make the tactic even more embarrassing to the patriots), the Baptists claimed that they were fighting for "No Taxation without Representation." Only it was a tax levied by their neighbors and not by Parliament that they were protesting: taxes collected annually from all inhabitants of the province for the support of the ministers and the maintenance of the meetinghouses of the favored Congregational churches. Thoreauvians before Thoreau, the Baptists fought for liberty of conscience by a method that had once brought hanging to an earlier group of Protestants in Massachusetts, the Quakers. In 1773 refusal to obey the laws for the support of the established church would not bring hanging, but the Baptists could certainly expect imprisonment, distraint of their property, and harassment of their families.

The nerves of the people of New England were taut in the fall of 1773. Relations with the king and Parliament had gone from bad to worse since 1770, and with the colonies on the eve of their war for independence it was hardly a propitious moment for this noisy minority of Baptists to put their own personal grievances above the general welfare of the colony—of the thirteen colonies. To attack their own government at this time would surely make their neighbors consider them Tories. What was it that led the Baptists to make such a fateful decision in September 1773?

The decision of the Baptists to refuse any longer to obey the laws requiring them to file certificates attesting to the fact that they were Baptists (if they wished to be excused from supporting the Congregational churches) was itself the result of a long train of abuses and usurpations. From the point of view of the Baptists this train of abuses was designed to reduce them under the despotism of religious tyranny. For years now they had protested that the legislature had usurped the power belonging rightfully to God alone to rule over his church. But their petitions had been answered only by repeated injury; their rulers had been deaf to the voice of justice and consanguinity.[1] Somehow the gigantic hypocrisy of the Sons of Liberty, who shouted so loudly for life, liberty, and the pursuit of happiness for themselves while denying it to their own minorities, pushed the Baptists beyond the point of further endurance. "These Sons of Liberty," said one Baptist who had suffered from their oppression, "ought rather to be called Sons of Violence!"[2] For they had violated the rights of their own neighbors and the most sacred of all human rights: the right to religious liberty.

The problem of certificates was peculiar to New England. It had started in the 1720s when, having granted toleration to dissenters from the established Congregational churches, the authorities decided to grant them exemptions from paying the religious taxes (or tithes) levied in each parish to support the Congregational church and its minister. By a series of laws, beginning in 1727, the legislature of Massachusetts had gradually worked out a system that it considered not only fair but generous.[3] Any Anglican, Baptist, or Quaker (no other forms of dissent were exempted) who filed an annual certificate, signed by his minister and a committee of respectable lay members of his church and attesting that he was "conscientiously" of their persuasion, was to be excluded by the parish tax assessors from the annual ecclesiastical tax levied for the support of the established church in that parish.[4]

The certificate system raised endless problems for the dissenters, of whom the Baptists were by 1773 the most numerous. In the first place it raised questions of administration: no parish was eager to exempt large numbers of its taxpayers because the more it exempted, the higher the tax the remaining members of the parish had to pay. Hence, parish tax assessors used every possible means of invalidating certificates: claiming that they were not properly written or not properly signed or submitted too late or even that the man who submitted it was not really a Baptist but merely a hypocrite posing as one to escape paying his parish tax. It was a common witticism in New England then to say that most Baptists had allowed themselves to be taken to the river (to be rebaptized by "dipping") not "to wash away their sins" but "to wash away their taxes." Sometimes, when a Baptist minister died or left his church

for some reason, all of the Baptists in that church were told that
their certificates were not valid because they had no minister to sign
them. Hence, Baptists were frequently taxed even when they tried
to obey the certificate law; and if they took their cases to court, they
faced Congregational judges and juries who took little interest in
their plight.[5]

In the second place, there was a clear social prejudice attached
to being "a certificate man" in a small New England town. In the
seventeenth century Baptists had been outlawed, banished from the
Bay Colony, and whipped at the stake for their heresies if they were
discovered. The Puritans commonly associated them with the sixteenth-century Anabaptists who had seized control of the city of
Munster in Germany and set up a Baptist theocracy, murdered non-
Baptists, and practiced polygamy. By the eighteenth century Baptists were no longer legally ostracized as "subverters of commonwealths," but they were socially ostracized, abused, and ridiculed
as ignorant crackpots, fanatics, and troublemakers (not unlike the
Jehovah's Witnesses and other fringe sects often abused by respectable Baptists today). By and large the Baptists in eighteenth-century
Massachusetts found their adherents among the lower classes, and
their preachers were not college-educated, often being farmers, tailors, or cobblers who simply felt "the call" to preach and were chosen as pastor by their lay brethren. Baptist meetinghouses were
seldom found in the center of a town on the village green but
usually on the outskirts where the ne'er-do-wells and scapegraces
lived (just as Rhode Island, "the sink-hole of New England," was
the haven for oppressed Baptists and Quakers on the fringe of the
respectable Congregational colonies). Baptist children were picked
on by their classmates in the public schools, and their parents were
seldom elected to town office (except perhaps as "hog reeve") and
almost never to the legislature. In short, they were an out-group
suffering considerable discrimination and prejudice as social deviants within their community.[6]

In the third place, the certificate system raised for most Baptists
a serious issue of conscience and religious liberty. Christ had said
that men should give to Caesar only that which was Caesar's. They
did not think Caesar had a right to ask them for a certificate before
granting them the right to support only that church and minister

to whom they felt conscientiously bound to adhere. Slender as it was, the certificate was an acknowledgment that the state had some control over the conscience of the individual, for without this pinch of incense on the altar of Caesar ("the certificate bow") to the idol of the state, as they called it—not unlike the refusal of Jehovah's Witnesses to salute the flag) the state would demand a tax to support its favored denomination. Many pious Baptists therefore steadfastly refused to submit certificates, and for forty years prior to 1773 these pietists were practicing an individual form of civil disobedience.[7] In consequence they were duly taxed for the support of the parish church. Upon refusing to pay the tax (for the same conscientious reason) these individuals were either put in prison or the constable took some item of their property and sold it at public auction to pay the tax. Many a Baptist saw his cow or horse taken from his barn by a tax collector; one man had his horse taken out from under him on the highway; another, his saddle; another, his winter's supply of beef. Carpenters had their tools taken, and women saw their pewter plates and spinning wheels sold for a few shillings' tax. There is a record of one woman in Raynham, Massachusetts, who spent thirteen months in prison for refusing to pay a tax of eight pence. And these families were fortunate compared to the ones whose breadwinner was taken off to jail for an indefinite stay while the family was left to fend for itself. Sometimes the tax collectors even sold a man's land. In the town of Ashfield in the year 1769, 398 acres of land owned by various Baptists who refused to pay their religious taxes were sold for £19 15s, though they were worth £396 13s.[8] The price of individual civil disobedience then, as now, came high. By 1773 many Baptists were beginning to look for a more effective means of expressing their grievances than individual martyrdom.

The man who instigated the Baptists' decision to confront the establishment with a concerted colony-wide demonstration of massive civil disobedience was Elder Isaac Backus, pastor of the First Baptist Church of Middleborough, Massachusetts. For the past four years Backus had been a leader of the Baptist Grievance Committee, and in 1772 he had been named its chairman, "the Agent for all the Baptists of New England."[9] He and his committee of Baptist ministers and laymen had tried by every means within their power to persuade the authorities that the ecclesiastical laws of the province were discriminatory, oppressive, and contrary to their charter rights—to say nothing of their inalienable natural rights and their rights as free-born Englishmen. On August 30, 1770, the Grievance Committee had published an advertisement in the Boston *Evening Post* calling on Baptists throughout New England to send the committee details of any cases of religious persecution they had suffered, "such as the taxes you have paid to build [Congregational] meetinghouses, to settle [Congregational] ministers, and support them, with all the time, money, and labor you have lost in waiting on courts, feeing lawyers, etc." trying to prove entitlement to tax exemption. "[You have long] felt the burden of ministerial rates; and when these would not satisfy your enemies, your property hath been taken from you and sold for less than half its value. These things you cannot forget." The time had come for united action, and the Grievance Committee was prepared to organize it: "measures will be resolutely adopted for obtaining redress from another quarter than that to which repeated application hath been made unsuccessfully." In short, as early as 1770 the Baptists were preparing to appeal to the king to help them. Little wonder that their neighbors began to suspect them of being allied with those Loyalists who wished to divide the colonists just when most patriots were beginning to realize that they must all hang together or they would al hang separately.

Isaac Backus had not always been a Baptist. In fact he was born in 1724 into one of the wealthiest and most influential Congregational families in Connecticut, the founders of the town of Norwich. His grandfather had been a representative to the legislature many times and was appointed a justice of the peace; his father was also a representative, and his family was related by marriage to the Huntingtons, the Girswolds, the Trumbulls, and other leaders of Connecticut's ruling elite; one of his uncles married the sister of Jonathan Edwards, and his cousin Eunice married a governor. The Backus Iron Works in Norwich and the Backus farms, mills, timber, sheep, and cranberries were the sources of great wealth. Backus stood to inherit both property and influence had he only remained within the respectable bounds of the Congregational Standing Order. Instead, he threw in his lot with the Baptists, a sect notorious for its fanaticism, its illiterate preachers, and its dedication to denouncing the Puritans' churches as anti-Christian because they baptized infants by sprinkling instead of adults by immersion.

Backus, like many other Congregationalists, came to the Baptists by way of the Separate movement of the Great Awakening, a schism within the Standing Order produced by the enthusiastic religious revivalism of George Whitefield, Jonathan Edwards, James Davenport, Gilbert Tennent, and a host of other itinerant New Light preachers in the 1740s.[10] Backus was converted in a revival in Norwich in 1741. He left the Congregational church in which he had been raised because its minister disliked the extravagant fanaticism of the New Light revivalists and refused to reform his church practices to suit their views. Backus, his mother, and several other relatives helped to form a church of their own on New Light principles (dubbed the Separate Church by those who disliked it). For refusing to pay taxes any longer to support the "corrupt" and "formal" religion of their old parish church, many of these Separates, including Backus's mother, eventually went to prison. But before this occurred, Backus had decided that infant baptism was an erroneous practice not sanctioned by the Bible and had joined the Baptists.

From the time of his founding the First Baptist Church of Middleborough in 1756, Backus was one of the leading spokesmen for his newly adopted denomination. In dozens of tracts, sermons, and public debates with Congregational ministers he defended the Baptist position and attacked the errors of infant baptism and of an established church system. In 1764 he also helped to found the first Baptist college in New England (later to become Brown University), but it had to be founded in Rhode Island and was known as Rhode Island College during most of his lifetime. The Baptists had grown rapidly after the Great Awakening; many of those who separated from the Congregational churches followed Backus into this fervent but despised denomination of pietists. To distinguish these "new" Baptists from the "old" Baptists (who had existed in New England since the 1640s) they were called Separate Baptists, indicating their recent schism from the established churches. In an effort to stifle and stamp on this new sect, the laws that had granted exemption from religious taxes to the Baptists in 1728 and 1745 were rewritten after 1750 to make it very difficult for the new Separate Baptists to claim that privilege. As far as most New Englanders were concerned, the Separates who turned Baptist were simply tax dodgers.

This was not only an unfair accusation, but it showed little understanding of the fervor and dedication of these pietists. Far from taking religion too lightly, they took it all too seriously. They left the respectable Congregational churches of their families, friends, and neighbors, because they felt compelled to obey the commands of God in all of their religious practices. Being literalists, they looked in vain in the Bible for any statement commanding infant baptism; and when they found none (for in fact there are no such explicit statements nor even any specific examples of infant baptism in the Bible), they concluded that the practice was another of those corruptions brought into Christianity by the papacy, and they refused to practice it. Like their Puritan ancestors, the Separate Baptists wanted to carry on Martin Luther's Reformation until Christianity was as pure in its doctrines and practices as it had been in the days of Jesus and his apostles.

The Standing Order waged a long and, on the whole, successful battle against those Separates who did not become Baptists. The Separate churches, which in the early 1750s had numbered more than one hundred and were the largest dissenting body in New England, were so firmly denied any legal status that by 1770 they had dwindled to a mere handful. Their members either returned to their parish churches or joined the Baptists. The unsuccessful fight the Separates waged against religious taxation and for disestablishment was taken up by the Separate Baptists under the leadership of Backus, James Manning, the first president of Brown University; Samuel Stillman, pastor of the First Baptist Church of Boston; and Hezekiah Smith, pastor of the First Baptist Church in Haverhill. But Manning, Stillman, and Smith were not native New Englanders. They had come to New England from the middle colonies after the Great Awakening. On the whole they took a less radical—a less pietistic—position than did Backus and the Separate Baptists in New England in the 1750s and 1760s.[11] Although these college-educated Baptists from Pennsylvania and New Jersey were willing to sign petitions for alleviation of the ecclesiastical tax laws, to pass resolutions calling for a more liberal system of toleration, and to raise funds for the purpose of fighting legal battles in the courts against discriminatory actions by sheriffs, constables, and tax assessors, they were not at all eager to antagonize the ruling elite in Massachusetts. They preferred to appeal to the Congregationalists' sense of justice and fair play. Hezekiah Smith had once been appointed by the Baptists' Grievance Committee to go to England and deliver a petition to the king, asking him to intervene on the Baptists' behalf, but he found reasons not to go. Samuel Stillman, in whose Boston church John Adams, John Hancock, and Sam Adams sometimes deigned to sit and listen to his eloquent sermons, tried his best to prevent Backus and his Separate-Baptist brethren from adopting radical measures. James Manning begged off from activities in Massachusetts because he lived in Rhode Island; besides, he was so concerned for the good reputation of his college among Congregationalists that he never published any sermon or tract on controversial issues.

Separate Baptists who, like Backus, had never been to college went along with the conservative methods of these learned men from "the western colonies" for several years. There is every indication that if the tax exemption laws had been administered fairly, the majority of the Baptists would have accepted the certificate system; it was the prejudicial and dicriminatory execution of those laws that finally convinced them that the higher principle of religious liberty through complete disestablishment was at stake. After all, the Separate Baptists were radicals only in religion; their social and political views were virtually identical with their neighbors', and on moral issues—such as idleness, gaming, dancing, theatergoing, tippling, and luxurious living—they were decidedly conservative. It might be said that, in one sense, it was Manning, Smith, and Sullivan who were the liberals of the denomination. They were on friendly terms with many Congregational leaders; they were eager to please and to imitate their manners of dress and behavior; they sought their respect and therefore tried to seem as sophisticated and urbane as possible. Samuel Stillman, in fact, had asked several Congregational ministers of Boston to participate in his ordination, which they did (much to the disgust of the Separate Baptists in the rural areas). It was said (and correctly) that Stillman wanted to pursue the policy of open communion with the Congregationalists—a kind of religious integration that no Separate Baptist would condone. So strongly did rural Baptists like Backus oppose any communion with pedobaptists that Stillman never dared to put his policy into practice. But he always hoped that the Baptists would someday abandon their provincialism and assume a friendlier, more urbane, more ecumenical stance toward their Christian brethren in the Standing Order.

Prior to the Great Awakening a number of the Old Baptists had attended Harvard and had begun the kind of ecumenical movement that Stillman wished to see carried out. Elisha Callendar (Harvard, 1710) had even become intimate with Cotton and Increase Mather and had so far presumed upon his place that he had tried to exercise his right (as a Boston minister) to sit on the Harvard Corporation. He soon found that this was considered too "pushy" and "uppity," and he ceased to attend the meetings. His successor, Jeremy Condy (Harvard, 1726), became so imbued with the intellectual liberalism of his day that he found the religious fervor of the Awakening disgustingly vulgar and would not participate in it. When Condy was asked to join the board of trustees of the new Baptist College in Rhode Island in 1764, he chose not to do so because it was not sufficiently friendly to Congregationalists.

After the Awakening the Separate Baptists reacted fiercely against this liberal or integrationist approach to their problem. Instead of trying to ape those who discriminated against them and gratefully accepting such crumbs of toleration as were granted to them as a privilege, they began to demand religious equality as a right. To be a Baptist became something to be proud of and to fight for, not to be ashamed of. It would be far-fetched and inaccurate to suggest that the prejudice and discrimination against the Baptists in colonial New England was anything like what the blacks suffered (though the experience of W. E. B. DuBois growing up in nineteenth-century rural Massachusetts has some parallels). However, any sociological analysis of social deviants within a community would find certain factors worth abstracting. Broadly speaking, any minority group, any out-group, has two choices in facing the in-group that controls the system and regulates the values of the community in which it exists: it can either seek to imitate the in-group, to curry favor with it, and to accept gratefully whatever privileges it can extract for its good behavior, hoping someday to be admitted into it (this might be called the assimilationist or integrationist approach); or it can seek to maintain its own identity, to resist as much as possible the values and customs of the in-group, and to cultivate its own distinctiveness or group pride, demanding to be accepted as equal on its own terms (this might be called the pluralistic approach). In American history a whole host of out-groups has alternated between various adaptations of these two approaches: Quakers, Catholics, Mormons, Jews, blacks (after 1865), Asians, Lutherans, and Jehovah's Witnesses, to name only a few.[12]

The Baptists in Massachusetts tried both methods at different times. From the attainment of toleration in the 1680s until the appearance of the Separate Baptists in the 1750s, the denomination, at least its leaders in the Boston area, tried the assimilationist approach. And to some extent the post-Awakening leadership of the western Baptists—Manning, Stillman, and Hezekiah Smith—carried on this approach. (That is probably why Manning allowed Ezra Stiles, a Congregationalist who later became president of Yale, to draw up the draft of the charter for Rhode Island College in 1763. Stiles found that the Rhode Island Baptists wanted to have the college controlled by Baptists, not by any ecumenical corporation made up of Congregationalists, Quakers, Anglicans, and Baptists.) But the persecution of the Separate Baptists by the establishment, plus their intense pietistic assurance that they, and they alone, had the Truth—the conviction that God had given them a particular mission to carry out his will on earth—led the grassroots leadership of the denomination after 1750 (men like Isaac Backus, Ebenezer Smith, and Asaph Fletcher) to take the second approach. After 1800, when the Baptists had more or less achieved the religious liberty they sought, they returned to the pre-Awakening, assimilationist view. But during the 1770s, their quest for self-identity led them to the poignant choice of following their own self-interest just when the colony was most in need of unity against the mother country.

Ironically, the revolutionary spirit of the colonists served to increase the revolutionary mood of the Baptists. Not only did they see their Congregational neighbors engaging in concerted civil disobedience against the English establishment (the Stamp Act riots, the burning of the *Gaspee*), but the Spirit of '76 gave popularity to the concept of a higher law of nature and of Nature's God, a law of inalienable, God-given rights that were dearer than life and more important to preserve then any traditional human loyalties—rights that were worth any sacrifice, even their lives, their fortunes, and their sacred honor. If the Sons of Liberty could "appeal to heaven" (to use John Locke's phrase) for the justice of *their* cause (i.e., the protection of their property from unjust taxation), how much more right had the Baptists to appeal to heaven for *their* right to worship God according to their consciences! Isaac Backus phrased the Separate Baptists "Declaration of Independence" in precisely those terms: "many who are filling the nation with the cry of LIBERTY and against oppressors [in Parliament] are at the same time themselves, violating the dearest of all rights, LIBERTY OF CONSCIENCE." If the Sons of Liberty could quote John Locke's *Second Treatise on Government* in defense of life, liberty, and property, Backus could quote John Locke's *Letters Concerning Toleration* in defense of religious voluntarism: "The Great Mr. Locke" says, "A church is a free and voluntary society. Nobody is born a member of any church, otherwise the religion of parents would descend unto children by the same right of inheritance as their temporal estates, and everyone would hold his faith by the same tenure he does his lands, than which nothing can be imagined more absurd."[13] Yet in New England everyone was considered to be born a member of the established (Congregational) denomination until he could prove otherwise; everyone therefore was taxed to support the Congregational church in the parish in which he lived unless he presented a certificate. That was the law the Baptists decided in 1773 they could no longer obey. They would no longer bear the discriminatory stigma of being called certificate men.

To the Congregationalists, the Baptists' complaints seemed absurd. They were reacting out of all proportion to their situation. As John Adams, Sam Adams, and Robert Treat Paine were to say in 1774, the establishment that existed in New England was "a very slender one, hardly to be called an establishment."[14] Did it not exempt any dissenter (well, any Baptist, Quaker, or Anglican; Shakers, Rogerenes, and Universalists were not exempt) from paying religious taxes to support the establishment if he merely provided the tax assessors with a small piece of paper to identify himself? What they were whooping up as a great infringement of conscience was "only a contending about paying a little money," said Robert Treat Paine. They were being oversensitive. No one was discriminating against them. They were separate but equal, and they were separate by their own choice.

In a sense the Congregationalists had a point. Baptists in Massachusetts were far better off in 1773 than they were in England and in Virginia; in both of those places they had no right to exemption from tithes to support the Anglican church. And how did a certificate infringe religious liberty? They were free to preach where they wanted, to build churches where they wanted, to worship the way they wanted, and even to practice their absurd form of baptism in any river or pond they wanted. But it was just this tone of voice that was the rub. The truth was that however fair the law seemed to the Congregationalists, to the Baptists it was evidence both of religious persecution and social discrimination. Baptist children were hooted at by their playmates, Baptist adults were ridiculed when they marched singing to the river to be baptized, and Baptist preachers were stoned, mobbed, and sometimes beaten or driven out of town. Amused spectators who lined the riverbanks to watch a baptizing were always treated to the spectacle of the town buffoons imitating the Baptist preacher by wading in to baptize a dog or two.

Social prejudice against the Baptists reached the point where they were pointedly unwelcome in newly settled towns. Sometimes proprietors in new towns refused to sell them land. If they somehow got land, they were frequently harassed by their neighbors until they left. New towns were a source of speculation in property values on the frontier. Too many Baptists in a town drove down property values. The law required that every new town or parish build a meetinghouse and settle a learned, pious, orthodox minister within a fixed period of time, usually three years. To this end heavy taxes were laid on all inhabitants when a new community was started; and the more exemptions granted to dissenters, the more the taxes on the Congregationalists rose. This being so, who would move into a new community full of Baptists or other dissenters?

A large landowner in Royalston, Massachusetts, Colonel John Chandler of Worcester, inadvertently agreed to sell some land to a

Baptist named Elisha Rich in 1768. When Chandler discovered Rich's denomination, he said he would cancel the agreement unless Rich would "alter his principles." Rich refused, and the Colonel "declared he would purge the town of Baptists."[16] The largest land-owner in Bennington, Vermont, Samuel Robinson, was reputed to have a clever plan of segregation to handle the problem: Anglicans were sold land only in one particular area of the town, Congrega-tionalists in another, and Baptists in a third.[17] In 1770 a Congre-gational deacon in the town of Warwick, Massachusetts, told two young girls in his church who had attended a Baptist service that "he should rather court a Negro than a girl who had been to a Baptist meeting."[18]

Isaac Backus, as a member of the Baptist Grievance Committee, had dealt with all of these problems for many years. He had himself been arrested once in Middleborough for refusing to pay a religious tax and would have gone to jail had not a well-to-do neighbor paid the tax for him. Some Baptists were so stubborn they refused to let anyone pay their taxes for them. They preferred to prove their loyalty to their principles by going to jail. For a Baptist, going to jail had become a very common and praiseworthy act by 1773. Jail held no fear for most of them.

Still, there were those who felt that one should obey the law. God had ordained governments, and although men might try to alter unjust laws by all legal means, God said, "Obey the powers that be." Perhaps God meant the Baptists to suffer as martyrs and wit-nesses for his cause; it was a serious matter to start flouting the law. Where would society be if everyone who disliked a law refused to obey it?

It was a tense group of Baptists who met in the small frame Baptist meetinghouse in Medfield, Massachusetts, on September 7, 1773. Forty-three of them, ministers and laymen, had been sent as delegates from the churches all over Massachusetts to vote on the question that Backus had raised. He had raised it by sending a circular letter to all of the churches on May 5, 1773, stating that the Grievance Committee had just voted to ask the Baptists to con-sider the possibility of massive civil disobedience. "Beloved Friends," the letter began, "We have received accounts that several of our friends at Mendon have lately had their goods forcibly taken from

them for ministerial rates, and that three more of them at Chelmsford . . . were seized for the same cause, last winter, and carried
prisoners to Concord jail; so that liberty of conscience, the greatest
and most important article of all liberty, is evidently not allowed as
it ought to be in this country, not even by the very men who are
now making loud complaints of encroachment upon their own liberties." The root of all of these difficulties, he went on, "is civil
rulers assuming a power to make any laws to govern ecclesiastical
affairs, or to use any force to support ministers." Christ did not say
that his Truth should be promoted by the civil sword but by spiritual
argument and preaching of his Word. Hence, we

desire you to consider whether it is not our duty to strike so directly at this
root as to refuse any conformity to their laws about such affairs, even so
much as giving any certificates to their assessors. We are fully persuaded
that if we were all united in bearing what others of our friends might for
a little while suffer on this account, a less sum than has already been
expended with lawyers and courts on such accounts would carry us through
the trial, and if we should be enabled to treat our oppressors with a christian temper, would make straining [i.e., distraint of goods for nonpayment
of taxes] upon others under pretence of supporting religion, appear so
odious that they could not get along with it.

Each church was asked to discuss the tactic and to instruct its
delegates, or "messengers," to the meeting to be held at Medfield
in September in order to form a consolidated policy for the denomination. Backus had been encouraged by the responses he had received from some of the Baptist churches. Asaph Fletcher said his
church in Chelmsford was ready to "suffer in a Good cause"; "It is
our opinion that if our denomination generally and unitedly agree
to refuse the exhibiting of certificates for the future, it might tend
to bring the affair to trial and decision in Parliament." Ebenezer
Smith of Ashfield wrote to say, "It is our minds not to carry in any
more certificates but to take our lot with our brethren in whatever
shall be the consequence." But Backus had no reply from Samuel
Stillman or Hezekiah Smith.

The meeting began in complete agreement as to one thing, "that
our Legislature had no right to impose religious taxes upon us."
But "some doubted the expediency of our now refusing any compliance with their laws." Samuel Stillman, for one, was reluctant to
pursue this course. He knew the temper of the Congregationalists.

He knew that they would see any such action at this time as an attempt to divide the colonists. Ezra Stiles had confided to his diary that he was convinced that the Baptists were seeking aid and comfort from the royal governors and the king's ministers and could not be counted on to fight with the patriots if it ever came to revolution. Had the Baptists not refused to join with Stiles and his Congregational colleagues in 1767 when they tried to form a united front against the Anglicans, who were planning to send a bishop to the colonies? And had not a Baptist minister in Philadelphia, Morgan Edwards (one of the prime movers in founding Rhode Island College for the Baptists), published a letter in the Philadelphia *Chronicle* in 1770 taking the Tory side, saying he thought the Baptists in New England would prefer Anglican to Congregational rule?[19] Stiles, and others, knew that Governor Thomas Hutchinson of Massachusetts had aided the Baptists in petitioning the king in 1771 against alleged oppressions in the town of Ashfield. And the king had bought the Baptists' favor by annulling a law passed to aid the Congregational church in Ashfield on the grounds that the law was unfair to the Baptists.

The delegates in Medfield argued all Tuesday afternoon, September 7, 1773, but Backus reported "since we were not all of a judgment in this case, they [the opponents] stood against our coming to any vote upon it lest our want of union therein should give an advantage to our adversaries."[20] Samuel Stillman was the principal opponent of the plan. It must have been amusing to see him, a small, frail man, barely five feet tall and weighing less than one hundred pounds, facing the giant Backus, six feet tall and weighing over two hundred pounds; one with a thin, pale, sharp face, the other large, fat, and florid; one dressed in the latest fashion—black silk short clothes, immaculate white neckpiece and cuffs, and polished buckled shoes—the other dressed in country homespun, rumpled, untidy, unfashionable. Stillman was a shrewd, witty, and polished speaker, holder of master of arts degrees from three different colleges; Backus was powerful but slow of speech, uneducated beyond the common elementary schools. It must have seemed like David and Goliath, a classic example of brains against brawn or the city slicker against the country bumpkin. Yet the two men were good friends and had great respect for each other. They had worked long and hard together on the Grievance Committee. They differed over tactics, not principles. No decision was reached that first afternoon.

The next morning Backus continued to press the delegates to vote for his plan. Was he naive in thinking that "their oppressors" would take pity on them if they all were distrained or sent to jail? Or did he calculate that their neighbors would yield to this pressure in the desire to keep unity against the king? He never said. There were at this time roughly twelve hundred Baptist church members in Massachusetts and probably four or five times that many who regularly attended Baptist churches. (To be a member one had to be converted, and being Calvinist predestinarians, the Baptists felt they had to wait upon the Lord for grace before they could become immersed and join the church. Many a devout Baptist waited all of his life for conversion and never received it in any form he could recognize.) In a few towns in Massachusetts there were particularly large congregations of Baptists: three churches of them in Middleborough, two in Swansea, three in Rehoboth, and two in Boston. They were the only church in Bellingham, and they were numerous in Haverhill, Dartmouth, Adams, Charlton, Dighton, South Brimfield, Wilbraham, and Lanesborough. If all of these refused to file certificates and then resolutely refused to pay their taxes, the authorities would have a serious problem on their hands. A few towns and parishes might no longer be able to support the parish church and minister. If the Baptists were imprisoned, the jails might not hold them all; the court dockets would be jammed. And how would it look in the other colonies? Perhaps more dissenters or sympathizers would join the protest. The Episcopalians and Quakers were known to be upset by the thought of separation from England and might find this a good occasion to embarrass the patriotic hotheads rushing needlessly toward revolution.

"Matters labored all day Wednesday" in the Medfield church. Backus found many as eager for action as he was, and by the end of the day "many of the brethren became very uneasy at being thus held back" by the more cautious element. However, Backus agreed to put off a final vote until Thursday, probably content that he had a majority and not wishing to railroad the minority if he could win them. But the next morning his plan was almost frustrated, as Stillman adroitly presented a compromise. "Mr. Stillman, who had been against our coming to a vote, brought in" a complicated substitute motion in order, he said, to keep harmony. First, he asked that the vote be a written one, so that those who opposed the majority would not be the butt of any animosity; second, that those who favored the plan of civil disobedience should do so "in a spirit of meekness"; third, that those who "think it expedient to give certificates" be asked by letter if next year they might be willing "to unite" with those who did not. Fourth, "that the churches allow each other entire liberty without any hard thoughts one of another"; fifth, that reports of any who suffered from adopting the plan be sent to the Grievance Committee to be acted on; sixth, that the opinion of Baptist friends in England be requested on the matter; and seventh, that all churches contribute funds to aid those who suffered under the plan.

The compromise perhaps saved the cautious from embarrassment, but it hardly provided the kind of united action Backus sought. If each church was allowed to go its own way, the plan could hardly be considered official denominational policy. It would lead to division where unity was essential. On the other hand, Stillman had a point in noting that the congregational polity of the Baptists did not entitle the Warren Association to pass binding votes on member churches—especially in social and political affairs. Backus, of course, argued that it was a matter of conscience and obedience to God's injunctions, not a mere matter of individual opinion. More discussion followed, and then a vote was taken. Thirty-four delegates were in favor of Backus's plan and "against giving any more certificates." Six wanted to continue to give certificates, and "three [were] at a loss how to act." But the vote was secretly taken, and those voting against it were not bound by the majority. Stillman, too, could claim a victory. However, Backus had better than a 5-to-1 majority in his favor. Moreover, the delegates raised funds to pay for the publication of a defense of the plan, which Backus had already written and read to them.

Titled *An Appeal to the Public for Religious Liberty*, it was printed the following month and widely distributed; in 1774 a copy was given to every member of the First Continental Congress. It still stands as the most forceful exposition of the pietistic theory of separation of church and state written during the colonial era. In it the Baptists declared their independence from an unjust and oppressive religious and civil authority in Massachusetts: "We are brought to a stop about paying so much regard to such laws as to give in annual certificates to the other denomination [i.e., the Congregationalists] . . . because the very nature of such a practice implies an acknowledgement that the civil power has a right to set one religious sect up above another . . . [and] emboldens people to judge the liberty of other men's consciences. . . ."[21]

Isaac Backus never signed another certificate for any of his church members in Middleborough, and neither did many other Baptist preachers throughout New England. But unfortunately, the plan of massive civil disobedience failed to attain its goal. It failed because the people of Massachusetts became too involved in their fight for independence to bother about the certificate law. Very few Baptists were arrested or distrained for failing to obey it. In a sense, therefore, their effort may be considered a moral victory. They got away without paying religious taxes and without making their certificate bow to Caesar. It might also be called a success in that when the people of Massachusetts came to write a state constitution in 1780 they abandoned the old system in which the Congregational churches held a favored position. The Massachusetts Bill of Rights specifically stated that "no subordination of any one sect or denomination to another shall ever be established by law."

However, the people who wrote the constitution of Massachusetts were not ready in 1780 to believe that the Baptist theory of voluntary support for religion could work. They believed that most men were too wicked, too selfish, to give enough money to support religion properly unless they were compelled to do so. The safety, good order, and morality of society depended on religion, and "religion cannot be diffused through a community but by the institution of the public worship of God," said the constitution. Therefore, it was the duty of the government to see that public worship was supported by public taxation. The new Massachusetts Constitution of 1780 required every citizen to pay religious taxes, though it provided that the taxes paid by Baptists and other dissenters should go to the support of their own churches. The difficulty was that, in order to ascertain to which church a man's tax should be delivered, all of those who did not belong to the parish church (the church of the majority of the inhabitants of any town or parish) still would have to file certificates. In that respect the Baptists' campaign of civil disobedience failed. The Revolution did not bring religious freedom or complete separation of church and state to New England.

Isaac Backus continued to fight against the certificate system and against compulsory taxes for the support of religion until he died in 1806. Some of his most important tracts on this subject were written after 1780, and many a vigorous court battle was waged on this issue for another half-century. Not until 1833 was the Massachusetts Constitution amended so as to abolish compulsory religious taxes. However, Backus did live to see the virtual cessation of imprisonments and distraints for failure to pay religious taxes. Most towns and parishes had, by the year 1800, given up trying to force Baptists and other dissenters to pay taxes merely to have those taxes turned over to the Baptist minister. It was easier to leave the Baptists alone. Perhaps this was an acknowledgment that the Baptists, despite their feelings of persecution, had fought as loyally and as hard as any Congregationalist for independence. Stiles and the Congregationalists were wrong in suspecting them of being Tories. In addition, the Congregationalists had to acknowledge that the Baptists were not simply tax dodgers. Going to prison is a hard way to avoid paying taxes.

There is one ironic conclusion to this episode in civil disobedience. Anyone who has recently reread Henry David Thoreau's *Civil Disobedience* will remember that Henry himself, a Harvard graduate, had to make a certificate bow to the state in the year 1838 to avoid arrest for nonpayment of religious taxes. Although the amendment to the Massachusetts Constitution in 1833 had permanently freed Baptists and other members of dissenting congregations from filing certificates, the law still assumed that anyone born of parents who belonged to the parish church was a member of that parish, and upon coming of age he was subject to taxation for its support. Thoreau's parents were Congregationalists, and when Henry reached manhood in 1838, the tax collector appeared and demanded that he pay the tax levied on him by the town for the support of his parents' church. Thoreau refused and would have been carried to jail had not someone paid his tax for him. But then, he said, "at the request of the selectmen, I condescended to make some such statement as this in writing: 'Know all men by these presents, that I, Henry Thoreau, do not wish to be regarded as a member of any incorporated society which I have not joined.'"

Backus's sentiments exactly: no Baptist wished to be considered a Congregationalist just because he had been born within the bounds of a Congregational parish. Backus also would have agreed with the rest of that famous essay, in which Thoreau (whose transcendentalism was about as far as one could get from Backus's Calvinism) urged the necessity for civil disobedience against a state that oppresses men's consciences. But Backus, unlike Thoreau, would have gone to jail before he condescended to make out a certificate for the selectmen.

[9]
Baptists Face the Revolution, 1776

Many contemporaries of the Baptists considered them unsympathetic to the patriot cause in 1776, as has been noted elsewhere in this volume. A few of them (located chiefly in the middle colonies) were. By and large, however, the Baptists proved to be ardent patriots, fighting and dying side by side with their Congregational oppressors in New England and their Anglican oppressors in the Southern colonies.

Historians, like contemporary patriots, have expressed doubts about the Baptists' position during the Revolution. Some historians consider them reluctant patriots at best. This chapter attempts to set the record straight. Fighting against the king, who had so often befriended them against their oppressors, was not an easy choice. Many Baptists expressed fears that if the patriots won, the Congregational majority in New England would only strengthen the Standing Order, and Baptists would then have no outside authority to appeal to as they had done in the Ashfield case. Other Baptists believed that the free exercise of religion was one of the natural rights for which the Revolution was being fought. Had they realized that it would be another half century before the old Puritan establishment fell, many might have chosen differently.

The Baptists began their history in the American colonies as rebels against the corruptions of the Standing Order in both old England and New England in the 1630s. They quickly established a reputation for turbulence, for obstinacy, and for stubbornly insisting on their own interpretations of church order and doctrine against all authority. The law banishing them from Massachusetts Bay in 1644 described them as turbulent and obstinate men. Cotton Mather called them "anti–New England in New England." When

Note: All of the instances of Baptist oppression mentioned in this essay can be found more fully described and annotated in W. G. McLoughlin's two-volume work, *New England Dissent: The Baptists and the Separation of Church and State, 1633–1833* (Cambridge: Harvard University Press, 1971). For Isaac Backus, see W. G. McLoughlin, *Isaac Backus and the American Pietistic Tradition* (Boston, 1967).

The original documents concerning the work of the Baptist Grievance Committee and its affidavits are among the large collections of Isaac Backus Papers at Andover Newton Theological School, Newton Center, Massachusetts, and at Brown University, Providence, Rhode Island.

they persisted in their efforts to worship outside the established church, the authorities nailed shut the doors of the meetinghouse they had secretly built in Boston in 1679.

But although their enemies thought of them as stubborn rebels, the Baptists thought of themselves as the most devout of people. They had a sense of their own moral and religious duty to God that made them willing to defend their principles against all odds. Believing that God was for them, they cared not who was against them. Acting from a righteous sense of moral outrage and indignation against the civil and ecclesiastical corruptions they saw around them, these pietistic rebels willingly suffered social and criminal persecution in obedience to what their consciences told them was a higher law. "We must obey God rather than men," they insisted when told that their principles were contrary to good order and learned authority.

It was in this context of dissent and the resulting persecution that Massachusetts Baptists would face the dilemma of the American Revolution. They would ask themselves whether the Revolution really was their war or the war of their oppressors.

Considering the Baptists dangerous to civil order ("incendiaries of commonwealths") and equating them with the fanatical Anabaptists who took over the city of Munster in 1535, the Puritans tried every possible means of exterminating this species of dissent when it first began to appear in Massachusetts in the late 1630s. Puritan authority could be very vindictive. What saved the Baptists from hanging was that most of them had been honest, hardworking farmers and artisans, good Calvinists, and devout members of the Massachusetts churches. The Baptists believed that the Puritans, who had continued the Reformation of Martin Luther, John Calvin, and Henry VIII in England, seemed unwilling in the New World to carry on that reformation to its logical conclusion. Specifically, Puritans refused to give up the practice of baptizing infants and to adopt baptism of adult believers by immersion.

The early Baptists in Massachusetts Bay Colony suffered much and often for their soul liberty. We have noted earlier the steady imposition of fines, whippings and jail sentences upon Thomas Painter, Christopher Goodwine, Benanual Bowers, and Obadiah Holmes in the 1640s and 1650s as well as the successful expulsion

of Lady Deborah Moody in 1638 and the quasi-banishment of
Thomas Goold and his followers to Noddles Island from 1668 to
1674. They were not only suspected of being heretical and disturbers of the peace but of relying upon their own spiritual righteousness instead of upon duly constituted authority in church and
state. When the Puritan minister, Thomas Shepard, Jr., told Goold
in 1668 that it was wrong for him to separate from the Charlestown
Church because it was God's temple, Goold answered, "Christ
dwelleth in no temple, but in the heart of the believer."

It was this kind of remark, indicating to the Puritans that Baptists
thought themselves to be in direct spiritual communion with God,
that made them seem dangerous fanatics, capable of fomenting a
rebellion against the commonwealth on the grounds that God commanded them to do it. Only a few years before, some Quaker
women had invaded Massachusetts from Rhode Island, claiming
that they had a revelation from God commanding them to take off
their clothes and parade stark naked into a Boston church during
the Sunday morning worship—and they did it. In the seventeenth
century, Puritans thought Baptist doctrines constituted a kind of
"creeping Quakerism." "Most of the Quakers that I have had occasion to converse with," said Cotton Mather, "were first Anabaptists."

Fortunately for Thomas Goold and his friends, it was not in the
best interest of the Puritans in Massachusetts to be too hard on
dissenters at that moment, for the more the Puritans persecuted
dissenters from New England, the more Charles II persecuted dissenters from the Anglican Church in old England. After 1660 the
English Puritans (or Independents) began writing to their friends
in Massachusetts pleading with them to go easy on the Baptists. So
finally, in 1682, the authorities in the Bay Colony decided to let the
Baptists worship freely in Boston despite the loud lamentations of
the Mathers and others that this kind of toleration for error would
surely bring down the wrath of God upon them. (In fact, a synod
of Massachusetts ministers in 1679 claimed that King Philip's War
probably was the result of God's displeasure with the colony for
allowing the Baptists to remain there.)

Thomas Goold died peacefully in bed in 1675. He was succeeded
as pastor of this first Baptist church by John Russell, Jr., whom

William Hubbard referred to as "the unstable shoemaker of Woburn." From the beginning the Baptists consisted of farmers, shoemakers, leather tanners, potters, sailors, mechanics, and even chimney sweeps—the weak, the foolish, and the despised of this world. Baptists had no inherent respect for heredity, wealth, social status, or learning.

The Baptists' anti-intellectualism stemmed from the belief that the spirit of God communed directly with all believers and granted special gifts indiscriminately to the poor and rich, the illiterate and the educated (1 Cor. 12:4; 13:2). God did not require that a minister of his Word know how to write Greek or Latin, or even English, but only that he should have "an inward call" to preach the gospel. The Baptists were particularly fond of the text, "But God hath chosen the foolish things of the world to confound the wise; and God hath chosen the weak things of the world to confound the things which are mighty; And base things of the world, and things which are despised, hath God chosen, yea, and things which are not, to bring to nought things that are" (1 Cor. 1:27–28). God did not mean to confine his Word to any elite but to bring light and comfort to all. If this doctrine helped make the Baptists democratic, it also made them bold; if it gave them comfort and assurance, it also gave them courage and commitment.

As the first heroic age of Baptist martyrs died out in Massachusetts, the new denomination tried desperately to win the respect and friendship of their former persecutors. In so doing, they gradually lost that old fervor and piety that had been their hallmark. The fifth pastor of the First Boston Church, Elisha Callendar, Jr., attended Harvard College (class of 1710) and asked Increase and Cotton Mather to participate in his ordination, which they graciously consented to do. A later pastor, Jeremy Condy, also attended Harvard (class of 1732) and became so respectable that in 1759 he was asked to deliver the election sermon to the General Court. Moreover, the Baptists, like many Congregationalists after 1720, gradually were losing their commitment to the strict doctrines of Calvinism when the First Great Awakening broke out in 1740.

The Great Awakening of the 1740s and 1750s brought into being a whole new group of Baptist converts known as New Light Baptists

or Separate Baptists (because like Thomas Goold they felt compelled to separate from the corruptions they found within the Congregational churches throughout New England). There was even a
separation from the First Baptist Church in Boston by some ardent
Calvinists who decided, in 1742, that Jeremy Condy had been polluted by the liberal professors at Harvard College and no longer
preached the true gospel.

While the Awakening brought new life and vigor to the Baptists
of New England, it also brought increasing fanaticism and a new
kind of persecution of dissenters. This time the punishment was
not the whipping post but the compulsory payment of religious
taxes to support the Congregational churches. Many who stubbornly refused to make this payment went to jail for conscience'
sake or saw the sheriff sell their household goods to pay it. The old
Baptists had finally won exemption from religious taxes to support
the established churches in 1729, largely because having become
respectable they had ceased to proselyte and therefore ceased to
grow. Baptists being small in number, the Congregationalists graciously agreed to free them from supporting their churches and
ministers. But when a new group of religious fanatics rejected infant baptism after 1740 and left the Standing Order by the hundreds, the authorities declared that these Separate Baptists were
not entitled to tax exemption because they were not really Baptists.
That is, the Separate Baptists were different from the quiet old
Baptists like Callendar and Condy. Because the authorities considered them to be some strange, new, turbulent, and obstinate enthusiasts or tax dodgers, they decided not to extend exemption from
religious taxes to them.

It must be admitted that some of these Separate Baptists really
were a bit eccentric. Some in Attleboro, Norton, and Easton claimed
in the 1750s that they had become so perfect that they would never
get sick and never die. Some of these perfectionists (or immortalists)
concluded that they were too saintly to be bound by mere human
laws and promptly abandoned their spouses in order to cohabit with
new "spiritual soulmates."

The old Baptists did little or nothing to help the new Separate
Baptists, considering them unworthy of fellowship. The new Baptists reciprocated by considering the old ones too corrupt theolog-

ically to be worthy of fellowship with them. The Separate Baptists were left at the mercy of the tax collectors; for if the old Baptists rejected them, the Congregationalists were able to argue that they were not true Baptists. So once again the Baptists became martyrs, stubbornly suffering persecution for their beliefs.

One of the earliest of these martyrs was an elderly widow named Esther White. She belonged to the Separate Baptist church in Middleborough but lived in the nearby town of Raynham. Mrs. White, taxed eight pence for the support of the established minister in Raynham, refused to pay it on the grounds that she was a dissenter from that church and had joined another. The town of Raynham refused to acknowledge the legitimacy of the Separate-Baptist Church in Middleborough, so the sheriff carried Esther White off to jail. When her Baptist pastor, Elder Isaac Backus, went to visit her shortly after her incarceration, he said, "She told me that the first night she was in there she lay on the naked floor and she said she never imagined that the floor was so easy to lie upon before . . . and she said that she was easy to stay there as long as God saw best she should." Though she could have paid the eight pence and been released at any time, Mrs. White remained in jail for thirteen months, until finally the Congregationalists in Raynham became so embarrassed that they released her from the charge. During her stay in jail she was visited frequently by her fellow dissenters, who joined in prayers and hymn singing to strengthen her spirit of resistance.

In 1748, in Sturbridge, a group of Separate Baptists chose John Blunt as their pastor and petitioned the town to exempt them from taxation to support the Congregational minister. Their petition was denied. When they refused to pay the taxes levied on them, the tax collectors came into their homes and distrained their property.

[The collectors] stripped the shelves of pewter, of such as had it; and of others that had not they took away skillets, kettles, pots, and warming pans. Others they deprived of the means they got their bread with, viz., workmen's tools and spinning wheels. They drove away geese and swine from the doors of some others; and from some that had cows—from some that had but one—they took that away. They took a yoke of oxen from one. Some they thrust into prison, where they had a long and tedious imprisonment.

In the town of Haverhill a wealthy merchant and graduate of Harvard, John White, joined the Baptist church led by Hezekiah Smith. However, the town refused to exempt him from religious taxes to support the establishment. When he refused to pay, the constable entered his dry-goods store in 1765 and seized "one piece of Black Taffety containing ten yards of the value of six pounds; seventeen yards of white Alamode of the value of six pounds, four shillings, and eight pence; one brass kettle of the value of one pound, eight shillings." These were sold at auction to pay his tax, and not even John Adams, whom White hired to sue the constables, was able to win his case for tax exemption.

Similar prejudice against Baptists continued through the 1760s and 1770s. The refusal of the proprietor of Royalston, Massachusetts, to sell land to Baptists was noted in the preceding chapter as well as the arrest of an itinerant Baptist minister in Warwick, Massachusetts, in 1774. When the deacon of the Standing Church in Warwick said that he would rather court a negro than a Baptist, the Baptists took the view that no decent Baptist woman would marry a persecuting Congregationalist. Separate Baptists tried to prevent such marriages by quoting the biblical text, "Be ye not unequally yoked together with unbelievers" (2 Cor. 6:14).

In a score or more other towns in these years the Separate Baptists were arrested, imprisoned, or had their household goods or livestock sold at auction to pay their religious taxes. It happened in Berwick, Leicester, Hadley, Sutton, Amherst, Sunderland, Montague, Princeton, Bellingham, Scarborough, Gorham, and Bradford, to mention just a few. In one town a man had his saddle taken from under him by the sheriff while he was out riding, and he had to get home riding bareback. In another town an itinerant Baptist book peddler had some Bibles taken from him to pay his tax. One Baptist in the town of Montague was approached by a constable who told him that if he did not pay his religious taxes at once he would distrain one of his swine. The Baptist responded sardonically, "Your claim to that animal may be good, for I have understood that your master took possession of that species of animals in the land of the Gadarenes many years ago."

Of all of the cases of oppression against these dissenters by far the most famous and most important was the affair in the town of

Ashfield. This case became a cause célèbre of Baptist persecution because it seemed to prove that Baptists were indeed second-class citizens whose very presence in a community was considered detrimental to progress. A Separate-Baptist church was founded in Ashfield in 1761 when the frontier community was still known as Huntstown. Two years later the Congregationalists in the town hired a minister and started to build a meetinghouse. Naturally, they taxed the Baptists to pay for the meetinghouse and for their minister's salary. This was perfectly legal until 1765, when the town was incorporated. The law read that once a town was incorporated it must grant tax exemption to bona fide dissenters. The Congregationalists in Ashfield refused to grant such exemption, claiming that these people were not really bona fide Baptists. When the Baptists protested, the legislature passed an extraordinary law requiring *all* inhabitants in this town to support the Congregational minister. The Baptists considered this law unconstitutional and continued to refuse to pay religious taxes. In Ashfield, however, instead of imprisoning them or distraining their livestock or household goods, the tax collectors began to auction off their land. Ten acres were taken from the Baptist pastor, Ebenezer Smith; twenty acres from his father, Chileab Smith; and various parcels from other Baptists, to the total of 398 acres of some of the best land in the town. These were sold for a pittance to gleeful Congregational neighbors. To make matters worse, the land taken from the Baptists was improved land on which they had a burial ground, apple orchards, and even houses. When the Baptists complained that the Congregationalists seemed determined to drive them out of the town by confiscating their land, the town replied that the Baptists were nothing but fanatics and tax dodgers whose church was "a kind of receptacle for scandalous and disorderly persons and . . . a sink for some of the filth of christianity in this part of the country." Finally, as if enough already had not been done, the Congregationalists accused Chileab Smith of manufacturing counterfeit money in his barn and had him arrested.

Historically, it is significant that these eighteenth-century Baptists refused to take all of this oppression lying down. They did more than simply suffer for conscience' sake. They stood up and fought back. And it is their fight for religious liberty that ties the Great

Awakening to the Revolution. It was a fight in which rural Baptists
bore the brunt of the effort, though they were ably assisted by some
of the more urban and urbane Baptists in Boston such as Samuel
Stillman and Isaac Skillman.

Their resistance against oppression took various forms. First, the
Baptists wrote petitions to their neighbors stating their principles
of religious freedom in terms as eloquent and important for the
history of religious freedom as those of Roger Williams a century
earlier or of Thomas Jefferson a generation later. Second, they
brought lawsuits against tax collectors, constables, assessors, and
town treasures to try to win their battle in the courts after losing it
in town or parish meetings. Third, they wrote protests to the General Assembly in Boston and tried to obtain changes in the laws
governing the religious establishments. Fourth, they formed a
Grievance Committee that (very much like the NAACP or the
ACLU today) gathered affidavits and witnesses for test cases, raised
funds, hired lawyers, and produced tracts or letters to the newspapers to educate the public at large. The Grievance Committee
also sent lobbyists to Boston to argue before legislative committees
to clarify the laws governing toleration and tax exemptions. After
1771 the tax exemption law was rewritten so as to include Baptists
who produced a certificate from their church saying they were baptized by immersion, but this was seldom fairly administered.

In addition, the Baptists occasionally sent appeals to the king in
London, asking him to intervene on their behalf, an action that, in
the case of the Ashfield Baptists, resulted in the king's overturning
the Massachusetts law that had led to the loss of their land. This
was in 1771. Thereafter, as the colonists began to reach the climax
of their own rebellion against the oppression of the king and Parliament, the Baptists adopted a new technique they had learned
from the Sons of Liberty and other patriots: the tactic of massive
civil disobedience. The most important example of this occurred
in 1773, when most of the Baptist churches in Massachusetts agreed
that they would no longer give in certificates of their membership
in dissenting churches as the law required for exemption from religious taxes. Arguing that certificates were themselves an illegal
action against religious freedom, the Baptists said they would fill

the jails of every town in New England rather than submit any longer to what they called "taxation without representation."

As the Revolutionary War approached, Baptists faced a dilemma. Did they stand to gain more by supporting the colonists against the king, or would they be better off to remain neutral or to support the king? The king, after all, had on several occasions helped the Baptists and other dissenters against religious oppression by the colonists. It was not an easy choice.

In 1774 the Baptists of Massachusetts, led by Isaac Backus of Middleborough, Chileab Smith of Ashfield, and James Manning of Providence, went to the First Continental Congress in Philadelphia to try to win support from the other colonies for their fight against the Congregationalists in New England. They made the tactical mistake of accepting support from the Philadelphia Quakers. John Adams, Sam Adams, and Robert Treat Paine, the Massachusetts delegates to the Congress, were astonished at the effrontery of these Baptists and their Quaker allies. They accused them of trying to split the colonists over a minor issue when the safety of the colonies required unity in defense of their liberties. Since the Quakers of Philadelphia were well known as opponents of colonial independence and were suspected of being Tories, the Baptist effort in Philadelphia probably did them more harm than good. But if they could no longer seek help from the king, and if the Continental Congress would not aid them, where could they turn for help?

Part of their dilemma lay in their pietism; for them, spiritual affairs were far more important than worldly affairs. They had taken little interest in the political furor over the Stamp Act. Their only interest in politics had been to obtain the right to worship God as they thought best. Isaac Backus, the leading spokesman for the Massachusetts Baptists, said in 1773, "For my part I am not able to get a pair of scales to weigh those two great bodies in, the Episcopal hierarchy and the New England Presbyterians [i.e., Congregationalists] so as to find out exactly which is the heaviest [oppressor of dissenters]." As chairman of the Baptist Grievance Committee, he had full knowledge of the Congregationalists' disregard for the rights of Baptists. However, as the controversy with England grew hotter, Backus came to see the impossibility of neutrality. In 1775 he wrote, "I perceived that things were likely to come to such a pass [soon] that there could be no neuters among us, and that my advice might frequently be asked by serious people about which side was right . . . for I was very sensible that bad men and bad actions were to be expected on both sides of the question in this sinful world."

Here is the epitome of the Baptists' dilemma between patriotism and pietism. As pietists they were prepared to believe both sides were wrong, but as patriots they were inclined to support those who had oppressed them most. Yet the quarrel with the mother country was not of their making. As opponents of the Standing Order, as members of the poor, the outcast, the powerless, the Baptists had not shared in the making of colonial policy. To solve the dilemma the Baptists had to emerge from their pietistic shell and decide just how they would stand in the secular world. "The result of my inquiry," said Backus, again speaking for the majority of his brethren, "was a full conviction that the claim of the British court was so unjust that all lawful means ought to be used to guard against them." But what happened when "lawful means" failed?

Between 1771 and 1775 the Baptists gradually came to realize that their search for Christian liberty was tied directly to their Congregational neighbors' search for political liberty. The tyranny and corruption that the Baptists had myopically seen only in the New England establishment suddenly loomed before them in broader and more horrendous terms from beyond the ocean. The tightening of British imperial policy in a series of Parliamentary acts after 1765 slowly evinced a design that penetrated even the pietistic mind—a despotic design to enslave all of the colonists. Once the Baptists recognized this new and greater danger to their freedom, the same arguments they had marshaled against the tyranny of Massachusetts were readily turned against the tyranny of Parliament. Civil disobedience against religious taxes could be applied to rebellion against tea and sugar taxes levied by a corrupt and unrepresentative Parliament. The higher law of God, utilized to flout the ecclesiastical constitution of New England when it subverted the religious rights of the Baptists, now became a justification for flouting the British constitution when it seemed subversive of the political rights of Englishmen.

When Backus agreed with John Locke that "truth certainly would do well enough if she were once left to shift for herself," he meant Gospel Truth. What he feared from Parliament and the Anglican episcopate was just what he feared from the Congregational Standing Order, a loss or hindrance of this freedom. Of course, Baptists also valued their rights of property, their natural rights, their right of local home rule and annual elections. But as pietists they did not see that these rights were threatened by the king until they came to believe that he threatened their religious liberty. But because it took them longer to see this, because until almost the last moment they felt the king was their principal bulwark against religious oppression, Baptists seemed to be Tories to their neighbors. The Baptists, therefore, became patriots after 1775 because they finally saw in the rise of imperial control a potential hindrance or obstruction to the free flow of God's grace, even a greater hindrance than that of the Standing Order in New England. If Parliament could pass any laws it wished to regulate the colonies, it could pass laws to hinder the freedom of preaching evangelical religion; it could establish an Anglican episcopate, institute tithing and ecclesiastical courts, and enact a Clarendon Code for colonial nonconformists. The streams of God's grace must not be dammed up again by the laws and institutions of men as they had been before the Great Awakening of 1740. As Backus put it, "The command of heaven is, *Let them run down*; put no obstruction in their way. No, rather be in earnest to remove everything that hinders their free course." When Backus said he agreed with the Sons of Liberty that "he is not a free man but a slave whose person and goods are not at his own but another's disposal," he was not so much concerned with life, liberty, and property in the Lockean sense as he was with Christian liberty: "The true liberty of man is to know, obey and enjoy his Creator and to do all the good unto and enjoy all the happiness with and in his fellow creatures that he is capable of."

Jefferson's phrase, "the pursuit of happiness," in 1776 bound the pietist and the rationalist, the deist and the dissenter, the Congregationalist and the Baptist more surely than any concept of constitutional liberty or the rights of Englishmen, for each could define happiness in his own way. To the pietistic Baptist, happiness was first and foremost obedience and service to God—the salvation of souls, the evangelization of the world. Civil liberty was always a means, not an end. Natural rights, social contract, the protection of property provided the milieu for the reception, distribution, and expansion of God's grace. But the pietistic mission was to all mankind, like Jefferson's proclamation of inalienable rights. Not an American nation but a Christian world was the ultimate goal. Toward this end the American Revolution was merely an important incident—and the French Revolution another—in releasing mankind from the dead hand of past corruption. The millennium had been on its way since the birth of Christ. The Revolution was a giant step forward toward that "Great Day."

The Baptists responded to the "shot heard 'round the world" less out of political than spiritual logic. The Spirit of '76 got into them just as the Holy Spirit got into them in revival meetings. When Backus heard of the Battle of Lexington, he quickly drafted a sermon, to be preached the next Sunday, in which he said that "the doctrine of passive obedience and non-resistance to kings" has brought America "upon the brink of popery and slavery." Rashly, he went on to say that George III had "violated his coronation oath" when he signed the Quebec Act and that Parliament had acted in "open violation of the essential rules of the English government." A few days later he noted more calmly in his diary that he might have gone a bit too far. Nevertheless, when the war came, Baptists readily and consistently enrolled in the revolutionary army and militia, and many of their minister served as chaplains. They shared the hope that any later dissenting groups have held in wartime—the Irish Catholics in 1861, the European immigrants and American Indians in 1917, the Nisei in 1941, the black Americans in all of our wars—that their free and voluntary participation in the defense of their homeland would win for them the respect of their neighbors and ultimately the full equality they earnestly desired. (However, some Baptists did feel that it was carrying patriotism too far when one of their women dressed in men's clothes and enlisted. For this she was disciplined by her church in Middleborough.)

But the respect and freedom that Baptists hoped for was much longer in coming than any of them could have realized. Backus, who lived until 1806, did not see the time when Congregationalism was disestablished in any New England state. In fact, in 1780 he discovered that in a fraudulent election-count the dominant Congregationalists had ratified a clause in the new state constitution of Massachusetts that made the plight of dissenters even worse thereafter than it had been before the Revolution. Not only did they fail to gain tax exemption, but also they found that as they increased in numbers they actually incurred even worse abuse at the hands of their neighbors.

For example, in May 1778 a group of Baptists in Pepperell, Massachusetts, met on the western bank of the Nashua River to witness the baptism by immersion of several of their newest converts. While they were assembled, a mob of angry townspeople, armed with clubs and sticks, arrived and broke up the ceremony. As the Baptists were dispersing, some local wits grabbed a passing dog and carried him into the river to perform a mock baptismal service to the great amusement of the mob. Although some in the crowd shouted that the meeting was a Tory plot, there is no evidence that any of these Baptists were Tories. A more sympathetic onlooker said of the riot, "Great God, is this the Liberties our country affords?" When Isaac Backus and the Grievance Committee of the Baptists arrived in Pepperell some weeks later to obtain affidavits for a lawsuit against the mob, Colonel Henry A. Woods, a hero of the Battle of Bunker Hill and one of the ringleaders of the mob, said at town meeting that if Backus came he would personally drive him out of town.

The real cause of the riot was that Baptists were not welcome in most rural towns. They lowered the social tone, and if large numbers of them were exempted from taxes, it made it more difficult for the Congregationalists to hire and pay the established minister. In Pepperell in 1778 the town was seeking a Congregational minister to replace one who had died. "We were sensible," said the townspeople, "that if we were reputed an irregular, disorderly people, no gentleman [of the cloth] of worth could chuse to come among us." So to prove how orderly and respectable they were, they decided to drive out the Baptists with clubs and sticks. Although the Baptists decided not to bring suit in this case, they felt they had to do so four years later when a mob in the town of Hingham forcibly ejected a Baptist preacher from a private home while he was conducting a service. Again this mob was led by some of the most respectable men in the town, leaders of the revolution for American liberty.

In May 1782 a mob broke into the home where Richard Lee was preaching to a few brethren, "seized Mr. Lee by his left arm and his collar and twitched him away with great violence, and others, taking hold of him, hauled Mr. Lee along clear out of town, cursing and swearing most terribly. . . . And one of them cast soft cow dung in Mr. Lee's face. Then one Captain Theophilus Wilder took a long club over Mr. Lee's head and swore that if he ever came into that town again he would take him & tie him up and whip him thirty stripes." To which Lee replied in good pietistic style, "That is not so much as they whipt Paul." This time the Grievance Committee not only hired a lawyer and brought suit against Wilder and the other mob leaders, but they won the case. However, as so often happens, the lawyers' fees were so large that Lee and his friends got very little of the damage money.

When the Revolution ended and the Baptists in Massachusetts discovered that under the new state constitution they were not any better off, and perhaps worse off, than they had been before, they were faced with a second dilemma: how were they going to make the United States a Christian nation? They were convinced that the nation and the states should have certain powers to protect religious liberty and to curtail unchristian behavior. Yet most Baptists, especially those in rural areas, favored a weak central government, believing they could make better headway toward liberty within their own town meetings than through a national Congress.

It is hardly surprising that many rural Baptists sided with Daniel Shays's brief rebellion in 1786 against the high taxes that eastern bankers and merchants were able to force through the legislature. For similar reasons most rural Baptists also opposed ratification of the federal Constitution in 1788. Several of the more prominent urban Baptists, however, such as Samuel Stillman and Thomas Gair in Boston and James Manning in Providence, favored the new Constitution. The Federalist leaders in Boston brought Manning to the convention there in hopes that he might persuade Baptist delegates to vote for ratification. (John Hancock asked Manning to deliver the closing prayer at the convention.) But the rural Baptists, especially those in the western part of the state, opposed ratification. In part they did so because they feared that a strong federal government would impose heavier taxes and restrict the freedom of local self-government; and many pointed out that the Constitution did nothing to guarantee religious liberty. (Even the passage of the first amendment to the Constitution in 1791 did not prevent Massachusetts from maintaining its system of compulsory religious taxes to support Congregationalism until 1833.)

More than twenty of the delegates to the Massachusetts ratifying convention were Baptists; five of them were Baptist ministers. Virtually all of them came with instructions from their towns to vote against ratification. Isaac Backus, chosen as one of the Middleborough delegates, reported in his diary, "Elder Alden of Bellingham, Elder Rathbun of Pittsfield, Elder Tingley of Waterborough . . . all voted against it and so did two-thirds of the baptist members of the Convention, of which there were above twenty. Elder Stillman and I, with twelve Congregational ministers, voted for it, though doubtless with very different reasons." When elected to the convention, Backus himself expected to vote against it. But after listening to the arguments he changed his mind. He believed that national unity was paramount, and he felt that the clause in the Constitution prohibiting any religious tests for federal officeholders was an important step toward religious liberty. However, when he returned to Middleborough, he found his constituents very unhappy about his decision: "some are very uneasy at my voting for the new Constitution," he wrote in his diary. He felt obliged to preach several sermons explaining his decision. More widely read, more sophisticated, and somewhat more conservative than the rural Baptists, Backus was not representative of their feelings in this matter.

However, Backus did express representative views in respect to the importance of making the new nation a Christian country. For example, he consistently opposed the incorporation of Baptist congregations even when the Massachusetts courts ruled in 1785 that incorporation would entitle dissenting churches to exemption from religious taxation. Noting that what Caesar could give, Caesar could take away, Backus argued strenuously that religious liberty could have no firm security in a system that required dissenters to ask permission of the legislature to be incorporated. Unfortunately, many Baptist churches thought Backus was needlessly quibbling on this question and applied for incorporation.

The separation of church and state in America was never a simple matter. Backus himself inconsistently signed a petition initiated by the Congregationalist clergy asking the federal government to license the publication of Bibles. He did so because he feared that inaccurate and heretical translations might lead people into heresy. But of course the power of license could become the power to refuse to license. It is worth noting in relation to missionary activity that the Baptists never had any qualms about taking the taxpayers' money to support their mission schools and churches among the Indians, just as they saw nothing wrong with the government's granting exemption from property taxes to all churches—an indirect form of government support for religion that recently has aroused much controversy.

Perhaps more difficult to understand was the willingness of Baptists to support the Massachusetts law requiring all persons to attend church on Sunday, and to accept the prevailing practice of having public school teachers inculcate religion in their pupils through the Westminster Confession of Faith. Backus even seems to have supported a clause in the Massachusetts Constitution that required all officeholders to take an oath stating, "I believe the Christian religion and have a firm persuasion of its truth." This oath clearly discriminated against Jews, deists, humanists, and perhaps Unitarians. He also defended test oaths, which many Catholics found discriminatory, such as oaths requiring them to forswear allegiance to any foreign power.

More important, but not necessarily more consistently, the Baptists (particularly rural Baptists) supported laws against theatergoing, blasphemy, disturbing the Sabbath, card playing, and gambling. They hedged somewhat in regard to the use of lotteries because the Baptist College in Rhode Island employed lotteries to raise money for its buildings. Only a few eccentric Baptists, like John Leland of Cheshire, opposed the use of public tax money to pay for state and federal legislative chaplains or the government's practice of proclaiming thanksgiving and fast days. (In New England, on such days all work was supposed to cease, and people

were expected to attend church as on the Sabbath.) When Backus
said that there should always be "a sweet harmony" between church
and state, he took a very different view from that of Jefferson and
Madison. They wanted the state to be absolutely neutral and secular; they believed religious faith was simply a matter of opinion
on which good men might differ. Jefferson did not do himself any
good with the Baptists when he said, "It does me no injury for my
neighbor to say there are twenty gods or no God. It neither picks
my pocket nor breaks my leg."

For the Baptists there was only one true religion and only one
true way to worship God. But being a minority, they had to believe
in religious freedom, and so they made a virtue of necessity. What
they really meant was that the clear truth of the Baptist persuasion
would quickly prevail over all other denominational forms in a free
marketplace for religious preaching. Jefferson, when seeking a
treaty with the Turks in Algeria, stated publicly that America was
not a Christian nation. The Baptists believed that if it was not Christian it should be. The fact that so many Americans joined the Baptists in the next century seems to indicate that they were more in
harmony with the true spirit of the Revolution than were Jefferson
and the deists.

Recent historical interpretations of the Revolution have pointed
out that in many respects it was a kind of civil revival, a crusade by
the American people to throw off the corruption that England was
forcing on the colonies and to establish here a republic that was
purer and more virtuous than any government the world had seen.
Sam Adams, though no friend to the Baptists, hoped that America
would become "a Christian Sparta," so dedicated to liberty and
justice for all that its farmer-citizens would, like Cincinnatus, altru-
istically leave their plows and families to rise to the defense of the
inalienable rights of man whenever they were threatened.

The Baptists fully shared this hope. It was expressed in their
egalitarian anticlericalism, in their millennial optimism, in their
inveterate individualism, and in their increasingly radical definition
of disestablishment (which we now define as voluntary support of
religion).

[10]

Mob Violence against Baptists, 1778

Part of the resentment against Baptists may have resulted from a general opinion that they were not ardent patriots. Part of it stemmed from the ancient Puritan prejudice against Anabaptists. But as new towns spread westward from the coast, a new source of antipathy arose on the grounds that they lowered real estate values and gave any community a bad reputation. To attract settlers, a new town had to convince them that taxes would be low. The major need for taxes in a new town came in building a meetinghouse and hiring a minister. If the townspeople were mostly Congregationalists, the religious taxes would be spread equally according to property evaluations. But if a town contained too many dissenters and if they succeeded in obtaining exemption from religious taxes and built their own meetinghouse, hired their own ministers, attracted other dissenters, then the religious taxes on the Congregationalists increased. Consequently newly formed townships did all they could to discourage settlers known to be dissenters.

Usually, the first sign that dissent was brewing in a town was the arrival of an itinerant Baptist preacher. He would hold meetings in people's homes or in an open field and then return periodically until he had converted

Note: This chapter is based primarily on the manuscript collections of Isaac Backus's papers at Andover Newton Theological School, Newton Center, Massachusetts, and at Brown University, Providence, Rhode Island. The Andover Newton collection contains the fourteen affidavits collected by Backus, his manuscript diary covering the years 1778 to 1783, the letter of September 8, 1778, from the Baptists of Pepperell to the Warren Baptist Association, and Backus's manuscript "History of the Warren Association." The Brown University collection includes the manuscript account of Richard Lee's mobbing in Hingham and Lee's own statements.

I have also consulted the following newspaper articles relating to the Pepperell Riot: Boston *Independent Chronicle,* October 15, 1778; November 12, 1778; December 3, 1778; and Boston *Gazette,* February 22, 1779; March 8, 1779.

Backus gave a brief description of the Pepperell incident in his tract, *Government and Liberty Described* (Boston, 1778) printed in *Isaac Backus on Church, State and Calvinism,* edited by William G. McLoughlin (Cambridge, Mass., 1968), page 345–65; he described the Hingham incident in *A Door Opened for Equal Christian Liberty* (Boston, 1783), also printed in *Isaac Backus on Church, State and Calvinism,* pages 427–438.

For anyone interested in the broader context of these incidents see my *New England Dissent, 1630–1833* (Cambridge, Mass., 1971), volume 1, pages 598–599, 640–642.

enough people to the antipedobaptist persuasion to form a church. The first
public sign that this was about to occur was a public baptism in the nearest
stream or millpond. Once a sufficient number had been baptized, according
to Baptist polity, they could hire their own minister or ordain one of their
own group. The next step was to appeal to the town clerk for exemption
from taxes to support the Standing Order. To avoid trouble, Baptists usually
tried to hold their baptismal ceremonies in out-of-the-way places. But some-
times they made a big show of it. In either case, they invited violent reactions
from both the respectable and disreputable members of the community.

We are enemies to disorder and unrighteousness.
—The Town of Pepperell, November 2, 1778

June 26, 1778, was a warm, sunny, midsummer's day in the small
town of Pepperell, Massachusetts, forty miles northwest of Boston.
The Revolution seemed to be proceeding smoothly. General Bur-
goyne had surrendered in the previous fall. Parliament had made
overtures of peace in the spring; the French had decided to lend
assistance to the rebellion. A farming community of 160 families
situated on the western bank of the Nashua River, bordering on
New Hampshire, Pepperell had not been the scene of any fighting,
nor was it ever to be. But it had been on the alert for trouble ever
since the day Colonel William Prescott had led the minutemen from
Pepperell and Groton to Charlestown for the Battle of Bunker Hill.

On this balmy afternoon a visitor to Pepperell could have seen a
small group of men and women gathered on the outskirts of town
on the edge of the river near a wooden bridge. There were about
a score of them listening intently to an energetic young man. Some
of the group seemed to be uneasy, shuffling their feet and glancing
apprehensively over their shoulders now and then toward the brow
of the hill where the road into town disappeared.

Suddenly the speaker stopped. His hearers turned around.
Shouts and cries came from the brow of the hill. A moment later
a man on horseback appeared on the crest where the road sloped
down toward the bridge. He pointed at the group by the river and
shouted, "There you are!" Several other horsemen joined him. The
shouting grew louder. As the small assemblage by the river watched
apprehensively, sixty or seventy people on foot surged over the hill
and down the road toward them. The crowd—a mob, really—car-

ried clubs and poles in their hands. A distinguished-looking man on horseback, brandishing a long horsewhip, was urging them on with shouts, while other horsemen rode back and forth beside the marchers. Obviously, the mob was well organized and well led. As they streamed down the dirt road, raising a cloud of dust in their wake, they "made the greatest clamor and tumult," said one on-looker, "and appeared and acted like men in a great rage." Some of them were "armed with staves and poles who seemed much enraged."

Apparently by prearrangement, the first of the mob to reach the bridge crossed over and blocked the other end so that no one could escape across it. But the men and women by the riverside made no move to run. They waited—some quietly, some tense, some angry, some afraid. Soon they were surrounded by the marchers "whose countenances and gestures portrayed their designs of violence." The men on horseback began shouting at the small group. Angry words were exchanged. One of the women argued with the mob, saying that she owned the land on which they were meeting, and no one would drive her off it. Someone from the mob shouted that the meeting was "a Tory plan, the work of the Devil." When a member of the group tried to answer him, one of the men on horseback shouted at him, "Hold your tongue, Davis, or I'll beat your teeth down your throat!" The mob grew more angry; some blows were exchanged. Amid the jeering and poking, several of the mob began kicking at those who argued back.

Realizing that they would not be able to continue their meeting, the smaller group, with the mob at its heels, slowly walked up from the bank of the river onto the road and trudged back toward town. As they walked, members of the mob continued to shout abuse, poke them with their staves, and kick at them. The crowd appeared to be "in a great passion," said an eyewitness; "the disturbers halloos and shouts as tho' they was following an enemy upon a retreat." Just as they got to the brow of the hill, there was a loud cry of laughter. Everyone turned to look back toward the bridge. Someone had fallen or plunged into the river and was yelling and splashing about much to the amusement of the mob. The group that had gathered by the river did not seem amused by the spectacle; they turned away and kept on walking. After they had gone about half

a mile, they came to a house owned by one of the group and gathered inside the gate. There was a small fenced enclosure where
they tried to continue their meeting. The mob stood nearby, yelling,
jeering, and interrupting. Toward the end of the meeting someone
in the mob shouted at the speaker, "That's a damned lie!"

The smaller group then went into the house. A few minutes later
three of the men on horseback dismounted, conferred with the
mob, and then entered the house. More angry shouting took place,
and the distinguished man with the whip called those who had been
speaking "ruffians" and demanded that they leave town at once.
He said that if they refused, he could not be responsible for their
safety at the hands of the mob. A visitor from out of the state
expressed his surprise at this kind of mob action and asked one of
the spokesmen for the town if he did not fear prosecution. The
spokesman answered that "there was no law that could take hold
of a mob."

As nothing more seemed to be about to happen, the mob began
to disperse, some to the nearby tavern and some to their homes.
An hour or so later the men and women inside the house began to
slip out in twos and threes, heading off in various directions. Spies
who had been left to watch them realized that they were simply
taking devious routes to reach another rendezvous. The town was
aroused again, and late in the afternoon the small group was found
newly assembled by another river where they baptized several.
Again they were forced to disperse. This time the distinguished-
looking man on horseback, who "appeared to be in a great passion"
at their temerity, rode his horse up to the group's speaker and,
waving his whip over the man's head, said "that he was a dirty,
mean fellow and if ever he came into town again in such a manner,
he would horsewhip him out."

A casual observer of these proceedings would undoubtedly have
assumed that the mob was a band of local patriots (indeed, many
of the leaders were members of the town's Committee of Safety)
riding herd on a group of loyalists. But in fact the incident had
nothing to do with the conduct of the Revolution. It was purely and
simply a case of religious bigotry. The people by the riverside constituted the first converts to the Baptist faith in Pepperell, and their
"ruffian" leaders were Baptist preachers from neighboring towns

who had come to administer the rite of baptism by total immersion. It was hardly a damnable Tory plot hatched by the Devil, though to some New Englanders who disliked the growing religious pluralism of their region, Tories and Baptists were equally damnable. This incident is worth noting, not because it was exceptional but because it was symptomatic of growing animosity toward dissenters from the prevailing Congregational way of life. Six years earlier, in the town of Ashfield in the western part of the state, Congregationalists had shown such malevolent intolerance against dissenters that the king felt compelled to override an act of the Massachusetts legislature to maintain their right of religious liberty. Four years later, as reported in documents that follow, the town of Hingham engaged in mob action against a Baptist preacher, bodily throwing him out of town after beating and kicking him and throwing soft cow dung in his face.

The affidavits, published here for the first time, provide vivid testimony to the depths of the anti-Baptist feeling in Massachusetts in the Revolutionary era. But what the affidavits do not indicate is why this feeling was so deep and so prevalent. On the face of it the Baptists had every right to be outraged and to attempt to bring suits against these mobs. The Baptist were breaking no laws. The Revolution had as one of its ostensible aims the securing of the inalienable right of liberty of conscience for all men. Baptists had worshipped freely in several Massachusetts towns since the 1680s, and since 1729 they had been excluded from paying religious taxes to support the established Congregational churches. Just a few months before the Pepperell Riot (as the Baptist affidavits called it) a new state constitution had been passed by the legislature guaranteeing liberty of conscience to all inhabitants; the leader of the mob in Pepperell, Colonel Henry A. Woods, a hero of the Battle of Bunker Hill and a member of the legislature, had voted for that constitution.

To the townspeople of Pepperell and Hingham (and of many other towns where anti-Baptist feeling was not so openly evident) the Baptists were pesky troublemakers and bold in challenging the traditional beliefs and customs of New England. At the very least, their illiterate preachers misled silly women and foolish men by their ignorant biblical literalism; at worst, Baptist itinerant exhort-ers went from town to town fomenting religious quarrels, attacking parish (Congregational) ministers, encouraging schisms in parish churches, and assisting tax dodgers, who were all too ready to claim that they were Baptists in order to be freed from the obligation of paying religious taxes to support the Congregational church and parson.

Further, the Baptists had claimed that liberty of conscience meant that Congregationalists did not have the right to lay taxes even on themselves to support their churches—that, in truth, God's word demanded that *all* true Christian churches, not just Baptist churches, must be supported by voluntary gifts or freewill offerings. They cared nothing for the time-honored traditions, the cherished beliefs, nor the liberty of conscience of Congregationalists who had just as many spiritual texts to prove that God's word was perfectly compatible with a system of religious taxation. Both the Massachusetts constitution of 1778 (though it was not adopted by the voters) and that of 1780 guaranteed liberty of conscience—the right of men and women to worship where and how they pleased—but both constitutions also required every town or parish to support the church of the majority by religious taxation. To the average New Englander, it was the Baptists who were promoting disorder and fomenting civil disobedience by arguing against these constitutional obligations.

Now that the Baptists are the largest single Protestant denomination in America and are considered to be eminently respectable and are respected everywhere, it is difficult to conceive of the intensity of the animosity against them in Revolutionary New England.

However, the Baptists in 1776 really did have a very different view of how the new nation should be constituted, and it ran counter to that of a great many Americans. Even though there were not more than a couple of thousand of them in Massachusetts at that time, the Baptists were able to stir up public opinion far out of proportion to their numbers. The issue they raised was an issue that continues to trouble America to this day: the separation of church and state. It was an issue that found most of New England curiously at odds with many of their compatriots in other states, among whom were Jefferson and Madison in Virginia. Most of the thirteen colonies quickly adopted the Baptist position on disestablishment after 1776, but Massachusetts retained its tax-supported religious system until 1833. Not even the First Amendment curtailed it, for that restricted only Congress, not the various states, from making laws respecting an establishment of religion.

Nevertheless, the proper relationship of church and state in the new nation was not an easy decision. The concept of complete separation or voluntarism was still a new one in the Western world, and outside of the exceptional examples of Rhode Island and Pennsylvania, it had never been tried. Most European observers considered disestablishment to be one of the most outlandishly radical aspects of the new political experiment in republicanism. New Englanders undoubtedly had the bulk of public opinion in Christendom on their side. The reasoning behind a tax-supported religious system was simple enough: the safety and welfare of any community rested on the morality and virtue of its citizens; Christianity was the best system of morality and religion ever revealed to man; therefore, the nation should, for its own good and the good of its people, use its taxing power to see that the Christian religion was supported and promulgated. This argument was doubly strong in America in 1778 because it was thought that a republic had greater need of a virtuous citizenry than any other form of government since in a republic it was the people who made and, in the end, enforced the laws.

Furthermore, most Americans shared at this time the Calvinists' pessimism about the innate depravity of human nature; both history and revelation testified to man's innate selfishness. And without a belief in God, an afterlife, a heaven and hell of rewards and punishments for actions in this life, few men would act rightly if it conflicted with their own self-interest. Article 3 of the Bill of Rights of the Massachusetts Constitution of 1780 put the matter in a nutshell:

As the happiness of a people and the good order and preservation of civil government essentially depended upon piety, religion, and morality; and as these cannot be generally diffused through a community but by the institution of the public worship of God, and of public instructions in piety, religion, and morality: Therefore, to promote the happiness and to secure the good order and preservation of their government, the people of this commonwealth have a right to invest their legislature with power to authorize and require, and the legislature shall from time to time authorize and require the several towns, parishes, precincts and other bodies politic, or religious societies, to make suitable provision, at their own expense, for the institution of the public worship of GOD, and for the support and maintenance of public Protestant teachers of piety, religion, and morality.

For the Baptists to argue that the support of religion should be left to the voluntary goodwill of the average man was to fly in the face of history, revelation, and human nature. Without compulsion, who would support religion adequately? Who would pay to hear ministers tell them how sinful they were if they could avoid such tongue lashings? Only the veriest dreamer or fanatic could advocate a system so subversive of the happiness and good order of the commonwealth. This was the kind of thinking that lay behind the wording of Article 3.

But if most citizens of Massachusetts believed in tax support for the public diffusion of piety, religion, and morality, and if so few people had been won over to the Baptist position since that sect first appeared in Massachusetts, why were the townspeople of Pepperell, Hingham, and elsewhere so fearful? One answer, of course, is that when people are fearful of a subversive element in their midst even the most minute evidence of it is apt to produce a great outpouring of animosity. How many Bolsheviks were there in America in the 1920s, how many Communists in the McCarthy era? Fearful people see the handful of dissenters in their midst not as isolated malcontents but as the advance guard of a major threat to undermine the morals and safety of the community; the best time to cut down such subversion is when it first appears. It is significant that the groups mobbed in Pepperell and Hingham were the first Baptists to appear in those towns. There was ample evidence that where this sect had gained a foothold in other towns they had quickly attracted all of the malcontents in the parish who, for whatever reason, had a grievance against the parish church or its minister. Once an alternative was open to such schismatics, the Baptist church was apt to grow larger and larger as the parish church grew smaller and smaller. And since it was cheaper to contribute what you wanted to support a Baptist church than to pay the heavy taxes levied by the parish for the support of the established church, the taxes on those who remained in the old parish church consequently grew larger with each defection from their ranks. The situation was not unlike the heated arguments that arise in towns and cities across the nation today over the support of parochial schools: if Roman Catholics wish to send their children to their own schools at their own expense, so the argument goes, that is their right; but it is also the duty of all citizens, whether Catholic or not, to pay compulsory taxes for the support of those public schools on which the welfare and safety of the community depends.

We need not deal here with the obvious religious friction that developed in a day when people took their denominational views with utmost seriousness, when Congregationalists were convinced that the Baptist doctrines and practices were heretical and would simply lead souls down to hell, and when Baptists considered infant baptism "a heaven-daring and God-provoking sin."

Equally strong was the feeling that Baptists were probably luke-warm toward the Revolution, if not actually loyal to the king. Baptists were considered among the three major dissenting groups in the colonies. The other two were the Anglicans (who had more loyalists in their ranks than any other denomination) and Quakers (who, because of their pacifism, took an avowedly neutral position in the war). Although the Baptists, through the course of the Revolution, proved to be as dedicated to the patriot cause as the Congregationalists and Presbyterians, there were good reasons for their patriotism to be suspect at first. For one thing, the Reverend Morgan Edwards, one of their leading denominational spokesmen in Philadelphia, had publicly proclaimed his loyalty to the English king in 1774, and later his son fought in the king's army. But more important, the Baptists in New England, through the long decades of their fight for religious liberty, had several times appealed to the king against the injustices of the various New England legislatures and townspeople. Such an appeal to the king against their neighbors was under consideration by the Baptists on the very eve of the Revolution, when any true son of liberty should have been willing to forget his denominational grievances and join in a united fight against the tyranny of king and Parliament.

But the Baptists had been outsiders for so long that they generally did not consider themselves part of the system (let alone of the establishment) in New England. It was well known that more than one royal governor in Massachusetts had used the Baptists' discontent as a means of rousing the king against the colony. Lieutenant Governor Thomas Hutchinson had personally urged the Baptists to appeal to the king against the Ashfield "persecutions" and gave their petition his support in 1772. To top it off, the Baptists of Massachusetts had sent a delegation led by James Manning, president of the Baptist College (later Brown University) in Rhode Island, and Isaac Backus (who collected the affidavits and pressed the suits against the mobs) to the First Continental Congress in 1774. Here, aided by leading Philadelphia Quakers, the New England Baptists had sought to embarrass the Massachusetts delegates by accusing them of religious persecution. John Adams, one of the Massachusetts delegates, said he could only conclude that the Baptists had joined with the Quakers to try to split the colonies and prevent their uniting against Parliament. On this occasion Adams told the Baptists that they "might as well expect a change in the solar system as to expect the people of Massachusetts to give up their establishment."

It was from such conviction of the rightness of their position that the "bourbon mobs" of Pepperell and Hingham acted. But it is necessary to add that their bigotry toward the Baptists exhibited also a snobbish disdain stemming from the lowly social position of most Baptists. Because the Baptists had always been looked down on, the denomination was not one that the educated and well-to-do associated with. And when the king forced tolerance for dissent on the colony after 1685, social discrimination remained one of the strongest forces preventing the spread of the baneful denomination. For the most part, the Baptists were the poorest people in any town and because they chose their ministers from their own ranks, caring nothing for the classical education and ministerial training of Harvard and Yale, their preachers were the butts of many a jibe by the learned parish clergy and others of the established churches. Cobblers, tinkers, tailors, and farmers, the Baptist preachers spoke as the Holy Spirit moved them; and although this brought spiritual comfort to the poor, it also brought ridicule and abuse from their neighbors. Parents spitefully prohibited their sons and daughters from marrying Baptists; schoolchildren made fun of Baptist play-

mates; learned ministers wrote tracts and sermons holding up the
Baptist faith to scorn. There is ample evidence that people did not
want to live near Baptists and that land speculators not only considered Baptists poor financial risks but felt that their presence in
a new town would lower property values. Few Baptists were ever
elected to office in local or state government, and almost none of
them were considered sufficiently responsible to serve on the Committees of Safety, Sons of Liberty, or Committees of Correspondence that provided the grass-roots organization for the Revolution
in New England. The Baptists, in short, were social pariahs, outcasts, and it was thus easy to arouse mob action against them in the
name of preserving the good order and self-respect of a town or
parish. As the following documents of the Pepperell riot indicate,
the townspeople saw nothing wrong with opening a letter addressed
to a Baptist in the town and reading it in a town meeting, while
ridiculing the Baptist preacher who had been invited to come to
immerse them in the river.

The following reports, found among the extant papers of the
Reverend Isaac Backus, have never before been published. The first
document was written by some of the Baptists in Pepperell and sent
to the Warren Baptist Association to be read at its annual meeting.
The Warren Association, formed in 1767, was a confederation of
about twenty-five Baptist churches, some in Rhode Island, some in
New Hampshire and Vermont, but most in Massachusetts. This
association had elected a Grievance Committee in 1769, of which
Backus became chairman in 1773. Its job was to gather information
about all cases of Baptist persecution and to take whatever action
necessary to protect the Baptists and to advance their cause. Not
unlike the National Association for the Advancement of Colored
People, the Grievance Committee gathered affidavits, waged legal
suits, and lobbied for legislation on behalf of a group who were
subject to social injustice. Isaac Backus was a most efficient agent
for his people, a constant goad in the flesh of the establishment; he
was often called a Tory because of his efforts.

As these documents reveal, Samuel Fletcher, an itinerant Baptist
exhorter from Chelmsford, Massachusetts, had first been invited to
Pepperell by Daniel Davis in March 1778 and was intimidated by a
mob at that time. Nevertheless, he returned in May and again for

the fateful day in June, at that time bringing with him Elder Isaiah Parker, pastor of the Baptist church in Harvard (Fletcher, not being ordained, was not entitled to perform baptisms). The Warren Association voted at its meeting on September 9, 1778, to instruct Backus as its agent to gather affidavits and bring charges against the mob's leaders. Backus visited Pepperell on September 12 for that purpose, and he too was threatened with dire punishment if he showed up again in the town: "I'll wring his nose and kick his arse," said Colonel Henry A. Woods, the leader of the mob. Backus gathered accounts from fourteen witnesses, and charges were brought against the mob's leaders at the meeting of the Middlesex grand jury early in October. "However," said Backus, "they [the jury] were prevailed with to suspend the matter until the town should vindicate themselves."

Backus published an account of the affair in the Boston *Independent Chronicle* on October 15. The town held a meeting and drew up its answer to the charges. This answer was published in the same paper on November 12. The gist of the answer was that Backus's "scurrilous" and "scandalous" account was "absolutely repugnant to the truth"; the town said that only a few youngsters and town derelicts had participated in the so-called riot and that "particular care was taken by the officers of the town to prevent riotous behavior and to maintain peace and good order. That we did, as a town, pay particular attention to the conduct of those dangerous persons is a fact we do not wish to be concealed." But the most revealing aspect of the town's justification was the reason it gave for considering Parker, Fletcher, and their "deluded" converts as dangerous.

Our situation at this time [June 1778] was very precarious. We were in pursuit of a gospel minister. We were deprived several years before of a very eminent one, the loss of whom taught us the importance of having the gospel re-established among us. Our all, as it were, lay at stake. We were sensible that if we were reputed as irregular, disorderly people no gentleman [minister] of worth would chuse to come among us; and it is notorious that these men [itinerant Baptists] endeavour to take advantage of such people's situations in order to rend and break them to pieces. Mr. Fletcher is evidently one of these pernicious ones; his extravagant, enthusiastic, and distracted behaviour in speaking against the constitution of other churches and condemning different denominations plainly evinces it. We shall point out an instance of his very impudent (and perhaps impious) manner of expression. He says, "It is a heaven-daring and God-provoking sin to offer an infant in baptism." Who but a madman would express himself in this manner? . . . We are not disposed to quarrel about the *ceremonial part* of religion, but we are enemies to disorder and unrighteousness.

Here, with no attempt to conceal it, was the truth underlying the incident: scorn for the Baptists, fear that the parish would be divided and hence unable to support a college-educated minister, and the worry that the town would get a bad name and its property values decrease if too many of these low people got a foothold. There was fierce pride in the prestige enjoyed by the established church and a misguided regard for pecuniary values.

Backus rebutted the town in an article in the *Chronicle* on December 3, having meantime returned to Pepperell on November 17 to obtain more information, including an account of the libelous attacks on himself and other Baptists made at the town meeting of November 2. Another attack on the Baptists, calling them liars, cheats, and Tories, appeared in the Boston *Gazette* on February 1, 1779, which Backus answered on February 22. But there the affair ended. No charges were ever brought against the mob leaders, and no Baptist church was formed in Pepperell during the Revolutionary era. For the time being, the matter ended in a draw.

Four years later, however, the Hingham riot did lead to a court action, in which the Baptists succeeded in having four of the mob's leaders arraigned for assault and battery. This riot, vividly described by Richard Lee, the Baptist preacher who was driven out of town, did come to trial. Backus, again acting as agent for the Grievance Committee of the Warren Association, hired James Mitchell Varnum, a Rhode Island attorney (though not a Baptist) to handle the case. Two aspects of the Hingham case deserve mention: first, the obvious dislike that Baptists had for lawyers (a feeling shared by many New Englanders), for most lawyers, like judges, were Congregationalists and hence not particularly sympathetic to the Baptists; second, the attempt to hold the Baptists up to ridicule by asking their preacher to debate with a black slave. Baptists, like blacks, were low on the social totem pole in New England, and it was often said that blacks preferred Baptist churches to those of the establishment. The subtle equation of evil and the Devil with the color black is also significant for the racial prejudices of New Englanders.

THE PEPPERELL RIOT

[Taken from the Isaac Backus Papers at Andover Newton Theological School, Newton Centre, Massachusetts]

A Trew account of the Lat[e] Transactions in the Town of Pepperell: one Daniel Davis of the Place asked one Saml. Feltcehr, a Late Baptis Preacher to Come and Preach a sermon at his home; and sd. Fletcehr agreed so; and was to send him a loyn [line] when he could attend; and accordingly he sent him a Letter that he would attend and preach at his home on March ye 17, 1778. The Letter came to Town on a Day when there was a Day appointed for Publick affairs; the Letter was Broken open and Delivered to one Nemh. [Nehemiah] Hobart, Town Clark, and sd. Hobart calld. a number Round & said, 'I have hear a Letter. I will Read it.' And after Reading sd. Letter one & another said, 'Who is this?' The Clark sd. 'It is old Timothy Fletcher's son, the fox hunter's son.' And many flouts & slings and laughts [were made]. And he [Hobart] was Ready to Call for a Vote whether he [Fletcher] should preach in sd. Town, but being aposed by one Dr. Lawrence [the clerk of the parish church] in a Liberal and Religious manner, 'Nay,' saith they, 'he [Fletcher] hath Don much Damag in other Towns.' And by this he [Hobart] gained the opinion of many, but the matter Dropt without a Vote but not without many Reflections.

But the Day appointed he Preachd. and Dr. Lawrence Invited him to Come the Next week and Preach at his house. Accordingly he came, Tuesday, Mar. 29 & Preached & in the Time of worship the house was assailld. by a Number of the Inhabitants of sd. Place and sum of the Principle men of sd. Place and they found one Temple, a Travler and he undertook to go in and Brake up the worship and the others stood without with a Poole [pole?] to take him as he Cam out. Sd. Temple came in and sd. he wou'd Brake up sd. meeting & spoke after this manner till he was put out of Doors and they all went to the Tavern and Rote Two Infimus Letters to Mr. Fletcher and in high Zeal said that if Ever he came their again he could be carried out upon a Rail and by Violence.

On ye 25 of June Mr. Isaiah Parker, Preacher of ye gospel & Pastor of a Baptis Church in Harvard, at the Desire [of] a Number of persons at Pepperell who Looked upon it to be their Duty to Receive the ordenance of Baptism by Emertion who went over their and preached a Lector [lecture] at one of their houses and after which gave Notice that the Next Day in the fore Noon there were Some Persons to be Examined respecting Their [religious] Experience and fitness to Receive the ordenance &c., and any Persons might have Liberty to attend that would. According sd. Business was attended upon without any objection, when six Persons offered them selves and were aproved of. Three of them were heads of families; two of them Males, ye other Femails.

The after Noon was appointed for the ordenance to be administered and a Discourse to Proceed it; accordingly they Repaired to a River Side and many attended & as they had Sang an hym and attended Prayers Mr. Saml. Fletcher that was to Preach had Named his Text & Inst. Began his Discours. There came up Lieut.-Col. Henery Woods, Capt. Nathaniel Lakin, Cornet Simon Gilson (Committee of Safty), Lieut. Jonas Varnom, Cap. Jeremiah Shattuck & Nehemiah Hobart (Selectmen as foresaid) with a Large Number to ye amount of 60 or 100 attendants whose countenances & gestures portrayed their Designs of Violence.

They Emediately forbid ye Preacher & Rushed upon the small audience without any parlying and absolutely forbid their Proceeding Either In Preaching or Baptising within ye Limits of ye Town, and [they] was so Loud and Noisey that they Entierly Interrupted the audience and Stopt. the Speaker. And when they were Desired by Mr. Parker to forbear their Violence, who [re]minded them of that Liberty of Conscience in manner of worship had Ever been allowd. by all Protestant Rulers, Even by the King of Brittan, and Coated [quoted] many Texts of Scripture to Prove his Proceeding, but the aforesaid Cort. Gilson said, 'Don't cout [quote] Scripture hear.'

(These men all sind. [signed] the Late form of Constitution or act of Court) and Mr. Parker asked them whether they had Sind. signed] sd. act and they would not answer but Still they persisted in their opposition and in ridicule took a Dog into the Water and Plunged him &c in Imitation of Baptism. When one of ye men who were Desierous of Receiving the Ordinance was accused by the above sd. Lakin of being a tory (tho very unjustly) Desired Liberty of Speaking in his own behalf [he] was answered by him 'Hold your Tongue or I will Beat your Teeth Down your throat' &c. They continuing in Such a Hostility the Party who was assembled for Religious worship was obleged to Retreat to a Privat house & had But just began their worship again before these opposers Pursued with the Same Sanguine Temper and in the time of worship stood with their hats on ridiculing, jearing, some times[s] Contradicting, mocking, &c.

After the Exercise was over, then they hiers [hired] for[with] strong Drink two Lude [lewd] fellows to go into the water, the one to Baptise the other who accordingly Did in a most Profain manner; after which a great Shout was made—after they flung in two Dogs more, when their head man said 'Their is one Dipt, their is Nother dipt' with a great Laugh and Shout. (Abraham Boynton dipt Jeremiah Lawrence.)

Then there came in [to the private house] three or four of their Chief [men] and Request to no whether they Intended to go forward in the ordenance & also admonished them Not to, as they Tendered ye Peace and order of the Town & their own Present Safty. And [they] was answered that as they [the Baptists] Lookt upon it, they had No good Design in asking, therefore they should Return them No Answer. After which the Persons [Baptists] seeing it impracticable to go forward in ye ordenance with Decency by reason of the opposition took a Second Retreat about two miles. But still [they] was Persued but Not so Close as to Prevent their Baptism. But those that Came Up before the ordenance was administered Sat by mocking in the time of its administration & as they were met by the above sd. Col. Woods & Capt. Lakin and a Considerable Number of the Party who seemed to be highly Displeased, shook their whips over them [Baptists] Threattend. and beat Som, Charging the Preachers to Depart the town that Night &c. and to Return No more as they would [not] Prevent their being Carried out on a Pole and Such taulk, Calling them Black, Dirty, mean Fellows, &c.

Since which Several of ye Chief men of ye Town and the Church in this Place met and Passd. Several Resolves as Votes among themselves in opposition to this work, Threattening violence to those Preachers if they came any more. The Church in Particular have manifested their Displeasure, Calling those meetings a Tory Plan, the work of the Devil, and Such Like &c. Sum of this Place have Denied any Dealings, with those that have imbraced the baptis worship and Even Denied to selle Corn to one that spake frindly of them. They also have Threatnd. the Lives of Som &c.

we Sine Our Names to These Truths as being
Ey witnesses to most of them and the others
we can Prove by Substancial Evidence Now
Living of These matters

Pepperell, September ye 5th, 1778   witness   Daniel Davis
Simeon Shattuck

LETTER TO THE WARREN ASSOCIATION

To the elders & messengers of the warren association to meet at Leicester, Sept. 8th, 1778:
Sirs,

if you Think Proper, we Pray you will Correct this for the Publick Press, and we, the above sd. Davis & Shattuck, together with a number of others in this town who are friends to the Baptists Denomination Request your earnest prayers to God for us and as we have Sent this account of the transactions of the town of Pepperell By Mr. Saml. Fletcher, preacher of the Gospel, who you find in the above account has suffered great per[se]cution in sd. town though we firmly Believe his labours have Been Blessed as a mean[s] of the Conviction & Convertion of Sinners to Jesus Christ & also for the edification of Saints in this place, we Desire you would Send us By sd. Mr. Fletcher the Best advice you Can and also that you would Send us help from your association to preach among us as soon as you Can & as often as possible. So we Conclude with wishing you Grace, mercy & pease through our Lord Jesus Christ.

The foregoing narrative was read to the Warren association at Leicester, Sept. 9, 1773, who ordered the same to be corrected and published by their agent [Isaac Backus] and [Grievance] Committee. The Agent therefore came to Harvard where on Sept. 11, 1778, Mr. Parker, pastor of the Baptist chh. in that place gave him an account of the following facts relating to the above Narrative, viz.

He testified that after their meeting on June 26 was interrupted by Col. Woods and others, as is above related, Mrs. Lydia Wright, who was the owner of the land they were met upon, openly spoke and ordered those interrupters of their worship to remove themselves off from her land; but they refused so to do. He also testifieth that after Mr. Fletcher had preachd. at Dr. Lawrence's, Col. Woods, Cap. Lakin and Mr. Hubbard came into dr. Lawrence's house and after some discourse Col. Woods said he advised said preachers immediately to depart out of the town of Pepperell for their own safety and welfare. Mr. Parker asked him if he meant that their lives would be in danger if they did not then depart? But they all refused to answer that question notwithstanding he told them that he must understand that to be the meaning of the words if they did not explain them otherwise. After some pause Col. Woods asked whether these people designed to go forward in baptism in that town? Mr. Parker replied that as he b[e]lieved they had no good design in asking the question he should not answer it. This they complained of as uncivil &c. At length he turnd. to those gentlemen and told them he did solemnly appeal to their consciences in the presence of God whether they had now come up against the Baptists with the spirit of Christ's disciples or Whether it was not like the persecuting Jews? To which they made no answer but went directly out of the house. Upon which he proposed to his friends privatly his aim in not telling those persecutors what he intended, viz. That they should part from each other, and by different ways, as imperceptably to their foes as they could, repair to a convenient place for baptism near two miles off. This was agreed to, and so the ordinance was administered, as is before related.

Lieut. Varnum gave a boll [bowl] of tody [toddy] to Boynton to dip Lawrence, & Lawrence afterwards boasted at Elijah Shattuck's that he had been dipt three times and did not believe yet. Susanna Fisk heard this last and Mr. David Wright's boys were in at Gilson's Tavern when the liquor was given.

While Dr. Parker was at prayers at Dr. Lawrence's, he blessed

God that there was none to make us afraid. John Green Junr. or Joshua Blood said, "That is a damned lie."

Varnum & Joseph Lawrence & Joel Hubbard gave [the] boys direction at the great river about putting a dog into the water. At the other river when they put in the dogs Clerk Hobart shouted and said, "There is one dipt. There is another &c." Woods, Lakin, &c were present.

Mr. David Wright says he stood near & heard this.

Note, upon examination since, the evidence does not appear clear that Varnum hired Boynton, or that Clerk Hubbard spoke said words, especially as to the latter 'tis likely the words were spoken by another. These two mistakes, if they be so, I was led into by Wright. All the other articles are fully proved.

I. Backus

STATEMENT BY SIMEON SHATTUCK, NOVEMBER 16, 1778

[Taken from the Isaac Backus Papers at Andover Newton Theological School]

March the 27, 1778 Mr. Samuel Fletcher Preached at Dr. Lawrence and his Hous was asalted by many of the inhabetence of the town thow [though] I saw them not till after meetin. I see Cap. Isaac Woods standing on a wall sum distance from the Hous others with him. I saw them have a rail or a pol. Cap. Woods cools [calls] to the company that was at the Hous to fetch him along. I wa[s] at a Church meeting and after meeting Mr. Jonas Varnum asked me if Sameuel Fletcher as agoin to Preach at your Hous. I told him he was. Says he, I am very sory that you invited such men as he into town to make such dissturbence. You may go out of town to heair him he says. He deserves to have a rope put round his neck and dragd out of town and that would be doin good jestess [justice]. June 26 Mr. Isaiah Parker Pastor of the baptis church in Harvard came with him [Fletcher]. In the afternoon they met by a river-side for Preaching and the Baptizing those Parsons satisfied account of Gods dealings With their Souls in order for Baptism. And as Mr. Fletcher had read a text and began to Preach Cor. Simon Gilson

Speaks and says let our Ministers alone. Then spake Leu. [Lt.] Jonas Varnum, you have no bisines hair. Then spake Cor. [Col.] Woods, Cap. Lakin and a number of others and saied that we should not have any pece their. Then as we re[t]yred to Dr. Lawrence to worship their folowed a great number of the oposers and mocked all the time of worship and the leading men of the town forbid Mr. Parker to Baptize any wheair in the Lymites of the town. Not with standing we retyered to another place in order to baptize but not with our mokers [mockers] Standing by, and Joseph Lawrence sayd to Mr. Parker when he was agoin into the water with Mr. Daniel Davis, take the Long Crock Devil in further, I hope you will keep him in so long that he wont come out again. And when we were returning back to my Hous we were met by the afore said Cor. Woods and Cap. Lakin and many more of the oposers of which Cor. Woods threatned of whiping Mr. Fletcher if you come into town any more says he you shall be cared [carried] out.

November 2 at a town meeting the twelth artical to see if the town Will take into consideration a late scandalas peace published in the new[s]paper sined Isaac Backus and act theiron as they shall think proper, and Cor. Woods being moderator of the meeting calls for vote and voted that they would act their on. Cor. Woods says as for his own part he did not so much care as I am so well known in most all the state but I Regard the caritur [character] of the town, for says he, if I came acrose this Backus i will have my recompenc but as for this Fletcher if I come acros him ill [I'll] ring his nose and kick his ass. Yes says Cap. Nuting that [is] what we will and many threatning words givin out by them. A haltor is to good for them and wheair are these Baptis if they have any thing to say why dont they spek and so on.

N.B. in July Dn. [deacon] Daniel Fiske came to me and as neer as I can Remember told me that the selectmen and comity off seafty met at Mr. Hobart['s] to see what was best to do conserning the affare the town was in and says he, we chose a comety of three men to go and Se those parsons that had invited Baptis Preachers as you call them into town and to discorse with them and se if we cant purswade you not to invite them in any more. For if you do we Expect that theair will be Vilance used and Cap. Nuting was to go

to Dr. Lawrence's and Cap. Lakin was to go and se Mr. Daniel Davis
and my self to see you and if you insist in it you must take what
folowes.

September the 12, 1778 Mr. Isaac Backus come to my Hous and
I asked him whether he was agoin to stay in town over the Saborth
and he said he was and he would Preach with us. I asked him
whether he wold Preach in the meeting Hous. He says I had as
leave as not. I told Mr. Backis that their was many in the town wold
hear the Baptis if they wold preach in the meating Hous and not
creep into Privit Houses. So Mr. Davis and I goes to Mr. Hobart as
he was the Clark and one of the Selectmen and told him that Mr.
Backis was in town and asked him whether he was wiling that he
Should Preach in the meating Hous. He says we have a minister to
seply our pulpit and shall not give leave. And theair was Mr. Willm.
Green theair with him one of the commety of safety and they began
to find falt with us for inviting such Preachers into town to make
such Disturbance and they sayd that they had prevented viliance
being used but they did not desire to any longer. Well said I, what
will you do? What will we do said Mr. Green, why we will fight them
said he. With what, said I? With these hands said he, making the
moshin, shaking his hands with spite in his countanence.

I being 40 years of age can Testify to the above
Truths. Pepprill, November 16, 1778.

Simeon Shattuck

STATEMENT OF JOSHUA AUSTIN

[Taken from the Isaac Backus Papers, Andover Newton Theological School]

Joshua Austin of Simsbury in the County of Hartford and State
of Connecticut Saith that last June, about the 27th Day 1778, that
He was in Pepperell and hearing that Mr. Fletcher and Mr. Parker,
Two Baptist preachers, were to preach that day and Administer
the ordinance of Baptism to Severel persons, my Cur[i]osity Lead
me to go and se and hear. Accordingly I went to the House of Mr.
Simeon Shattuck's in sd. Pepperill: From whence I went to a River
in said Pepperell to hear the Sermon that were to be Deliver'd there,
and se the ordinince of Baptism Administer'd when a large Body

of People were Conven'd together. After Prayer &c. Mr. Fletcher Read His Text, open'd his Sermon and began to preach thereform. Then open'd to View (to my thoughts) An awful Sceane. One Cornet Gilson (as I was inform'd was his name) spook aloud and bid him be silent and not to speak against the Standing Ministers [i.e., parish ministers]. Was then seconded by Col. Woods and Capt. Laken, when a General Clamour Insued among the people. He (Mr. Fletcher) assaid [essayed] to go on with his sermon when he was interrupted again with the most Scurrelous Language. Then [he] Desir'd for humanities sake not to be interrupted, but those Gentlemen still proceded in their unchristian Manner, for so Justly I think I may term it. When Mr. Parker addrest them, to my thought in the Language of a Christian and Scholar, and reminded them of Liberty of Conchence that were allowed By all Prodestent Nations and even by Great Briton with wom we are at war with and that they had approv'd to the Late Constitution wherein that was allow'd Viz. Liberty of Conshence which they had now acted inconsistent with that Constitution and even the Laws of God and humanity. Mr. Parker Cited them many Texts of Scripture to prove that their Conduct was not to be justified, to which One Cornet Gilson (As I was inform'd that was his Name) reply'd do not Mention Scripture hear. By this and other Expressions it appear'd to Doct. Lawrence and others that those Gentlemen was determin'd that the Exercise of the Day should not be allow'd. Doct. Lawrence then desir'd them to go to his house which was Compli'd with.

Then proceeded many of the people to the said Doct.'s house and Many others to Mr. Gilson's Tavern, among the latter I went In Company. When set on our seats a Dispute Arose about the Conduct that was transacted at the river side, when Col. Woods, Capt. Laken took a part to Justify there own and other perseding he opposing the Two Baptist preachers in perseding to preach and Exercise the rights of their Religion. In said dispute I took an Active part myself and ask'd those Gentlemen if they thought they acted upon principles of religion. Too which they did reply they should. I told them in my Oppinion they had Acted Inconsistent with the principles of Religion as taught by our Saviour, or even the principles of Common Sense and sound policy. Then Insued a warm debait upon the latter assertion. Viz. Common Sence and sound policy. I told them we ought to be Extreamly Causious how we made Enemies at this all important Crysus, when the Liberties of America were Envaded by a powerful enemy. And told them Liberty of Conchance was allow'd them By the King of Briton from whom we had Justly revoulted. Then [I] asked them if that perswation might not enjoy the liberty of Conchance and Worship the God of heaven According to the rights of their religion if they thought they for the futer [future] would Venture their [the Baptists] Lives in the high places of the field, face the Weapons of Death, brave the Danger that ever was attendant on War, fight, bleed, and die as many of the perswation (to my knowledge) have done. To which they reply'd to this Effect that it was no matter whose side such fellows was on. Then I Exclaim'd in this Manner to the best of my Memory: 'Good God! is this the Liberties our Country affords?' To which Capt. Laken reply'd that he had heard Villians in the army that was justly brought [to] the whipping poast [for such talk]. I told them I would put five hundred Dollars in stake that Neither the General Court of this State nor the Grand Continental Congress would Countenance their Conduct. But the Matter was wav'd and the dispute Brook off with thretning to take me up as I was a Stranger in the Country.

Then I went immediately out of the house and to my Amazement and very great astonishment I saw a Young Man in Contempt to the Baptists [form of] baptism Emmerse a Dog and shouts of the people in Acclamation of Joy at the horrid Action was beyond Description. Capt. Laker or Mr. Hubbard said, "Their is one Dipt." I also saw one Man Dipt another admist the acclamation and shouts of Joy of the people. I must acknowledge that Col. Woods and Laken seem'd to me to be the head of this Scandalous affair.

STATEMENT OF WILLIAM PARHAM

[Taken from the Isaac Backus Papers, Andover Newton Theological School]

I, William Parham, of Ashby in the County of Midsx. & State of the Massachusetts Bay, of Lawfull Age Testafie and Say that on or about the 27th of last March, I being at the House of Dr. Ephraim Lawrence in Pepperell hearing Mr. Saml. Fletcher preach. There being a Disturbance in the House amongst the People in time of Exercise. After which I made an Enquiry who made the Disturbance and one Mr. Temple of Molborouogh said, "It was the Doctor in turning me out of Doors for which I will be revenged of him, for I had good Authority to do what I did, as I was Employed by this Town to break up Such Disordily meetings." Then Querying of him about his Authority so to do—there being a Number of said Pepperell People about him who Countenanced him in his Assertions whereupon at first I took it to be that he was an officer and had a Warrant from Authority therefor—Yet soon after by observation I perceived they meant to Do it by their Threats &c. amongst whome was Mr. John Shattuck Jnr. (whom I am informed is one of the selectmen of the Town this year) Mr. Jona[than] Shattuck, and Mr. Patrick White. Said White had but a few Days before told me as I was going to hear sd. Fletcher preach at Mr. Daniel Davis's that the Select-Men had undertaken to prevent his Preaching there—whereupon I replyed that I did not think that they had any Right to prevent People worshiping god according to ye Dictates of their own Consciences—whereupon he replyed that if they did not Do it, he believed the Town would let the Consequences be what they would. At said meeting at Dr. Lawrence's there was gathered a considerable Number of People in the Yard and about ye House that Manefested a Spirit of opposition and Thretned Violence on said Fletcher's Person if they Could git at him who was in the House.

About the same time as [I] fel into Company with Mr. Thos. Shattuck of said Town he told me that there was a Mob that had agreed to prevent any such Preaching in the town. To which I replyed that such proceeding[s] were Dangerous. And he Answered that there was no Law that Could take hold on a Mob.

Soon after at Different times I was told by Mr. Simeon Green and Mr. John White of said Town, that they had been Invited by the opposers to Joyn them in order to break up said meeting at said Lawrence's but refused to go.

Sometime in ye Latter End of the month of June following, as I was just Joyning the Socicty that was gathered to worship at the Riverside where they had met in order to Baptizing in said Pepperell, when Mr. Isaiah Parker, Pastor of a Baptist Church at Harvard was over for to preach & to Baptize with said Fletcher, I was met by one that Come out from amongst those that had gathered about ye Audience that had met for Religious worship, who told me that there was one Baptized—soon after there was another that said it was only a Dog dipt. And as I then Came up to them there was a very great Clammor and Noise—some Saying we will have no Baptizing here & such Like—amongst which opposers I saw Lieut. Col. Henry Woods, Capt. Nathl. Lakin, Cornet Simon Gilson, Mr. Nehm. Hobart—who absolutely forbid their Proceeding either in preaching or Baptizeing in the Town. I also at the same time was within hearing of the said Capt. Nathl. Lakin who appeared to be in a Passion, who was talking with Mr. Daniel Davis of said Pepperell (who I understand was, and that then meant to be Baptized) Callimg him Tory & ye Like and as said Davis was making some defense said Lakin saith to him, "Hold your Tongue or I will beat your Teeth down your throught." And as this society of worshippers was so interrupted and forbid, Dr. Lawrence Invited them to His House whereupon they went & said Mr. Fletcher began his sermon again (as I understood he had been broken off by opposition at ye Riverside) in a yard at said Lawrence's and these opposers who beat them at ye River, followed & gathered near in time of Exercise, who made open Disturbance & behaved with great indecency—one calling out a Loud as said Mr. Parker was returning Thanks in his last Prayer that there was none suffered to make them a Fraid, "That is a damn'd lie." After Exercise said Col. Woods, Mr. Hobart & Capt. Lakin Came into the House & Calling for said Parker & Fletcher & informed them that it was ye mind of ye Bigger part of this Town that they should not proceed to Baptize any in ye Town & Did warn or causion them in ye behalf of ye Town not to, as they regarded ye Peace and order of ye Town & their own Safety. After some words between these Men & Mr. Parker they went out of ye House and I followed them out. About which time, as I was out abraud, I saw one Man lead another into the Water and Dipt him at which Time there was a great Shout made by the Opposers. Soon after these Ministers & the Persons that was Desirous of haveing Baptism retired to another Water, & I with them & while Mr. Parker was baptizing them, there was some Persons Come up who mocked & ridiculed. One said out Loud,

"Take her in further for she is a Long Crocked Devil" and as we were returning from ye Water to Mr. Simeon Shattuck's (who was one that was Baptized) there met us sd. Col. Woods & Capt. Lakin, and a Number with them, it now being Evening & Darkish, and as said Woods met ye said Mr. Fletcher, who was on Foot, he turned & rid along by his side assalting him with reproachful words & shaking his Horse whip over him & threatning him that if ever he came into Town again & he should Come a Crost him, he would Horsewhip him all the way out, if it should cost him half his Estate. And such Like Language, till they Came up to said Shattuck's house. Where said Fletcher went in and Mr. Parker had arrived before him, who Escaped ye Fury of their persuers at this time by passing by them as I Suppose unknown. Here they stopt at ye House and Capt. Lakin said if they would go out of Town that Night & promise never to Come into Town again he would do his Endeavour that they might go in safety. Upon which I asked him if they did not, wether he would do his Endeavour that they should not go out in Safety, and he Answered me, "It is none of your Business," and further saith that "We are Determined not to Leave ye House till we Clear it of those Preachers." And as I was Endeavouring to Convince them of the Evil of this their procedure one of the Company kicked me on the Stomock and struck me on ye Head. Another of Ye Company tells me if Ever I came into Town again he would see to it that I should not go out without having my hide well Sooked.

About this Time I perceived Col. Woods to be missing from his Company. I soon went into ye House myself and Left ye rest of them there near the House. But after we had been in ye House a Considerable Time and attended Singing & Prayers &c. I see no more of them that Night. I further well remember that at ye Baptizeing that I saw a Number that was Armed with Clubs & Poles on ye opposit side of ye River as ye other End of ye Bridge.

Since the above affair as I was down at Pepperell on Nvemr. 2nd on my own Business, there Happened to be a town meeting that Day and in the Evening I stopt into yet Meeting House to see some Persons that my Business lay with. Soon after they took under Consideration an Article in their Town warrant which was in these words, or very near (viz. "to see if the Town will take into their

Consideration a scandelous Piece in the News-Paper Signed Isaac Backus and to act thereon as they shall think proper"). The aforesaid Col. Henry Woods Being moderator of said Meeting after reading the Article, one of ye Inhabitants (who a little after was Chose ye first Committee man to Consult a Piece that Col. Woods produced to print in answer to ye account that Mr. Backus had Published) riseth and saith, "I motion that ye next time that Mr. Backus Come in to Town, he and all his Company be whipt out." Others say that ye Backus was now in ye House & talkt. of searching for him with a Candle. And some said that he had no Business here, upon which Capt. John Nutting saith that these Men were after Women &c. and as there was many Jeers and ye like Cast by the House, Col. Woods tells them that it was a waitey matter and if ye account of ye Town should be believed they were an undone People—that he did not Value his own Carecter in the matter so much, as he was known by Gentlemen & the account would not be allowed A Broad [of him], but he was most Concerned for the Credit of ye Town, that the matter under Consideration ought to be treated with Solemnity & Contempt & that ye account as set forth by Mr. Backus was a Pack of Lies, &c. Upon which the Narrative was read that Mr. Backus had published by ye aforesaid Mr. Hobart, the Clerk, and remarks made by him & Col. Woods & others as they went thro. & these persons whose Conduct had been exposed to the publick. Denyed parts and Explained matters as they thought proper. Col. Woods saith in respect to his thretning Fletcher & Shaking his whip over him, it was very likely to be true and that he did tell him if he ever Catched him in town again he would horse whip him and he believed he should still (there was none in the House that made any opposition to their Handling ye matter). Said Hobart saith that the Yong men had applyed to us for leave and they would through [throw] them all into the River. Mr. Wm. Green, one of the Comtee of Safety, saith that he would make some Apology for that young men's Zeal in the matter, which was this (viz) "They seeing ye Fathers of ye Town Suffer such Disorders to take place as these Sort of People [Baptist preachers] did not regard the Town lines &c., they saw Nothing but inevitable ruin [for the town] &c except they should take ye matter into their own Hands in their way &c" and much talk of this sort passed in ye

House, and Col. Woods saith further that this method that they were going to take would bring out ye betrayers of their Town &c that ye Halter was too good for Such persons Let them be whome they would, that Should thus presume to hurt ye Honour of this Town. Another saith that they Should be hang'd & that their Dead Corpses should hang under ye Trees so thick as People should run against them as they past ye Roads. About this time Col. Woods produces a Paper & ye Clerk and himself reads it, it being an Answer to Mr. Backus's Narrative in ye Papers. Then it was mentioned by some whether they would Except [accept] it or not or whether ye meeting should be adjourned to Consider ye Same. But it was soon agreed upon that there Should be a Committee chosen and they might report upon it in a few Minutes & accordingly they Did & ye Town excepted it immediately as soon as ye Vote was Called & voted it should be signed by ye Clerk in ye Name of ye Town & be published. Farther, said Woods, while ye Matter was Debating before ye Town, said he knew how he should git his recompence of Mr. Backus if Ever he Should come acrost him and as to his Informers, he would kick their asses and wring their Noses and would advise others as Individuals to Do the same. The above is the truth to ye best of my Memory which I am ready to sware to if Called.

Ashby, November 5, 1778   William Parham

THE HINGHAM RIOT

[Taken from the Isaac Backus Papers at Brown University]

We whose names are here subscribed testify that on May 28, 1782, hearing that Mr. Richard Lee was going to have a meeting for divine worship at David Farrar's in Hingham in the evening, we went there, and just as he was going to begin it, Captain Theophilus Wilder and Nathaniel Damman came into the fore room & sent for Mr. Lee and Mr. Brown into that room and asked Mr. Lee if he was going to preach there? He said he came therefor for that intent. They said he and his company had better go out of town immediately or it would be much [the] worse for them, for they were a chosen committee sent to prevent any such fellows preaching in that town. Mr. Lee asked if they had any greator law than that holy

Bible? if they had he should be glad [if] they would make it appear. They told Mr. Lee he had better go out of that town, and if he did not, they would carry him out immediately. He asked them if they had any law for so doing? If they had, he should be glad [if] they would make it appear. They did not, and he turned and went into the other room having the Bible in his hand, and desired the people not to be afraid of men, for our blessed Lord has said, fear not them that can Kill the body, but rather fear him who can destroy both soul & body in hell.

By this time Captain Walter Hatch came in and asked Mr. Lee if he intended to preach? He said yes, and he desired that they might have their meeting in peace. Hatch then went out to a great company near the door, and Captain Wilder came in and asked Mr. Lee if he intended to go forward or not? he said yes. Capt. Wilder then said, "Men, come in." Under which a number came in, and Zechariah Whiting being stript to his shirt sleeves by Wilder's order seized Mr. Lee by his left arm and his collar and twiched him away with great violence, and others, taking hold on him, halled Mr. Lee along clear out of town, cursing and swearing most terribly. In doing of which they tore one of the armholes of his coat about half round & tore buttons off his jacket.

About the time they got over the town line we came up, and a Hingham man said Mr. Lee might go and hold a meeting at his house, but some of them said if he did, they would carry him out of town and burn his house down. And if Mr. Lee went to mention any scriptures they would set to hallooing with loud voices to drown his [voice]. And one of them cast soft cow dung in Mr. Lee's face. Then they presented Prince Wilder, a large negro man, & said, there is your disputer, and some said "Here he is, as black as hell!" And Captain Wilder shook a long club over Mr. Lee's head & swore that if he ever came into that town again he would take him & tie him up and whip him thirty stripes.

Mr. Lee said, "That is not so much as they whipt Paul."

"What, damn you," said one; "Do you compare yourself to Paul?"

Mr. Lee asked them to let him have his horse and things.

"What," said some of them, "have you got a horse?"

Lee said, "Yes."

Then one of them said, "Yes, damn you, and you stole him too!"

After his horse and things were afterwards brought to him & Mr. Lee went and held a meeting in Scituate that night. But as the effect of the violence used with him, he was ill in body several days after.

Abijah Brown
Jaccheus Lambort
Betty Brown
Molly Loring
Rith Simmons
Lucy Loring

RICHARD LEE'S STATEMENT

I, the subscriber, not only give my joint testimony to the foregoing facts, but also to the following. By the way, when sundry of my friends were at a distance, namely, that as the mob carried me along, when I said I pitied and could pray for them, or mentioned any scriptures, they repeatedly smote me on my mouth with the palms of their hands, cursing and calling me by [as] many bad names they could think of. Some of them pulling me by the arms & others pushing me with their staves, and as one of them who had hold of my right hand fell down, others shook their clubs over my head & swore that if I flung another of them down, they would sink me to hell in a moment. I told them I did not fling him down. I then said, "I look upon this holy Bible to be the very best law that ever I heard of." One who had me by the left hand, seeing it in my right hand, said, "What have you this damned thing here for," and he spitefully struck at it, and the second time he knocked it to the ground, and then stamped violently with his foot and kicked it along upon the ground saying, "God damn the Bible to hell."

Richard Lee

LEE'S STATEMENT CONTINUED

As a lawyer accused me of prosecuting these men out of spite, on purpose to undoe them, I would further say that I let the matter rest for about two months, and then was informed that those men who had abused me in Hingham gloried in what they had done, & even thretned my life if I came there again, upon which many people of various denominations advised me to enter a complaint against them as a necessary means of securing the public peace and liberty of mankind, for if they were alloed to do so there, they might other places also.

I then went with Mr. Backus to Boston and took the advice of several gentlemen of note who all agreed that I ought to enter a complaint to the grand jury of Suffolk county. I then went and conversed with Mr. Benjamin Hammet, foreman of said jury, who advised me to come with my witnesses to their court at Boston in October, and enter my complaint. I did accordingly, taking pains to go from my home seventy miles to Scituate and took four witnesses from thence, and went 23 miles to Boston, where all five of us gave in our testimony upon oath before the grand jury, and then withdrew into another room, where Mr. Mason, the lawyer soon came to us and told us that we might go home, & they would send for us when they wanted us. We questioned him upon it, but he repeatedly asserted we might go home. This was October 1, and that evening we all return'd to Scituate. But hearing that a friend had said that I ought to have stayed & seen what the court did upon it, I went again to Boston, October 3, when Mr. Mason seemed sensable that he had erred before and he and the court ordered me to appear there on the tenth with all needful evidences. So I had to take another journey to Scituate and returned to Boston on October tenth with seven more witnesses, when we found that notwithstanding all this pains & cost which we were at, for the public good, these breakers of the peace had not been so much as summoned to appear at court; and the case was adjourned two days, and we were obliged to wait upon costs so long.

On October 12, four of the mob appeared in court and pleaded not guilty and then the trial of the case was put off till January 14, 1783, when they were bound in large bonds to appear. and we were also bound then to appear upon penalty of ten pounds each.

Snow, ice, and severe cold weather caused that to be a very difficult season. Yet I appeared in Boston with other witnesses. But behold, the guilty party did not appear, and in favour to them the case was adjourned two days, in which we had again to stay upon costs, with a promise from the court that the case should then be tried. Yet on January 16, the lawyers prevailed to have the case put off till April when we are again bound to appear.

BACKUS'S DIARY ON THE HINGHAM CASE

[Taken from the Isaac Backus Papers at Andover Newton Theological School]

Lordsday, July 14, 1782). Preacht a 3d time at Ebnr. Hooper's. The 15th I went and preacht at Joseph Dammon's in Abinton; the 16th twice at Abijah Brown's in Scituate; the 17th at old Mr. Lambert's and baptized Marcy Dammon. Brother Richard Lee was there who has been instrumental of considerable [religious] awakening in these parts within a year past; and we had evident tokens of God's powerful presence in these meetings.

The town of Hingham has been barred against this work [i.e., Baptist preaching] for these 40 years, and as brother Lee went to preach within its borders on the evening of May 26th, capt. Theophilus Wilder, a church member, at the head of a large mob, came and seized him, and with great violence, carried him out of town. He now came and lodged with me at Mr. Isaac Wilder's in Hingham, and the 18th we went to Boston where our [Grievance] committee advised him to prosecute them.

Thursday, May 8 [1783]. Preacht at deacon Eames's in the north of Bridgewater; met with brother [Richard] Lee there in his return from Scituate, and concluded to publish an account of his case with that of [one in] Attleborough last year. The referees who met upon his case the 6th [of May] at Col. Howard's were Walter Spooner, Joseph Gardner, and Wm. Baylies esqrs. But Gen'l Varnum, Lee's council [counsel] and Benj. Lincoln, jur. council for the rioters, got Lee away up chamber and prevailed with him to make up the matter without any public hearing and without consulting his friends. Varnum is to have £32.8.0 for attending once at Boston and now here, without pleading openly at all. Lee is to have but £44.14.2 for himself and all of his friends.

The Balkcom Case, 1782: A Short-lived Victory for Religious Liberty

Soon after the Declaration of Independence, most of the original thirteen colonies of British North America formed new constitutions based on the revolutionary ideology of republicanism. Most of these constitutions included a Bill of Rights that explained the fundamental natural rights that belonged to all mankind and that no government could take from them without inviting a revolt. Massachusetts adopted its new constitution in 1780. It contained two articles in its Bill of Rights that dealt with religion; Article 2 granted freedom of conscience and Article 3 stated that, nevertheless, every town was authorized "to make suitable provision" for "the support and maintenance" of religion. This ambiguity caused the Baptists to wonder on what grounds they might now be exempted from taxes to support the Congregational churches. When the town of Attleborough laid a heavy tax on all property owners to repair and enlarge the Congregational meetinghouse, the Baptists refused to pay their share of the tax. The sheriff seized some of their cows, sold them at auction, and used the money to pay the tax. The aggrieved Baptists brought a test case, arguing that under the constitution they were guaranteed liberty of conscience. A local judge gave them a favorable ruling, and for a brief moment the Baptists believed that after 150 years of struggle they were free at last. Their triumph proved very short-lived.

Fifty years before the date conventionally assigned for the separation of church and state in Massachusetts a court decision in effect disestablished the old Puritan ecclesiastical system. But the decision in the Balkcom case, though recognized by the attorney general of the state and by all others concerned as of crucial importance, has been almost totally neglected by historians. In 1783 the Baptists publicly hailed the decision as the culmination of their long fight for religious liberty in New England. It preceded by three years the passage of Jefferson's famous bill for religious liberty in Virginia. Had the precedent set by the Balkcom case been followed, perhaps Isaac Backus and Massachusetts rather than James Madison and Virginia would now be enshrined in history books as the source of the unique American principle of separation. And perhaps the pietistic theory of separation would have prevailed over the deistic theory in American constitutional law. The reasons this case should not have been neglected deserve some attention.

The Balkcom case was a test case under the newly adopted state constitution of 1780. Unlike the famous Quok Walker case, which now appears not to have been based on constitutional issues,[1] the Balkcom case was acknowledged throughout to hinge on the courts' interpretation of Article 3 of the Declaration of Rights, which was an integral part of the Massachusetts Constitution. This article, which John Adams had found too difficult to write in his preliminary draft, concerned the role of religion in society and the relationship of one sect to another. It was a compromise article that attempted to satisfy both those who wanted to continue the old Puritan tradition of an established, tax-supported church system and those who wanted a voluntaristic church system. It satisfied neither group and was the most hotly debated article in the newspaper controversies and town meetings preceding the ratification of the constitution. Samuel Eliot Morison has demonstrated that Article 3 was not, in fact, ratified by the required number of voters, though it was declared so by the committee that counted the votes.[2]

The Baptists of Massachusetts had been fighting to disestablish the standing church, the Congregationalists, since the 1640s, though by disestablishment they meant primarily the abolition of compulsory religious taxes—a definition the Puritans considered totally without merit. The most the Baptists had obtained was a system of tax exemption for themselves, the Quakers, and the Episcopalians. Adopted in a series of temporary laws after 1727, the tax exemption system required dissenters from Congregationalism to present certificates from their churches attesting to their being bona fide members of the congregation in good standing.[3] After the rise of the Separate-Baptist movement in the 1750s the Baptists, led by Isaac Backus, had waged a much more aggressive campaign for voluntarism. By 1780 they thought they had victory within their grasp. But despite the liberalizing temper of the Revolution, they had been unable to persuade their neighbors to put an end to the special privileges the Puritan system had bequeathed to the Congregationalists. Whereas Article 2 of the Declaration of Rights stated that "no subject shall be hurt, molested, or restrained in his person, liberty, or estate, for worshipping GOD in the manner and season most agreeable to the dictates of his own conscience, or for his religious profession or sentiments," Article 3 had gone on to assert the right of every town or parish "to make suitable provision, at their own expense, for the institution of the public worship of GOD, and for the support and maintenance of public Protestant teachers of piety, religion and morality." This meant that compulsory religious taxes were still to be laid in the new state.

The constitution did not mention the Congregational churches. In fact it explicitly accepted the possibility that any "Protestant teacher of piety, religion, and morality" might be chosen by the majority of voters in a town or parish as their standing minister. Theoretically, a Baptist, Quaker, or Episcopalian church could become the established or standing church in a parish, and the Congregationalists would then be the dissenters who would have to provide certificates if they did not wish their religious taxes to go to the support of the denomination of the parish majority. This was the concession the constitution had made to the opponents of the old Puritan establishment or, if you prefer, to Protestant pluralism. As the final sentence of Article 3 put it, "Every denomination of Christians, demeaning themselves peaceably, and as good subjects of the commonwealth shall be equally under the protection of the law; and no subordination of any one sect or denomination shall ever be established by law."

However, this concession was seriously undercut by the fact that minority groups in any parish or town were no longer to be exempt from religious or ecclesiastical taxes. Every male inhabitant or property owner had to pay for the support of religion under the terms of Article 3. This did away with "tax dodgers" who had formerly claimed to be dissenters in order to escape religious taxes under the terms of the old exemption laws. This was the concession demanded from the voluntarists. And they did not like it. For in actual fact the Congregationalists were a majority in almost every town and parish. Besides, the Baptists and Quakers were unwilling to accept tax support even where they obtained a majority. The best the dissenters could do in the few towns or parishes where they were numerous was to band together to prevent the laying of any religious taxes. But this itself was contrary at least to the spirit of Article 3, which stated that "the happiness of a people, and the good order and preservation of civil government, essentially depend upon piety, religion and morality and . . . these cannot be generally diffused through a community but by the institution of the public worship of God and of public instructions in piety, religion and morality" supported by compulsory religious taxes. In short, the Congregationalists still believed that men were too depraved to support voluntarily the proper number of churches with properly educated ministers. In their view a good society justified taxes for the support of religion just as it did for the support of law courts, highways, or public schools.

It is true that in some towns and parishes public sentiment had turned against religious taxes even among the Congregationalists, and Article 3 permitted any community that could support religion voluntarily to dispense with them. But the general effect of Article 3 was to reinstitute a system that had fallen into disuse since 1775. The new constitution virtually inaugurated a new ecclesiastical system.

In place of the old tax exemption system, Article 3 offered dissenters the opportunity to have their religious taxes paid over to the ministers and churches of their own denomination. Thus, even the dissenters, who admittedly had difficulty raising money to support their churches, now had an assured income. But Article 3 did not specify how transfer of religious taxes was to take place. Most towns and parishes assumed that dissenters still had to file certificates with the parish clerk so that he or the parish treasurer might know who they were and to what church or minister their taxes were to be paid. The burden still rested on the taxpayer to prove that he was a bona fide dissenter. Parish treasurers were usually reluctant to see any ecclesiastical taxes go to support any church but the Congregational one because this raised the tax burden on the Congregationalists. The epithet "certificate man" still indicated a man so ignorant, malicious, or fanatical as to be deluded into "warping off " from the true faith of the founding fathers and the accepted standards of the community.

To the Baptists the great objection to the certificate system was that it meant rendering to Caesar what was not Caesar's. It indicated at least a tacit acknowledgment that religious taxation was a proper duty of the civil sword. But according to Baptist teaching "Christ's kingdom was not of this world." And in the view of Baptist leaders of the day, like Isaac Backus, James Manning, Samuel Stillman, and Hezekiah Smith, the state did not have the right to lay religious taxes on all citizens nor on any group of them. To them religious liberty meant disestablishment, and disestablishment meant voluntarism. Isaac Backus, pastor of the First Baptist Church of Middleborough, had been one of the leading opponents of Article 3 since it was first broached at the constitutional convention. And all of the Baptist churches petitioned against it when it was adopted. Some of the Baptists knew that the votes that ratified Article Three had been juggled, because Noah Alden, the Baptist minister of Bellingham, had been a member of the committee that counted the votes.[4]

A test of its constitutionality was the last resort in the Baptists' fight for disestablishment. The lawsuit of Elijah Balkcom against the tax assessors of the east parish of Attleborough in December 1781 provided that case.

In December 1780, three months after the new constitution had gone into effect, the east precinct or parish of Attleborough voted to raise £23,000 in paper money ("at the rate of 75 of paper for one of silver," or six dollars per £134) for enlarging and repairing the parish (Congregational) meetinghouse.[5] A small number of Baptists in the parish who worshipped at the First Baptist meetinghouse in Attleborough were among those taxed for this purpose. When they refused either to file certificates requesting exemption or to pay their taxes, the tax collector took cows from five of them and sold them at auction, using the proceeds to pay the taxes and returning any money left over to the owners. But evidently Elijah Balkcom had no cow, or else the tax collector wished to make an example of him, for he was told that if he did not pay his tax of £0.17.6.3 (in silver) he would go to jail. Balkcom still refused, and on December 17, 1781, the constable, Eliphalet Wilmarth, came to his home and marched him off "towards Taunton gaol." Balkcom balked and finally decided to pay his tax under protest. He was released and returned home. Shortly afterward he consulted a lawyer and decided to bring suit against the tax assessors, John Wilkinson, Elkanah Wilmarth, and David Richardson, for illegally taxing him.

In the case that followed, Balkcom urged as his defense that it was unconstitutional for Baptists to be forced to give certificates either to be exempted from religious taxes or to have their taxes paid over to their own church because Article 3 stated that no one sect should ever be subordinated to any other. If he won this point, he would effectively undermine the intent of Article 3 and the plan of religious taxation that the Congregationalists thought was secured by it. Unfortunately, only a brief and uninformative official record of this case appears to have survived.[6] But from the diary and papers of Isaac Backus it is possible to reconstruct in considerable detail the trial and its outcome. Backus was at this time serving his tenth year as agent for the Grievance Committee of the Warren Baptist Association. As agent he was the chief lobbyist, propagandist, and advisor for Baptists throughout New England who suffered in any way from the existing ecclesiastical laws. Naturally, he took an active interest in Balkcom's suit.

His first mention of it occurs in his diary on February 24, 1782, a Sunday, when he preached "at Elijah Balkcom's in Attleborough, who was seized for a precinct tax on Dec. 17 and sued the assessors therefore before Wm. Holmes esq. Feb. 22 who turned the case against him, and Elijah has appealed to Taunton Court; 4 men more have each had a cow taken away for the same tax."[7] Two days later Backus took some notes "from the papers laid before said court" by Balkcom's lawyer, Colonel George Leonard, on February 22. According to these notes, Balkcom had been born in Attleborough of Congregational parents who had baptized him as an infant in the parish church of which they were members.[8] But in May 1780 he had become convinced of the truth of antipedobaptism and "left the parish meeting and went to the Baptists." The Baptist church in Attleborough had been founded in 1769 and had been under the pastorship of Elder Job Seamans since 1773.[9] This church was Calvinist in its theology and admitted to baptism and membership only those who had experienced conversion as evidence of their predestined election to heaven. Balkcom, though convinced of the truth of Baptist principles, had not yet received the grace of God; and because he had not experienced conversion, he was not eligible for church membership. He was, however, welcomed as a member of the congregation in the hope that he soon would receive grace. At his trial before the justice court of William Holmes in Norton on February 22, "Elder Seamans, Levi Maxcey, and Joseph Guild testified upon oath that Elijah Balkcom had attended their meeting ever since May, 1780, and had done his part in supporting the worship to their satisfaction."[10]

Backus also wrote in his notes of the case that neither "Brigadier George Godfrey, council for the parish, nor the judge" could "say as any certificate law had been in force since September 1779" when the old certificate law had lapsed. Nevertheless, "the judge turned the case aginst the bap[tist]s without hesitation." Apparently, the parish claimed that it would have let Balkcom out of his tax if he had had the courtesy to ask the Baptist church to provide him with a certificate of his new affiliation. Balkcom claimed that since the old certificate law had lapsed and the General Assembly had enacted no new one under the constitution, this proved that Article 3 did not permit the taxing of Baptists or any other dissenters.

When Judge Holmes ruled against this claim, Balkcom appealed to the County Court that was to be held in Taunton in mid-March. Backus decided to attend these proceedings and also to give the case some publicity. He wrote a letter to John Carter, editor of the *Providence Gazette,* that appeared on March 2, 1782. It is worth quoting in full for the combination of social, political, and religious pietism that animates its appeal. It is also worth comparing with James Madison's Remonstrance of 1785 for the difference in its tone and emphasis:

> The unalienable rights of mankind were so well defined by our public leaders, in the former part of our contest with Britain, and the rights of conscience in particular, that many gentlemen in other States thought that those here who were earnest to have our religious rights well secured while they were engaged with their countrymen to defend our civil liberties, were too jealous in that matter; but do not the following facts evince the contrary?
>
> Our new constitution took place in October, 1780; which declares it as an essential right, "that no subordination of any one religious sect or denomination to another shall ever be established by law." And it excludes all former laws contrary hereto. And the compilers of the constitution in

their address to the people, to move them to receive it, say, "religion must at all times be a matter between God and individuals;" which truth shines with a meridian brightness through the holy scriptures. Yet the majority, in many parishes in our State, still assume the power to judge for the rest about religious worship, and to tax the minority for its support. And for such a tax, made in the east precinct of Attleborough, in December, 1780, Elijah Balkcom was seized on December 17, 1781, and carried some distance towards Taunton gaol; but being obliged to take care of his aged father, who was then exposed to like treatment, he paid the money, taking a receipt therefor, and sued the assessors who taxed him, before William Holmes, Esq; of Norton, on February 22, 1782; when and where he proved, that he has usually attended public worship with the first Baptist church in Attleborough, ever since May, 1780, and has done his part toward the support thereof to their satisfaction, by the testimony of the pastor and two principal members of that church. Yet judgment was given against said Elijah, that he should pay costs; from which he has appealed to their county court. Five men more, who profess to be of the Baptists sentiments and attend their worship, were taxed in the same bills, and have each had a cow taken from them, and more are threatened; and all this without producing any other law for so doing, but such as were made in former days of ignorance, when one religious sect presumed to act as lawgivers and judges for the whole State, about soul-guides.

Now let these matters be calmly and solemnly considered. As religion must ever be a matter between God and individuals, because *every one must give account of himself to God*, nothing can be religion which is of a contrary nature. Religion is of infinite importance, and greatly concerns our present, as well as future happiness; but to call any thing religion which is not so, is the way to deceive mankind; and will any dare say, that deceiving them is necessary for the public good! Whenever any have been judged, and set at nought, because they would not act contrary to the dictates of their conscience, they have ever looked upon themselves abused; and much more, if civil penalties have been added thereto. And, say the scriptures, *happy is he that condemneth not himself, in that thing which he alloweth.* Rom xiv. 12–22. And may we not hope, that our honored legislators will soon take effectual methods to remove the above described encroachments upon the rights of conscience, and that all orders of men among us will henceforth be in earnest after such *happiness,* as not to be *self-condemned?*

Clearly, Backus is speaking out of a different tradition from the reasoned deism of Madison. Where Madison's argument is abstract, rational, and legalistic, Backus relies directly on scripture, faith, and the pietistic temper of the Baptist persuasion.

On March 13, 1782, Backus mounted his horse and rode to Taunton to hear the case argued and to serve as an advisor to Balkcom. He wrote two versions of what happened. The shorter version appears in his diary:

. . . the 15th lawyer Paine moved to have Elijah Balcom's case taken out of the court and referred to particular men; but in the morning of the 16th we met with John Dagget esquire and others from Attleborough, who owned that referees were not tied up to points of law as a jury are, therefore we could not consent to a reference because our aim was to know how the judges understood the present laws in these matters, and both parties agreed to refer the case to them; who were the honorable Walter Spooner, Thomas Durfee, Benjamin Williams, and Wm. Baylies esquires; and our cause was pleaded in a learned and elegant manner by the honorable William Bradford and James Mitchel Varnum esquires; the opposite cause by Robert Treat Paine esquire, attorney general of this state; and after a fair and full hearing the judges unanimously gave Balkcom damages and costs of court; which is a great step towards putting an end to that controversy, and calls for our unfeigned and heavy praise.

In other words, the Baptists and their lawyers refused to accept Robert Treat Paine's plan for keeping the constitutional issue out of the affair. If they had agreed to referees, or arbitrators, the matter would have been settled out of court and have had no legal force in determining the constitutional issue. The choice of the judges rather than a jury was, of course, in the best interests of both sides because the most learned minds were needed to weigh the fine points of such an issue. Their "determination" was agreed "to be final." The fact that Paine had taken charge of the case for the parish indicates the importance that he and the defenders of the establishment gave to it.[11]

Backus wrote a longer version of this when he returned from Taunton, which he headed "Attleborough Sufferings, 1781, 2 and deliverance." It provides some valuable insights into the arguments presented by both sides as well as revealing Paine's inveterate dislike for the Baptists:

Varnum opening the case, Paine answered him, and Bradford replied. Paine owned expressly that Religion must ever be a matter between God and individuals, and that he disclaimed all subordination of one sect to another, but pleaded that giving certificates was not a subordination to any sect, but to the government and that Balkcom was born and baptized in the second precinct in Attleborough, and that it was uncivil and [as?] well as unlawful to leave that society [congregation] without giving them notice of it, and insinuated that he left them to save his money. Bradford declared this last to be ungenerous and unjust, for he had paid toward repairing their meeting house before he left them, and they did not begin the work till afterward. After the judges had deliberated upon it they unanimously gave judgment, that the appelant recover damages and costs. A very important event![12]

So important an event did it seem to Backus that he wrote a tract about it on May 10, 1783, to inform the general public of its significance: *A Door Opened for Equal Christian Liberty, And No Man Can Shut It. This Proved by Plain Facts* (Boston, 1783).[13] He explained the crux of the case in these terms: "The east parish in Attleborough, supposing that our laws about worship were the same as formerly, taxed and made distress upon several persons, for the support of their worship, who did not attend thereon. One of them thought proper to try how our laws now are in that respect." Balkcom's contentions in the case were

. . . that RELIGION was prior to all states and kingdoms in the world, and therefore could not in its nature be subject to human laws; that the certificates heretofore required, were given to parish officers, officers of one particular sect, and not to officers of government; and as our constitution says, "No subordination of any one sect or denomination to another, shall ever be established by law," those laws are repealed thereby. And as the constitution was established by the people, it is stronger than any law the assembly can make, it being the foundation whereon they stand. Also the society to which the appellant [Balkcom] joined [i.e., the Baptist congregation in Attleborough] is as regular a society as the other [the parish or Congregational society] that taxed him.

The judgment of the justices in Balkcom's favor, Backus wrote, "not only settled the controversy in Attleborough, but has been extensively beneficial elsewhere." Backus and the Baptists claimed that Massachusetts' general assessment system for the support of religion erred because it assumed that every citizen belonged to the parish church unless he could prove otherwise.

If natural birth, and the doings of others [i.e., infant baptism by one's parents] could make a person a member of a religious society, without his own consent, we should have no obligation against the way of withdrawing from such a society that our opponents plead for [i.e., by means of a certificate]. But since religion is ever a matter betweem God and individuals, how can any man become a member of a religious society without his own consent? And how can a man who believes it to be impossible, practically say, that it is possible without contracting guilt to his conscience?

This was the individualistic-pietistic approach of the Baptists and of the nineteenth-century evangelicals toward religion. Whereas

Article 3 continued, or even extended, the Puritan principle of the
territorial parish and tried to fix it as a fundamental political institution recognized in the new state constitution, Backus and the
Baptists wished to move in the other direction. As they themselves
put it, they wished to return to the original principles of John Robinson and the Scrooby Pilgrims in favor of a gathered church of
true believers whose membership was open only to the converted
person who could give convincing public testimony of the inward
change the Holy Spirit had wrought in his heart. Robert Treat Paine
"accused the Baptists," said Backus, "of refusing to subordinate to
government" in their opposition to certificates. But the Baptists
turned the charge around and asserted that the government was
seeking to subvert the individual conscience and to usurp power
over the kingdom of God.

In this tract Backus sought to place the blame for the Revolution
on the Puritans who had misconstrued the concept of a gathered
church and turned Massachusetts into a theocracy:

The first, and most essential article in the order of Christ's kingdom, is
that no man *can see it,* nor have any right to *power* therein, until he is born
again. John i.12, 13.iii.3. And the fathers of the Massachusetts government
paid such a regard to this truth, that, during their first charter, none were
admitted to full communion in their churches, nor to govern in the choice
and support of ministers, without a credible profession of that change. In
their excluding of all others from a vote in civil government, and yet com-
pelling of them to attend and support their worship, gave the most plaus-
able handle that the British court ever had, to rob us of the stipulated
privilege of choosing our own governors, while they demanded our property to support governors arbitrarily set over us. And contentions upon
this point was the root of the late bloody war.

But the successful conclusion of this war and the recent decision
in the Balkcom case had convinced Backus of "the arrival of more
agreeable times' in which "the prospect of a much greater reformation [lies] before us." His interpretation of the Balkcom case was
that "all former taxes to support worship, were imposed in each
government [colony or province] by a particular sect who held all
others in subordination thereto; which partially is now expressly
excluded from among us." "All the power that the constitution gives

our legislature in this respect . . . is a voluntary obedience to God's revealed will."

This being the case, Backus was willing to withdraw his former objections to the constitution. He went so far as to say that he did not even wish to quarrel with the constitutional requirements for compulsory attendance at public worship and compulsory observation of strict Sabbatarianism: "We believe that attendance upon public worship, and keeping the first day of the week holy to God, are duties to be inculcated and enforced by his laws, instead of the laws of men; but we have had no controversy with our rulers about that matter." Presumably the further reformation in the "more agreeable times" ahead would gradually solve this problem too. "And a faithful improvement of our privileges will weaken it [tyranny] more and more, till there shall be no more use for *swords*, because there shall be *none to hurt or destroy in all God's holy mountain.* Isaiah xi, 9. Micah iv.1–4."

Backus's millennial optimism in this tract was reflected in the circular letter adopted by the Warren Baptist Association on September 10, 1783, in which the Balkcom decision was linked to the signing of the Treaty of Paris as a sign of the times: "For so much was said in the third article of our bill of rights, about the exercise of civil power in religious matters, as raised their [Congregational enemies'] expectations and appeared very threatening to us. But it now appears upon trial that the last clause of that article overthrows the superstructure which was intended to have been built thereon."[14]

Unfortunately for the Baptists, their moment of triumph was short-lived. The religious establishment was not so easy to defeat as was the institution of slavery. The decisions of one county court were not considered binding on the others nor even on itself. In 1785 another test case, for which the Baptists had had high hopes, produced a decision exactly opposite to that in the Balkcom case; this plunged them into despair. It was the case of *Cutter* v. *Frost*. A Baptist church had been founded in the second, or west, parish of Cambridge (then called Menatomy Parish) in 1781; in 1783 Elder Thomas Green was ordained over it. The members of Green's congregation refused to pay the religious taxes levied on them by the parish. In 1784 several of them were distrained and one, Gershom Cutter, was imprisoned for two days. Cutter, acting on the advice of James Sullivan and Levi Lincoln, brought suit against the assessors, Ephraim Frost, Jr., and Amos Warren, for trespass

for that the said Ephraim and Amos at said Cambridge on the thirtieth day of December last past with force and Arms an Assault on him the said Gershom did make and him the said Gershom did beat and Imprison and then the said Ephraim and Amos did then and there with force and arms as aforesaid unlawfully restrain him the said Gershom of his Liberty for the Space of two days and Carried him about four miles to the Common Gaol in said Cambridge and therein Closely Confined him until they compelled him to pay the sum of two pounds one shilling and sixpence two farthings to regain his liberty and other Enormities and outrages they then and there did to the said Gershom and against the Peace.[15]

The case came before the court of common pleas in Concord in September 1784. The court found for Cutter and awarded him sixty pounds in damages and costs. After this, the parish, acting on the advice of its lawyer, Perez Morton, appealed to the Supreme Judicial Court (the case at this point became *Frost et al.* v. *Cutter*). A few weeks before the case came to trial, Elder Green wrote fearfully to the Warren Baptist Association:

They have made distress upon three persons, two of them members of the Society and one of the Church. We have sued their assessors, and have attended upon two courts without getting a hearing. And next tewsday we shall give our attendance once more; but Brethren, we are under a disadvantage, our enemies will be our Judges. We ask your united prayers in our behalf, that God would influence our Judges and to judg righteously.

He added in a postscript, "They have rated us, meaning our opposers, towards carrying on the Lawsute against ourselves; and gave their list to their Constable in order to collect the money—was the like ever known in a land of light?"[16] Green meant that the parish had levied a civil tax on all inhabitants to defray the cost of their appeal against the decision in favor of Cutter, and thus the Baptists were forced to pay, as members of the parish, for a suit against themselves. This was not as uncommon as Green thought. Backus, writing at this time about the case, said, "As they are near the first University in America, all the arts of the politicians of church and state have been employed against them."[17] This was typical of the Baptists' persecution feelings.

Backus reports the charges of the judges given to the jury in the Supreme Court on October 26, 1785: "Judge [Nathaniel P.] Sargeant declared their old laws to be in force and that they knew no society in the Commonwealth but corporate bodies; with whom Judge [David] Sewall concurred, and the jury turned the case against the Baptists the next day. The other judges said little upon the case."[18] A letter from Elder Green to Backus on October 28 revealed the shock the jury's verdict (in accordance with these charges) gave the Baptists throughout the state:

We have lost our case ... The Judges gave a most shocking arbitrary Exposition upon ye Third Article of ye Bill of Rights. They declare no Society that is not under corporate Power is known in the Law in this Commonwealth[;] also that ye Temporary Acts for the Quakers and Baptists and Churchmen are still in forse and that the Third Article is perfectly conformable to said Laws—also that the Jewrors were obliged to determine our cause upon such Principals.[19]

As a result of this verdict, he continued, "The Parish Treasurer has given orders to these Collectors amediately to strain [distrain] upon the rest of my Hearers for Taxis which will amount to *100* dollars."

Green must not have reported the Cutter decision accurately, for if the old exemption laws were still in force, that would have been a direct contradiction of Article 3. It was impossible to exempt dissenters on receipt of certificates (as the old laws stated) and as well to require them all to pay taxes and then have those taxes returned to their ministers (as Article 3 specified). What the court seems to have meant was that dissenters were still obliged to give in certificates to the parish so that the parish might have a means of determining which persons were entitled to have their tax money turned over "to the support of the public teacher or teachers of his own religious sect." But the most important—and for the Baptists and other dissenters, the most devastating—aspect of the decision was the ruling that only religious societies or congregations that were incorporated by law (i.e., by act of the legislature) were entitled to receive the tax money paid in by their members to the town or parish.

The key phrase in Article 3 read "the several towns, parishes, precincts, and other bodies politic, or religious societies" should have the right of electing their own teachers and contracting with them for their support. What the Supreme Court said in effect in the Cutter case was that the phrase "religious societies" in this clause was simply a modifier of the term "bodies politic." This meant that the only legally recognized religious societies (congregations or churches) were those that had corporate status as bodies politic, that is, bodies created by act of legislature. Since all standing parishes were created by such acts, they were of course incorporated. But none of the dissenting congregations in Massachusetts had ever applied to the legislature for incorporation, and therefore they were legally private, not public, bodies. And what right had any private body to lay claim to public taxes?

The dissenters, even some of those who, like Samuel West, had voted for and defended Article 3 in the convention, had not found this interpretation in its words. They had assumed throughout the debate in 1780 that "other bodies politic or religious societies" meant other religious congregations than the Congregational churches or parishes. No one had ever thought it necessary for dissenting groups to be incorporated before they could take advantage of the tax exemption laws. And there does not appear to have been a single Baptist or Quaker congregation in Massachusetts that was incorporated before 1785. Under the existing English laws against dissenters, the colonies may well have believed that they had no more right to incorporation than they had in England, though individual members of such congregations were allowed to hold property in the name of the congregation. This latter concession had been written into Massachusetts law in 1755 by an act that enabled deacons or other specially chosen persons to act as trustees for money or property left as endowment to any religious body.[20]

If the verdict in the Cutter case were to stand, then dissenters faced an entirely new situation. Every one of their congregations would have to petition the legislature for incorporation, and literally hundreds of such acts would be required. This seemed as extreme a position for the courts to take against dissenters as the Balkcom case had been against the establishment.

Four days after the Cutter decision Backus called a meeting of the Grievance Committee in Boston to decide what further action should or could be taken. Before this meeting someone among the Baptists had consulted "a great lawyer" (perhaps James Sullivan) concerning what action could be taken so that the Baptists might, as Article 3 allowed, reclaim the money they had paid for support of their own minister, Elder Green. The lawyer, strangely enough, did not say they must follow the court's decision and seek incorporation from the legislature. Instead, according to Backus, he advised them "that if they would give in certificates to the ruling sect, that they belonged to said Baptist society, and would have their money go to the minister thereof, he might sue the money out of the hands of those who took it."[21] This advice, if Backus was correct, was based on a strange reading of Article 3. The article said: "All moneys paid by the subject to the support of public worship, and of public teachers aforesaid, shall if he requires it, be uniformly applied to the support of the public teacher or teachers of his own religious sect or denomination" where "he attends." The lawyer whom the Baptists consulted in 1785 "constructed the word HE to mean the teacher who was to receive the money and not the man who paid it," which was certainly a strained and ungrammatical reading of this sentence.

Actually, what the lawyer meant was that it would be more proper, legally speaking, for the dissenting minister to bring suit by action of *assumpsit,* claiming that the parish treasurer was withholding sums of money due him, than for the dissenting taxpayer to bring suit to try to force the parish treasurer to pay his religious tax to his minister.

The Grievance Committee considered the lawyer's advice and voted 4 to 1 to advise Elder Green to proceed to "sue the money out of the hands" of the parish treasurer in West Cambridge. Backus gave the one negative.[22] He believed that to take this action was as bad as turning in certificates in that it clearly acknowledged the right of the towns to levy the tax and to collect it from dissenters. He also thought it would make Baptist ministers look greedy and litigious, suing for the money from their adherents. But Elders Stillman, Skillman, Hezekiah Smith, and Caleb Blood chose to ignore his arguments and to fight the matter out on more pragmatic lines. Their reasoning was understandable. If Elder Green won his suit, he would get around the problem of incorporation, and this would save the Baptists much time and trouble. It would also obviate another matter of principle: whether incorporation itself was an acknowledgment of unjust civil power over the church. Perhaps, if Green won, the towns and parishes would stop collecting religious taxes from Baptists. So Green sued. "As many as were strained upon, he sued for the money in three cases before three different justices of the peace & recovered judgment; then their enemies appeared to concord court [Middlesex Common Pleas] where after a full hearing on March 18, 1786, the cases were turned in the baptists favour: upon which the parish made up with them. Tho' the money adjudged was not paid" very promptly.[23]

The Green cases were, as it turned out, an inconclusive victory. The Baptists had to yield on the question of certificates, and then they had to be prepared in every parish to go to law to obtain money that, according to Article 3, was to be turned over to them "uniformly" on the request of the individual paying the tax (or the request of his minister). Eventually, many towns chose the obvious way out. They ceased even to assess those Baptists who turned in certificates and thus placed the matter back where it had been before 1780. But other towns were particularly stubborn about the matter and forced the Baptists to wage long and costly suits year after year to win back a few dollars in taxes, hoping in this way to wear down Baptist resistance. It was reported that "it required in one instance fourteen suits at law before a town treasurer yielded the taxes, and in another an expense of one hundred dollars and four years' time to get four dollars out of his hands for the use of a Baptist minister."[24] Probably, in many cases the Baptists had neither the funds nor the aggressiveness to fight for their rights. And many towns continually returned to the verdict in the Cutter case to claim that they need not turn back tax money to dissenting congregations that were not incorporated. From 1785 until 1811, when the Act of Religious Liberty was passed by a Jeffersonian-Republican legislature under Governor Elbridge Gerry, the incorporation problem remained crucial in the Baptists' struggle.

The Balkcom case might thus be considered a legal fluke that historians have quite rightly neglected. But a second thought will reveal that it has more significance than that. For a time, in the crucial years 1775 to 1785, the whole question of religious establishment in America hung in the balance. It was possible that the failure of Article 3 to receive the necessary two-thirds vote for ratification in 1780 might have forced a reconsideration of the whole nature of the religious establishment in New England. It was possible that the Balkcom case in 1782 might have set a precedent for voluntarism. Both incidents confirm the fact that the issue was much more uncertain than a superficial study of the mainstream of events implies.

In addition, both incidents indicate that Massachusetts and Virginia did not differ so much on this issue as historians have supposed. The victory of Jefferson's bill for religious freedom in Virginia over the General Assessment bill supported by George Washington, Patrick Henry, and Richard Henry Lee was just as close and uncertain in these years. The fact that the balance tipped one way in Virginia and the other in Massachusetts deserves closer scrutiny. What precisely did make the difference in each case? And how "inevitable" was each result?

The whole debate over the Balkcom case, as revealed in the writings of Backus and the Baptists, brings home once again the fact that there were two or perhaps three different theories of church–state relations at work among those who advocated separation. The view of Madison, Mason, and Jefferson, as expressed in the great debates over this issue in Virginia, has been assumed to be the primary or fundamental one. Most historians and most recent decisions of the U.S. Supreme Court have drawn on the eloquent and logically consistent reasoning of these learned, latitudinarian Anglicans and deists in defining the tradition of separation. But in actual fact the position of Backus and the pietistic Baptists and evangelicals has been far more pervasive in the popular mind.[25] The loud outcry against the Court's recent decisions on Bible reading and prayer in the public schools testifies to this. The pietists, as has been said, wanted separation in order to keep religion free from interference by the state. The deists wanted separation in order to keep the state free from interference by religion. Backus insisted that the United States of America was and should be a Christian nation. Thomas Jefferson said it was definitely not a Christian nation. Backus wanted friendly cooperation, not a rigid wall of separation between church and state, and he had a very fuzzy view of precisely where the civil enforcement of Christian morality ended and the religious freedom of Christ's kingdom began. Jefferson wanted a high wall and had a very clear view of the line on which to build it. In the twentieth century a secular society finds Jefferson's view much more congenial. In the nineteenth century an evangelical society preferred that of Backus.

And finally, the debate over the Balkcom case should lead historians to ask what happened to that view of separation expressed by New England Unitarians like Robert Treat Paine and Virginia Episcopalians like Patrick Henry. Unlike the deists and the pietists, these men thought that religious liberty was perfectly consistent with compulsory tax support for religion on a nonsectarian Protestant basis. So many people, North and South, considered this the wisest course for the new nation that it is really not surprising that Massachusetts tried to make it work for fifty years after the Balkcom case. All of these questions need to be reconsidered before we will really understand what happened in the so-called Second Great Awakening, when America finally shuffled off both its Puritan remnants and its Revolutionary flirtation with the Enlightenment's secularism to emerge with an evangelical, voluntaristic establishment that was *sui generis* in Western civilization.

APPENDIX 1

[The following summary account of the Balkcom case is found in the bound manuscript volume of the Inferior Court of Common Pleas dated 1773–1782 in the Bristol County Courthouse, Taunton, Massachusetts, case #39, March Term, p. 410. None of the loose papers in the case could be found.]

Elijah Bolkcom of Attleborough in our County of Bristol, Yeoman, Appellant v. John Willkerson, Yeoman, Elkanah Willmorth, Gentleman and Daniel Richardson, Gentleman all of said Attleborough Appellees from the Judgment of William Homes Esq one of the Justices of the Peace for said County rendered at a Justice Court held at his dwelling House in Norton in said County on Friday the twenty Second day of February last, when and where the said Bolkcom was plaintiff and the said John, Elkanah and Daniel were Defendants In a plea of the Case, for that the said John, Elkanah and Daniel at Attleborough aforesaid were Assessors in the second Precinct in said Attleborough for the Year of our Lord seventeen hundred and Eighty and the same Elijah was the same Year an Inhabitant in said precinct and professed himself to be one of the Sect or Denomination of Christians called and known by the Name of Babtist and so by Law and the Constitution of said Commonwealth exempted and entirely excused from paying any Rates or taxes toward the support of any Minister of any other Denomination of Christians, or repairing any Meeting-House belonging to said Different Denomination and not liable by Law to be assessed therefor, whereof the said John, Elkanah and Daniel were well knowing; Yet they contriving to injure and wrong the Pet: and to cause Money to be extorted from him unjustly, did on the thirtieth day of December in the same Year at said Attleborough illegally make an Assessment among others on the Plaintiff for the sum of Seventeen shillings and six pence and three farthings for the Pole and Personal Estate to the said Precinct for the defraying the necessary Charges arising in said Precinct and for the payment of the several debts contracted by the enlarging and repairing the Meeting-House in said Precinct not belonging to the Sect or Denomination of Christians called Babtist and the said Assessors afterwards at said Attleborough on the same day last mentioned delivered said Assessment on the Pet: to one Eliphalet Willmarth a Constable of said Town for said Year with a Warrant in Form as by the Law of said Commonwealth is prescribed in such cases requiring and commanding the said Eliphalet to levy and collect the same Assessment according to Law and afterwards, to wit on the seventeenth day of December last past, at said Attleborough in pursuance of said Warrant and List of Assessment for the nonpayment of said Sum illegally assessed as aforesaid on the Pet: the said Eliphalet seized the Body of the plaintiff and him detained in Custody for the Space of three hours and until the said Plaintiff in order to obtain his Liberty was obliged to pay said sum of seventeen shillings and sixpence three farthing illegally assessed as aforesaid and also the further sum of one shilling besides other grate Expences and loss of time. Now the Pet: in fact saith that long before and at the Time of the making of the Assessment aforesaid so made on him as aforesaid he was and ever since has been and now is a professed Member of that Society of Christians called and known by the Name and Denomination of Babtist in said Attleborough under the Pastoral Care and Instruction of Elder Job Simmons and that the Pet: doth usually frequently and conscientiously attend with said Society on the Lords days, for the public Worship of God and that the said Elijah hath contributed to the support of the said Elder and so by Law and said Constitution is exempt and excused from paying any Rates or Taxes and Assessments towards the Necessary Charges of said Precinct and repairing an enlarging said Meeting House, and of all this the said Assessors were well knowing and also that the said assessment on the said Elijah was illegal, Arbitrary and vexatious all of which is to the Damage of the said Elijah Bolkcom as he saith the sum of Forty Shilling. At which Justice Court Judgment was rendered that the said John, Elkanah and Daniel recover against the Pet: their Costs occasioned by this suit. Both Parties now appear and agree to argue the Cause here, Now, in Court, before the Judges of the Same Court, and their Determination to be final—who are a full hearing of the Causes, the Pleas, Evidences and Allegations of the Parties, say, that the Appellant recover against the Appellels the Money sued for and Cost. It's therefore considered by the Court that Elijah Bolkcom recover from John Wilkerson, Elkanah Willmarth and Daniel Richardson the sum of Eighteen shillings and sixpence three farthings Lawfull Money Damage and Cost of Court taxed at Six pounds Eighteen shillings and Sixpence.

APPENDIX 2

[The following shorthand notes on the testimony at the trial are transcribed from the papers of Robert Treat Paine, "Minutes and Trials of Law Cases," Bristol Session, March Term, 1782, Baulcom v. Wilkerson, et al. These papers are currently being edited by Mr. John D. Cushing, and I am indebted to him and to the Massachusetts Historical Society for locating them and permitting their publication here.]

THE BALKCOM CASE

Elijah Baulcom v *Wilmarth and al*
    cas. cur: [the case as presented at court]
    Mr. Varnum
in May 1780 Baulcom became a regular Baptist—in Decr. 1780 the Tax made
Prov: Law 1757:
Chap. 6 of Const:
    6: Laws to continue in force till etc.
    Religion is Anteriour to Government and therefore can't be controled by it . . . —so is Philosophy—
This doth not adopt the [Power of Certification?]

no Law in force but what is introduced
Therefore they must prove it

are not certificates contrary to equality

can a Baptist call on a Congregationalist for a Certificate

would the Congregation[alist] wish it if the Baptists were more numerous

if no Subordination, then no Certificate

2: Lill. Ab: 298 A man[?] is obliged to give notice to another of that wch. he may [otherwise] inform him. . . . . .
he that gives notice must be subordinate as he car[ries?] the certificate to his equals

Prov. Law Parsons[?] obliged to go to memb[ers?]
Black: p. 87
Job Simmons, Elder. Mr. Baulcom has usuall[y] attended 1st Baptist Chh since May 1780
Levi Maxey, May 1780 he [baulcom] attended and signed the agreement
Jos: Guild junr, he has attended our meeting
John Richardson the people [?] taxed [?] offered [?] to have it

Isaac Backus and Thomas Jefferson

If a public opinion poll had been taken in the United States at the time the Constitution was ratified in 1788, most Americans would have responded yes to the question "Is the United States of America a Christian country?" However, many of the Founding Fathers were hardly orthodox Christians. Thomas Jefferson has generally been described as a deist; John Adams was a Unitarian. When Adams was president, the United States concluded a treaty with the Moslem nation of Tripoli (now Libya) in which one article read in part: "As the government of the United States of America is not, in any sense, founded on the Christian religion . . ." That treaty was ·ratified by more than two thirds of the U.S. Senate and signed by John Adams. Thomas Jefferson concurred that this was not a Christian nation and was elected in 1800 and again in 1804 without any difficulty. In 1802 he wrote the famous statement to the Danbury Baptist Association in Connecticut that there should always be "a wall of separation between Church and State."

Elder Isaac Backus, a leading spokesman for the Baptists at the time, believed in separation of church and state, but he was also among those who thought the United States was and should be a Christian nation. That would be true as soon as all those outside the churches were persuaded to become members. Religious liberty would create an open marketplace for preaching the various forms of Christianity and, in his opinion, the United States would ultimately be a Baptist nation, for the Bible says that "the Truth is great and shall prevail."

This chapter attempts to clarify the important differences between the deistic view of the new nation held by Jefferson and the Christian view of it espoused by Isaac Backus. Neither view was wholly wrong nor wholly right, but in the nineteenth century, the United States (under what some historians have called "the second establishment") was closer to the view of Backus.

The role of Isaac Backus (1724–1806) and the Separate Baptists in the development of the American tradition of separation of church and state has not yet been given its due. Yet any careful evaluation of this tradition must acknowledge that neither the position of Roger Williams nor that of Thomas Jefferson and James

Madison adequately defines it. The basic premises of William's position were far too Puritan in theology and too anti-institutional in
polity to be typical, and the basic premises of Jefferson's and Madison's position were far too rationalistic and anticlerical. Or to put
it another way, Williams was too great a perfectionist about religious
purity, and Jefferson and Madison were too indifferent, if not hostile, toward revealed religion to be entirely representative of the
American approach to church–state relationships.[1]

In the secular mood of the twentieth century the U.S. Supreme
Court has drawn heavily on Jefferson and Madison in its increasingly rigid interpretation of the "no establishment" clause of the
First Amendment, but throughout the nineteenth century most
Americans firmly believed that the United States was a Protestant
nation, and that as such its laws and customs should conform to
the will of the evangelical majority.[2] Because the Baptists and the
Methodists were the most widespread and numerous denominations in that century, it seems essential to include their evangelical
theory of Separationism in any attempt to define that tradition. It
is hardly logical to expect that the views of a seventeenth-century
deistic Episcopalian like Jefferson or Madison would accurately rep-
resent the views of these evangelical pietists. The Methodists, who
were still part of the Anglican Church during the Revolution, produced no spokesman for their views on this tradition during its
formative period. But the Baptists found in Backus a most energetic
and eloquent spokesman. In his long, active career and his tren-
chant tracts he provided a dedicated, effective leadership for eighteenth-century pietism that entitles him to rank with Williams,
Jefferson, and Madison as a key proponent of this fundamental
tenet of the American democratic faith.

Backus was born in 1724, the son of a well-to-do farmer and a
member of one of the most distinguished Congregationalist families
of Norwich, Connecticut. Baptized as a child into the parish church
of his parents, he grew up without ever questioning its orthodoxy
or its practice of the Halfway Covenant. But after his conversion,
under the New Light preaching of James Davenport and Eleazar
Wheelock in 1741, he began to notice how many of the church's
members were not really visible saints. And when the parish minister would not agree to exclude such reprobates from communion,

Backus and several of his relatives, together with a large number of the most respectable people in his congregation, left the parish church and formed a Separate church in Norwich in 1745.[3] A year later Backus felt called to become an itinerant New Light preacher, and in 1748 he was ordained pastor of a Separate church in Middleborough, Massachusetts. In 1751, after two years of spiritual doubt, he adopted antipedobaptist views and was rebaptized by immersion. He then tried to conduct his Separate church on open-communion lines for five years. Finding this impossible, he dissolved the Separate church in 1756 and organized the First Baptist Church of Middleborough on closed-communion and evangelical Calvinist principles. He remained pastor there until his death in 1806, devoting himself tirelessly to itinerant evangelism, denominational consolidation, and the fight to overthrow the established system of the Congregational churches in New England.

The history of separation of church and state in Massachusetts from 1692 to the Great Awakening, so ably told by Susan Reed in her neglected monograph on this subject,[4] is a story of how the Quakers, Baptists, and Anglicans fought, each in their own way, to establish their right to exemption from paying compulsory religious taxes for the support of the Standing (Congregational) churches. But in this early period it was the Quakers and Anglicans who carried the main thrust of the movement. The Baptists played a secondary role, fighting mainly for the preservation of their privileged position in the town of Swansea. The Anglicans, of course, did not oppose religious taxation out of any commitment to the principle of voluntarism. They frankly coveted the privileged position of the Congregationalists. The Quakers, although committed to voluntarism, rested content after 1729, when the Massachusetts General Assembly granted exemption from paying religious taxes to all members of their persuasion who could prove that they were bona fide Quakers.

The Baptists did not come forward to lead the fight for voluntarism until after the Great Awakening. Their theory of Separationism evolved slowly and painfully during the years 1748–1773. But the place to begin a discussion of their views is in the year 1739, just before the Great Awakening began. At that time the Massachusetts ecclesiastical laws stated that three kinds of dissenters were to be tolerated as persons exempted from supporting the establishment: "Anabaptists," "Quakers," and "Churchmen." All three terms had pejorative overtones indicating that the weight of public opprobrium was cast so heavily against joining one of these "dissenting sects" that even the opportunity to evade the high costs of religious taxation seldom persuaded a man to do so except out of the strongest conscientious scruples.

The law required anyone who claimed to be a member of the Anabaptist or Quaker persuasion to provide a certificate signed by his minister stating that he did regularly attend and contribute money to that church; the minister and two leading members of that church or congregation had to swear that such persons were "conscientiously of their persuasion," not simply tax dodgers.[5] The Standing Order considered this, and rightly so, a most generous arrangement. Compared to the status of dissenters in those colonies where the Anglican Church was established or to those in England, the dissenters of Massachusetts were indeed far better off. Due credit has not been given to the Congregationalists of "the Glacial Age" for the advance they made toward toleration by these laws—albeit the advance was made grudgingly and under strong pressure from England.[6] Many Congregationalists, however, resented the fact that dissenters received this special tax exemption, especially since every exemption to a dissenter raised the tax burden for the rest of the community. Hence, local authorities often made it extremely difficult for dissenters to obtain certificates, and the term "certificate man" was one of scorn and resentment throughout the eighteenth century.

Because the tax exemption laws in Massachusetts were temporary and had to be renewed approximately every five years and because some Baptists complained that they were not fairly administered, a committee of the leading Baptists in the vicinity of Boston, under the leadership of James Bound and Joseph Callendar, was organized in the 1730s to negotiate with the General Court over revision and improvement of the laws. In 1739, when the exemption law of 1734 was about to expire, the legislature consulted with this group and permitted it to submit a bill on the subject. It is significant that this group, describing itself as "Agents for the people called Baptists," told the General Court that they found the tax exemption system satisfactory in principle but wished that it could be a permanent rather than a temporary law. They said, however, that they would be satisfied if the current law were extended for ten years. Their petition humbly thanked the court for the exemption system which "hath been much to the relief and comfort of the said people called Baptists, as well as an honourable Characteristick of the mildness, moderation and Christian Spirit of the Legislators."[7]

The Great Awakening, however, produced a wholly new kind of Baptist in Massachusetts (and throughout the country) who was not so humble or acquiescent. These "new Baptists" or "Separate Baptists" began as radical New Lights converted during the Great Awakening; finding that the Old Lights were successfully thwarting their reforms, they separated from the Standing Order and eventually adopted antipedobaptist views. More than 125 such separations occurred in New England, but to their dismay the Separates discovered that the General Assembly declined to recognize them as bona fide dissenters. The legislators argued that the Separates had no distinctive marks as a persuasion or denomination to differentiate them from the Congregational churches of the establishment; to grant them the same tax exemption privileges as had been granted to Anabaptists, Quakers, and Churchmen would, therefore, lead to utter confusion and the total breakdown of the prevailing system.[8] Consequently, the Separates found themselves saddled with double taxation: they had to support their own churches and those of the Standing Order as well. And if they were so adamant as to refuse to pay taxes to support the Standing Order, they were imprisoned or had their goods distrained and sold at public auction.[9] Under this pressure the Separate movement gradually disintegrated; of the 125 Separate churches existing in 1754, only about a dozen remained by 1776.

Meanwhile, many of the Separates moved from their original position of "Strict Congregationalism" into the position of antipedobaptism. The theological reasons for this shift are complex, but suffice it to say that the question of infant baptism had always been one of the most awkward and inconsistent aspects of New England Congregationalism; the Puritans professed to believe that a church should be made up only of visible saints admitted to communion on profession of their faith after conversion. But this left undefined the role that those baptized in infancy were to play in the church when they came of age if they had not yet become visible saints. The Separate movement began in large part out of a reaction against the Halfway Covenant and Stoddardeanism, which were efforts to solve this problem but which, in the eyes of the new pietism of the Great Awakening, had only made it worse.

There was a certain logical consistency therefore in moving from the Separate position to the antipedobaptist position and arguing that a voluntaristic church of visible saints could only mean a church in which adult, professed believers should be granted the seal of baptism and the privileges of church membership. As the Separate movement began to crumble from outside pressure by the civil authorities, it simultaneously disintegrated internally from the dissensions arising among those moving into the antipedobaptist camp. Naturally, there were many in the Standing Order who looked upon this movement as an effort by the Separates to claim the right of tax exemption granted to Anabaptists. But few pietists were so hypocritical as this, and fewer would have been willing to bear the double onus of being schismatics and Anabaptist "certificate men" just to "wash away their taxes" by immersion.

Anyone reading the diaries and letters of men like Backus, who made the painful transition from Separate to Baptist between 1749 and 1756, will soon be convinced of the tortuous trial of conscience involved. In fact, Backus said that he at first opposed the idea of antipedobaptism because he thought the Devil was tempting him and his Separate brethren by offering them an easy way out of persecution. Like most Separates, Backus was ready to go to jail rather than pay religious taxes to support the Standing Order, but he was not ready to let his fear of jail lead him into religious error.[10]

The evolution of Backus's First Baptist Church of Middleborough from strict Separate to open-communion Separate to closed-communion Baptist principles in the years 1748–1756 was typical of many such transitions throughout the province. And it was from the new evangelistic drive of these Separate-Baptist churches that the Baptist denomination in New England derived its vigor and growth in the late eighteenth century. Backus, who quickly became a leading spokesman for these Separate Baptists, was aware of the evolutionary development of his own views. Writing in 1781, he said, "I was such a dull scholar in Christ's school that I was thirty-two years in learning a lesson of only six words, namely, 'One Lord, one faith, one baptism.'"[11] By this he meant that having started his spiritual life as a pedobaptist New Light in 1741, he then took ten years to evolve to the position of antipedobaptism, five more years to acknowledge the truth of closed communion, and then seventeen more years to decide that he could no longer acquiesce in the New England system of tolerated tax exemptions for dissenters. It is important to keep in mind the evolutionary and often pragmatic development of the Baptist position on church and state if we are to distinguish it from the more ideological and consistent positions of Williams, Jefferson, and Madison.

While Backus fought vigorously for the right of Separates and then of Separate Baptists to be exempt from compulsory support of the standing church and ministry, his early efforts were limited to broadening the definition of a bona fide dissenter to include the new Baptists, whom the legislature tried to classify as Separates, and to increasing the effective and honest administration of the tax exemption laws for Baptists. Liberty of conscience and freedom of religion represented for him, and for most Baptists prior to 1773, essentially a self-centered and denominationally oriented goal rather than an absolute or clearly enunciated principle. Nowhere did Backus argue on behalf of dissenters in general, as Williams and Jefferson so often did; nor did he join forces with other dissenting groups to work for separation on an interdenominational basis.[12] Always the Baptists worked with and for the Baptists. If their principles had a broader application, that was secondary to them, and it is as misleading to read our current theory into them as into the principles of Williams or Jefferson. Like all radical reformers, the Separate Baptists occasionally exalted their immediate personal claims into broad abstract principles. But in practice their goals were limited, their practices expedient. For example, they showed little concern for other new dissenting groups that arose in New England after the Great Awakening; in the opinion of the Separate Baptists, the Universalists, Shakers, Sandemanians, and Methodists were merely corrupt and dangerous heretics, not allies against the establishment. One of the most noted Separate Baptists, Valentine Rathbun, a minister who worked closely with Backus for the abolition of compulsory religious taxes, actually tried to persuade the people of Pittsfield in 1781 to banish all Shakers from that town.[13] Nor is there a word in all of Backus's published or unpublished writing concerning the famous lawsuit of 1783–1786 by which John Murray, the founder of the Universalists in America, won toleration and tax exemption for his sect in Massachusetts. Backus was positively vitriolic in his tracts attacking Universalists, Shakers, and Methodists, all of whom he considered as dangerous heretics to a Christian commonwealth as the Puritans had considered the Munsterite Anabaptists to be. He did not specifically urge their persecution, but neither did he urge their toleration. The same implacable hostility was displayed by nineteenth-century Baptists and Methodists against Mormons, Catholics, and Christian Scientists.[14]

Nor did Backus argue at first for complete disestablishment of church and state, for that would have committed the Baptists to opposing the established status of the Church of England at home. But the Baptists often found the king to be their strongest bulwark against persecution in Massachusetts, and they did not want to alienate him by attacking the church of which he was the head. It was only under the stimulus of the incipient revolt against England, and after the examples of civil disobedience provided by the Sons of Liberty against the Stamp Act, that Backus finally led the Baptists to adopt an uncompromising attitude against mere religious toleration.[15] It was not until September 1773 that the Baptists of New England finally took a stand for freedom of conscience as a natural or supernatural right and began a campaign of massive civil disobedience by refusing any longer to submit annual certificates of their dissenting persuasion in order to obtain exemption from religious taxes. And even then the line between church and state was drawn specifically in terms of compulsory religious taxation.

Many aspects of Separationism that we now associate with the tradition were still unresolved among the Baptists even at the time of Backus's death. Throughout the nineteenth century, in fact, the Baptists, like other evangelicals and the public at large, were quite ready to use the state to enforce their superior claims against Freemasons or the heathen Indians and Orientals. Francis Wayland, the

Baptist president of Brown University, virtually preached a doctrine of religious survival of the fittest in the 1840s, and other evangelicals were still preaching Christian imperialism at the end of the century.[16] Few nineteenth-century evangelicals saw any inconsistency in supporting laws to enforce the Protestant Sabbath or Prohibition, laws against blasphemy and profanity, laws against lotteries, gambling, theatergoing, dancing, and, ultimately, laws against the teaching of evolution. In recent years staunch nonevangelical supporters of separationism have cried out against the decisions of the Supreme Court preventing Bible reading and prayer in the public schools. Certainly, Jefferson would have approved of these Court decisions, and so would Williams. But it seems certain that Backus would not. And it is the pragmatic middle ground of Backus on church and state, not the more consistent positions of Jefferson and of Williams, that prevailed in practice throughout most of American history.

As a Baptist, Backus might be expected to have drawn on the work of his illustrious predecessor, Williams, in evolving his pietistic theory of separationism. Being a contemporary and later a political supporter of Jefferson, he might also have been expected to share some of his views about this matter. But in fact he drew little from either of them and developed his separationist views on very different grounds. Although he shared Williams's Calvinistic theology, he had no use for his Seekerism. Although he shared Jefferson's Lockean defense of voluntarism, he deplored his deistic theology. Sidney Mead has rightly pointed out that the positive ideological thrust of Baptist Separationism from Reformation principles was less important in achieving Separationism in America than the practical necessities of the New World situation. But his claim for a "rationalist-pietist alliance" is subject to serious qualifications, especially in New England.[17] The rationalists in New England were Unitarians, and the Unitarians, as Backus knew, were stout defenders of the establishment. Backus evolved his principles and wrote his tracts against the New England establishment before he had even heard of Jefferson or Madison. As for Williams, he had held Baptist views for only about four months in 1639, and his repudiation of their views for the more radical stance of the Seekers made him no authority for the Baptists of New England.[18] His books were a rarity in America, and Backus agreed with most Congregationalists that Rhode Island was a poor example of the results of separation of church and state because its religious institutions were so poorly supported; he frankly called that colony "irreligious" and preferred to cite Pennsylvania as a more prosperous and respectable example of the blessings of voluntarism.[20]

But even setting aside the question of direct influence on Backus of Williams or Jefferson, it is plain that there are striking differences in their respective approaches to the proper relationship of church and state.[21] Granted that all three opposed an establishment of religion that required conformity of conscience and uniformity of worship and that laid taxes on all citizens for the support of one state church, but this kind of establishment existed nowhere in the American colonies in the eighteenth century. Williams had to fight against total conformity and uniformity in seventeenth-century New England, but neither Jefferson nor Backus faced that situation.[22] What was in existence in most of the colonies by 1750 was a preferred or privileged church that received official aid from the state but that granted broad toleration to dissenters. These dissenters were totally exempt from supporting the privileged Congregational churches in New England after 1730, and the collection of religious tithes was notably lax in the Anglican colonies. The problem of religious liberty consequently was more practical than ideological, especially after 1776. As Mead points out, the pietists and rationalists agreed that social morality and order, not conformity of belief and worship, was the only real church–state issue to be settled.[23] On this point the Unitarians of New England agreed with those latitudinarians in Virginia—like George Washington, John Marshall, Richard Henry Lee, and Patrick Henry—who believed that a general assessment tax on all citizens to provide support for the church of the individual's own choice was the only feasible system in a poor country. Voluntarism was simply inadequate to build sufficient meetinghouses and support sufficient ministers to inculcate the principles of morality and obedience essential to a stable, honest, orderly social system. Williams had faced virtually the same situation in England in 1652 when the tolerant Protectorate also sought to lay religious taxes for the support of a variety of sects.[24]

In opposing the concept of a general assessment tax (Jefferson and Madison successfully, Backus and Williams unsuccessfully) the advocates of voluntarism may seem to have had much in common. Yet a closer examination of their statements on an ideal church and an ideal state indicates marked variations in their fundamental outlooks. Williams, for example, denied that there was any ideal church ordained by God, though he was convinced that the word of God had revealed Calvinism as the true form of orthodox belief.[25] Backus clearly believed that closed-communion Calvinistic Baptists, organized in a congregational polity but united in association, were the ideal "gospel church."[26] Jefferson passionately hated Calvinism and the priestcraft and believed that voluntarism would undermine the power of churches, priests, and superstitious creeds and would free American minds for a natural theology without ministers or churches;[27] he denied flatly that America was or should be a Christian nation. Backus and the Baptists, like most nineteenth-century evangelicals, were convinced that America was not only a Christian nation but a Protestant one. Backus looked forward to the day when Baptist ministers and evangelists would convert all Americans to antipedobaptism. Williams denied that short of a new revelation or the millennium any form of church or denomination should be formed; he even denied that God had called any men to be ministers, pastors, or evangelists since the days of the Apostles, and hence no man should make his living by preaching the word of God.[28]

Unlike Backus and Jefferson, Williams had an essentially pessimistic and premillennial view of history; the world was in the hands of Antichrist and would shortly come to a disastrous Day of Judgment.[29] This was far from the optimistic mood of the rationalist Jefferson or the pietistic Backus, each of whom foresaw the rising glory of America in his own terms. Nineteenth-century Americans preferred the pietistic vision of Backus to the secularistic one of Jefferson. And despite Jefferson's hope that Americans would all be deists by 1830, the fact that in the 1790s Congress supported chaplains in the army, navy, and Congress, placed "In God We Trust" on the coins, and happily supported the national days of fasting, prayer, and thanksgiving proclaimed by Presidents Washington and Adams indicates that Backus's vision was the more typical.

If Backus's difference with Jefferson is not obvious enough in these respects, one has only to contrast the bill Backus proposed for the Massachusetts Constitution of 1780 regarding religious freedom with the statements of Jefferson and Madison on this principle:

As God is the only worthy object of all religious worship, and nothing can be true religion but a voluntary obedience unto his revealed will, of which each rational soul has an equal right to judge for itself; every person has an inalienable right to act in all religious affairs according to the full persuasion of his own mind, where others are not injured thereby. And Civil rulers are so far from having any right to empower any person or persons to judge for others in such affairs, and to enforce their judgments with the sword, that their power ought to be exerted to protect all persons and societies within their jurisdiction from being injured or interrupted in the free enjoyment of this right under any presumption whatsoever.[30]

Jefferson and Madison never defined "true religion" as "a voluntary obedience" to God's "revealed will" in Scripture. They wished to free men's minds from superstition and to measure true religion in terms of the universal laws of nature. As Mead points out, "Religion was defined as one's 'opinion'" in Jefferson's bill for religious freedom.[31] For him the Bible was neither more nor less God's revealed will than the books of Euclid and Isaac Newton. But disestablishment for Backus meant leaving Christ's kingdom free to propagate itself through the evangelistic ministry of the Word and the supernatural grace of the Holy Spirit. Both Jefferson and Backus wanted separation of church and state so that the truth would prevail, but for Backus truth came through the heart by grace, whereas for Jefferson it came through the head by reason.

The views of Williams and Jefferson on Separationism have often been expounded, but the manner in which Backus evolved his position and the various inconsistencies in the Baptists' pragmatic approach to this problem in New England need more careful elaboration. Backus first became engaged in the movement for separation of church and state in 1748, when the parish in which his Separate church was located laid a tax to build a meetinghouse. Backus and all of his congregation were assessed for this tax to support the established Congregational church, and when the parish refused to heed their request for exemption, Backus called a conference in Attleborough in the spring of 1749 to which he invited the members of four Separate churches in the vicinity. At this meeting a petition to the General Court was drawn up, asking that the Separates be granted the same privileges of tax exemption as the Baptists and Quakers. The petitioners pointed out that under the charter of 1691 "liberty of conscience is granted to all Christians except Papists," yet "if we pass not under the denomination of Churchmen . . . or Anabaptists or Quakers and do not worship on the Sabbath with the major part of the town or precinct where we live," then they "imprison some and put some in the stock[s] and also take away some of our goods and chattles."[32]

It is significant that neither in this petition nor in any subsequent petition did Backus and the Separates or Baptists ever state that they wished to have full religious liberty granted to "Papists." In 1655 Williams had specifically stated that "Papists, Protestants, Jews or Turks" should have the same freedom of religion, and the charter of Rhode Island made no exceptions in this regard nor denied any civil privileges to Roman Catholics. But Backus and the Separate Baptists, being children of Puritan heritage, looked upon Catholics the same way the Puritans had looked upon Anabaptists: as dangerous heretics and subverters of civil order. At most Backus held that their peaceable presence might be tolerated, but he saw no need at this time to grant them religious liberty in the form of exemption from religious taxes.

Backus's petition of 1749, limited though it was in its quest for toleration, was not granted by the General Court. Five years later this same petition was again presented by Backus and his brethren, and again it was turned down. So far as I can discover, Backus made no further pronouncements in public on church and state until he published A Fish Caught in His Own Net (Boston, 1768). This tract was a polemic in answer to the charges of the Reverend Joseph Fish, the standing minister of Stonington, Connecticut, that the Separates and Separate Baptists were ignorant fanatics who deserved no countenance by the state. Here Backus first spelled out his theological position against compulsory religious taxation, quoting Biblical texts that he construed to ordain voluntarism and insisting that since Christ's kingdom was not of this world all man-made laws governing ecclesiastical affairs were contrary to divine laws: "For no man can serve two masters." However, he devoted less than 15 of the 129 pages in this tract to the question of Separationism; most of the work sought to deny Fish's charges that the Separates were heretical in faith and disorderly in practice.

Two years later Backus published *A Seasonable Plea for Liberty of Conscience against Some Late Oppressive Proceedings Particularly in the Town of Berwick* (Boston, 1770). Of the forty-eight pages in this tract, three are devoted to some general statements on liberty of conscience and the remainder to protesting against the censure of some antipedobaptists in the Standing Church of Berwick. Since antipedobaptism was, in his eyes, commanded by God, it astounded him that a minister should censure a Christian who followed his conscience in adopting this principle. The thought uppermost in his mind here and throughout his writing was that the state, by forcing men to pay to support the false doctrine of pedobaptism, was thwarting or hindering the spread of Gospel truth and aiding in the spread of error.

Finally, Backus issued his first and major treatise devoted wholly to the subject of religious liberty: *An Appeal to the Public for Religious Liberty against the Oppressions of the Present Day* (Boston, 1773). It is a strong and forthright statement of the Baptist or pietistic position on separationism and deserves to rank with Williams's *Bloody Tenent* and Madison's *Remonstrance* as one of the great American expositions of this principle. It owes something to John Locke,[33] a little to Williams,[34] much to Backus's reading of the Bible, but most of all to the historical experience of the Separate Baptists since 1748. This tract may be described as the declaration of independence of the Separate Baptists against the ecclesiastical tyranny of the Standing Order, for it was written to justify the policy of civil disobedience adopted by the Baptist churches at their annual association meeting that September. At this meeting the delegates from most of the Baptist churches in Massachusetts voted overwhelmingly to refuse any further compliance with the system of certificates and to suffer mass imprisonment if necessary to affirm their conscientious objections to compulsory religious taxes.

The gist of Backus's argument can be discerned in the five reasons he gave at the conclusion of this tract for the Baptists' decision to oppose the certificate laws:

1. Because the very nature of such a practice [giving in certificates] implies an acknowledgment that the civil power has a right to set up one religious sect above another.

2. Our legislature ... claims the right to tax us from *civil obligation* as being the representative of the people. But how came a civil community by any ecclesiastical power?

3. Their laws require us annually to certify to them what our belief is concerning the conscience of every person that assembles with us as the condition of their being exempted from taxes to other's [*sic*] worship.

4. The scheme we oppose evidently tends to destroy the purity and life of religion ... bringing an *earthly power* between Christ and his people.

5. The custom which they want us to countenance is very hurtful to civil society. ... when temporal advantages are annexed to one persuasion and disadvantages laid upon another. ... Not only so, but coercive measures about religion tend to provoke emulation, wrath, and contention.

Backus himself never signed another certificate for any of his church members, but this test of massive civil disobedience was thwarted by the events leading to the outbreak of the Revolution. For the sake of unity most towns ceased to prosecute Baptists when the war began, and after 1778 the problem took an entirely new turn with the drafting of a new constitution for the state. Backus was never able to persuade the people of Massachusetts or of any other Puritan colony to abandon the system of compulsory religious taxation. Instead, Massachusetts adopted a general assessment system in 1780 very similar to the one Patrick Henry proposed in Virginia several years later.

There is not space here to pursue the historical account of this problem. The point I wish to stress is that Backus and the Baptists of eighteenth-century New England thought primarily of religious liberty in terms of ending compulsory religious taxation, not in terms of a high wall of separation. To indicate how fuzzy the line between church and state remained for Backus and the Baptists, a few examples may be cited.

In 1766 the Separate Baptists came to constitute a majority of the parish in South Brimfield, and as such they were able to block the election of any minister of the Standing Order as the settled pastor of the parish. To resolve this problem the Congregationalists joined with some of the leading Baptists and agreed to vote for their pastor, James Mellen, as the Standing, or official, minister and to pay his salary by taxing all of the property owners of the parish. Mellen accepted this proposal and was elected. Religious taxes were assessed for his support; those who refused to pay them, some of whom were Baptists, were arrested and taken to jail. The opponents of this scheme, however, fought back by taking the matter to court, where they succeeded in proving that Mellen was not entitled to be a parish minister because he lacked a college degree or approbation by the Standing ministers of the county, which the law required for all parish ministers.[35] In 1770 Mellen's church, which considered itself Baptist, apologized to the other Baptists in the province for having agreed to allow their minister to be elected parish minister.

Backus, it must be said, deplored the whole incident, but obviously even the issue of compulsory religious taxation was not so clear-cut to many Baptists as some of their historians would have us believe. If Mellen had won his case, perhaps Baptists elsewhere would have tried to emulate "the South Brimfield Plan." The truth is that many Separate Baptists agreed with the Congregationalists that voluntarism simply was not an adequate method of providing support for religious worship. Backus himself admitted that the Baptists were frequently unable or unwilling to provide sufficient freewill offerings to build a meetinghouse or to pay a decent salary to their ministers.[36] One of the leading Separate-Baptist ministers of Massachusetts, Ebenezer Hinds of Middleborough, a close friend and associate of Backus, went so far as to petition the legislature in 1788, requesting the civil authorities to force his congregation to pay his back salary.[37] Even though most Baptist ministers engaged in farming or some other trade to supplement their incomes, countless Baptist churches broke up and disappeared in these years because they could not provide subsistence for their minister and his family.

Backus might assert that God would "preserve His church even against the gates of Hell," but the fact was that the Baptists were in feeble circumstances in most New England communities. And being good Calvinists, they recognized that human nature was too inherently selfish to part voluntarily with much money even for so good a cause as ministerial support. A secularist like Jefferson, who ultimately placed his hope for democracy in a tax-supported public school system, could ignore this problem. Seekers, like Williams, who declared (as Jehovah's Witnesses do today) that all denominations were wrong and all ministers lacked valid ordination, could be equally cavalier about the decay of church institutions; Williams said as much in his famous statement that the civil state would not be affected if all of the churches broke up and disappeared.[38] But the Baptists, who insisted, as Backus did, that a true government must be a Christian government in which there was "a sweet harmony" between church and state,[39] had difficulty in refuting the hardheaded, practical arguments used against a voluntaristic system.

Another example of the Baptists' willingness to take advantage of state aid for religion in this period can be seen in the history of the town of Ashfield. The Ashfield affair is famous in Baptist history as an example of the worst kind of persecution of the Separate Baptists, and Backus worked hard to persuade the king to invalidate a Massachusetts law of 1768 that made the Baptists in Ashfield responsible for paying support to the parish minister despite the general tax exemption law. Yet part of the resentment against the Baptists in Ashfield stemmed from the fact that in the early years of the settlement of that town, when the Separate Baptists had been a majority of the inhabitants, they had elected one of their brethren, Ebenezer Smith, to be the settled minister of the town and laid claim to the plot of land reserved in all new townships for the first settled minister. They also claimed the right to the income from the plot of land laid aside for the support of the parish church, and they may even have had hopes of raising money by taxation for their Baptist meetinghouse. In addition, they claimed that Smith, as the settled minister of the town, was exempt from paying civil taxes, just as Congregational parish ministers were. The Congregationalists in Ashfield took the matter to law, however, and the courts ruled that Smith lacked the qualifications to be a parish minister. Thus, the plans of the Baptists were thwarted, and the "persecution" began. But the fact remains that these Baptists too were not above attempting to derive such benefits from the state as they could get and from claiming the legal status and privileges of parish ministers.[40]

In the less rigid ecclesiastical systems of Maine, New Hampshire, and Vermont there are many examples of Baptist ministers who made good their claims to the ministerial plots in new towns because they were the first settled ministers in those towns. Elias Smith relates several instances in the 1790s of Vermont towns offering him their ministerial plots, and Job Seamans was actually installed as the settled minister of New London, New Hampshire, in 1788, and for several years he permitted the town to lay taxes for his support.[41] Backus disapproved of Seamans's being paid by taxation, but there is no record of his opposing the granting of ministerial plots to Baptists who were the first settled ministers in new towns.

After 1790 the Baptists, like other dissenters in New England, began to claim the right to use the parish meetinghouses and to share proportionately the income from the town's ministerial lands. There were numerous lawsuits involving such claims, and in many towns the Baptists were permitted to use the town meetinghouse for a certain number of Sundays each year in proportion to the number of their adherents in the parish. It all seemed perfectly just to the Baptists; since public tax money had built the meetinghouses and since the ministerial plots were a public provision for the support of religion, why should they not receive their fair share?[42]

But of all of the issues on which the Baptists found themselves most bitterly divided in the latter part of the century, that of seeking incorporation by the legislature was the most hotly contended. The principal purpose of incorporation was obviously to compel Baptist congregations to provide adequate compensation for their pastors. Baptist leaders like Hezekiah Smith, one of the wealthiest men in Haverhill, flatly disobeyed the resolution of the Warren Baptist Association in seeking incorporation for the church of which he was pastor in 1793.[43] Many other Baptist ministers did the same during the next forty years. The legislative records reveal that by 1820 more than forty Baptist churches had obtained legislative acts of incorporation.[44] Some incorporated Baptist churches in the 1790s and early 1800s sued their own members in court and distrained their goods for failing to pay their duly assessed share of the minister's salary.[45] The Congregationalists doubtless enjoyed the spectacle and delighted in seeing the Baptists admit the failings of voluntarism. Backus, let it be said, bitterly opposed incorporation, pointing out that the right of the legislature to incorporate some churches implied its right to deny incorporation to others. But his arguments were not always heeded.

Though Backus was consistent in opposing the actions of Baptist elders like Mellen, Ebenezer Smith, Seamans, and Hezekiah Smith, he was nevertheless far from having a clear-cut position on the precise line to be drawn between church and state. For example, he sided with the majority of the Baptists in the Warren Association in 1791 in voting to petition Congress (along with the Congregational clergy) for the establishment of a federal commission to license the publication of all Bibles in the United States. It never occurred to him that here also the right to license carried with it the right not to license.

Backus similarly praised the Constitution of Massachusetts because it required a religious oath of all officeholders: "No man can take a seat in our legislature till he solemnly declares, 'I believe the Christian religion and have a firm persuasion of its truth.' "[46] Many Baptists disagreed with Jefferson, Madison, and Williams that religious liberty should include the right to hold office even for Jews, Mohammedans, deists, atheists, and infidels.[47] Backus defended test oaths requiring Roman Catholics to forswear their spiritual allegiance to the pope before they could assume public office or, as he put it, to "disclaim the principles which are subversive of a free government."[48]

Similarly, it never seems to have occurred to him that the inculcation of the Westminster Confession in the public schools of New England was in any way an infringement on the rights of parents to bring up their children in their own religious faith. Backus, being a strict Calvinist, firmly believed that the Westminster Confession contained the only true interpretation of Scripture. To him the banning of religious training from the public schools of New England would have been the greatest wickedness—though he did not, of course, care to have infant baptism taught in those schools.[49]

Backus and the Baptists were also strong believers in the necessity of the so-called Puritan blue laws, which punished persons for profanity, blasphemy, or profanation of the Sabbath. In an unpublished sermon written some time after 1784 he praised and quoted a tract by a Baptist minister of London in which it was "deemed a kind of persecution by connivance when, for want of putting the laws into execution against Sabbath breaking, our magistrates permit the profane to disturb them that fear God in their closets and families."[50] He went so far as to condone the actions of his grandfather who, as justice of the peace in Norwich, had condemned two members of the seventh-day sect called Rogerenes to be whipped in 1725 because they were apprehended traveling through his jurisdiction on the Sabbath.[51]

And of course, Backus saw nothing wrong with laws requiring public adherence to his own puritanical conceptions of morality; laws against gambling, card playing, dancing, and theatergoing. There is an amusing entry in his diary at the time of the burning of the Grand Theater in Boston in 1798. Backus had noted earlier that this theater had opened in direct violation of the laws against stage plays in Boston, and when it burned to the ground just as the company was planning a grand spectacle of the destruction of Sodom and Gomorrah, Backus wrote that this was "a plain testimony against mocking God."[52]

The Baptists were also perfectly willing that the state, through its chief magistrates, should require certain days of fasting, thanksgiving, or prayer to be observed throughout the year, thereby turning weekdays into Sabbaths when everyone was supposed to stop work or travel, close his business, and resort to religious worship in the meetinghouses. Backus regularly read the governors' proclamations of such days from his pulpit and observed them in his church. This was part of the harmony between church and state about which he and Jefferson would have violently disagreed. Jefferson and Madison, as presidents, pointedly refused to issue fast and thanksgiving day proclamations as Washington and John Adams had done.[53]

There is some difficulty in finding a quotation in all of Backus's forty-two published works and his many unpublished letters and papers in which he directly and forthrightly opposed the law requiring compulsory church attendance by all citizens on the Sabbath. His only reference to this was published in a tract of 1783 when he said that he and his brethren did not necessarily agree with the law, but, he added, "we have had no controversy with our rulers about this matter."[54] If Backus, who was among the most radical of the Baptists on this subject, did not wish to push such a controversy, it seems clear that most of his brethren probably agreed with the Standing Order that such a law was essential to the good order of a Christian commonwealth.[55]

There is no neat way to sum up the respective contributions of Backus, Williams, Jefferson, and Madison to the development of American tradition of separation of church and state. Williams, it would appear, was the least influential of the four and probably the least representative, for few Americans since 1750 have been pessimistic premillennialists, Calvinist typologists, and anticlerical Seekers. Jefferson and Madison spoke for a rationalist-humanist element in American thought that has become increasingly influential in the twentieth century but that throughout most of our history has been the view of a small minority. But Backus probably represents most adequately the evangelical view of Separationism—the "sweet harmony" of a Christian nation—that has predominated. Historians would do well to reexamine his position and to give it its rightful place in future evaluations of this notable tradition.

[13]

A Learned Baptist Founds an Ivy League College

In 1764 the Baptists in Rhode Island, with help from the Baptists in the Middle Colonies, obtained a charter from the legislature of Rhode Island to establish a college. They hoped it would do for them what Harvard and Yale had done for the Congregationalists—provide them with a learned ministry and learned lay leaders. They yearned for respectability in civil society as much as for religious freedom in spiritual society.

Called at first the College of Rhode Island (and after 1805, Brown University), the charter required that its president should always be an ordained Baptist minister—a rule that was not altered until the 1930s. Although open to students of any persuasion, the majority of the college's trustees were by charter Baptists. To the Congregationalists it was always "the Baptist College," and the Baptists were proud of it.

The college caused some distress among pious rural Baptists who had long opposed a learned and "hireling" ministry. They prided themselves on calling their pastors "Elder," not "the Reverend Mr. So-and-So." They insisted that the pastor was only the first among equals. Baptist churches chose and ordained their own pastors and had the power to dismiss them. In short, they considered themselves ecclesiastical democrats. Most of their early ministers were artisans (cobblers, carpenters, cordwainers) or farmers. Most of them received no pay. At first, therefore, many Baptists would not send their sons to the college (it was not open to women). A spirit-filled minister was more important than a learned minister.

Nevertheless, the first president of Rhode Island College, James Manning, who was educated at a Presbyterian college (Princeton), proved to be remarkably successful in overcoming this popular prejudice against learning. He helped to raise the Baptists to respectability and renown. Today Brown is a member of the prestigious Ivy League.

The following obituary notice of James Manning was written by Isaac Backus in 1791 and has only recently been discovered in manuscript. It is published here for the first time. Isaac Backus (1724–1806) was a close friend of Manning and served as a trustee of Brown University from 1765 to 1799. The pastor of the First Baptist Church in Middleborough, Massachusetts, Backus was the leading figure in the movement to separate church and state in eighteenth-century New England. The author of forty-two tracts, sermons, and historical volumes, Backus is best remembered for *his three-volume history of the Baptists in New England (referred to in this obituary as "our History" because he wrote it as the official history of his denomination).* But his contemporaries knew him best as "the Agent for the Baptists in New England" and their foremost spokesman for the disestablishment of the Puritan (Congregational) churches.

The obituary was written for The Baptist Annual Register, *a compendium of Baptist information published annually in London by John Rippon from 1790 to 1802. Backus was a frequent contributor to this series of volumes, and Rippon relied heavily on him for news about the Baptists in New England. Why Rippon did not publish this obituary is not known. Perhaps he found it too long. More likely it arrived in London after Rippon had already printed (or set in type) the shorter and anonymous obituary that may be found on pages 241–43 in* The Baptist Annual Register *of 1792.*

The manuscript of Backus's obituary notice is still among the collection of Rippon Papers, in the Angus Library, Regents Park College in London, England, but microfilm copies of all of the Backus papers in this collection are now among the Backus collection at the Brown University Library.

Backus, being a good Calvinist, thought it significant that not only Manning but two other important benefactors of Brown all died in 1791. Hence, he appended to his obituary of Manning a brief sketch of the lives of John Jenckes and Nicholas Brown, also printed for the first time. In order to preserve something of the flavor of Backus's style, the original spelling, capitalization, and punctuation have been retained throughout this transcription.

Apart from Backus's general admiration for James Manning, there are two points in this obituary that are of special interest. First, Backus here explains why Manning, although one of the most learned and well-read Baptists of his time, never published anything of consequence. Second, he demonstrates the intense pride of the Baptists in the progress of their college under Manning's leadership, which led them to rank it above Harvard ("the University at Cambridge") for the ability of its students in "the gifts of public speaking."

The reader who wishes to know more about Manning's career is referred to the two well-documented studies Life, Times and Correspondence of James Manning and the Early History of Brown *(Boston, 1864) and* History of Brown University *(Providence, 1867), by a former librarian of Brown, Reuben A. Guild.*

OBITUARY NOTICE FOR JAMES MANNING

James Manning was born in Elizabethtown, Newjersey, October 23, 1738. And he was educated in the college at Princeton in that

government, where he took his first degree in September, 1762. He
was a member of the Baptist church in his native town, who soon
called him into the great work of the gospel ministry. The Baptist
Association in Philadelphia also esteemed him to be a proper person to begin a college in Rhodeisland government, where equal
religious liberty had been always enjoyed. Therefore, in a voyage
to Halifax in Nova-Scotia, in 1763, he called in at Newport, and
proposed the design to a number of gentlemen, who readily concurred with the proposal; and they procured a Charter for a College, from their Legislature, in February 1764. In the summer
following, Mr. Manning removed with his wife to Warren, in Bristol
County, where a baptist church was soon constituted, and he became their pastor. He also began a school there; and in September
1765, he was chosen President of the college, in which seven young
gentlemen took their first degree in September 1769. But the Corporation of the college met in February 1770, and voted to remove
it to Providence, where a large brick Edifice was built for it in the
year following.

The Baptist Church in Providence, the first in America, had long
been under Arminian teaching, and also held the laying on of hands
upon every member, as a term of their communion. Such darkness
had prevailed therein, that no regular church records could be
found. Mr. Manning was invited to preach in their church, and a
blessing was granted upon his labours; but their former minister,
and those who held to their former principles, afterwards drew off,
and formed a church in Johnston, three miles from Providence;
and Mr. Manning was called to take the pastoral charge of the old
church. And such a revival of religion was granted therein, near
the close of the year 1774, as added above an hundred members
to that church in ten months, as well as many more to other
churches in the town.

But as the American war commenced in the midst of that time,
and the college edifice became a barrack for soldiers, both human
and divine learning were greatly obstructed thereby. And though
the removal of the enemy from that State, enabled the President to
renew the affair of education in the college edifice, yet, by order
from a council of war, it was seized for a French hospital, on Lord's-
day, June 25, 1780, while Mr. Manning was gone to preach the

gospel to his people; and it was held as such until March 1782. And no recompence hath ever been made for the great damages which were done to the house, though no government on earth ever gave a farthing towards building it. Other places of education have had large grants from Legislatures; and both education, and religious teaching, have been engines of power and gain, in all ages, and in all countries. But as this place of education was erected upon truly liberal principles, it could not be acceptable to men who were fond of *commanding* others in religious matters. Neither could any like it, who meant to make their own *inclinations* the rule of their conduct. In the spring of 1786, the legislature of the state of Rhodeisland, elected President Manning a delegate to Congress; and a hope of obtaining a grant from thence, to indemnify the college which he served, for their sufferings in the war, induced him to accept of the office for six months. But, though he was received there with great respect and honor, yet the Congress did not judge it to be expedient, in the circumstances of public credit at that time, to grant any recompence to Rhodeisland college. Neither could our President obtain but part of his salary, as what funds we had for it, were chiefly in public notes of the state of Rhodeisland, the credit of which was sunk very low. Yet he persevered in his noble design, of establishing a place of education, where the highest degrees of human learning might be obtained, without subscribing to any religious tests invented by men. And in 1788 he greatly rejoiced, in seeing a Constitution adopted for all America, which excludes all such tests.

For extensive knowledge, fervent piety, and a constant labour to hold up light to mankind in general; with a dignity of behav[i]our towards those in the highest ranks, while the lowest had easy access to him upon all occasions, he hath exceeded most men that have ever been in our land. Yet his *humility* was so great, and his concern for the honor of our University, that he never could be prevailed with to publish any one discourse to the world. He knew how envious many were, and how ready they would be to make use of the least mistake they could discover, against the honor of the Institution for learning which he served; and he gave this as the reason, to his peculiar friends, why he refrained from appearing to the world in print. Though few men in America have held a more extensive correspondence by letter, or with greater esteem and confidence, than was held by President Manning; and his memory will be precious to succeeding generations, who will reap the happy fruits of his labours, and of his sufferings in a good cause. Indeed, his success, and the applauses of multitudes was so great, near the close of his life, that many are ready to say, "What were his sufferings!" But if they had seen the shafts of envy, which were cast at him, and the deceitful methods which many took, to obstruck his pure designs, and to turn all that he had done into measures that might gratify fleshly lusts which war against the soul, they would account his sufferings unspeakable. For nothing is so grievous to a pious person, as the opposition which is made against his pious desires and designs, by his inward and outward enemies, of whom *traitors* are the worst. The deceit of our own hearts, is the most dangerous to each of us, and the deceit of others is the next. *Deceit, is the poison of asps*, Rom. iii.13. It makes many teachers and professors of religion, *serpents, and a generation of vipers*, Mat. xxiii.33. And no men will know in this world, how much he suffered from such.

Yet he lived to see our college arise in esteem for learning, especially for the gift of public speaking, above the University of Cambridge, so that many young men were sent to it, from all parts of the country, and from all denominations. And he was enabled to govern the schollars with such dignity and condesiention, authority and mildness, as to be both feared a[nd] beloved to all, to an extraordinary degree. And his preaching was in the pure language of the gospel, and so plain as to manifest truth in every conscience, being as easily understood by the lowest, as by the highest capacities. He was a chief mover in forming the Warren Association, which has been a great means of uniting the Baptist churches in New England, and of spreading knowledge, purity and love through the land; and also of defending the rights of conscience, against superstition and licentiousness. For we have had abundant evidence, that a pretence of *liberty*, hath often militated again[s]t a conscientious regard to *truth,* as much as a pretence of *orthodoxy or godliness.* Indeed the counterfeits of all virtues, have been carried to an amazing height in our country, against which

Dr. Manning was a noble witness, both in public and private, in profession and practice. He was a burning and shining light, and his extensive benefits were greatly admired and rejoiced in, when he was suddenly removed from our world, on July 29, 1791, about 4 o'clock in the morning, by an apoplexy which seized him five day[s] before.

A gentleman in Providence published the following character of him, a few days after his death. "In his youth he was remarkable for the symmetry of his body, and gracefulness of his person. His countenance was stately and majestic, full of dignity, goodness and gravity; and the temper of his mind was a counterpart to it. He was formed for enterprise. His address was pleasing, his manners enchanting, voice harmonious, and his eloquence almost irresistible. Having deeply imbibed the spirit of truth himself, as a preacher of the Gospel he was faithful in declaring the whole counsel of God. He studied plainness of speech, and to be useful more than to be celebrated. Over the College, he presided with the singular advantage of a superior personal appearance, added to all his shining talents for governing and instructing youth. From the first beginning of his Latin school at Warren, through many discouragements, he had by constant care and labour assisted to raise that seat of learning to notice, to credit, and to respectability, in the United States. Perhaps the History of no other College will disclose a more rapid progress of greater maturity, in the course [of] 25 years.

"His death is a loss not only to the College or Church, but also to the World. He is lamented by the youth under his care, by the churches, by his fellow-citizens, and wherever his name has been heard of in every quarter of the civilized earth."

I am very sensible that men have been so often extravagant, in drawing characters of the dead, that many will imagine the above character to be of the same kind; and, though none may appear to contradict it publicly, yet it will be discredited by great numbers, who are unwilling to have their own conduct reproved thereby. For if the best of human learning can be obtained, and pure religion be promoted, without the least help from any civil government upon earth, then all the use of party tes[t?]s, and of secular force in such affairs, are injurious both to knowledge, and to pure religion. And whether they are not so, is freely referred to every rational mind,

> By their humble servant,
>   Isaac Backus.

Middleborough
November 11, 1791.

N. B. Mr. Jonathan Maxcy, who was educated in the College at Providence, was ordained the Pastor of the Baptist Church in that town, with great unanimity and solemnity, September 8, 1791. So that there is hope of their having good teaching, and a heavenly blessing in that place, after their Fathers are gone to eternal rest.

THE DEATHS OF JOHN JENCKES AND NICHOLAS BROWN

The families of Brown and Jencks have been exceedin[gly] useful in Providence. Mr. Chadd Brown was was an early proprietor of that town, History, vol. I, p. 93. His son, John Brown, was a magistrate in their government, and a teacher in Providence church. Vol. 2, p. 116. Elder James Brown's four grandsons were Nicholas, John, Joseph, and Moses. The last of them is a Quaker, though he has done much for our College at Providence. The family of Jenckes came from England after the death of Oliver Cromwel, and have been very useful in Rhodeisland government ever since. Governor Jenckes, and his brothers, Ebenezer and William, are mentioned in our History, vol. 2, p. 48, 91, 98, 396, etc. Daniel Jenckes esq; was son to Elder Ebenezer Jenckes, a member of the baptist church in Providence, and a useful ruler in their government. He was a member of their Legislature when the charter was granted for their College, and gave liberally towards it. His son John Jenckes, was also a member of that church, and liberal to the College, as well as often a member of their Legislature, and he was much esteemed, both in religious and civil society. But, alas! death removed him from all his connections here, on January 1, 1791. Mr. Nicholas Brown was also taken away on May 29, 1791, universally lamented. For two such members of the Corporation of the College, and then the President, to be all removed by death in one year, is a strikeing demonstration of the uncertainty [of] human prospects, and a loud call to every one to seek the kingdom of God, and his righteousness without delay.

[14]

A Baptist Autobiography
in Verse, 1820

Born in 1747, Jabez Cottle of Tisbury, Martha's Vineyard, began life as a Congregationalist. By the time he decided to write his autobiography, in 1820, he, like many other New Englanders, had transferred his faith to the Baptists. Cottle's life, as he tells it, recounts the ordinary events of an ordinary man who came of age in the Revolution (after spending some years as a whaler, like so many born on Martha's Vineyard). He describes his part in the Revolution, his efforts to establish a home on the frontier, his conversion to the Baptist persuasion, and his years as an itinerant preacher after his ordination.

Though in most respects his life was uneventful, he chose to see in all of it, the hand of God leading him to save the souls of the people of the new nation. Though the versification is crude, its sincerity is obvious. Cottle represented the kind of honest, blunt, hardworking citizens who made up the bulk of the Baptist persuasion as it grew, by 1820, to be a major denomination throughout the United States—a far cry from the days when Baptists were whipped, jailed, and banished.

This hitherto unpublished and unknown autobiographical poem has recently come into the possession of the Harris Collection of American Poetry and Plays of the Brown University Library. It is an excellent example of an unexplored genre of American folk art that flourished throughout New England in the late eighteenth and early nineteenth centuries—the spiritual autobiography in verse. Not only is it a striking primitive poem, but it also provides illuminating insights into American religious and social history.

When Jabez Cottle decided in his seventy-third year to record his life for posterity, he provided us with a forthright, moving expression of the feelings of the so-called common man and captured the spirit of a large slice of American life in 294 lines. Although Cottle participated in a general way in the important events in the birth, establishment, and early development of the United States of America, his own role in these events was, he knew, small and unimpor-

tant. What motivated him in writing this poem was his devout
Calvinistic belief that all events, great and small, in the history of
man were directed by the providential hand of God. If he mixes
here the intimate personal trials and tribulations of himself and his
family with the more imposing trials and tribulations in the birth
of the American republic, it is because he sees God's will at work
in the little as well as in the great happenings of this world. His
controlling purpose was to advance the Kingdom of God, to display
his life as a warning and an example to others (as God meant it to
be), and perhaps, God willing, to bring others into the saving faith
of Christianity. With great pains the old man lined out those events
that led him from vanity to salvation and those that brought about
the triumph of American virtue and valor over the tyrannical
oppressions of "old John Bull" as lessons for the spiritual salvation
of souls and witnesses to the glory of God. Freedom from Satan's
bondage seemed implicit in both victories, and the poem thus em-
bodies that subtle mixture of pietistic fervor and patriotic pride
that characterized the millennial impetus of early nineteenth-
century America.

   This poem has a spontaneous, simple, yet moving power that
conveys the piety and integrity of the writer.[1] Here and there it is
crude, strained, and somewhat unclear. For an unlettered poet,
however, Cottle displays a remarkable sense of feeling for "ryme,"
and although the verse is extremely uneven, it will stand comparison with the more formally correct work of Joel Barlow or Timothy
Dwight. Cottle shows sufficient sophistication to depart from the
neoclassical rhymed couplet and iambic pentameter by occasionally
writing triplets or short and long lines. Often, obviously, his depar-
tures in rhyme or in meter come as the result of his inability to find
the right words. But the strength of the poem lies in his unwillingness to sacrifice content to form. He is more interested in expressing
his thoughts accurately than in making his lines scan.

   Jabez Cottle was born in Tisbury, Martha's Vineyard, February
22, 1746/7.[2] He was the third of seven sons born of Sylvanus Cottle.
Sylvanus Cottle's great-grandfather, Edward Cottle, had been born
in Wiltshire, England, about 1628 and emigrated to Massachusetts
in 1650. Jabez Cottle's mother, Abigail Sherman, was Sylvanus's
second wife. She was descended from the families of William Brad-

ford and Edward Winslow of the old Plymouth Colony. Sylvanus
Cottle was, like most of the settlers of Tisbury, a poor and pious
husbandman. He was sufficiently respected by his neighbors to be
chosen deacon of the Tisbury parish church. Jabez and his brothers
and sisters were raised in the atmosphere of Calvinistic piety stim-
ulated by the first Great Awakening. But he did not discover that
he was one of the elect until long after he had reached manhood.[3]

As he reports in this poem, Jabez Cottle received permission
from his parents to become a sailor at the age of fifteen. For six
years he lived a hard but exciting life aboard a whaler in the great
days of whaling, when spermacetti "oil resembling honey . . . never
fail'd to bring the ready money." In 1768 he gave up the sea to
become a farmer. And on November 9, 1772, he married Sarah
Arnold of Rochester, Massachusetts (the Cottles having moved from
Tisbury to Rochester in 1760). They had five sons and five daughters. The next year he and two of his brothers moved to Woodstock,
Vermont, then a frontier community. The rest of the large Cottle
family moved to Woodstock in subsequent years. It should be noted
that Deacon Sylvanus Cottle (Jabez's father) became a Baptist in
1774 and joined the Third Baptist Church of Middleborough,
where he played a leading role until moving to Woodstock in 1778.[4]
According to the town records, the Cottle family became the first
settlers in South Woodstock, and owned most of the land in that
area. By 1790 there were forty-seven Cottles, young and old, living
in South Woodstock; the village was known locally as Cottle Town.

During the Revolution, Warren Cottle (Jabez's brother) became
a captain in the militia, and Jabez himself went "to meet the haughty
foe" as a militiaman but evidently was never engaged in any fighting.[5] In 1778 he built a log house and cleared his land for farming,
and in 1779 he built a gristmill with his brother Warren, which he
later converted to a fulling mill and clothier's works. That same
year, 1779, he was elected a selectman of the town and often served
in that capacity and as moderator of the town meetings in succeeding years. He built a second gristmill lower down the stream on his
farm in 1781, which "would help the owner and the publick too."

In 1782 and 1784 Jabez Cottle was elected town representative
to the General Assembly of New York (Vermont still being claimed
as part of New York State), and later he served several terms as a

representative to the Vermont legislature. He subscribed toward the salary of a schoolmaster who conducted a winter school in South Woodstock, and in 1797 he became the first president of the Woodstock Social Library. In 1801 he was appointed justice of the peace, performing most of the civil marriages in the town during his last twenty years.

The great turning point in his life came in 1785, when he was converted at a revival meeting and joined the Second Baptist Church of Woodstock. A few years later this church merged with the First Baptist Church, to which most of the Cottles belonged.[6] Cottle shared the views of those members of his church who stated in a public letter to the established church in 1793 that they would not pay taxes to the parish for the support of a Congregational church that they could not in conscience attend and whose tax-supported ecclesiastical system smacked too much of the same kind of tyranny they had just thrown off in the Revolution.[7]

As he explains in his poem, Jabez Cottle was received into the Baptist church on a public profession of his conversion, but at first his faith was weak. It was not until the Lord chastised him in the year 1800 by striking his wife with lightning and sending her permanently out of her mind that he came to accept the arbitrary grace of a sovereign and unfathomable God. Thus, "at last a wise, a holy God, / Did visit me with his chastiseing rod / That he his wand'ring sheep might now reclaim."

Soon afterward he was made a deacon of the church, and in 1803, when the church lost its pastor, he was ordained as Elder (the Baptists never required that their ministers be college-educated, only that they be converted, orthodox, and have the gift of preaching).[8] This church belonged to the Woodstock Baptist Association, which formed a missionary society in 1806 and commissioned volunteers like Cottle for missionary tours of two months' duration or more to the frontier areas of Vermont, New Hampshire, and Canada.[9] In 1811, as a result of a schism in the Woodstock Baptist Church, Jabez Cottle transferred to the East Windsor Baptist Church, where he was again ordained pastor.[10]

In 1799 his brothers, Warren and Joseph, moved west to the Louisiana territory and settled in Missouri, where most of the restless Cottle family soon followed them. Jabez, however, remained in

Woodstock till his death. He built a solid brick house which is still standing. He completed his spiritual autobiography on his seventy-third birthday, three months before his death on June 4, 1820.

Life of Eld. Jabez Cottle
  from the original manuscript
  Written by himself
  March 5th A.D. 1822[11]

On Marthas-Vineyard Island it appears
I first began my few and evil years.
In seventeen hundred forty Six and one
My mother first embrac'd her first born Son.[12]
To love the cause and bear the cross of Christ
According as I advanc'd in age
To act my part on this lifes busy stage
Unwearied pains they took to lead my mind
From vain pursuits substantial good to find[;]
Gods holy word was daily read with prayer
That they its precepts might observe with care[.]
But when arriv'd to fifteen years or more
My disposition led me from their door
In chase of false delights;—Obtained consent
Then ship'd a voyage and out to sea we went[.]
From Carolina's shores, off 'Hatteras
We crus'd the gulf stream down. Our business was
To seek and take the Spermacetti Whale—
Bring her 'long side, hall down our forward sail
Scuttle her head and then prepare a pail
And from it fill three hogsheads, sometimes four
Sometimes a little less and sometimes more
As was their size, of Oil resembling honey
Which never fail'd to bring the ready money.
And now perhaps we think it best to try
Our luck beneath an East and Northern sky[.]
Passing the guy of Canso, we explore
The craggy coast of Labradore
Passing the straits of the great Hudsons mouth

South from the coast of Green land seek our prey
Among those icy islands make a stay
Whose lofty summits towring towards the skies
And their broad bases speak their pond'rous size[.]
Standing a Southern course in search of whales
Leaving the vast mountainous Newfoundland
Bearing far off upon our starboard hand
Perhaps a distance from its nearest shore
At least one hundred leagues and perhaps more[.]
East of the grand bank we our voyage complete
Put up our helm and then cast off main sheet
And now our sails all fill'd a Western course we stand
The isle of Sables on our Starboard hand
We shape our course for Marthas-Vineyard sound
Perhaps on Georges bank we may find ground
Crossing the shoals and up the sound proceed
The tide being fair we're carried through with speed
Steering due North which brings us into port
Where all our owners and our friends resort[.]
Our Colours flying at mast head will tell
As far as seen that all on board are well[.]
We now heave out our boat and go on shore
Give up the chase and go to sea no more.
Thus six long years unprofitably spent
Because my mind on vanity was bent.
I served here in this marritime school
With wisdoms lessons urg'd, but what a fool
I was. And had no heart for to improve
The precious lessons sent me from above[.]
But now I see my folly and repent
That so much time in vanity I spent[.]
My present age is twenty one and more—
'Shall now my fortune try upon the shore[.]
My aged parents now in their decline
Wishing their worldly cares to resign
Into my hands to do as if they all were mine
Pay up their debts and some things specified
And have their worldly int'rest when they died[.]

To which at last I gave my full consent
And all my calculations to that object bent.
Thinking it no longer best to be alone
Rememb'ring two is better far than one.
I made my choice—She readily consented
With which I ever since have been contented[.]
I now was almost twenty Six years old
And now (if ever) strong[,] courag[e]ous, bold[.]
Soon after which the war broke out and rag'd
Yankees and Brittons often were engag'd[:]
One in the cause of liberty and life
Love of his Country, children and his wife,
Step'd forth a volunteer courag[e]ous bold
While the other's greatest stimulus was gold
No love of patriotic ardour in his breast
By British press gangs into service press'd
With beauty, booty for the countersign
Their brutal lusts to foulest deeds incline[.]
In such a case t'was easy to divine
Who won the field, whose robes in vic'try shine
And whose bold brows the laurel wreaths entwine[.]
During this war I took an active part
According to my sphere with all my heart
Led out my men to meet the haughty foe
And from our country to ward off the blow
Yet never could our courage fully test
By meeting foes in battles breast to breast.
My faith was strong we should at last prevail
The cause of justice sure will never fail[.]
A figure struck my mind and I will try
The idea plainly to exemplify[:]
A pair of ballances from the heavens suspended
The beams of which far East and West extended[;]
From both these ends a large scale was let down
To weigh the cause betwixt us and the Crown[:]
In one end justice, liberty and all
Such heavenly weights to Brittain looking small[;]
The other, gold, pride, power and old John Bull

Oppression Tyranny pil'd up and heaping full
Of such trumpery, and all
Flew up, shew'd tekel wrote upon her wall.
After seven long years and more had roll'd on[.]
Our armys led by the great Washington
As if to bring the contest to a close
And humble low our mercenary foes[,]
Cornwallis and his army all were taken
At York town if I am not much mistaken
And Brittain being greatly disappointed
When come to see her colonies disjointed
And she with all her Germanick attendants
At last compell'd to own our independence
And she together with her boasted Navy
Forc'd to knuck under and cry out pecavy[.]
About this time I moved into Vermont
Purchas'd wild land and built a log house upon't[.]
The town and Country all around was new
Inhabitants and neighbours very few[.]
Fore seeing these and many other ills
I preparation made for building mills
Which when completed verry well I knew
Would help the owner and the publick too[.]
About this time my father's sick and died
His children gathered round his bed and cried[;]
But since it's God who gave—he takes away
Let us be still—his sovereign will obey[.]
His body in the silent grave shall lay
Untill the great the resurrection day
When it shall rise all glorious to behold
Refin'd from sin and purified like gold[.]
About this time our fields with worms abound
Armies of insects crawling on the ground
Enter our meadows and destroy our grass
Then all in rank into our cornfields pass[.]
The hand of God in this appear'd so clear
Which made the hearts of some to quake and fear[.]
Among the rest I view'd myself to be

Fit food for worms and nothing could I see
Why I was spar'd while others ceas'd to be[.]
I saw my time that's pass'd was spent in vain
Beloved self 's the object. Worldly gain
And all the blessings I enjoy below
Freely from God the living fountains flow
My worldly int'rest, children and my Wife
And all my mental powers, Yea and my life
I ow'd to God. Ten thousand talents more
And still was adding to th'enormous score[.]
I see that all my vows made in distress
If God would help me I would do no less
Than love and serve him while I liv'd below
Reform myself and be religious too
In stead of which when worldly prospects fail
Those wicked murm'rings in my heart prevail[.]
I see 'twas vain to trust to reformation
I lean upon as hope of my salvation[;][13]
The sovereign power and grace of God alone
Abounding through his well beloved son
My only hope the anchor of my soul[.]
And here I trust he made my spirit whole[.]
A diff 'rent prospect open'd to my view
Old things were done away, all things were new[.]
A publick declaration now I found
My duty 'twas to make, in conscience bound,
Of what I thought the Lord had done for me
That friends and neighbours, every one, might see
That mercy, pardon's[14] all divinely free
God had in store for sinners such as we.
The saints appeared beautiful to me[;][15]
I thought Christs image in them I coud see[.]
Gave my relation to the church, expecting
To be set by, but found no one rejecting[.]
Some time I strove to keep my conscience clear
By faithfullness according to my sphere
And found Christs yoke to be exceeding light
When I his humble footsteps kept in sight[.]

But O alas how soon I got away
And verry little could I say
About the cause of Christ, but still did go
On with his children with my mind so low
Untill at last a wise[,] a holy God,
Did visit me with his chastiseing rod
That he his wand'ring sheep might now reclaim
And bring it home into his fold again[:]
My bosom friend the partner of my life
A tender mother and a virtuous wife
The mother of ten children, five of whom were sons
And now alive in health save one is not
Which di'd in infancy—almost forgot[.]
A husband—nine children round our board
With plenty crown'd for which we bless the lord
Our prospects clear the skies exceeding bright
When lo a heavy cloud appears in sight
A flash of lightning stream'd before our eyes
Lights on my wife—our worldly comfort dies
She's now derang'd in all her pow'rs of mind
My wife is lost—a Bedlemite I find.
Ye children who have mothers, husbands wives
Precarious is their reason and their lives[;]
Therefore be wise and learn to love the giver
More than the gift and you shall live forever[.]
But to return, our worldly prospect's blasted
The grievous wound near twenty years hath lasted
But all is right, it was the hand of God
I'd bless his name and wish to kiss his rod[.]
Soon after this afflictive providence
My brethren thought it duty to advance
Me to a Deacon—poorly qualified
To take the care and wait upon the bride.
But since it was my lot I must needs yield
And not a coward prove and quit the field[.]
After some years had rolled on and pass'd
My baptist brethren were agreed at last
And call'd me forth once more to take a stand

Upon the walls of Zion, trump in hand
Proclaim salvation free to dying men
And with the bread of life to feed the brethren[.]
This heavy trials brought upon my mind.
Can I submit to this and be resign'd?
The least of all the flock and ignorant
A stammerer likewise with learning verry scant[;]
And many such like things did cause me trouble sore
Beyond what I had ever felt in all my life before[.]
Seeing no other way to keep my conscience clear
I gave the matter up to God with trembling fear[.]
I then was set apart by Ordination
And thus was qualified to fill the station.
I served the church of Christ according to my measure
And with a willing mind which often gave me pleasure[.]
Permit me here a little to digress
And in a proper manner to express
A trying scene where I was call'd to mourn
As one for a first born—or only son
In prime of life of twenty Six years nigh
A useful member of society
In all his dealings just in every action
Which gain'd a universal satisfaction[;]
But he's brought down by sickness to the grave
And gone to him who first the blessing gave[.]¹⁶
May I be still and know that he is God
And hear and kiss his just and holy rod[.]
So in our garden early doth appear
A beautious flower which doth our spirits cheer
But in the height of all our expectation
Untimely frost destroys the vegetation[;]
We pass the place where once the flower grew
Which brings pass'd Scenes afresh into our view[;]
We drop a tear and then we vainly try
Some other sweet, the vacance to supply[.]
But to return again from this digression
And speak of what transpired in succession
Once, twice, yea thrice I to the Northward went

As missi[o]nary I was thither sent[.]
I went from town to town as I proceeded
Preaching the gospel free to all that needed[.]
Some evidence I thought did obtain
That all my labour was not spent in vain[.]
About this time I found a house we needed[,]
Collected the materials and proceeded
With brick and lime made every calculation
And with large stones I laid a firm foundation[;]
And as we progress made can truly say
The Lord did bless our labours every day.
The spotted fever rag'd and swept off many
Among our neighbours round was scarcely any
But what were call'd to mourn
The loss of friends which to the grave were borne
While we enjoyed health and prospered[.]
May all Gods goodness unto us be noticed[.]
At the same time the war commenc'd and rag'd
We and the Brittains often were engag'd
In battle sore, untill the lord at last
Appear'd, the schemes of all our foes to blast[;]
Jackson at Orleans gave the final blow
Which laid the pride of Brittain verry low[.]
The war is o'er[,] the noise of Cannon cease
And we enjoy an honorable peace[.]
Nor of our prowess or our heroes boast
But only in the Lord the God of hosts.
Now to return, our house is finish'd we move in
Which a great comfort unto us hath been[.]
And now by reason of infirmity
My strength is greatly weaken'd in the way
Which gives me opportunity and time
This narrative to write, and that in ryme
Being this day exactly Seventy three
When this you read you will remember me[.]
                    March 5, 1820[17]

[15]

Conclusion: Disestablishment at Last

The final stage in the separation of church and state in New England obviously did not come with the First Amendment to the U.S. Constitution in 1791. That amendment applied only to Congress: "*Congress* shall make no law respecting an establishment . . ." Not until well into the twentieth century did the Supreme Court, utilizing the Fourteenth Amendment, begin to apply the First Amendment to state and local laws affecting religion. In fact, the Supreme Court case that actually cited this part of the First Amendment with respect to religious freedom was not decided until 1940 in *Cantwell* v. *Connecticut*.

Disestablishment within the old Puritan states therefore had to be fought by dissenters through state legislatures and state courts, just as in the colonial era. The history of these struggles in Vermont, Connecticut, New Hampshire, Maine, and Massachusetts is complex, and space is not available here to do them all justice.[1] For the most part these disestablishments collapsed not with a bang but a whimper. There was no last storming of the barricade, no triumphal victory march, no headlines, cheers, or dancing in the streets. The old established systems were whittled away bit by bit until they finally tumbled down by the weight of their own rotted timbers.

In Vermont, where the majority of settlers were Congregationalists from Connecticut and Massachusetts, many towns laid religious taxes for the support of that denomination and expected everyone to pay them. The constitution of Vermont (adopted in 1777) declared that "any man who professes the protestant religion" should have freedom of conscience, but "every sect and denomination of Christians ought to observe the Sabbath . . . and keep up and support some sort of religious worship." In 1783 and again in 1797 the legislature passed bills allowing the majority in each township to lay taxes to support its church and permitting those not of

the majority persuasions to be exempted from this tax upon filing
a certificate of his or her membership in another denomination.
The certificate was to be signed by the dissenter's minister. If there
was no church of his persuasion in the town, he then had to pay
taxes to support the denomination of the majority (which in most
cases was Congregational). By implication these laws required the
dissenting or minority churches to be incorporated by acts of the
legislature in order to qualify their members for exemption. The
Baptists fought to have this law repealed as contrary to their principle of voluntary support and a hindrance to the free exercise of
religion. Their efforts failed until 1801, when the legislature
amended its certificate system by allowing each dissenter to present
his own certificate. But not until 1807 was the certificate system
ended and true voluntary support of every church permitted. Prior
to that, the state of Vermont kept its hands on religion.

In Connecticut the Standing Order waged a much longer and
more successful battle to sustain religious tax support for the Congregational churches. A small step toward toleration was made in
1784, when the Saybrook Platform of 1708 (which had united state
authority to the Congregational associations and consociations) was
repealed. A Toleration Act was adopted at this time, permitting
dissenters from Congregationalism to be exempt from ecclesiastical
taxes upon filing a certificate signed by a Justice of the Peace attesting to the fact that the dissenter was a bona fide member of
another church and not simply a tax dodger. Because all justices of
the peace were Congregationalists, it was not easy for dissenters to
obtain such certificates. In 1791 the legislature amended this requirement and allowed dissenters to file their own certificates under
their own signature with the clerk of the Congregational church in
their town—a galling requirement for many. Again the Baptists
protested that this required obeisance to the state and gave a favored position to the Congregational churches. These protests were
ignored until the Baptists received additional support from the
Episcopalians in the state. Episcopalians (descendants of the Anglicans, or Church of England) were more highly respected, wealth-
ier, and usually better educated than most dissenters. They too
recognized the advantage that the tax system gave to the Standing
Order. With their help a law was passed in 1816 that finally ended

the law requiring church attendance on the Sabbath, but the certificate system remained in place.

In 1817 a new political party, the Toleration party, was formed in Connecticut, with the specific goal of ending any form of established preference for congregationalism. Its opposing party, the Federalists, were in bad repute, not only for opposing the War of 1812 but for calling the infamous Hartford Convention in 1815; this body had come close to advocating the secession of New England from the Union (just on the eve of Jackson's glorious victory in New Orleans). The shoe was now on the other foot; in 1776 it was the dissenters who had seemed unpatriotic. The Toleration party, which included Episcopalian candidates, won the election. Once in office it altered the ecclesiastical tax system to allow any denomination to lay taxes on its own members and have them collected by state authority—a compromise that satisfied the Episcopalians but not most of the other dissenters (especially the Methodists, who had now separated from that church, and the Baptists). This act also amended the certificate law so as to allow dissenters to file their own certificates with the town clerk.

In 1818 the Toleration party received an even greater majority of the votes, and a constitutional convention was called to revise the old colonial charter under which the state had lived with only minor changes since 1776. The new constitution contained a bill of rights stating that "no preference shall be given by law to any Christian sect or mode of worship" and "no person shall be compelled to join or support nor by law be classed with or associated to any congregation, church, or religious society." This finally did away with the old territorial parish system and the ecclesiastical taxes to support them. Connecticut had finally achieved disestablishment, at least in the colonial sense of that term.

In New Hampshire the Dartmouth College case and its connection with party politics finally put an end to religious taxes in 1819. In the state constitution of 1783 "the several towns, parishes, bodies-corporate or religious societies" were given the power "of electing their own public teachers and of contracting with them for their support and maintenance."[2] Under this clause the legislature passed a law permitting every town (as an incorporated body) to lay taxes for the support of "public Protestant teachers of piety, religion and morality." Those dissenting groups whose members filed certificates of membership were exempted from paying this tax to support the minister chosen by the majority (again, almost always Congregationalists). Nonetheless, in 1803 a Presbyterian was jailed for failing to pay a tax to support a Congregational minister, and only a judicial ruling that Presbyterians were truly a different denomination and hence entitled to dissenting status (and tax abatement) won him his freedom. A year earlier a Baptist named Isaac Smith was imprisoned for failure to pay a tax of fifty cents to the Congregational minister in his town; the court ruled that although he was in fact in regular attendance at the local Baptist church he was not entitled to tax abatement because he had not been baptized (which was hardly his fault because Baptist churches admitted to full membership only those to whom God, in his arbitrary wisdom, had sent grace; despite his prayers and exemplary conduct, Smith remained unconverted).

These and other similar cases in New Hampshire seemed to the dissenters from Congregationalism to indicate unequal treatment under the certificate system. The Republican party decided to capitalize on this after 1815 by portraying the Congregationalists associated with Dartmouth College as enemies of religious freedom. Isaac Hill, a leading Republican and editor of the *New Hampshire Patriot,* was among those who wanted to transform Dartmouth from a private college (led by Congregationalists) into a public college with no denominational ties. The Federalist party defended Dartmouth's right to be a sectarian college, and the issue became central to the political campaigns of 1816–1818. Victory for the dissenters came in 1818, when the legislature, now dominated by Republicans, passed the Toleration Bill. By this act, which went into effect in 1819, any citizen was permitted to "sign off " from the parish register and thus exempt one's self from any tax laid by a town or parish to support its minister; it also provided a simple system of incorporation for any religious society of any denomination. Although Daniel Webster won the Supreme Court case in 1819 that preserved Dartmouth as a private college, the Republican party had made effective use of it to end the preference for Congregationalism inherent in the old ecclesiastical tax system.

The struggle in Maine was similar to that in Massachusetts because until 1820 Maine was included as part of the state of Massachusetts. However, Maine, as the northern frontier of Massachusetts, had over the years attracted many dissenters and thus had developed a more tolerant spirit than was evidenced in the old Bay Colony. Dissenters in Massachusetts and Connecticut had constantly moved northward as well as westward to seek new land and new freedom. By 1816 Maine had such a heavy concentration of Baptists that it was able to receive state aid for a Baptist college at Waterville (later Colby College). After Maine was separated from Massachusetts in 1820, as part of the famous Missouri Compromise, its first legislature passed an act to eradicate the last traces of ecclesiastical taxes for the support of religion. Called "An Act Concerning Parishes," this law took from the townships the power to allow the majority to assume the prerogative of being the established church of that town and to levy taxes on everyone who could not provide a certificate of membership in another incorporated religious society. It also allowed any church of any denomination to incorporate itself by applying to the nearest justice of the peace. In short, Maine followed the pattern already set in Vermont, Connecticut, and New Hampshire.

As might be expected, the last state to hold out against disestablishment was Massachusetts, where it had all begun. Two factors led to the ultimate demise of the Standing Order there: the rapidly increasing number of dissenters (by 1820 they equaled or exceeded in number the members of the old Puritan churches) and the split within Congregationalism that divided the Unitarians from the Trinitarians. The history of Unitarianism stretches back at least to the mid-eighteenth century and beyond that to the Enlightenment in Europe. The seventeenth century has been called "The Age of Piety," the eighteenth, "The Age of Reason." As the Enlightenment, with its new faith in rationalism and scientific progress, gathered force after 1750, it spread rapidly among the educated elite of the English colonies. From this movement came the ideas that made deists of such Americans as Benjamin Franklin and Joel Barlow, latitudinarian Anglicans of Thomas Jefferson and James Madison, and New England Unitarians of John Adams and his son John Quincy Adams. Unitarians received their name because they did not consider the doctrine of the Trinity reasonable or rational; to speak of the deity in three different forms (Father, Son, and Holy Ghost) resembled, in their opinion, either superstition, theological obscurantism, or "tri-theism." Gradually, many college-educated Americans rejected not only this aspect of Christian orthodoxy but most of the doctrines of Calvinism—predestination, election, perseverance of the saints, limited atonement, salvation by the miracle of sovereign grace, and the inheritance of original sin from Adam's fall. But although the educated, upper-class people of Massachusetts quietly dropped these beliefs, they did not drop out of church (any more than Franklin or Jefferson did). They believed churches were necessary to give consolation to the grieving, moral order to the common people, and the fear of God to potential lawbreakers. Consequently, the Unitarian elite remained pillars of the Standing Order in Massachusetts; they stayed within the Congregational churches and staunchly upheld the necessity for religious taxes. They did not trust the common man to support religion voluntarily—not so much because of "original sin" (though that was the Calvinist name for it) but because "history taught" that human nature is always guided more by self-interest, passion, and lust for power than by benevolence, charity, and generosity. "The first want of man," John Adams said, "is his dinner, the second, his girl." The average man was not just "a little lower than the angels" but closer to being a tool of Satan. "Government, like dress, is the badge of lost innocence," said Tom Paine. "If men were angels, no government would be necessary," said James Madison. Rational men of all persuasions agreed that checks and balances were needed in a democracy to keep the mob from creating first anarchy and then tyranny under some demagogue. To the Unitarians (most of them members of the Federalist party) as to the Congregationalists (also Federalists for the most part), the most important check on human depravity was the morality, piety, and fear of God taught in the churches of every town, and it required attendance at church every Sunday.

Consequently, the "orthodox" or "Trinitarian" Congregationalists and the "rational" or "Unitarian" Congregationalists were in total agreement about the need for state support of religion. The third article of the Massachusetts Constitution explained why every town must be responsible for laying taxes "for the support of public

Protestant teachers of piety, religion and morality" and must "enjoin upon all the subjects an attendance upon the instruction of the
public teachers aforesaid" on Sundays, fast days, and thanksgiving
days: "As the happiness of a people and the good order and preservation of civil government essentially depend upon piety, religion
and morality, and as these cannot be generally diffused through a
community but by the institution of the public worship of God and
of public instruction in piety, religion and morality, therefore . . ."
The constitution went on to sustain the old ecclesiastical tax system.
Unitarians, however, did not favor conformity of belief and practice; they believed in toleration for dissenters provided they supported their own "Protestant" pastors. Consequently, after 1780 the
certificate system was presumed to remain in force, and bona fide
members of dissenting churches were entitled to exemption from
taxes to support the Congregational majorities in each town.

Between 1776 and 1820 more than 126 parishes in Massachusetts
(most in the vicinity of Boston, where the educated elite were most
numerous) came under the sway of Unitarians. In 1805 Harvard
University chose a Unitarian as its professor of divinity. When Unitarians in a parish chose a Unitarian Harvard graduate to become
the town's minister, the Trinitarian Congregationalists were outraged. They found themselves being taxed to support and required
to attend churches in which they heard the heresies of Unitarianism
preached from the pulpit every week. As good Calvinists, the Congregational trinitarians began to question the validity of the ecclesiastical tax system. They felt the spur that had so long bloodied
the dissenters from Congregationalism. Not until 1825 did the Unitarians break away and establish themselves as a new and distinct
denomination. Meanwhile, a long contest continued within the
Standing Order, as well as between the dissenters and the Standing
Order.

Following the Cutter Case in 1785,[3] the problem of interpreting
the rights of toleration for dissent bogged down in a variety of court
cases. Only the courts could adjudicate the meaning of the clauses
firmly embedded in the state's constitution, and each case had its
own distinct implications. Furthermore, over the period from 1785
to 1820 more and more Unitarians rose to prominence in the Federalist party and were appointed to important judicial positions.

The Supreme Judicial Court of Massachusetts was the court of last resort for appeals from the lower courts. To it came the cases in which dissenters claimed that they were unfairly denied tax certificate or that their ecclesiastical taxes were not paid over to the support of their own ministers.

The first important case to be decided on this issue was that of the Universalist John Murray and his followers in the town of Gloucester. Universalists as a denomination were, like the Unitarians, part of the rationalist or anti-Calvinist movement associated with the Enlightenment and had their origins in England. On the whole, however, they were not from the educated elite but from the artisan and middle classes. Their chief quarrel with Calvinism focused on the doctrine of divine retribution or hellfire for the non-elect (supposed to include from two thirds to three fourths of humankind, including even small children) who died with no visible signs of conversion. "Murrayites" (as this sect was called at the time) held that God was a loving, benevolent father, not a vindictive, angry tyrant. He did not send his only son to earth simply to die for a few saints arbitrarily chosen. They found in the Bible the doctrine of "universal salvation"—Christ died to save "whosoever" would accept Christianity. They replaced the Calvinist view of a limited atonement with a general atonement. However, the Universalists denied the existence of eternal hellfire for those not converted during their lives. They preached that there would be a probationary period after death for the souls of the unconverted, during which they would be purged of their sins and finally admitted into heaven. (Some Calvinists referred to the Universalists as "no-Hellites.") Even Unitarians, though anti-Calvinist, believed that the doctrine of universal salvation was unsound because it took away the fear of damnation that alone held many unruly people in check. Universalism was not therefore a religion that would contribute to the good of society as the constitution required.

But the Universalists in Gloucester made a more serious error. When Murray came from England and was chosen as their minister or leader, his congregation did not perform any standard ritual of ordination. Hence, when taxed, they came before the Supreme Judicial Court in 1785 with two strikes against them.[4] The court had to decide first whether this new sect was truly "Protestant" and second whether Murray was truly ordained as a "teacher of piety, religion and morality." Only if both were allowed could his congregation be exempt from religious taxes to the town minister. Justice William Cushing ruled that it was not up to the courts to decide whether Murray's tenets were orthodox, and he ruled that it was not necessary for his congregation to be incorporated. However, he and the other justices did conclude in 1786 that Murray had not been ordained by any acceptable Protestant form. This then raised a thornier question. If he was not a minister, were the various marriages he had performed for his followers valid? Fearing that those couples might bring suit against him for impersonating a minister, Murray left Gloucester and fled to England. Universalism continued to flourish nonetheless.

This case did not resolve the critical and vexing question as to whether all dissenting congregations had to be incorporated in order to have their taxes abated or returned to them (or their pastor) after being collected. The judges usually said this was required, but some, like Cushing, disagreed; and when the matter was referred to a jury, the jury usually insisted on it. To clarify the situation, the state legislature passed a law in 1800 that specifically required all dissenting groups seeking recovery of religious taxes to first become incorporated; only "public" sects (those publicly recognized), not private religious groups, could come before the law to recover taxes.

As a result of this law (and in fact ever since the Cutter case in 1785) many Baptists and other dissenting denominations decided to seek incorporation. But Isaac Backus vigorously opposed this both in pamphlets and in discussions before the various Baptist associations. Backus considered the seeking of corporate status from the state to be acceptance of the right of the state to "license" which people were free to worship according to their consciences and which were not; it placed man's authority over the Christian's God-given right of religious freedom. Furthermore, because some incorporated churches used the civil power thus granted to accept taxes raised from their own members (or to tax their own members), they were doubly guilty of yielding to Caesar what belonged to God. Despite his arguments, many of the Baptist churches in Massachusetts did seek incorporation.

Meanwhile, dissenting churches that did not seek incorporation continued to bring suit in court for the abatement of these taxes. Despite the law of 1800, at least six cases are on record in which juries awarded recovery of ecclesiastical taxes to unincorporated religious societies.[5] This was worrisome to the Standing Order, for as Justice William Cushing had noted in the Murray case, "proliferation of voluntary sects might leave many corporate parishes unable to fulfil the constitutional mandate to support a minister."[6] Finally, in 1810 a case was heard by the Supreme Judicial Court that seemed to settle the matter once and for all. In *Barnes* v. *Falmouth* Chief Justice Theophilus Parsons and the court ruled flatly that unincorporated religious societies could not sue for recovery of religious taxes because they had no standing in law.

This decision outraged those Baptists and other new sects who had kept faith with the principles of voluntarism and had refused to seek incorporation. By this time the concept of equal religious liberty was gaining ground even in Massachusetts. So many religious dissensions were wracking so many towns that a movement began to abandon the courts for political action. Jeffersonian Republicans saw in this issue a way to undermine Federalist political power. After considerable lobbying, the dissenters persuaded the Massachusetts legislature to pass the Religious Freedom Act in 1811. This act specifically overthrew Parsons's decision by permitting unincorporated religious societies to recover ecclesiastical taxes. The only requirement was that each society file a list of its members with the clerk of the town in which they lived so that the clerk would know how much tax money was to be returned to that church. Some Baptists still considered this little more than a modified certificate system. Others spoke of it as a "general assessment" tax on all property holders for the support of religion (each denomination's share of that tax being distributed to it on a pro rata basis). Certainly, it served to make the dissenters distinguish themselves from the churches of the establishment. In the case of *Adams* v. *Howe* in 1807 the Supreme Judicial Court had described unincorporated churches as "extra-legal," which to some implied "illegal" or at least less than fully legitimate.

By 1820 the rapidly increasing number of dissenting churches and the intensifying quarrels between Unitarians and Trinitarians for control of parish churches contributed to the decision to call a

constitutional convention in Massachusetts. The problem of religious taxes was now a matter of concern to the ruling elite as well
as to the minorities. This became evident in the case of *Baker* v.
Fales, which was decided just prior to the convention. In that case
(sometimes called the Dedham case) Justice Isaac Parker of the
Supreme Judicial Court (a Harvard graduate and a Unitarian)
ruled that even when the majority of members in a parish church
were Trinitarian and chose a Trinitarian minister (from Yale or
Andover) the church was not the controlling public, or incorporated, body. The parish or property owners and voters in each town
or parish were the only legal body able to choose a minister and
lay taxes for his support. This horrified the Trinitarians because
traditionally the practice had been that both the church members
(the visible elect) and the voters of a parish or town must concur
in choosing the town minister. Under Parker's rule the secular (non-
members) citizens could overrule the communicants (the members)
of the church. This was the system of Erastianism from which the
original Puritans founders of Massachusetts had fled to the New
World—the state as superior to the church. The Trinitarians had
no recourse in such situations but to become "dissenters," to leave
their old parish church and file their list of members with the town
clerk just as any Baptist, Methodist, or Universalist had to do. It
was a bitter pill to swallow. In town after town in the neighborhood
of Boston, Trinitarian Congregationalists were forced to build their
own meetinghouses and pay their ministers out of their own pockets
while the Unitarians took over the town meetinghouse and levied
ecclesiastical taxes to supported a Harvard-educated minister who
preached heresy.

The constitutional convention of 1820 failed to resolve this problem, for in most of the Massachusetts towns west of Boston the
Trinitarians were still in control; and much as they sympathized
with their brethren around Boston, they still wanted to maintain
ecclesiastical taxes. The convention did propose to the voters an
amendment to Article 3 of the constitution allowing more latitude
toward dissenters than did the Religious Liberty Act, but it was
rejected. Dissenters thought it did not go far enough; Congregationalists and Unitarians thought it went too far.

Five years later the Unitarians, having gained control in more and more parishes, formally separated from the Congregational denomination and formed their own denomination. This proved to be the straw that broke the back of the establishment. Denominational diversity now replaced the simple dichotomy between the Standing Order and the dissenters. The effort of the Trinitarian Congregationalists to retain the old tax system was no longer worth the candle. After bringing several futile cases in the hope of reversing the Dedham decision, the Trinitarians joined the dissenters in calling for an end to the general assessment plan of public tax support for "religion, piety and morality." In 1833 the legislators passed an amendment to the constitution stating that "all religious sects and denominations, demeaning themselves peaceably and as good citizens of the commonwealth, shall be equally under the protection of the law and no subordination of any one sect or denomination to another shall ever be established by law."

This did not mean that religious taxation ended in Massachusetts in 1833. But taxes now could be laid only by religious societies that wanted to lay them on their own members. Any individual in any town could "sign off " (i.e., ask to have his name deleted from the parish list) and remain untaxed simply by telling the town clerk that he or she no longer wished to be considered a member of the Congregational parish (into which every citizen of Congregational parents was born, with the right to vote on parish affairs). Towns and parishes ceased to lay taxes on dissenters (and then return them); and many Congregational churches, as well as dissenters, relied wholly on the voluntary principle for support. Ironically, some incorporated Baptist congregations entered into legally binding agreements with their members to assess them for a contribution each year, and when a member failed to pay such an assessment, the deacons took him or her to court in a civil suit for breach of contract. But technically this was a private suit and had nothing to do with any established church system. The civil law of contract had replaced the Puritan law of public support for religion. Other churches made contracts to rent pews or auctioned off pews, and the church could bring suit for failure to pay pew rents or could repossess pews not paid for; those unable to afford pew rent or purchase had to sit in the gallery or on benches behind the pews. Other Baptist churches resorted to spiritual discipline, censuring or excommunicating for the sin of covetousness those who refused to contribute their fair share to church support; and sometimes ministers had to sue the church for failure to pay their salaries. Voluntarism was not easy.

The history of the Baptists' struggle for religious liberty in New England can be summarized in terms of six distinct stages: First, the period from 1630 to 1691, when the Baptists (and other dissenters, like Roger Williams, Anne Hutchinson, the Quakers, and Anglicans) struggled merely for toleration. Second, having won toleration (the right to attend the church of their choice) through irresistible pressure from England as well as their own efforts, the Baptists, Anglicans, and Quakers then struggled from 1690 to 1734 to obtain exemption from paying religious taxes to support the established Congregational churches. When this was achieved under the certificate system (which satisfied the Anglicans and Quakers), the Baptists went on to the third phase, during which they sought to make that system operate in a fair and uniform manner. The fourth phase began in 1773, when the Baptists concluded that the certificate system would never work because it was inherently discriminatory in a society so strongly dominated by the Standing Order; they then launched their campaign for total disestablishment and the implementation of voluntary religious support. That effort was sidetracked after the Revolution by the efforts of the Standing Order to substitute a general assessment system for the certificate system. Here the Baptists (and other dissenters) split over whether to seek incorporation of each congregation in order to make a general assessment feasible under law. The sixth and final stage in the struggle (during which the Universalists came to play a leading part) took place from 1811 to 1833: divisions within the Standing Order (in Connecticut between Congregationalists and Episcopalians and in Massachusetts between Trinitarian and Unitarian Congregationalists) finally compelled abandonment of the old system of ecclesiastical taxes laid and collected by state power. The success of the Jeffersonian Party and the weakening of the old Federalist Party contributed to this, as did the growing number of dissenters from Congregationalism and the religious movement known as the Second Great Awakening.

Most historians date the Second Great Awakening as spanning

the generation from 1800 to 1830. It was a national movement of religious revitalization, producing a modification of the Calvinist ideology that had dominated New England theology for so long. God ceased to be defined as an angry, vindictive sovereign who arbitrarily saved a small elect through whom civil and ecclesiastical order were to be maintained; the new definition portrayed God, through Christ, as a benevolent and loving father who sent his son to earth to atone for Adam's original sin and thereby opened the possibility of salvation to everyone. The doctrine of predestination (with its fatalistic overtones) gave way to a new optimistic belief in free will and a partnership between God and man that would lead to a never-ending perfection of America until the millennium should arrive here. By 1828, when Andrew Jackson of Tennessee was elected president, a new faith in the innate divinity within the average person led to the decline of rule by the *aristoi*; a change in the flow of authority popularized the claim that "the voice of the people is the voice of God."

The positive thrust of this new evangelical Arminian ideology swept across the new nation, bringing with it a new faith in self-reliance and a new era of moral reform that pervaded every aspect of society. The tremendous growth in church membership and a new voluntaristic cooperation between pastors and laity in spreading the truth of Protestantism provided at last the conviction that, in America at least, the churches could and should be supported by the free will of the believers rather than the power of the state. Christianity, in losing its Calvinist interpretation, became democratized.

Sociologists might describe this mighty shift in civil and religious polity as the unforeseen consequences of purposive action. Historians would simply say that changing circumstances change ideologies. What Puritan could have foreseen the pertinacity of dissent, the king's determination to support toleration in the colonies, the Glorious Revolution of 1688 and its law for religion toleration, the tremendous influx of scores of new dissenting sects, the gradual loss of piety among the original Puritans, the rise of the Enlightenment, the success of the colonial rebellion, and the new democratic order that arose with Jefferson and Jackson? Or to put it another way, how could the Puritans have guessed that a few concessions to dissenters (forced by unforeseen contingencies) would eventually lead to the total demolition of the old Standing Order? And more important, did the Baptists themselves ever expect things to turn out that way? Their struggle was heroic in its persistence, but the principles behind it seem to have been altered by the same unforeseen contingencies.

However arrived at and however perplexing to preserve, the principles embedded in the first clauses of the First Amendment of the Bill of Rights are well worth upholding. Today the world is full of scenes of internecine violence among people of opposing faiths unwilling to grant the free exercise of religion and religious equality to those who dissent from them. Those who struggled so hard for so long to implant these principles in our Constitution deserve at least our commitment to sustain them.

Notes

1. Quoted in James H. Moorhead, *American Apocalypse* (New Haven, Conn., 1978), p. 223.
2. See W. G. McLoughlin, *New England Dissent, 1630–1833*, 2 vols. (Cambridge, Mass., 1971).

Introduction (pp. 1–12)

1. Ezra Stiles wrote a good deal about the coolness of the Baptists toward the Revolution prior to 1776. His diary is cited in W. G. McLoughlin, *New England Dissent* (Cambridge, Mass., 1971) 1:561–562, 576–582, 585. This quotation is on p. 579 in vol. 1. One reason Stiles and others in New England suspected the Baptists of being Tories was that Isaac Backus, James Manning, and Chileab Smith, among others, went to the Continental Congress in Philadelphia in September 1774 and accused John Adams, Robert Treat Paine, and other delegates (all Congregationalists) from New England of denying freedom of religion to the Baptists. New Englanders considered this an effort to create dissension in the colonial ranks at a very crucial moment. Ibid. 1:552–562.
2. Ibid. 1:505.
3. Ibid. 1:505–506.
4. Ibid. 1:664–665.
5. For the important role of Isaac Backus in the Baptist movement for separation of church and state, see W. G. McLoughlin, *Isaac Backus and the American Pietistic Tradition* (Boston, 1967).
6. See chapter 15 for a discussion of this final phase.
7. *The Christian Watchman* (Boston), 1 August 1828, p. 122; 14 August 1829, p. 130.

Chapter 1. The Rise of the Antipedobaptists in New England,
1630–1635 (pp. 13–36)

1. Elder William Brewster of Plymouth predicted of Roger Williams in 1633 (two years before he was banished from Massachusetts and six years before he temporarily adopted Baptist views) that "he would run the same course of rigid separatism and Anabaptistry which Mr. John Smith the Sebaptist of Amsterdam had done." Nathaniel Morton, *New England's Memorial* (Cambridge, Mass., 1669), p. 78. Geoffrey Nuttall (*Visible Saints* [Oxford, 1957]) quotes Francis Cheynell on the loose use of the term Anabaptist in 1643: "Every man is now counted an Anabaptist if he does not maintain Monarchy to be *iure Divino*" (p. 2).
2. John Cotton and Cotton Mather both claimed to know persons who held Anabaptist views in the colony during its early years but who were

tolerated because they did not openly express them. The Cambridge Platform specifically forbade the magistrates from punishing "erroneous opinions not vented."

3. The origins of these churches are discussed below. The best history of the Baptist movement in New England is Isaac Backus, *History of New England*. It was originally published in three volumes between 1777 and 1795; however, I have cited throughout the more useful two-volume edition edited by David Weston and published by the Backus Historical Society, Newton, Mass., 1871. Some accounts list the Rogerenes of New London, Connecticut, among the early Baptists because they originated in 1674–1675 as a branch of the Seventh Day Baptist Church in Newport. But by 1685 this eccentric group had "declined into Quakerism" and was excluded from fellowship by the Baptists. See John R. Bolles and Anna B. Williams, *The Rogerenes* (Boston, 1904) and chapter 15 this volume.

4. Mrs. Scott, who, like many of the other Hutchinsonians "declined" into Quakerism, was whipped in Boston in 1658 when she returned there to express her new views (Joseph B. Felt, *The Ecclesiastical History of New England* [Boston, 1862], 2:202).

5. In 1649 Williams stated of the Baptists, "I believe their practice comes nearer the first practice of our great Founder Christ then other practices of religion doe, & yet I have no satisfaction neither in the authorities by which it (baptism) is done nor in the manner [immersion]; nor in the prophecies concerning the rising of Christ's Kingdome after the desolation of Rome &c" (Letter to John Winthrop, Jr., 9 December 1649, in Massachusetts Historical Society, *Collections*, 4th ser., 6 (1863): 274). Williams's views are discussed more fully below.

6. For John Clarke, see Thomas W. Bicknell, *The Story of John Clarke* (Providence, 1915); John Callendar, *An Historical Discourse . . .* (Boston, 1739), pp. 27, 63ff.; Clarke's autobiographical remarks in *Ill-Newes from New England* (London, 1652); Backus, *History*, 1:77–78, 97; and I. E. Richman, *Rhode Island* (New York, 1902), 1, chapter 4.

7. Lukar split off from Henry Jacob's Non-Separatist Congregational Church in London in 1633 and joined John Spilsbury's Separatist group. In 1641 he was rebaptized by immersion along with Spilsbury and others. Shortly after that he went to Rhode Island, where he joined Clarke's church and became a ruling elder in it. He died in 1676 (A. H. Newman, *A History of the Baptist Churches in the United States* [New York, 1894], p. 50. John Winthrop states that as early as the summer of 1641 some of Anne Hutchinson's followers "turned professed Anabaptists," but his description of them indicates that they were not the predecessors of Clarke's group. See his *History of New England*, ed. James Savage (Boston, 1828), 2:38. Unfortunately, there are no extant records for either the Providence or the Newport Baptist churches in the seventeenth century, and what little is known of them comes from indirect sources, many of them hostile.

8. For the best discussions of the Puritan theory of church and state, see George L. Haskins, *Law and Authority in Early Massachusetts* (New York, 1960), and E. S. Morgan, *The Puritan Dilemma* (Boston, 1958). Cotton's remark is quoted in Perry Miller, *Orthodoxy in Massachusetts* (Cambridge, Mass., 1933), p. 240.

9. Thomas Cobbett, *The Civil Magistrates Power in Matter of Religion . . . Together with a Brief Answer to a Certain Slanderous Pamphlet Called 'Ill-Newes from New England'* (London, 1653), p. 34.

10. In Samuel Willard, *Ne Sutor Ultra Crepidam* (Boston, 1681), Preface.

11. C. M. Andrews, *The Colonial Period in American History* (New Haven, Conn., 1934), 1:450, n. 1. In The Body of Liberties adopted by the General Court in 1641, section 95 was devoted to "the Liberties the Lord Jesus hath given to the churches," and the fifth among these indicates clearly the anti-Erastianism of the New England Puritans: "No injunctions are to be put upon any Church, Church officers or members in point of Doctrine, worship or Discipline whether for substance or circumstance besides the Institutions of the Lord." (W. W. Whitmore, ed., *The Colonial Laws of Massachusetts Reprinted from the Edition of 1660* [Boston, 1889], p. 57).

12. Williston Walker, *The Creeds and Platforms of Congregationalism* (New York, 1893), p. 237.

13. Walker, *Creeds and Platforms*, p. 237.

14. Backus, *History*, 1:88; Felt, *Ecclesiastical History*, 1:403–404. In 1772, Elder John Davis, pastor of the Second Baptist Church in Boston, tried to discover who was the first Baptist in Massachusetts. In a letter to Isaac Backus, August 3, 1772, Davis claimed that Seth Sweetser of Charlestown deserved that title. According to Davis, Sweetser and his family came from Tring, in Hartford, England, in 1638. Because of his Baptist views he was denied the right of inhabitant and could not share in the common land, yet he was required to pay taxes for the support of the Congregational ministers in Charlestown. His son, Benjamin Sweetser, became an early member of Thomas Goold's Baptist church in Boston. Davis's letter is among the Backus Papers, Andover Newton Theological School, Newton Center, Mass.

15. Felt, *Ecclesiastical History*, 2:427.

16. Winthrop, *History*, pp. 123, 136. "Many others infected with anabaptism removed there also," Winthrop adds. See also Backus, *History*, 1:486; Alonzo Lewis and J. R. Newhall, *History of Lynn* (Boston, 1865), p. 187; George E. Ellis, *The Puritan Age* (Boston, 1888), p. 381.

17. Winthrop, *History*, 2:174–175. Winthrop also noted under this entry, July 5, 1644, that it was at this time that "Anabaptistry increased and spread in the country which occasioned the magistrates, at the last court, to draw up an order for banishment such as continued obstinate after due conviction."

18. See David Pulsifer's transcript of the Middlesex County Court Records, 1:232, 287, in the Middlesex County Court House, Cambridge, Mass. Hereafter referred to as Pulsifer Transcript.

19. Ibid. 1:301, 3:205; Nathan E. Wood, *The History of the First Baptist Church of Boston* (Philadelphia, 1899), p. 113. See the loose files of the Middlesex County Court in the courthouse under dates April 6, 1666; October 3, 1663; April 5, 1681; 1(2) 1655; April 6, 1693. Bowers appears to have held Quaker views in 1661, but in 1666 and thereafter he attended the Baptist Church in Charlestown, though he is not recorded in its records as a member. It is not clear why he was never banished.

20. Wood, *History*, pp. 113–114. See also Bowers petition of April 5, 1681, in the loose files of the Middlesex County Court.

21. One of the few other cases of whipping involved William Baker, first mate of a London ship, who was whipped in Cambridge in 1657; see Backus, *History*, 1:400; and Jonathan Sprague, *The Answer of Jonathan Sprague to a Scandalous Libel* . . . (Providence, January 24, 1722/23), a broadside in vol. 155, p. 3, of the Providence Town Papers, Rhode Island Historical Society.

22. For Witter's arraignments, see Felt, *Ecclesiastical History*, 1:482, 568; Ellis, *Puritan Age*, pp. 381–382; and Lewis and Newall, *Lynn*, p. 231. For his excommunication on July 24, 1651, see Felt, *Ecclesiastical History*, 2:46. Isaac Backus is the authority for the fact that he was "a brother of the church" in Newport before the summer of 1651 (*History*, 1:178), although the Newport church records that Backus cites are now lost. It is possible that he was not yet a member when he requested a visit from the Newport church and that he was asking to be immersed in order to join the church at that time. Although those who visited him in July 1651 did perform some baptisms at his home, it is not clear whether Witter's was one of them, and all contemporary accounts are obscure on this point.

23. For Clarke's version of this incident, which seems reliable, see his *Ill-Newes from New England* (London, 1652); for the Puritan side of the story, see Cobbett, *Civil Magistrates*. John Gorham Palfrey, the nineteenth-century historian of New England, claimed that Clarke had ulterior political motives in staging this invasion of Massachusetts at that particular moment. For an examination and refutation of Palfrey's claim, see H. M. King, *A Summer Visit of Three Rhode Islanders to the Massachusetts Bay in 1651* (Providence, 1896).

24. There is no way to clear up the confusion regarding the precise sequence of events. Clarke states in his account that after being apprehended on Sunday they were watched by constables overnight "as theeves and robbers" and the next day were arraigned and taken to jail in Boston. But the date of the order committing them to jail is Tuesday, June 22. Moreover, the sentence of the court states that "upon the day following" their arrest, "being then in the custody of the law," they did "meet again at the said William Witters . . . and did there receive the Sacrament" and "Baptize such as were Baptized before." See also Cobbett, *Civil Magistrates*, p. 39. Obadiah Holmes, in his account of the incident in Clarke's tract admits to having baptized "Goodwife Bowdish" and defends himself against the charge that he baptized her naked—a common canard against the Baptists. Mrs. Bowditch had been presented to the county court for Baptist views in 1646. Felt, *Ecclesiastical History*, 1:576. In November 1651 Witter was brought before the Salem County Court on charges of denying infant baptism and "being re-baptized" (H. L. Osgood, *The American Colonies in the Seventeenth Century* [New York, 1904], 1:266).

25. Clarke, *Ill-Newes*, pp. 5–6.

26. As in most of the details, there is confusion over the payment of these fines. Clarke says that he did not want anyone to pay his fine, but the court accepted the money tendered for him despite his wishes. Why the court would not accept the fine money offered by Holmes's friends is

also unclear. Clarke's account says that Crandall's jailer later had to pay his fine. Other accounts say that Crandall's fine was paid for him over his objection at the time he was released. Undoubtedly, the authorities wanted to make an example of someone and Holmes was the most likely candidate.

27. Clarke, *Ill-Newes*, p. 122.

28. Ibid., p. 22; Backus, *History*, 1:184ff. The two men involved, John Spur of Salem and John Hazel of Rehoboth, had both been admitted as freemen in Boston in the 1630s and had been admonished before the courts for openly venting their Baptist views in the 1640s (Backus, *History*, 1:195, n. 2). Spur was excommunicated from the Salem church for anti-pedobaptism on July 13, 1651 (Felt, *Ecclesiastical History*, 2:46).

29. For an account of this debate and selections from it, see Jeremiah Chaplin, *Life of Henry Dunster* (Boston, 1872), pp. 122–131. See also Pulsifer Transcript, 1:74–75, 132.

30. There has been considerable debate among historians as to whether Dunster actually preached to a group of antipedobaptists in Scituate—perhaps they were some whom Charles Chauncy had indoctrinated with the necessity for baptism by immersion. There is no concrete evidence for this, and it appears more likely that on occasion he preached before perfectly orthodox members of the regular Congregational church there.

31. John Cotton, *The Bloody Tenent Washed and Made White in the Bloud of the Lambe* . . . (London, 1647), p. 64.

32. This law is quoted in Backus, *History*, 1:126. In the revised edition of the General Laws published in 1660 this law was combined with a law of 1646 against heresy; see Whitmore, *Colonial Laws of Massachusetts*, p. 154. It should be noted that John Winthrop was not enthusiastic about this law (probably because it made Massachusetts seem too intolerant in the eyes of many friends in England). He appears to have favored a petition asking for its repeal, which was sent to the legislature in October 1645. That the Commissioners for Plantations had ordered toleration in the West Indies and Bermuda that year and had advised New England to follow suit may also have encouraged this petition. However, the following year an even stronger petition called for strengthening the law, and the legislature decided to let it stand unchanged. See Winthrop, *History*, 2:250–251; Ellis, *Puritan Age*, p. 386; Morgan, *Puritan Dilemma*, p. 188; Backus, *History*, 1:145.

33. This law is quoted in David B. Ford, *New England's Struggles for Religious Liberty* (Philadelphia, 1896), pp. 34–35; it was slightly revised in the book of General Laws in 1660. See Whitmore, *Colonial Laws of Massachusetts*, p. 148.

Chapter 2. The Baptist-Puritan Debate of April 14–15, 1668 (pp. 37–92)

1. A discussion of this shorthand account, its transcription, and editing is in the Transcriber's Note, which follows this introduction.

2. For Mary Goold's account, see Isaac Backus, *A History of New England*, 2d ed., ed. David Weston, 2 vols. (Newton, 1871), 1:305–308. Mary Goold's feeling that the debate was to no purpose probably sprang from her rec-

ognition that the Puritans were not open to conviction and were interested only in demonstrating to the spectators how culpable the delinquents were. She may also have felt that in denying moderators to the Baptists the authorities made the debate unfair. And finally, she no doubt thought, as the Baptists did, that because they were told that they might be subject to additional punishments if they spoke "so offensively against God and man that you can't be suffere therein," they had to speak guardedly and could not make the best defense of their position. It should be noted that in 1651 the Massachusetts authorities had agreed to a public debate with John Clarke, pastor of the Baptist church in Newport, but he declined to enter it for fear that he would be prosecuted for what he might say. See ibid. 1:184–185, 204, n. 2.

3. See especially the tracts written in the 1640s by John Cotton, George Phillips, Thomas Cobbett, and Thomas Shepard, Sr., attacking infant baptism.

4. The best general accounts of the founding of Goold's church are to be found in Backus, *History*, 1, chapter 6, and Nathan E. Wood, *The History of the First Baptist Church of Boston (1665–1899)* (Philadelphia, 1899); the original records of this church are in the vault of Andover Newton Theological School, Newton); there are other manuscripts dealing with the legal aspects of their trials in the Massachusetts Archives (State House, Boston), 10:214–224, 227–228, 229–230; the records of the Middlesex County Court (Cambridge); and the Suffolk County Court (Boston).

5. Some accounts of the formation of this church have suggested that John Myles, pastor of the Baptist church in Swansea (Plymouth Colony), which was formed in 1663, may have come to Charlestown to rebaptize Goold and his friends, but the transcript of the Debate indicates that they rebaptized themselves. Probably the recent arrivals from Baptist churches in London took the lead in this. The Debate also clears up any doubts about their being immersed; the failure of the church records to specify the mode of baptism had previously left this question in some doubt.

6. Wood, *First Baptist Church*, provides what little biographical information is known about most of these men and women. It is clear that they were not the disinherited and the unstable; the early members included men who had been freemen, deacons in Puritan churches, selectmen and constables in the towns, and solid yeoman farmers, shipmasters, and artisans for the most part. Only John Thrumble, who was not a member of the church, was entitled to be called "Master" in the Debate. Only Bowers was so unstable as to have been whipped; he died insane.

7. Richard Mather, *A Defence of the answer and arguments of the Synod in . . . 1662* (Cambridge, 1664), pp. 13, 19.

8. Thomas Hutchinson, ed., *A Collection of Original Papers* (Boston, 1769). p. 378. The king meant by this only to grant religious freedom to Anglicans in Massachusetts.

9. The full text of the resolution, dated September 18, 1666, is in Miscellaneous Bound MSS (Massachusetts Historical Society), 1663–1674; but the official decision, omitting the threat of banishment and merely sustaining the fines and previous injunctions, appears in Nathaniel B. Shurtleff, ed., *Records of the Governor and Company of the Massachusetts Bay*, 5 vols. in 6 (Boston, 1853–1854), vol. 4, pt. 2, p. 316.

10. Ibid., 4, pt. 2, pp. 373–374.

11. Massachusetts Archives, 10:221, 223.

12. Printed in Backus, *History*, 1:314–315.

13. See Edward C. Starr, *A Baptist Bibliography* (Chester, Pa., [etc], 1947–etc.), for a list of books and tracts dealing with the Baptists.

14. John Clarke, *Ill Newes from New-England* (London, 1652), contains a brief statement of his Separate-Baptist views but is devoted primarily to recounting the details of the whipping of Obadiah Holmes in Boston in 1651 for preaching and baptizing among the Baptists in Lynn. John Russell, Jr., *A Brief Narrative* (London, 1680), contains a brief answer to eight charges leveled against the First Baptist Church of Boston; it repeats some of the points made in the Debate but is chiefly concerned to prove that the church did not contain or admit scandalous persons.

15. Printed in Backus, *History*, 1:300–301.

16. The Puritans never quarreled with the Baptists about the validity of immersion as a mode of baptism. "I willingly acknowledge," said John Cotton in 1647, "that Dipping is a lawful manner of Baptism" (John Cotton, *The Ground and Ends of the Baptisme of the Children of the Faithful* [London, 1647], p. 3. The reason the Puritans gave for not baptizing by immersion was their fear that in a cold climate it would injure the health.

17. The law of 1644 against Anabaptists made this specific: "Forasmuch as experience hath plentifully and often proved that since the first rising of the Anabaptists, about one hundred years since, they have been the incendiaries of the commonwealths and . . . if they should be connived at . . . must necessarily bring guilt upon us, infection and trouble to the churches, and hazard to the whole commonwealth" (Backus, *History*, 1:126).

18. Russell, in his *Brief Narrative*, argues that the Baptists had tried in vain to remain within the Puritan churches and mentions the case of Thomas Foster of Billerica. Thomas Goold, in the account he wrote after the Debate of his own case, points out that he was forced from the church when he wanted to commune with it (Backus, *History*, 1:290ff.). John Myles, the Welsh Baptist who had served on the Board of Triers in Cromwell's National Church System, founded his church in Swansea in the Plymouth Colony on an open-communion basis, and during King Philip's War he became the acting pastor of the First Baptist Church of Boston; see Henry M. King, *Rev. John Myles and the Founding of the First Baptist Church in Massachusetts* (Providence, 1905). But probably the most significant evidence relates to the case of John Pierce, who seems to have persuaded some of the ministers to help him draft an appeal to the Woburn church to admit him to communion though he had been rebaptized by immersion in Goold's church; see Prince Papers (Massachusetts Historical Society), 1:90–91, and Middlesex County Court Records, No. 85, 1679.

19. One or two of those who joined Goold's church gave as one of their reasons for doing so their dislike of the persecution of the Quakers, but this was not a common reason, for the Baptists generally tried to dissociate themselves from the radical views of these heretics.

20. See Wood, *First Baptist Church*, pp. 113–115. Bowers and his wife

also attended Quaker meetings. They never joined Goold's church. For his insanity, see Middlesex County Court Records, April 6, 1693.

21. Backus, *History*, 1:302.

22. It is significant also that no New England Baptist in the seventeenth century specifically attacked the system of compulsory religious taxation. The issue is not raised in the Debate nor in any of the documents relating to the early years of Goold's church. Presumably, this was because even in England dissenters were required to pay tithes to the Church of England, and there seemed no hope of avoiding them in New England. Not until toleration was obtained did the Baptists proceed to the next step toward religious freedom.

23. For the Puritans' fear of Separatism and individualism, see Edmund S. Morgan, *The Puritan Dilemma: The Story of John Winthrop* (Boston, 1958), chapter 9, "Separatism Unleashed"; for Puritan collectivism, see Samuel Eliot Morison, *Builders of the Bay Colony* (Boston, 1930), chapter 5, "John Hull."

24. For the implications of hereditary sainthood and aristocracy in the covenant theology, see Edmund S. Morgan, *The Puritan Family*, 2d ed. (Boston, 1956), chapter 6, "Puritan Tribalism."

25. Printed in Massachusetts Historical Society, *Collections*, 4th ser., 8 (1868):292.

26. Massachusetts Historical Society, *Proceedings*, 1 (1791–1835):174.

27. Massachusetts Historical Society, *Collections*, 2d ser., 8 (1819):46–112.

28. The note by "C.H.S."—with two ellipses (indicating sentences omitted because containing shorthand symbols that cannot be rendered typographically)—reads as follows:

March, 18. 1829

After considerable labor I despair of being able to decipher the short hand minutes of the conference, without other help than this book alone affords. I ascertain by comparison with other writing of the same period, that the alphabet is peculiar—but I find in both that the writers were *not* accustomed always to join *all the letters* of the same word together, as is modern practice, but in many instances to separate them even in short words. . . .

From the passages of Scripture quoted we may gather the drift of the arguments, and possibly, in time, the whole alphabet. . . .

At best, it is bad chirography. Possibly some other by the same hand may be found plainer.   C.H.S.

29. Edmond Willis, *An Abbreviation of Writing by Character* (London, 1618). See also William P. Upham, "History of Stenography," Essex Institute, *Historical Collections*, 14 (1876):1–48.

30. Most of the information on the Baptist participants is contained in Wood, *First Baptist Church*, and in Backus, *History*. Additional information is in the records of the First Baptist Church of Boston at Andover Newton Theological School.

31. Sources for these Congregational sketches are *Dictionary of American Biography*; James Savage, *A Genealogical Dictionary of the First Settlers of New England*, 4 vols. (Boston, 1860–1862); and John Langdon Sibley and

Clifford K. Shipton, *Biographical Sketches of Graduates of Harvard University* (Cambridge and Boston, 1873–).

32. Samuel Eliot Morison, *Harvard College in the Seventeenth Century*, 2 vols. (Cambridge, 1936), 1:306–307.

33. James 5:20. There are so many instances in the Debate where specific Bible texts are referred to directly or indirectly that we have annotated only those we consider of real significance to understanding the flow of the argument.

34. Because polygamy was practiced by the Munsterite Anabaptists in 1535, all Baptists were tarred with this brush.

35. 1 John 4:1.

36. Jer. 29:26–27. Allin apparently means that false teachers accused Jeremiah of being insane and a false prophet.

37. When Goold was brought to court on September 5, 1665, after the formation of his church, he presented the court with a copy of the Articles of Faith and Order that he had drawn up and his members had signed. See manuscript records of the First Baptist Church of Boston at Andover Newton Theological School, also printed in Wood, *First Baptist Church*, pp. 65–66.

38. The question defined by the General Court order instituting the debate: "Whether it be justifiable by the word of God for these persons and their company to depart from the communion of these churches, and to set up an assembly here in the way of Anabaptism, and whether such a practice is to be allowed by the government of this jurisdiction."

39. Perhaps Turner means, "We account ourselves guilty if the charge were correct that we depart from the churches of Christ."

40. Probably a reference to 1 Cor. 8.

41. The text occurs in 2 Cor. 6:17.

42. Rev. 3:16.

43. Since baptism was an ordinance, not a sacrament, Goold implies that the Baptists would differ only from the Standing Order on this point. Henry Jacob is said to have persuaded John Robinson, the Scrooby Separatist, to so far withdraw his objections to the Church of England as to admit that it was proper to commune with them in word and prayer. John Cotton said he was willing to go farther than that; see John Cotton, *The Way of the Congregational Churches Cleared* (London, 1648), pt. 1, pp. 8, 10–11.

44. Perhaps a reference to John Owen (1616–1683), dean of Christ Church, London, one of the leading Independents of the seventeenth century, who wrote a tract favoring limited toleration in 1648 and whose introduction to the Savoy Declaration in 1658 was a similar plea. Hull probably saw the latter. For Owen, see W. K. Jordan, *The Development of Religious Toleration in England* (Cambridge, 1938), and William Walker, *The Creeds and Platforms of Congregationalism* (New York, 1893), pp. 352–353.

45. An obvious reference to the Halfway Covenants, which enlarged the right of baptism by permitting the grandchildren of saints to be baptized if their parents owned the covenant. Some argued at this time that any parent who owned the covenant was entitled to have his child baptized. See Walker, *Creeds*, pp. 238ff.

46. Danforth did not transcribe or make any notation of this confession of faith, but presumably it is the same as that referred to in note 37 above. There is no record that Turner was ever ordained over Goold's church, but he may have been a lay elder, and he certainly preached to the group.

47. This may be a reference to the petition of several Independents made to the Westminster Assembly, December 4, 1645, requesting the Presbyterians "that they might not be forced to communicate as members in those parishes where they dwell; but may have liberty to have congregations of such persons who give testimonies of their godliness, and yet out of tenderness of conscience cannot communicate in their parishes" (Backus, *History*, 1:147).

48. It was the custom among the more radical Separate Baptists in Massachusetts to walk out of their parish churches when infants were baptized and on occasion to stand up in the congregation and denounce the practice as antichristian or "the badge of the Whore." Thrumble is obviously dissociating the members of Goold's church from such disturbers of the peace and admitting such persons deserve civil punishment. Goold states that in the 1650s he did this when he first became convinced of the error of infant baptism, but when he found that it grieved his brethren, he stopped doing it. See Wood, *First Baptist Church*, p. 46.

49. Presumably a reference to the Freeman's Oath.

50. See Zech. 5:1–4.

51. A reference to the Cambridge Platform, which quotes William Ames's *De Conscientia*: "If any (saith he) wronged with unjust vexation, or providing for his own edification or in testimony against sinn depart from a church where some evills are tollerated, & joyn himself to another more pure, yet without condemning of the church he leaveth, he is not therefore to be held as a schismatick, or guilty of any other sinn" (Walker, *Creeds*, p. 198). See also chapter 13 of the Platform for a similar list of lawful reasons for withdrawing.

52. Possibly a phonetic rendering of ἀπαρχομαί, to offer first fruits of sacrifice.

53. Though a censure or admonition did prohibit him from taking communion, it was not the same as excommunication. Goold wrote a more elaborate account of his censure, for which see Wood, *First Baptist Church*, p. 48. (The original manuscript is in the Rhode Island Historical Society.)

54. For a somewhat different version of this record, see Wood, *First Baptist Church*, pp. 39–42.

55. Thomas Lynde was a deacon of the church at Charlestown.

56. Obviously, John Farnum, Sr., who was one of the three Baptists then in prison. For a defense of his actions and his later recantation, see Wood, *First Baptist Church*, pp. 160, 188.

57. See note 5 above.

58. The use of typology (i.e., finding prefigurations or symbols of New Testament concepts in the Old Testament) was common to both Puritans and Baptists, but the Baptists repudiated it as a basis for defending infant baptism. Thrumble's reliance on it here seems inconsistent with his rejection of it below.

59. Heb. 10:34.

60. Another reference to the Preface or to chapter 13 of the Cambridge Platform. See note 51 above.

61. Probably a reference to the fact that in Goold's church it was the practice to let all of the brethren "prophesy" or exhort and not confine the preaching simply to the ordained elder. The Puritans had, in the 1630s, also permitted laymen to prophesy on certain occasions, but by 1665 this practice had almost ceased. The rise of the Baptist movement may well have been in part a pietistic resurgence against this and other increasing formalizations that provided less means for self-expression and participation among the laity.

62. See John 9.

63. The text occurs in Isa. 66:5.

64. 3 John 9.

65. This was the Puritan claim to punish only "open heresy" or disorderly conduct that threatened the civil peace and not simply "erroneous opinions not vented." By this subterfuge Puritans claimed to practice both a due separation of church and state and also liberty of conscience. They always denied that they persecuted any man because only the righteous could be persecuted.

66. This seems to be a reference to the fact that the ministers of the Puritan churches made a contract for their salaries with the parish before they assumed the pastorship of a church. To many Baptists this practice of "a hireling ministry" was contrary to Scripture, but this is the only hint in the Debate that the Baptists opposed the religious taxes that were laid to pay these ministerial salaries.

67. Perhaps a general reference to Calvin's accession in Geneva in 1536.

68. Presumably a reference to earmarking animals.

69. Eph. 5:8–10.

70. See Preface to the Cambridge Platform, Walker, *Creeds*, p. 197.

71. This refers to the first and ninth paragraphs of the section on ecclesiastical law in *The Book of the General Lawes and Libertyes* (Cambridge, 1660), reproduced in William H. Whitmore, ed., *The Colonial Laws of Massachusetts* (Boston, 1889), pp. 146–147.

Chapter 4. Separate Baptists and the "Free Love" Problem, 1748–1749 (pp. 100–123)

1. See appendix 1. Unless otherwise noted, all documents quoted are from diaries and papers of Isaac Backus at Andover Newton Theological School, Newton Centre, Massachusetts.

2. See appendix 2 for this and other documents from Rhode Island State Archives relating to the divorce case of Joseph Bennet.

3. C. C. Goen in *Revivalism and Separatism in New England, 1740–1800* (New Haven, Conn., 1962), pp. 200–203.

4. These and other records from the Norton Separate church are quoted in George F. Clark, *History of the Town of Norton, Massachusetts* (Boston, 1859), pp. 443–456.

5. Isaac Backus, *History of New England with Particular Reference to the Denomination of Christians Called Baptists*, ed. David Weston (Newton, Mass.,

1871), 2:446. Original edition published in three volumes in 1777, 1784, and 1796.

6. Bartlet's affidavit is quoted in appendix 3. See also Backus, *History*, 2:88–89, 111.

7. Ezra Stiles, *Extracts from the Itineraries*, ed. F. B. Dexter (New Haven, Conn., 1916), p. 418; Backus, *History*, 2:462.

8. Quoted in J. M. Bumsted, "Presbyterianism in 18th Century Massa-chusetts: The Formation of a Church at Easton, 1752," *Journal of Presby-terian History* 46(4) (December 1968): 251.

9. David Buchdahl, "American Realities: Anthropological Reflections from the Counter-Culture" (Ph.D. diss., University of Chicago, 1974), chapter 2.

10. Virginia R. Cummins, "Finneytown, Original and First Families," *Bulletin Historical and Philosophical Society of Ohio* 11(4) (October 1953): 331–341. I wish to thank Catherine F. MacDougal of Norton, Massachusetts, for this and other helpful genealogical material relating to the Ward and Finney families.

Chapter 5. Arminian and Calvinist Baptists (pp. 124–133)

1. See *The Diary of John Comer*, Rhode Island Historical Society Collec-tions (Providence, R.I., 1893), 8:68–69; and Richard Knight, *History of the General or Six Principle Baptists* (Providence, R.I., 1826), p. 307.

2. Isaac Backus, *A Church History of New England* (Boston, 1796), p. 261.

3. *American Baptist Magazine* (Boston, 1827), 7:152–154. See also David Benedict, *A General History of the Baptist Denomination* (Boston, 1813), 1:528.

4. The best study of the Separate-Baptist movement in New England is C. C. Goen, *Revivalism and Separatism in New England* (New Haven, Conn., 1962), but he does not mention this association.

5. The standard biography of Backus, Alvah Hovey's *Memoir of the Life and Times of Isaac Backus* (Boston, 1859), makes no mention of this impor-tant aspect of his career, nor do two more recent studies of Backus: Thomas B. Maston, *Isaac Backus: Pioneer of Religious Liberty* (Rochester, N.Y., 1962); and Milton V. Backman, "Isaac Backus: A Pioneer Champion of Religious Liberty" (Ph.D. diss., University of Pennsylvania, 1959).

6. This is a reference to the famous Stonington Conference of May 1754, at which the pedobaptist Separate churches and the Separate-Baptist churches had voted to cease open-communion fellowship, thereby splitting the pedobaptist Separates from the antipedobaptist Separates; see Isaac Backus, *A Church History of New England* (Providence, 1784), pp. 211–215.

7. I.e., the Five Principle, closed-communion, Separate-Baptist churches of New England.

8. There is an unpublished manuscript (sermon or lecture) in Backus's hand at the American Baptist Historical Society in Rochester, New York, titled "Thots about Laying on of Hands. Feb. 1764." It is probable that this was brought by Backus to this conference and read to the assembled members of the association. Backus used three lines of argument to indi-cate that the ritual of laying on of hands was at best an optional or circum-

stantial one that ought never to be a bar to communion: First, because although the Bible describes Jesus' "laying hands on some distrest objects and healing them. . . . I haven't discovered any precept of his injoining ye laying on of hands upon all believers as a standing ordinance of his Church." Second, although Paul, Ananias, and the Apostles "laid on hands in ordinations" and on several "extraordinary" occasions, the very exceptional nature of these occasions proved that the practices were "peculiar to ye apostolick age." Third, the injunctions in Hebrews 6:1–2, "which I take to be ye great hinge on which ye whole controversy turns," had been taken, out of context, as a summary of Christian principles and practices; whereas in fact it was a description of how to go on "unto perfection" by leaving behind this and other doctrines and practices mistakenly carried over from "the Old Testament dispensation" by Jewish converts. Here Backus relied on extensive quotations from "ye pious & learned Dr. Gill" of England to prove that in this letter to the Hebrews Paul was not instructing them about the necessity of laying on of hands but advising against it.

Backus used the occasion also to warn these New Light Calvinistic Baptists that when the sixth principle prevailed among the pre-Awakening Baptists of Rhode Island, it caused them to decline from the orthodox Calvinism of Roger Williams so that these "Old Baptist churches" were now "very dark about the doctrines of free grace and very negligent as to ye daily practice of devotion and piety." Backus's accusation would make an interesting study, for it is clear that the Baptists of Rhode Island did become very lax in practice and Arminian in doctrine after 1656, when the laying on of hands began to prevail among them.

Backus had to fight constantly against the unsophisticated literalism of the Baptists, and there are two other unpublished manuscripts in the American Baptist Historical Society, one dated as late as 1788, attacking this sixth principle on similar grounds.

9. It is not clear that Elders Peter Worden (Werden) of Coventry, Nathan Young of Foster, and Ezekiel Angell of North Providence were actually members of the association. Nor is it clear who Elder Bennet was. (Perhaps it was Josiah Benit, whom Backus listed in his manuscript "Account of Ordinations" as "a Baptis . . . ordained at Situate in Rhod-Island Government April 11: 1750." This manuscript is at Andover Newton Theological School.) It is also not known which of these elders was beginning to waver on the sixth principle.

10. Ebenezer Hinds was elder of the Second Baptist Church of Middleborough, a five principle Calvinistic Church.

11. The "Result," or official decision, of the council was signed by Backus, Hinds, Alden, and three lay messengers from their churches, Ezra Clark, Silas Wood, and Ebenezer Holbrook.

12. Ellen Larned also lists as members of this association in the 1750s the Chestnut Hill Baptist Church in East Killingly, Connecticut, and the Baptist Church in West Woodstock, Connecticut (*History of Windham County, Connecticut* [Worcester, 1874], 1:466–468).

13. L. K. Wroth and H. B. Zobel, eds., *The Legal Papers of John Adams* (Cambridge, Mass., 1965), 2:32–47.

Chapter 6. A Poetic Plea for Religious Liberty, 1772 (pp. 134–145)

1. For contemporary accounts of the Ashfield affair, see Chileab Smith, *An Answer to Many Slanderous Reports Cast on the Baptists at Ashfield* (Norwich, Conn., 1774), and Isaac Backus, *A History of New England*, ed. David Weston (Newton, Mass., 1871), 2:149–166; for subsequent accounts, see Frederick G. Howes, *History of the Town of Ashfield* (Ashfield, n.d. [1913], pp. 14–86; Bernard Bailyn, *Pamphlets on the American Revolution* (Cambridge, Mass., 1865), pp. 163–164; W. G. McLoughlin, *New England Dissent* (Cambridge, Mass., 1971), 1:531–546.

2. On the cover of the manuscript is written, in Backus's hand, "Mr. Smith's Narrative of Ashfield"; the text itself, however, is in Chileab Smith's hand.

Chileab Smith (1708–?) was a deacon in the Congregational Church in South Hadley, Massachusetts, until 1751, when he turned against the Standing system and, after consulting Jonathan Edwards, became a Separate. He purchased land in Huntstown (later Ashfield) in 1751 and moved there with his eight children. There was then no church or pastor in the new settlement, so Smith held meetings in his home. In 1761 a group of the settlers, including the Smith family, became Baptists and formed a Baptist church over which Ebenezer Smith, Chileab's son, was ordained pastor in 1761. When the Congregationalists in Huntstown founded a church of their own and brought in an educated pastor in 1763, taxes were laid on the Baptists for his support, and the Ashfield troubles began. In 1786 Smith led a schism from his son's church and became the pastor of the Second Baptist Church in Ashfield. In 1798 the two churches reunited under the pastorship of Enos Smith, another of Chileab's sons. The date of Smith's death is unknown.

3. Comparison of the handwriting of the poem with letters written by Ebenezer and Chileab Smith reveals that it is in Chileab's handwriting, though there is no doubt that Ebenezer was its author. His father simply had clearer handwriting.

Ebenezer Smith (1734–1824) was born in South Hadley, Massachusetts, and moved with his family to Ashfield (then Huntstown) in 1751. Like his father, he was first a Separate and then a Baptist. In 1761 he was ordained over the new Baptist Church in Huntstown and remained its pastor until 1798. He played an important role in the efforts of the Baptists to gain exemption from paying taxes to support the Congregational church in Ashfield after 1765. In addition, he was one of the few New England Baptists to strongly advocate the abolition of slavery (see his letter to Isaac Backus, 16 October 1773, among the Backus Papers, Andover Newton Theological School, Newton Center, Mass.) In 1786 he requested that his church pay him a fixed salary because voluntary support was insufficient. At this his father led a schism and formed a second Baptist church in Ashfield. Smith continued as pastor of the first church until 1798, when he moved to western New York state. In 1816 he was preaching at Stockton at the age of eighty-six. There are almost two dozen of his letters among the Backus Papers, as well as several accounts by him of the Ashfield affair, but he apparently published nothing; this is the only known example of his efforts in poetry.

4. It is another irony that the leading figure in the persecution of the Ashfield Baptists was Judge Israel Williams, a proprietor of Ashfield and one of the leading men in the Connecticut Valley; Judge Williams sided with the king during the Revolution and was imprisoned by his townsmen in 1777 for his loyalism. See *Dictionary of American Biography* (New York, 1936), 20:266.

5. Though Smith was not involved in counterfeiting, there was a ring of counterfeiters operating in Ashfield at this time. Its leader was a Congregationalist, but some Baptists were also involved. See Backus, *History*, 2:180–181; Ebenezer Smith's letter to John Davis, 30 December 1771, in the Backus Papers at Andover Newton Theological School; and Isaac Backus's notes on a conversation with Ebenezer Smith about the counterfeiters, 20 February 1775.

6. For the role of Isaac Backus and John Davis as lobbyists and pamphleteers for the New England Baptists at this time, see W. G. McLoughlin, *Isaac Backus* (Boston, 1967).

7. In transcribing this poem I have retained the original spelling throughout but have changed the capitalization, added some punctuation, and broken the poem into sections in the interest of clarity.

8. Probably a reference to "Bloody" Mary (1553–1558), made infamous by one of the most popular books of evangelicals in the colonies, John Foxe's *Book of Martyrs* (1559).

9. A reference to the persecution of Baptists and Quakers in seventeenth-century New England. Baptists were banished by law in Massachusetts in 1644 and whipped in 1751, but only Quakers (and witches) were hanged.

10. After 1700 most New Englanders were willing to admit that their forefathers were wrong to inflict corporal punishment or banishment on dissenters, and by the charter of 1691 (mentioned nine lines below) the king required toleration in Massachusetts for all denominations of Christian "except Papists." The problem for dissenters after 1691 was to convince the authorities that toleration meant exemption from religious taxation to support the established Congregational system.

11. After 1729, Baptists, Quakers, and Anglicans were exempt from taxes to support the Congregational churches if they provided a certificate to the local authorities that they belonged to a bona fide dissenting church. But then the question became, what was a bona fide Baptist church, and who was a bona fide member rather than a mere tax dodger? By 1772 many Baptists had decided that even the requirement of a certificate by the state for exemption from religious taxes was an infringement of freedom of conscience. But if they refused to supply a certificate (or if it was declared fraudulent), they were subject to imprisonment or confiscation of their estates to pay the religious taxes levied on all inhabitants by each town or parish.

12. The Congregationalists could rightly claim that by the law of 1768 no Baptist in Ashfield was exempt from religious taxes. Hence, even those disposed to exempt Baptists from these taxes adopted the "we would if we could, but we can't" attitude Smith describes here.

13. The king disallowed the peculiar Ashfield Law of 1768 in July 1771; the news of this reached Boston in October 1771, and Chileab Smith was arrested for counterfeiting on November 8, 1771.

14. The General Court, or legislature, of the province.

15. Ebenezer Smith did go to the General Court himself in 1768 and in 1770 to petition for exemption from religious taxes for the Baptists in Ashfield.

16. A reference to his father's imprisonment on November 8, 1771, on false charges of counterfeiting, for which he was kept under heavy bonds to appear in the superior court the following spring.

Chapter 7. Baptist Opposition to Slavery, 1773 (pp. 146–156)

1. For a discussion of antislavery views in the colonies at the time of the Revolution, see Winthrop D. Jordan, *White over Black* (Baltimore, 1969), pp. 169–311.

2. See John M. Bumsted and Charles E. Clark, "New England's Tom Paine," *William and Mary Quarterly*, 3rd ser. 21 (October 1964): 561–570.

3. Rufus D. Jones, *The Quakers in the American Colonies* (New York, 1966), pp. 164–165.

4. For general discussions of the New England Baptists and slavery at the time of the Revolution, see W. G. McLoughlin, *New England Dissent* (Cambridge, Mass., 1971), 2:764–769; and Thomas B. Maston, "The Ethical and Social Attitudes of Isaac Backus," (Ph.D. diss., Yale University, 1939), pp. 137–157.

5. See Frederick G. Howes, *History of the Town of Ashfield* (Ashfield, Mass., n.d. [1913], pp. 95–96.

6. It is not known precisely how late in 1773 this fourth edition of Allen's tract was issued, but quite possibly it was after October 16.

7. For the story of the Ashfield Baptists' fight with the Congregational establishment, see Howes, *Ashfield*, pp. 63–86; and McLoughlin, *New England*, 1:531–536.

8. McLoughlin, *New England*, 1:516–517; L. Kinvin Wroth and Hiller Zobel, eds., *Legal Papers of John Adams* (Cambridge, Mass., 1965) 2:32–47; and Isaac Backus, *A History of New England with Particular Reference to the Denomination of Christians Called Baptists*, ed. David Weston (Newton, Mass., 1871) 2:150–151.

9. See William O'Brien, "Did the Jennison Case Outlaw Slavery in Massachusetts?" *William and Mary Quarterly*, 3rd ser., 17 (1960): 219–241.

10. "I.B." was Isaac Backus, to whom the letter was addressed. In editing this document I have retained the original spelling but added some punctuation and capitals. The original is among the Isaac Backus Papers at Andover Newton Theological School, Newton Center, Massachusetts. The heading is not part of the original document.

Chapter 8. *Massive Civil Disobedience As a Baptist Tactic in 1773 (pp. 157–177)*

1. For a contemporary account of Baptist "persecutions" and their efforts to obtain religious liberty and disestablishment in New England, see Isaac Backus, *A History of New England with Particular Reference to the Denomination of Christians Called Baptists*, ed. David Weston (Newton, Mass., 1871).

2. See the letter of Elder Ebenezer Smith of Ashfield to Elder Samuel Stillman of Boston, 5 December 1770, in the Isaac Backus Papers, Andover Newton Theological School, Newton, Massachusetts.

3. For a list of these laws, with relevant quotations from them, see the appendices in David B. Ford, *New England's Struggle for Religious Liberty* (Philadelphia, 1896).

4. The Anglicans (who did not object in principle to religious taxes) were required to pay religious taxes, but the taxes of duly certified Anglicans were turned over by the parish authorities to the rector of their church. Duly certified Baptists and Quakers were exempted from such taxes.

5. Many documents attesting to these and other legal difficulties that thwarted a fair application of the tax exemption laws can be found among the papers of the Grievance Committee of the Warren Baptist Association, in Isaac Backus Papers.

6. Kai T. Erikson, in *The Wayward Puritans* (New York, 1966), a sociological study of religious dissenters as social deviants in Massachusetts, unfortunately does not deal with the Baptists, but his general observations are relevant.

7. For a discussion of the various religious, legal, and political arguments used by the eighteenth-century New England Baptists in their petitions and tracts regarding tax exemption, see W. G. McLoughlin, *Isaac Backus and the American Pietistic Tradition* (Boston, 1967).

8. For a general account of the Ashfield case, see Frederick G. Howes, *History of the Town of Ashfield* (Ashfield, Mass., 1913).

9. The Grievance Committee was an agency of the Warren Baptist Association. Its first chairman was Elder John Davis of Boston, but Backus had been an active member since its founding in 1769.

10. The best account of the Separate movement and its connection with the Separate-Baptists is C. C. Goen, *Revivalism and Separatism in New England, 1740–1800* (New Haven, Conn., 1962).

11. Manning, Stillman, and Smith were, however, New Lights, or Evangelical Calvinists, who warmly endorsed the work of Edwards and Whitefield and tried to direct the pietistic fervor of the Awakening and its aftermath into Baptist channels.

12. There are, unfortunately, too few sociological studies of religious groups as social deviants. I have cited one in note 6 above; two others worth mentioning are J. J. Loubser, "Puritanism and Religious Liberty: A Study of Normative Change in Massachusetts, 1630–1830" (Ph.D. diss., Harvard University, 1964); and George DeVos and Hiroshi Wagatsuma, *Japan's Invisible Race: Caste in Culture and Personality* (Berkeley, Calif., 1966).

13. Isaac Backus, *A Seasonable Plea for Liberty of Conscience against Some*

Late Oppressive Proceedings (Boston, 1770), pp. 3, 12; and Backus, *A Letter to a Gentleman in the Massachusetts General Assembly* (Boston, 1771), p. 506.

14. Quoted in Alvah Hovey, *A Memoir of the Life and Times of the Rev. Isaac Backus* (Boston, 1858), pp. 210–211.

15. Of course, to the devout Baptist it was hardly a "choice" in the sense of being merely a personal whim or opinion; for them, being a Baptist was the only possible persuasion for an orthodox Christian. To be anything else was to oppose the will of God.

16. The Rich case is described in a manuscript in the hand of Elder John Davis, titled "Mr. Rich's Case at Roylston, 1769," among the Isaac Backus Papers.

17. For Samuel Robinson, see Henry Crocker, *History of the Baptists in Vermont* (Bellows Falls, Vt., 1913), p. 15.

18. See the manuscript from Thomas Rich of Warwick to Elder Noah Alden of Bellingham, May 27, 1774, titled "Some Short Account of the Baptis att Warwick," in Isaac Backus Papers.

19. See Ezra Stiles, *The Literary Diary of Ezra Stiles*, ed. F. B. Dexter (New York, 1901) 1:168–169, 472–474.

20. Backus's account of the Medfield meeting in a letter to Samuel Stennett of London is reprinted in Hovey, *Backus*, pp. 190–194.

21. This tract is reprinted in W. G. McLoughlin, ed., *Isaac Backus on Church, State, and Calvinism* (Cambridge, Mass., 1968); see p. 333 for this quotation.

Chapter 11. The Balkcom Case, 1782: A Short-lived Victory for Religious Liberty (pp. 228–248)

1. See William O'Brien, S. J., "Did the Jennison Case Outlaw Slavery in Massachusetts?" *William and Mary Quarterly*, 3rd ser., 17 (1960): 219–241.

2. Samuel Eliot Morison, "The Struggle over the Adoption of the Constitution of Massachusetts, 1780," Massachusetts Historical Society, *Proceedings*, 50 (1917): 353–412.

3. For the background of the certificate system, see L. K. Wroth and H. B. Zobel, eds., *Legal Papers of John Adams* (Cambridge, 1965), 2:32–47; Susan M. Reed, *Church and State in Massachusetts, 1691–1740* (Urbana, Ill., 1914); Jacob C. Meyer, *Church and State in Massachusetts from 1740 to 1833* . . . (Cleveland, Ohio, 1930).

4. On the back of a letter that Alden wrote to the Warren Baptist Association on September 9, 1780, he gives the total tabulation of votes as 6,298 opposed to Article 3 and 8,585 in favor. By the rules of the convention every article needed a two-thirds majority to be accepted. Alden's letter is among the Isaac Backus Papers at Andover Newton Theological School, Newton Center, Mass.

5. This information and that which follows in this paragraph, is on a loose sheet in Isaac Backus's hand among the Backus Papers. On September 25, 1780, the parish had also voted "to make up the fall of money to their minister" by levying a tax of £70 in silver. This sum may have been

lumped with the £23,000 for the meetinghouse when the tax was assessed. Unfortunately, the original records of the east parish are missing.

6. See appendix 1.

7. Backus's unpublished diary was written in fourteen separate volumes. Volume 10 covers the years 1780 to 1784 (Backus Papers).

8. As will be seen below, Balkcom's father later left the Congregational church to become a Baptist, but the circumstances of his shift are unknown, and the records of the Attleborough Baptist Church are missing.

9. For the complicated history of this Separate-Baptist church, see John Daggett, *Sketch of the History of Attleborough* (Dedham, Mass., 1834), pp. 65–67.

10. These notes are in the Backus Papers.

11. There are some brief notes for this case in the extant papers of Robert Treat Paine at the Massachusetts Historical Society, printed here as appendix 2.

12. Backus Papers.

13. The title was characteristically based on proof texts: (1) "For, brethren, ye have been called into liberty, only use not liberty for an occasion to the flesh, but by love serve one another" (Gal. 5:13); (2) "behold, I have set before thee an open door, and no man can shut it" (Rev. 3:8). Both texts were printed on the title page.

14. The Baptists, however, had no objection to the oath of office that the constitution required of all state officeholders, and this same circular letter calls on the Baptists to thank God "for now no Governor, Councellor, Senator or Representative, can take a seat in our government till he solemnly declares, 'I believe the Christian religion and have a firm persuasion of its truth.'" September 9, 10, 1783, *Minutes of the Warren Association in their Meeting at Charlton* (n.p., n.d.).

15. This charge is in the files of the Supreme Judicial Court of Massachusetts for June to November 1785, October Session, pp. 260–261. Frost and Warren must have acted as both assessors and collectors for the parish.

16. Green's letter, dated 8 September 1785, is among the Backus Papers.

17. Backus's manuscript, "History of the Warren Association," which he wrote in 1784 and which is among the Backus Papers. See also his *History*, 2:328–329.

18. Backus, manuscript, "Diary," 11 (31 October 1785): 21. The judges (including William Cushing, Francis Dana, and Increase Summer) were undoubtedly influenced by the decision they had rendered several months earlier in the case of John Murray (discussed below). I also wish to note here that in my article on the Balkcom case in the *William and Mary Quarterly*, I erroneously gave the date of *Cutter v. Frost* as 1784 instead of 1785.

19. Thomas Green to Backus, 28 October 1785, in Backus Papers.

20. *The Acts and Resolves, Public and Private of the Province of Massachusetts Bay* (Boston, 1869–1922) (abbreviated as Mass. Prov. AR), 3:778–779. This act, passed January 10, 1755, was titled "An Act for the Better Securing and Rendering More Effectual Grants and Donations . . . for the Better Support and Maintenance of Ministers of the Gospel and Defraying Other Charges Relating to Publick Worship." It specified that "the deacons of all the several Protestant churches" and Episcopal church wardens "are and

shall be deemed so far bodies corporate as to take in succession all grants and donations whether real or personal" made to support ministers or maintain meetinghouses. This act also allowed pews to be taxed for the charge of public worship "according to the convenience and situation thereof." Though it was intended primarily to aid the established churches, the act was sufficiently broad to include the dissenters. The essential features of this law were reenacted on February 20, 1786.

21. Backus, *History*, 2:328–329.

22. Backus's manuscript "Diary," 11:21.

23. Backus's notes on the back of the letter from Thomas Green dated October 28, 1785, in the Backus Papers.

24. Edward Buck, *Massachusetts Ecclesiastical Law* (Boston, 1865), p. 43. In many cases the Baptists were required, as in West Cambridge, to pay civil taxes laid to defray the town's costs in defending the suits that the Baptists were waging.

25. In my opinion the position of John Leland, who is often cited as the leading eighteenth-century Baptist spokesman for separation of church and state, is far closer to that of Madison and Jefferson than to that of Backus and the Baptists. The failure to recognize his eccentric (from the Baptists' point of view) theological stance on this issue has contributed greatly to the confusion of these two distinctly different viewpoints.

Chapter 12. Isaac Backus and Thomas Jefferson (pp. 249–269)

1. Perry Miller seems to me quite right in arguing that Williams came to his final position "because he was driven by religious passion and not because he was mollified by the religious indifferentism of a Jefferson. He preached liberty of conscience not because he thought it the least destructive or most economical way for men to live together, but because of a vision which for him was a never-ending ecstasy. He did not look forward to a free society as the goal of human endeavor; instead he looked down on it, in pity and sorrow, seeing in freedom only a preliminary requirement for the Christian pilgrimage" (*Roger Williams: His Contribution to the American Tradition* [Indianapolis, Ind., 1953], pp. 27–28; see also Edmund S. Morgan's excellent study, *Roger Williams: The Church and the State* [New York, 1967], which amplifies and in places corrects Miller's view.)

2. James Bryce captured the prevailing view of Americans on this question in the nineteenth century when he said, "The matter may be summed up by saying that Christianity is in fact understood to be, though not the legally established religion, yet the national religion" (Quoted in John F. Wilson, ed., *Church and State in American History* [Boston, 1965], p. 154.) By the increasing rigidity of the Court's interpretation, I mean in contrast to the nineteenth-century American attitude described by Lord Bryce. I recognize that many strict separationists feel that since 1948 the Court has permitted considerable breaking of the wall of separation.

3. For a discussion of the Separate or Strict Congregational movement in New England, see C. C. Goen, *Revivalism and Separatism in New England, 1740–1800* (New Haven, Conn., 1962). It should be noted that, on the

whole, most Separates favored Separationism; the latter is a modern short-hand term for the principle of separation of church and state (or voluntarism), which has no specific relationship to the Separate movement.

4. Susan M. Reed, *Church and State in Massachusetts, 1691–1740* (Urbana, Ill., 1914).

5. The requirements for signatures on the certificates varied from time to time, but throughout most of the century three signatures were required. See *The Acts and Resolves, Public and Private, of the Province of the Massachusetts Bay* (Boston, 1869–1922) 2:714. Anglicans also were required to obtain similar certificates, but this did not entitle them to tax exemption; it merely gave their minister claim to their religious taxes for his support.

6. See Reed, *Church and State in Massachusetts*, for the pressure Anglicans and Quakers were able to bring upon Massachusetts from England. In 1739 there were only nine Baptist churches in Massachusetts, with perhaps three hundred members, most of them in the area of the old Plymouth Colony around Swansea and Rehoboth.

7. Massachusetts Archives, Ecclesiastical, 12:96, 127, Secretary of State's Office, Boston. It appears that the legislature, fearing tax dodging, was preparing to revise the tax exemption law so that Baptists and Quakers would have to pay religious taxes, as the Anglicans did, and then have these taxes turned over to their own ministers. Hence, the Baptist agents may simply have been settling for the lesser of two evils.

8. The Standing Order was, of course, correct in its view that to grant tax exemption to Separates whose doctrines and practices differed from that of the established churches only in the intensity of their pietistic fervor would have destroyed the ecclesiastical system. Baptists, Quakers, and Anglicans could be tolerated and given tax exemption only because they were so few. But if 125 towns and parishes were divided into competing Congregational factions of almost equal size, most would not have been able to provide adequate support for both. The Separate movement had to be crushed.

9. Backus himself was threatened with jail for this reason in 1748, and four years later his mother and brother were imprisoned in Norwich, Connecticut, for refusing, as Separates, to pay religious taxes. See W. G. McLoughlin, *Isaac Backus* (Boston, 1967), pp. 22, 49.

10. The diary, letters, and other papers of Backus, which are now being edited for a letterpress edition under a grant from the National Historical Publications Commission, are owned principally by Andover Newton Theological School, Newton Center, Massachusetts. The best proof that the Standing Order feared tax dodging among the Separates was the new tax exemption law of 1754 that was designed specifically to exclude the "new Baptists" from the tax exemption privileges of the old Baptists. It proved impossible, however, to maintain the distinction, and the law did not function as expected.

11. Isaac Backus, *Truth Is Great and Will Prevail* (Boston, 1781), appendix 7.

12. The one exception to this occurred in 1774, when the Baptists accepted an invitation by some leading Quakers in Philadelphia to join them in a protest to the Continental Congress. But this joint endeavor was limited

to the one specific occasion, and it was prompted by the ulterior motives of the Quakers, who hoped to thwart the radical efforts of the Congress by injecting this divisive note. See McLoughlin, *Isaac Backus,* pp. 128–132.

13. The motion supported by Rathbun in the town meeting at Pittsfield in 1781 is quoted in J. E. A. Smith, *History of Pittsfield* (Boston, 1869) 1:454.

14. Backus referred to Mother Ann Lee of the Shakers as "a common prostitute" and called John Wesley a Tory and a liar. Of course, Williams bitterly attacked the Quakers, and Jefferson was equally hostile toward Calvinists and Catholics; but what Backus lacks is any clear-cut statement that, despite their theological errors, these new dissenters equally deserve religious liberty. Somehow, he could not bring himself to include them as true religious believers.

15. Even as late as the spring of 1775 Backus was urged by many Baptists to be cautious in taking the patriot side lest it lose them the goodwill of the king (McLoughlin, *Isaac Backus,* p. 134).

16. See Francis Wayland, *The Elements of Political Economy* (Boston, 1852), pp. 131–132; and Josiah Strong, *Our Country* (New York, 1886), chapter 14.

17. See Sidney E. Mead, *The Lively Experiment* (New York, 1973), pp. 19, 40–44.

18. Morgan argues that Williams was not, properly speaking, a Seeker (*Roger Williams,* p. 152). But whether or not he shared all of the official tenets of this group, there still seems no other adequate term for his position after 1639. Williams's famous statement to John Winthrop after having left the Baptist denomination is also worth quoting here: "I believe their practice comes nearer the first practice of our great Founder Christ than other practices of religion does, & yet I have no satisfaction neither in the authorities by which it [baptism] is done nor in the manner [immersion]; not in the prophecies concerning the rise of Christ's Kingdome after the desolation of Rome &c" (Massachusetts Historical Society, *Collections,* 4th ser., 6 [1863]:274).

19. Backus first mentions reading Williams in his diary, 2 February 1773, Backus Papers: "Met now with some writings of old Mr. Roger Williams which I was very glad of." The first publication in which Backus quoted Williams was his *Appeal to the Public for Religious Liberty* (Boston, 1773), pp. 25–26. For some of the reasons that Backus did not often quote Williams, see Thomas B. Maston, *Isaac Backus: Pioneer of Religious Liberty* (Rochester, N.Y., 1962), p. 76.

20. Isaac Backus, *Policy as Well as Honesty* (Boston, 1779), p. 10.

21. I agree with Miller's statement that "although Williams is celebrated as the prophet of religious freedom, he actually exerted little or no influence on institutional developments in America: only after the conception of liberty for all denominations had triumphed on wholly other grounds did Americans look back on Williams and invest him with his ill-fitting halo" (*Roger Williams,* p. 29).

22. It should be noted here that the Congregationalists of eighteenth-century Massachusetts always denied that their system was in fact an establishment of religion. They defined an establishment in terms of a confessional state in which conformity to a specific creed and ritual was required

of all churches supported by law. Congregational churches were autonomous in creed and ritual.

23. Mead, *Lively Experiment,* pp. 59–70. Mead claims that under voluntarism the churches proved inadequate "to define, articulate, disseminate
the basic religious beliefs essential for the existence and well-being of the
society"; thus, they had to turn the task over to the state via the public
schools. I would argue that most nineteenth-century evangelicals saw the
schools as merely an adjunct to the churches and placed their faith in
revivalism to convert the nation to Christian morality and order. They
relied, meanwhile, on the power of moral suasion from the pulpits and the
passage of wholesome laws to maintain the well-being of society.

24. For Williams's opposition to this system, see his *Fourth Paper Presented
to Maior Butler* (London, 1652).

25. For Williams's stalwart Calvinism, see Miller, *Roger Williams,* p. 28.
Again I would agree with Miller that Williams never speaks "in the tones
of modern liberalism. For him the ideological issue [of separationism] is
not central: the question is the meaning of Scripture. Were Cotton correct
in saying that such-and-such is clearly demonstrable, Williams would have
to agree that a good conscience ought to submit and allow the magistrate
to help, just as we today believe that a judge can sentence unrepentant
thieves" (ibid., p. 104). In *The Bloody Tenent Yet More Bloody* (London, 1644)
Williams makes this concession to the Puritans: "Let Master Cotton now
produce any such nation in the whole world whom God in the New Testament hath literally and miraculously brought forth of Egypt, or from
one land into another, to the truth and purity of his worship—then far be
it but I should acknowledge that the seducer is fit to be put to death"
(quoted in Miller, *Roger Williams,* p. 183).

26. Backus devoted much of his energy to overthrowing the Arminian,
Six-Principle Baptist position that grew up in and around Rhode Island
after Williams's death, and he was a strong advocate of associationism for
maintaining the good order and orthodoxy of his denomination of closed
communion, Five-Principle Calvinist Baptists.

27. It is hardly necessary to reiterate Jefferson's disdain of "the moun-
tebanks calling themselves the priests of Jesus" and his fear of "the power
and the profit of the priests. Sweep away their gossamer fabrics of factitious
religion, and they would catch no more flies. We should all then, like the
Quakers, live without an order of priests, moralize for ourselves, follow the
oracle of conscience, and say nothing about what no man can understand,
nor therefore believe" (quoted in Saul K. Padover, ed., *Thomas Jefferson on
Democracy* [New York, 1954], pp. 117–18).

28. As Williams put it in his *Hireling Ministry None of Christ's* (London,
1652), p. 4, neither "the Begetting Ministry of the Apostles . . . or the
Feeding and Nourishing Ministry of Pastors and Teachers . . . are yet re-
stored and extant." He also denounced here the man who "makes a Trade
of Preaching" and who demands "a maintenance" or "explicitly makes a
covenant or bargaine" for his salary as a preacher (ibid., p. 8). Yet Backus,
in his *The Liberal Support of Gospel Ministers, Opened and Inculcated* (Boston,
1790), explicitly defended the right of the minister to demand a fair salary
from his congregation and even to excommunicate for covetousness any
who failed to provide their proportionate share.

29. For Williams's prediction that the true testimony of God's prophets and witnesses "is probably neer finished" and "the slaughter of the Witnesses, Revel. 11" is about to begin, "after which and their shame three years and a halfe, followeth their most glorious and joyfull Rising," see his *Hireling Ministry*, p. 2.

30. The manuscript of Backus's proposed "Bill of Rights" for the Massachusetts Constitution is in Backus Papers; it is printed in Maston, *Isaac Backus*, appendix C, pp. 121–123.

31. See Mead, *Lively Experiment*, p. 57. It must be admitted that in the years 1775–1785 Jefferson and Madison tried not to exaggerate but to play down their differences with the pietistic dissenters who supported disestablishment. It was in the years after 1800 that their deism became most pronounced in its hostility toward revealed religion and priestcraft.

32. Massachusetts Archives, Ecclesiastical, 12:626.

33. What it owes to Locke derives from his *Letters Concerning Toleration*, not from his *Second Treatise on Government*, for in this tract, Backus specifically repudiated the contract theory of government, another fact that highlights his divergence from the thought of Jefferson and Madison.

34. He quotes two short paragraphs from *The Blood Tenent Yet More Bloody*. Backus, who rediscovered Williams's forgotten works, quoted him sparingly, and other writers on separationism in this period almost never mention him.

35. Isaac Backus, *A History of New England with Particular Reference to the Denomination Called Baptists*, ed. David Weston (Newton, Mass., 1871) 2:143–144.

36. See Backus, *History, passim*, and Backus, *Liberal Support of Gospel Ministers*.

37. A copy of Hinds's petition is among the Backus Papers. Hinds also praised the Massachusetts Constitution of 1780 as "the Best Constitution that the Baptist[s] have been under Since the Massachusett[s] Began," although Backus denounced it as making the Baptists' position worse than it had been since 1729. See Hinds's letter to the Warren Baptist Association, 3 September 1781, Backus Papers.

38. Quoted in Miller, *Roger Williams*, p. 117.

39. See Isaac Backus, *A Fish Caught in His Own Net* (Boston, 1768), p. 23.

40. For the Ashfield case, see Frederick G. Howes, *History of the Town of Ashfield* (Ashfield, Mass. [1913]), and *Acts and Resolves*, 4:1036ff.

41. For Smith, see Elias Smith, *The Life, Conversion, Preaching, Travels and Suffering of Elias Smith* (Portsmouth, N.H., 1816), pp. 205, 206; for Seamans, see Backus, *History*, pp. 537–538.

42. The result of this was often ludicrous as four or five denominations tried to divide up the fifty-two Sabbaths among themselves. Gradually, after 1810, the towns decided that the town hall should be a wholly secular or civil building and that each denomination, including the Congregationalists, should build its own house of worship.

43. For an account of the confrontation between Hezekiah Smith and Backus on this matter, see Smith, *Life*, pp. 233–234. Another reason often given to justify incorporation of a Baptist church was that a series of court decisions after 1780 ruled that unincorporated dissenting churches in Mas-

sachusetts could not claim exemptions from religion taxes. But most Baptist ministers found other ways around these decisions than by incorporation.

44. It should also be pointed out that there was some confusion in the constitutional clauses concerning tax exemption, implying that only an incorporated church or congregation could obtain the religion taxes paid by its members under the new general assessment procedure. The courts were not consistent about this, however.

45. "The society at Haverhill was incorporated and from this it spread till cattle and horses were taken by force to pay baptist ministers for preaching" (Smith, *Life*, p. 234).

46. Isaac Backus, *A Door Opened for Equal Christian Liberty* (Boston, 1783), p. 12. However, Backus later applauded the fact that the federal Constitution prohibited any such oath of office for federal officeholders.

47. The man who succeeded Backus as the leading spokesman for the Massachusetts Baptists, Elder Thomas Baldwin of Boston, stated in the Massachusetts Constitutional Convention of 1820 that "he was willing that parishes should have power to tax all persons within their limites who are not enrolled in any other [religious] society." That is, he was willing that persons who belonged to no church or congregation should be taxed to support the parish church (*Journal of Debates and Proceedings of the Convention* [Boston, 1853], p. 422).

48. Backus, *Truth Is Great*, p. 33.

49. See *Life . . . of Smith*, pp. 119–123, for an interesting example of the way in which public school teachers imposed the Westminster Confession on all children even against the will of the parents. Backus has no recorded statement on this issue.

50. This manuscript sermon, titled "The Man of Sin Revealed," also quotes a sermon by Benjamin Wallin, a Baptist minister in London, dated 9 October 1774, pp. 31–32, in which Wallin bemoans the fact that a recent "petition, signed by a great number of respectable persons, for some further check to the horrid impiety [of Sabbath-breaking] not barely failed of success but was treated with derision [by Parliament]." Wallin complained that "little regard is now paid to a day once held sacred through the nation, the pollution of which is an inlet to all manner of disorder and wickedness and proves fatal to millions." Backus agreed (see Backus Papers).

51. "I saw a Book write by John Bolls of New London Printed 1734 in the latter end of which was set down 2 Copies of record from under my grandfather Backus's hand of his punishing said Bolls and Sarah Colver 2 Quakers on July 26, 1725 for their traveling on the day before, which was Lordsday. . . . Both were whipt for breach of Sabbath, which they called Persecution" (Backus's unpublished diary, 4 August 1754, Backus Papers).

52. Backus's unpublished diary, 11 February 1798, Backus Papers.

53. It is not clear whether Backus opposed the payment of chaplains by the state and federal legislatures, though in 1793 he did express displeasure with the U.S. Senate for paying five hundred dollars each to two Episcopal bishops for this purpose (see Isaac Backus, *Testimony of the Two Witnesses* [Boston, 1793], p. 46).

54. Backus, *A Door Opened*, p. 6.

55. Some historians consider John Leland a more radical exponent of

separationism among the Baptists than Backus; others more or less equate the views of the two men. In my opinion Leland was too eccentric to be typical of the Baptists, especially of those in New England. Leland spent his most productive years in Virginia, where he imbibed much of the spirit of the most radical dissenters, and his views of separationism were decidedly nearer to those of Jefferson and Madison than to those of Backus. His eccentricity is indicated by the fact that after his return to New England to settle in Cheshire, Massachusetts, in 1792 he refused to perform the Lord's Supper in his church because it seemed to him an empty ritual. (See the records of the Cheshire Baptist Church, Pittsfield Athenaeum.) Like Madison and Jefferson, Leland wanted a high wall of separation between church and state, opposing not only public fast and thanksgiving days but even laws against dueling, lotteries, or for the enforcement of the Sabbath. In sharp contrast to Backus, who believed that America was and should be a Christian nation, Leland stated, "The Notion of a Christian commonwealth should be exploded forever" (L. F. Greene, *The Writings of John Leland* [New York, 1845], p. 107). Leland became a scandal among the New England Baptists, when, after Backus's death, he opposed the foreign mission movement, the Sunday school movement, and the effort to persuade Congress to prohibit the delivery of mail on Sundays.

Chapter 14. A Baptist Autobiography in Verse, 1820 (pp. 277–288)

1. For suggestions concerning the literary qualities of this poem, I am indebted to Professor Hyatt H. Waggoner of Brown University.

2. Most of the biographical material about Jabez Cottle and his family can be found in a paperbound, hectographed book titled *The Cottle Family*, compiled and published by Mrs. Velma Cottle-Musick of Kingfisher, Oklahoma, in 1961. Mrs. Musick relied chiefly on printed sources, and most of her information about Jabez Cottle came from the following works: Charles E. Banks, *The History of Martha's Vineyard* (Boston, 1911); Henry Swan Dana, *History of Woodstock, Vermont* (Boston, 1889); Lewis C. Aldrich and Frank R. Holmes, *History of Windsor County, Vermont* (New York, 1891); and Grace Canfield, *The Valley of Kedron* (Kedron, 1940). Some additional information is contained in David A. Benedict, *A General History of the Baptist Denomination in America* (Boston, 1813), Henry Crocker, *History of the Baptists in Vermont* (Bellows Falls, Vt., 1913), and Elias Smith, *The Life, Conversion, Preaching, Travels and Suffering of Elias Smith* (Portsmouth, N.H., 1816).

So far as is known, Jabez Cottle did not publish anything during his life, and his letters or papers are not extant. I am indebted to Mr. Roger E. Stoddard, curator of the Harris Collection; Rev. Harold F. Worthley; Miss Sara Lee Silberman; and Mr. John M. Bumsted for assistance in tracking down information about Jabez Cottle.

3. That Sylvanus Cottle was a New Light is shown by his requesting Elder Isaac Backus, a Separate-Baptist minister of Middleborough, to preach in Tisbury in 1753. For this and other references to Cottle, see the

manuscript diaries and travel journals of Isaac Backus in the Andover Newton Theological School, Newton Center, Massachusetss.

4. A record of the baptism of Sylvanus Cottle and of his admission to church membership (as well as records of other church activities in which he engaged) is contained in the manuscript records of the Third Baptist Church of Middleborough in Andover Newton Theological School, Newton Center, Massachusetts.

5. See *Rolls of the Soldiers in the Revolutionary War 1775 to 1793 for the State of Vermont*, compiled and edited by John E. Goodrich and published by the authority of the legislature (Rutland, Vt., 1904). Although these records show that five members of the Cottle family were at one time enrolled in the militia, they do not mention Jabez Cottle.

6. References to Jabez Cottle's activities in this church can be found in Crocker, *Baptists in Vermont*, pp. 179, 244, and in the printed minutes of the Woodstock Baptist Association for 1789, 1790, and 1802–1806.

7. For quotations from this letter see Dana, *History of Woodstock*, pp. 375–376.

8. A record of his ordination is contained in the unpublished manuscript of Isaac Backus entitled "Account of Ordinations," which is among the Backus Papers at Andover Newton Theological School.

9. See Crocker, *Baptists of Vermont*, p. 233. For an autobiographical account of one of Cottle's missionary tours, see the published minutes of the Woodstock Baptist Association for 1811.

10. See Crocker, *Baptists in Vermont*, pp. 244; and Dana, *History of Woodstock*, pp. 373ff. See also the published minutes of the Woodstock Baptist Association for 1806–1809 and for 1819, which mention the troubles in Cottle's church.

11. This is the date on which someone (probably one of his children) transcribed the manuscript he had written two years earlier (see date at end of poem). The whereabouts of the original manuscript is unknown.

12. Sylvanus Cottle had had two sons and six daughters by his first wife, Mary Hatch. She died about 1742, and he married Abigail Sherman in 1745. Jabez was her first-born son.

13. He means here that it was vain for him to rely on his own willpower to reform himself. Salvation can come to the Calvinist only through the grace of God.

14. The apostrophe here seems to have been a mistake.

15. "The saints" were the visible elect; i.e., the member of the church who, to all earthly appearance, had been converted and hence were among those predestined for heaven.

16. Jabez Cottle, Jr., died about 1797.

17. He is evidently figuring his birthday by the new-style calendar and thus has added eleven days to February 22, 1746/7. The person who copied the poem on March 5, 1822, obviously did so as a birthday remembrance. It suggests that perhaps the family read the poem aloud each year to observe his birthday.

Chapter 15. Conclusion: Disestablishment
at Last (pp. 289–303)

1. For a more extensive discussion of the details of disestablishment in each state, W. G. McLoughlin, *New England Dissent,* vol. 2. All quotations in this chapter are from this source unless otherwise noted.

2. Anson Phelps Stokes, *Church and State in the United States* (New York, 1950) 1:429.

3. The significance of the Cutter case is discussed in chapter 11 of this book.

4. The best discussion of the Murray case is in John D. Cushing, "Notes on Disestablishment in Massachusetts, 1780–1833," *William and Mary Quarterly,* 3rd ser., 26 (April 1969): 169–190.

5. Ibid., p. 183.

6. Ibid., p. 179.

Index

267, 301; banished from Massachusetts, 20, 25; as a Baptist, 19, 22,
257; Calvinist theology of, 259, 269;
and separation of church and state,
vii, 19, 257–58, 262
Willis, Edmond, 54
Wilmarth, Eliphalet, 232
Wilmarth, Elkanah, 233
Wilson, John (c. 1651), 31

Wilson, John (c. 1712), 96
Winthrop, John, 18, 22, 28, 34, 50
Witter, William, 30–31
Wolcott, William, 26
Woods, Henry A., 191, 197–200, 207
Woodstock, Vt., 279–80
Woodward, John, 115
Woolman, John, 148
Wordsworth, William, 118
Wright, Frances, 12